Contents

v

FIVE CENTURIES
OF FAMOUS SHIPS

Robert G. Albion

FIVE CENTURIES
OF FAMOUS SHIPS

From the Santa Maria to the Glomar Explorer

with a foreword by Benjamin Labaree

McGraw-Hill Book Company

*New York   St. Louis   San Francisco   Auckland   Bogotá
Düsseldorf   Johannesburg   London   Madrid   Mexico
Montreal   New Delhi   Panama   Paris   São Paulo
Singapore   Sydney   Tokyo   Toronto*

DEC 1978

Library of Congress Cataloging in Publication Data

Albion, Robert Greenhalgh, 1896–
Five centuries of famous ships.

Includes index.
1. Ships—History.   I. Title.
VM15.A5   387.2'09'03   77-4904
ISBN 0-07-000953-8

1234567890 KPKP 7654321098

The editors for this book were Robert A. Rosenbaum and Joan Zseleczky,
the designer was Elliot Epstein, and the production supervisor
was Frank P. Bellantoni. It was set in Palatino by University Graphics, Inc.

Printed and bound by the Kingsport Press.

Foreword

Maritime history has always been dominated by a fascination for the ships that have been constructed for exploration, travel, and warfare upon the sea. In no other branch of transportation has the vehicle itself commanded so much interest; neither wagons, nor automobiles, nor even locomotives or airplanes have approached the vessel in its power to attract our attention. This circumstance derives in part from the very challenge that ships have faced from the sea—its great distances, its wild storms, its hidden dangers. Compared to land vehicles, the ship has always had the greater task to perform. In part this interest also stems from the grand scale on which so many vessels have been built, with towering masts, billowing canvas, and massive smokestacks. For centuries ships were the largest objects made by man; today they remain our largest moveable works. Who can forget those pictures of the *Queen Mary* standing on end alongside the Empire State Building, the two like a pair of growing children matching heights? Whatever their size, ships have been among the most graceful of man's creations, the ultimate fulfillment of the dictum best stated by Horatio Greenough that form follows function. In this respect ships have only recently been challenged by high-speed aircraft.

But most of all, our attraction to ships has come from the fact that they have been perceived as individuals with distinct physical characteristics and patterns of behavior, as recognized by the ceremony of christening them with distinctive names. Even such cookie-cutter products as liberty ships at least had names, and their crews would insist, as sailors have always insisted of their vessels, that each had a distinctive personality as well. When a passenger took a trip by water, he boarded the *J. T. Morse* or the *Aquitania*. In contrast, when a passenger boarded a train, it was merely "the 5:45 to Rye," or at best *The Twentieth Century Limited*. No one who has been to sea would ever doubt that ships have life, as surely as do horses, pets, or even people.

In their enthusiasm for ships, however, some maritime historians have been carried away by minutiae about the vessels themselves, forgetting that all history involves people, places, trends, and change. When asked to prepare a reference work on famous ships, Robert G. Albion, the dean of American maritime historians, made no such mistake. Each essay briefly describes the vessel and then gets to the point of its significant contribution to maritime history. In some cases a ship won fame by carrying an explorer on a pioneering expedition, in **vii** others by participating in a critical battle. Some vessels were included because their design introduced a significant innovation, others because they represented an important type, still others because their loss brought heavy casualties. Each essay emphasizes the role played by the people involved in the vessel's career—designer, master, crew members, passengers—and the tale is often spiced with lively anecdotes and episodes unknown or long-forgotten. Romanticism aside, Albion's vessels are the creatures and instruments of men after all. Ship and man together make maritime history, and it is this relationship which vitalizes these sketches.

Albion would himself admit that at least fifty other vessels could easily have been added to the 160-odd covered in the book. Indeed, the selection of almost *any* finite number of vessels for such a volume is bound to bring the inevitable question "Why not include the good old S.S. So-and-so?" We all have our own favorites, for such is our nature as lovers of ships, but this is a book on *Albion's* favorites. He has been writing on maritime history for over fifty years and was an established authority in the field when most of us were still pushing toy boats around the bathtub. His knowledge and understanding embrace five centuries of time and most of the world's oceans. Not many maritime historians can match that range.

By arranging his essays chronologically in order of the chief performances of their subjects (rather than by launching dates) and by grouping the essays into logical sections, Albion has given his book a sense of continuity that runs throughout its various essays. By reading it from beginning to end, one can acquire a real sense of historical development. As maritime frontiers are opened, new and improved vessels are required. Merchant ships increase in size, warships become more deadly, steam challenges and then conquers sail. And finally nuclear energy, an insatiable demand for oil, and the search for mineral resources on the seabed bring types of ships that only Jules Verne could have imagined a century ago. *Five Centuries of Famous Ships* is at once a useful guide to the histories of the world's most significant vessels and at the same time a cohesive and readable history of important maritime developments since 1492. It is a fitting gift to us all from a distinguished scholar.

BENJAMIN W. LABAREE

Director
Williams College–Mystic Seaport Program
in American Maritime Studies

FIVE CENTURIES
OF FAMOUS SHIPS

I

THE DAWN OF THE MODERN ERA

(1492–1660)

Santa Maria

San Rafael

Mathew

Mary Rose

Great Harry

Victoria

Jesus of Lubeck

San Pablo

Golden Hind

Revenge

Virginia of Sagadahoc

Half Moon

Unitie

Mayflower

Vasa

Sovereign of the Seas

Naseby (Royal Charles)

I

THE DAWN OF THE MODERN ERA
(1492–1660)

The vessels sailed by Christopher Columbus, Vasco da Gama, John Cabot, and other explorers of the late fifteenth and early sixteenth centuries were the first to have their names preserved in history. The *Santa Maria,* the *San Rafael,* the *Mathew,* and the *Victoria* provide, therefore, a convenient starting point for a volume on famous ships. Their fame is a result of the voyages that they made rather than innovation of design or construction. Other vessels, such as the *Mayflower,* gained immortality by carrying European settlers to colonize the New World.

The sixteenth century brought two major changes in the appearance of warships. The old, unwieldy warships had high profiles with fore and stern castles bristling with guns to ward off boarders; the new warships had lower profiles with cannon mounted in the hull. The new vessels were far more maneuverable and could engage the enemy at some distance by firing a "broadside," the simultaneous discharge of several guns along one side. England's *Revenge,* built in 1577, marked the emergence of this new class of warship. By the mid-seventeenth century, with the *Sovereign of the Seas,* came the three-decked ship of the line, a design that would remain dominant for 200 years.

Santa Maria

The *Niña, Santa Maria,* and *Pinta,* Spanish replicas which sailed to America for the Columbian Exposition of 1893. *(N. Ponce de Leon, The Caravels of Columbus, 1893)*

The *Santa Maria,* flagship of Christopher Columbus, made the most important sea voyage in history. It was from her deck in the early morning of October 12, 1492, that Columbus first saw the New World; he went ashore later in the day to take possession of the new-found island in the name of Ferdinand and Isabella of Spain. The *Santa Maria* did not long survive that famous day: 10 weeks later she became a total loss on the coral reefs off Hispaniola. His two smaller vessels, the *Niña* and *Pinta,* returned to Spain; Columbus later made three more voyages to the New World. Incidentally, the *Santa Maria* has one other claim to distinction: she is just about the first vessel in history (except perhaps Noah's Ark, and the mythical *Argo*) whose name became well known.

In the first four months of 1492, Ferdinand of Aragon and Isabella of Castile initiated three actions that had a profound effect on Spanish history. On January 2 the capture of Granada marked the expulsion of the Moors from Spain, who in 711–719 had conquered most of Spain; there was frequent warfare in the intervening years as the Christians pushed southward. Three months later, on March 30, the pious Isabella banished from Spain all Jews who refused to become Christians. Finally, during April, the rulers agreed to support Columbus in his project to reach Asia by sailing westward into the Atlantic instead of around Africa. These three important events were interrelated. The end of the centuries of wars with the Moors left thousands of soldiers available for the occupation of the new lands that Columbus would   3 discover. The expulsion of the Jews left Spain with fewer merchants to take advantage of the lands beyond the seas.

The voyaging of Columbus ushered in the Age of Discovery; in 30 years (1492–1522) three great voyages revealed a new world map to an astounded Europe. Following the Atlantic voyaging of Columbus, the Portuguese under Vasco da Gama in 1497–1498 made their way around the Cape of Good Hope to India. Finally, in 1519–1522, one of Magellan's ships circumnavigated the earth, having found the full extent of the Pacific. Interestingly enough the same years of discovery saw the climax of the High Renaissance with the work of the great artists Leonardo da Vinci, Michelangelo, and Raphael and the writings of Machiavelli.

Columbus was born near Genoa, Italy, as Cristoforo Colombo. He went to sea at an early age and soon became a skilled navigator. Because of the valuable cargoes carried to Venice and Genoa, captains had to be skillful navigators and their ships had to be well equipped. Captains often sailed under different flags; it was the nationality of the ruler or owner, not that of the captain, which counted. Columbus's efforts to find someone to finance his project of getting to the East by sailing due west were not repaid until 1492, when Isabella of Castile finally agreed to put up the $14,000 or so to pay the expenses.

The little port of Palos on the Rio Tinto played a leading part both in ships and men. Portugal cut off much of Isabella's Castile from the sea and except for the Galician-Basque region in the far north, most of the Castilian maritime activity was centered in the ports of Cadiz, Seville up the Guadalquivir River, and Palos on the Rio Tinto. In order to ease the financial costs, Isabella decreed that because of some delinquency, Palos would have to furnish two caravels. The Pinzon family of Palos, as ships' officers, played a major role in command under Columbus. The crews were mostly from the same area; there were only four non-Spaniards.

The third ship in Columbus' fleet, the *Santa Maria,* a vessel of about 100 tons, had a different background. Columbus chartered her because she happened to be lying in the river near Palos. She came from Galicia in the far north and had the unofficial nickname of *La Gallega,* or Galician. Her captain and owner, Juan de la Cosa, also a Galician, served as pilot of his ship in the voyage. Unlike the slender caravels *Niña* and *Pinta,* the *Santa Maria* was a *nao,* or full-rigged ship. (As with most of these early vessels, there is no way of knowing exactly how the three ships looked, but efforts have been made to reproduce their appearance. Replicas, built in Spain, sailed across the Atlantic in 1893 for the Columbian Exposition.) Columbus took the *Santa Maria* as his flagship because of her size, but he was not enthusiastic about her—he much preferred the little *Niña.* Both caravels, about 4 or 5 tons in size, were considerably faster than the *Santa Maria.*

The little fleet set sail on August 3, 1492, dropping down the Rio Tinto from Palos to the sea on ebb tide. The course was set for the Canary Islands, well to the southward. Whether or not he knew of the prevailing Atlantic winds beforehand, Columbus managed to get following winds westward, and also later when homeward bound. The northeast trades blew fairly steadily from the latitude of the Canaries well over toward the Caribbean, just as the westerlies would provide support from the latitude of Bermuda homeward past the Azores; to have sailed in the opposite direction would have meant constant battling of heavy winds.

Stopping at Gomera in the Canaries, which Spain had recently acquired, Columbus had a chance to round out his provisions, to change the rig on the *Pinta,* and to flirt briefly with the charming widow who was governing the islands. On September 6 he headed out into the Atlantic, confident that in less than 3000 miles he would reach the "Indies." His preliminary calculations had been faulty in underestimating the distance to Asia, which was actually some 11,000 miles.

For a while, conditions aboard ship were almost idyllic, with the steady following trade winds making nearly all work unnecessary. Things fell into a pleasant routine, following customs already well established. The duties on deck were divided between two watches, which alternated every four hours. Time was kept by cabin boys (grummets) who watched the sand run out of the half-hour glass, turning it when empty with an appropriate verse—that was the beginning of the "eight bells" arrangement for changing the watch. There were religious overtones in the daily routine, from the Pater Noster and other prayers to the evening hymn Salve Regina. Because of the blue skies and white clouds overhead and the refreshing breeze, the sailors were able to enjoy the days at sea.

Eventually, as they moved farther westward, the pleasant atmosphere changed. With the wind always from the eastward, the sailors began to wonder how they were ever going to get back to Europe, and the farther they sailed out into the unknown the more troubled they became. The Spanish crew began to question the judgment of the Italian commander, however impressive his titles might be. (Magellan, a Portuguese, would have even greater difficulty with his Spanish crews.) Not only were the ordinary mariners concerned, but the closely knit group of Palos officers also questioned the authority of the Genoese commander. Most troublesome of all was Martin Alonso Pinzon, prominent in the life of Palos and captain of the *Pinta,* and jealous of the top position of the Italian with his radical ideas. The Galician Juan de la Cosa, owner and master of the *Santa Maria,* was also jealous.

The discontent mounted until October 10, the most critical day of the voyage, when Columbus was faced with almost open mutiny just short of the West Indies. It was finally agreed between Columbus and Pinzon that if nothing was discovered in three days they would turn back. Pinzon later claimed that Columbus was so discouraged that it was Pinzon himself who urged him to go on.

By the night of October 11 there were indications that land was near at hand. Columbus claimed that he saw a single light ahead for a brief while but that it disappeared. There was a large reward for the first to report a landfall, and Columbus later secured the award for that spurious claim. About 2 A.M. on October 12 the real landfall came. The lookout on the forecastle of the fast little *Pinta* cried, "Tierra! Tierra!," and the fleet all came to life. The wind had been blowing strongly, and in the general excitement the fleet had been bowling ahead at good speed, contrary to general practice for a night approach. To avoid the possibility of piling up on a lee shore, Columbus had the fleet jog on and off until daylight.

When daylight came, the "New World" was in sight. It was one of the Bahama Islands, called Guanahani by the natives, piously named San Salvador by Columbus, and later called Watlings Island by the English. Reefs surrounded a considerable part of the island, so the fleet went around the south end to a harbor of sorts on the western side. Although reaching land was a joyous occasion in itself, a climax came later in the day when, as the old record says:

> Presently they saw naked people, and the Admiral went ashore in the armed ship's boat with the royal standard displayed. So did the captains of the *Pinta* and *Niña,* Martin Alonso Pinzon and Vinente Yanez his brother, in their boats, with the banners of the Expedition, on which was depicted a green cross with an F on one arm and a Y on the other, and over each his or her crown. And having rendered thanks to Our Lord, kneeling on the ground, embracing with joy the immeasurable mercy of having reached it, the Admiral arose and gave the island the name San Salvador. Then he summoned to his side the two captains . . . as witnesses, and in the presence of many natives of that land assembled together, took possession of the island in the name of the Catholic Sovereigns with appropriate words and ceremony.

Because of his achievements Columbus was now honored by the crews. On the way across the Atlantic, he had been referred to as Captain General, now "the Christians hailed him as Admiral and

October 12, 1492, represented the pinnacle and climax for Columbus. He had accomplished the great achievement for which he would be remembered—the discovery of America. From that time on, there would be nothing quite equal to that feat. There would be mild disappointment for a while and then graver developments, climaxing in his being brought back in chains from America in 1500. (One could almost say that, in view of their reputation, some men died at the peak of their achievement—Lord Nelson and Abraham Lincoln, for instance—while others—such as General Grant and Columbus—lived too long.)

From then until his death, Columbus believed that he had reached Asia—he felt that Cipangu, or Japan (described by Marco Polo as Zipangu), was just around the next bend. His error has been perpetuated in the phrases "Indians" and "West Indies." After two days of pleasant relations with the "Indians" of San Salvador—gentle and peaceful people of great simplicity—he sailed southwest for Cipangu. He made stops at some of the Bahamas, then reached Cuba, which he named *Juana* for the young princess of the Spanish rulers. Hoping to establish diplomatic relations with the "great khan," he optimistically sent a trained linguist, armed with Latin letters of introduction, into the interior. The envoys found a simple, hospitable Indian caique; the only tangible result of the mission was the discovery of tobacco. The fleet continued down the north coast of Cuba with no important findings. There was, however, a very troublesome defection. So far, there had been no discovery of gold; Martin Alonso Pinzon, in the *Pinta*, simply deserted on November 22, hoping to get at the gold first, and did not rejoin Columbus until mid-January.

Crossing over the Windward Passage to the great island which Columbus named "La Isla Española" (now Haiti and Santo Domingo), gold suddenly became obvious in the decorations of the natives, who reported that there was much more gold not too far distant. Columbus was received warmly by the caique Guacanagari, who ruled northwestern Haiti, and there was prospect of much more gold to come. Reaching Cape Haitien, he received enthusiastic demonstrations of hospitality. For two nights, just before Christmas, natives arrived by canoe to swarm aboard the *Santa Maria*, bringing gold and other gifts. Columbus estimated that more than a thousand natives came aboard.

By Christmas eve those two days of hospitality had left the entire personnel of the *Santa Maria* in a state of utter weariness. Columbus retired to his cabin and so did the master, Juan de la Cosa. Man after man tumbled into sleep until shortly after midnight, the only person still awake was a boy to whom the helmsman, contrary to regulations, entrusted the tiller. Because of these shocking conditions, the *Santa Maria* slid onto a shelving coral reef, with a groundswell driving her further onto it. The boy sounded the alarm; Columbus and the crew rushed on deck and tried to haul the ship off the coral, but to no effect. Juan de la Cosa, second in command and owner of the ship, tried to desert in the only boat and headed for the *Niña*, but was turned back. The coral punched holes in the hull, which filled with water. The mainmast was cut away in an effort to lighten the ship, but the situation grew worse. Guacanagari's Indians helped to salvage what they could from the ship. They stole nothing from their guests, but rather brought still more gold.

It was clear that the *Santa Maria* was a total loss, and Columbus had to make plans to meet the crisis. With the *Pinta* still away, it was obvious that the *Niña* could not absorb the 40-man crew of the flagship. He decided to leave the men ashore to form a colony at Navidad, on the edge of the gold country. It has even been claimed that Columbus, wanting to establish a colony but knowing that he could probably get no volunteers, deliberately arranged the shipwreck, but that is hard to credit. During the next few days a fort was built with timber and fastenings from the ship. Columbus shifted his flag to the *Niña*, which was his favorite ship. She sailed on January 2, nine days after the wreck, and soon joined the *Pinta*. Pinzon, arrogant as ever, made some lame excuses, and the two returned by the northward route, with its following westerlies. After falling into the hands of the Portuguese at the Azores, the *Niña* was back at Palos in mid-1493. Columbus took her again for his second voyage later that year.

(See J. M. Martínez-Hidalgo, *Columbus' Ships*, 1966; S. E. Morison, *Christopher Columbus, Mariner*, 1955.)

San Rafael

The second of the three great voyages of exploration was made by Vasco da Gama, who opened the sea route around Africa to India between July 1497 and September 1499. It was the culmination of eight decades of Portuguese sailing down the coast of Africa, starting with Prince Henry the Navigator's initiative. Da Gama's experience thus differed from that of Columbus in the first great voyage of exploration in 1492 and from that of Magellan in the third great voyage in 1519, both of whom had to persuade the Spanish crown to back them. In contrast,

da Gama was suddenly called upon by the king of Portugal to carry
through the longstanding Portuguese search for a new route to India.

The Portuguese caravels had been beating their way down the coast of Africa since 1415. By the time of Henry the Navigator's death in 1460, the caravels had rounded the Cape Verde Islands and reached as far as Sierra Leone. The Crown had continued its support, and in 1487–1488 Bartholomeu Dias had actually rounded the stormy tip, which the king decided to name the Cape of Good Hope, because now the way seemed clear to reach India. Then, strange to say, the Crown waited nearly a decade before following up Dias' discovery. And during that decade, Columbus had made for Spain his great voyage of discovery. The only consolation to the Portuguese was that Columbus had brought back no spices.

Another special aspect of the da Gama voyage was that the Europeans already knew somewhat of the distant country. For several centuries, the Malabar Coast of southwest India had profited richly as an entrepôt, collecting its toll on the spice trade from eastern seas, and thence on through the Persian Gulf or Red Sea and over to the Mediterranean, where Venice and Genoa picked up the precious cargoes and distributed them throughout Europe. That trade was well organized in the hands of Moors, a general term which included Arabs and other Moslems. They realized that if the Portuguese could load a cargo of spices on the Malabar Coast and deliver it nonstop to Lisbon, they could avoid the high transshipment costs. That consideration would provide tense drama for da Gama out on the Malabar Coast.

Da Gama's ships were about the same modest size as the *Santa Maria* of Columbus and the *Victoria* of Magellan, about 100 tons. The Portuguese ships were new vessels, specially built for the expedition under the watchful eye of the king, who named them the *San Rafael*, da Gama's flagship; the *San Gabriel*, commanded by his brother Pedro; and the *San Miguel*, or *Berrio*, with young Nicolas Cohelo in command; the *San Miguel* would be scrapped and burned on the outward passage.

The squadron sailed from Lisbon on July 9, 1497; large crowds saw them off, not all of whom were cheering. In the lengthy poem, the *Lusiads*, the great Portuguese poet Camões told how numerous people lamented the possibility that so many of these young men, facing the perils of the sea, might never return. In fact, barely half the 150 men did survive the voyage; scurvy, in particular, took a very heavy toil.

One aspect of the outward voyage had an important lasting effect. The earlier Portuguese African voyages had headed down along the coast and had to beat head winds much of the way. Da Gama, instead, took advantage of the ocean winds by heading southwest almost to the coast of Brazil and then turning southeast for the Cape of Good Hope.

No one is certain as to just why da Gama took this step, since he had little experience in exploration. It seems likely therefore that this route was suggested by someone else. At any rate, when the next Portuguese expedition set out for India, it actually hit the tip of Brazil and established Portugal's claim to the area. Throughout the age of sail for another four centuries, the sailing directions gave this as the approved route.

The squadron doubled the Cape of Good Hope in November and put in on the east coast on Christmas Day, naming their landfall Natal. Then they encountered the same sort of vicious storm which had caused da Gama's officers and crew to insist on turning back. The Portuguese crews panicked and were on the verge of mutiny. The three captains met this with a combination of force and guile. Each ship handled its own trouble, without allowing the crews to get together. The officers threw the navigating instruments overboard, to point up the difficulty of getting home without them. Shortly afterward, finding a suitable shelter, they careened their battered ships and broke up the worn-out *San Miguel.*

An important difference between this voyage and the voyages of Columbus was that the Portuguese encountered sophisticated, highly developed Moors whereas Columbus encountered simpler, less cultured natives. On the east coast of Africa the Moors were not only worldly-wise, but often tricky and treacherous, causing some difficulties at Mozambique and Mombasa. At Malindi, on the other hand, the "king" was cordial and cooperative, and provided three months of lavish entertainment. The king then furnished them with an able pilot for the three weeks' crossing of the Indian Ocean to the Malabar Coast.

On August 26 the *San Rafael* had a climactic experience similar to that of Columbus' men approaching San Salvador. As Camões expressed it:

"Pale shone the waves beneath the golden beam;
Blue o'er the silver flood Malabria's mountains gleam;
The sailors on the maintop's airy round.
Land, land, aloud with waving hands resound;
Aboard the pilot of Malindi cries,
Behold, O chief, the shores of India rise!"

They were approaching Calicut (not to be confused with Calcutta), the most active seaport-entrepôt of the Malabar Coast. The king of Portugal had earlier sent out one Pedro de Covilham to scout the port and its trade. It was one of those west coast city-states, whose king or "zamorin" had a major interest in its trade.

Da Gama's men soon ran into difficulties: first suspicion of their trade intentions and then open hostility. The well-entrenched Moors, composing a sort of chamber of commerce, determined to fight this threat to their rich trade. They had an influential, well-bribed ally in the zamorin's director of the exchequer, who was ready to throw every obstacle in the way of the Portuguese. They sneered at the gifts da Gama brought. When the trading started, the zamorin saw a chance to unload on the Portuguese inferior spices that the Moors would not buy. The Moors protested, pointing out that anyone stupid enough to pay full price for such material could not be real traders, but were probably spies. When the Moors saw that the Portuguese were going ahead with the trade anyway, they tried to persuade their bribed officials to kill da Gama's men, imposing one intolerable insult after another in the hope that the Portuguese would start a fight and could thus be cut down. But da Gama played his cards well and was able to slip out to sea with a cargo of mediocre spices, planning revenge when the Portuguese would return.

On his homeward passage, da Gama stopped in at the nearby port of Cannanore, whose king with his eye on the next Portuguese voyage treated them cordially and generously. And more of that pleasant treatment came at Malindi; no time was wasted on the hostile ports. For once, there was decent weather in the usually storm-wracked waters near Good Hope. The ships, in increasingly bad condition, reached the island of Terceira, where Pedro da Gama died. The two ships limped on to Lisbon, having lost many of their crews from scurvy.

Their arrival marked one of the happiest days in Portugal's history. Prince Henry the Navigator's dream had finally led to success, and the country was on the eve of a glorious but exhausting colonial adventure in the East. Portugal made no attempt to extend its authority far inland in Africa or India; its whole colonial empire could be seen from the decks of passing vessels, consisting as it did of fortified trading posts. The plan was too ambitious. Not enough trained Portuguese were available to man such an empire, and a century later much of it fell to the Dutch and the English. Da Gama was richly rewarded for his success and returned twice to India, the second time as viceroy. But his flagship *San Rafael* did not hold together for those later voyages.

(See K. G. Jayne, *Vasco da Gama and His Successors, 1460–1580*, 1970.)

Mathew

For an exploring voyage of the highest significance, the records are amazingly meager about the crossing of John Cabot to America in 1497 in the little *Mathew*. The voyage gave England a claim to North America, and it also led to the rapid growth of the cod fishery of the Grand Banks. Yet the story has to be pieced together and still has many gaps.

Cabot was probably born in Genoa about 1450. His father took him to Venice as a boy and he was naturalized there in 1476. Cabot was a mariner and, as partial background for his exploring, had visited Mecca, where the spice trade suggested going direct to the source of the spices. He had moved to Bristol by 1495, apparently feeling that England offered the best chance for backing. On March 5, 1496, he received letters patent from King Henry VII granting sweeping powers in whatever unknown lands he might discover, but the voyage was to be at his own expense.

He had only one little 50-ton vessel for this venture. The *Mathew* had square rigs on the fore- and mainmasts, with lateen on the mizzen—a conjectural model at Bristol shows a solid rather than graceful build; the poop and forecastle were not as high as on many vessels of the day. Her crew numbered only 18.

The ship sailed from Bristol about May 20, 1497, and made its landfall, presumably at the northern tip of Newfoundland, on June 24. This was good time for a westbound North Atlantic crossing. The passage was apparently uneventful and the *Mathew* proved herself a good sailer. Samuel Eliot Morison, in his *Northern Voyages* says, "So let us supply a little imagination to bridge the few known facts." He manages to build up a quite convincing story.

Cabot's landfall was close to the Strait of Belle Isle, which separates Newfoundland from the Labrador mainland, near Cape Degrat and, in Morison's estimate, barely five miles from where Leif Ericson had made his temporary settlement in 1001. At any rate, on the one occasion when he went ashore, Cabot, with proper ceremonial, took possession in the name of Henry VII, displaying the banners of England and of Venice. At no time on this side of the Atlantic did he encounter any natives.

Somehow—the evidence is not clear—he made a run to the southward and encountered the Grand Banks, which were swarming with codfish, so plentiful that one had only to lower a bucket over the side to have it filled. Then, after possibly returning north to Cape Degrat, he headed for home, making a quick 15-day passage to the Breton coast and then doubling back to Bristol, where he arrived on August 6.

He proceeded at once to London, where King Henry was most appreciative. The accounts of the royal household show that on August 11, Henry gave "£10 to hym that founde the new Isle" and later settled on him an annuity of £10 to be charged against the Bristol customs. Cabot had a real heyday with his royal grant, strutting around in London with crowds who "run after him like madmen."

Cabot proceeded at once to plan a new voyage, with new letters patent from the king. He had one ship at royal expense and four others

backed by Bristol merchants. (There is no record as to whether the
Mathew was included) They sailed in May 1498; one ship returned fairly soon, the rest were never heard from again. Cabot's son, Sebastian, had made the first voyage but did not go on the second. He would have a long and prominent career in the Spanish service, helping to develop the Plata region and serving as a pilot general. Eventually, in Mary's reign, he returned to England and helped promote the quest for a northeast passage.

(See S. E. Morison, *The European Discovery of America—Northern Voyages, 500–1600,* 1971.)

Mary Rose

When Henry VIII started the transition to the modern big gun broadside, with gunports cut in the hull, the first two ships so constructed were the *Great Harry (Henri Grace à Dieu)* and the somewhat smaller *Mary Rose.* The latter was named for Henry's sister Mary, a lively girl who was briefly queen of France; after her husband died, she married the man she wanted. It is not certain which ship first had holes cut in the hull to accommodate the heavy bronze guns placed in the hold. The *Mary Rose* was launched in 1509, five years before the *Great Harry,* but the guns and gunports may have come later. She was rebuilt in 1536, and her tonnage was increased from 500 to 700.

The record of her sudden end, however is well recorded. In 1545, when a French fleet attacked Portsmouth, the king was in the *Great Harry,* flagship of the defending English fleet, which included the *Mary Rose.* There had been strong skepticism in naval circles about the safety of cutting those gunports in the hull. That skepticism was confirmed when the *Mary Rose* heeled over in the breeze. The water rushed in through the open ports, which were barely 16 inches above the waterline, and she sank quickly. Only 45 of a crew of some 600 survived. The victims included the captain, Sir Henry Carew, whose wife was ashore and witnessed the disaster. The flooding of the ports a century later caused a similar wreck of the big new Swedish warship *Vasa.* The *Mary Rose's* big brass cannon were recovered, and the whole ship was raised and restored. The nature of her loss did not prevent further cutting of gunports in the hull, but there would be frequent occasions when the big ships were unable to use the lower tier of guns in heavy weather. As with so many of those Tudor ship names, there would be seven other *Mary Roses* down to World War II.

(See E. H. Archibald, *The Wooden Fighting Ships in the Royal Navy, A.D. 897–1860,* 1968.)

Great Harry (Henri Grace à Dieu)

King Henry VIII has been credited by some as being the father of the English navy because he started the conversion of the clumsy tubs into effective fighting craft. His special drastic innovation came in 1514, when he introduced heavy cannon into the hold of the *Great Harry*, having holes cut in the sides of the ship so that the cannon could be fired against the enemy ship. This was possibly before the *Mary Rose* was altered and may have marked the beginning of the broadside, which became the principal naval force for more than four centuries.

Earlier warships had guns, but they were light guns scattered through the high towers at bow and stern. They were called "man-killers" because, in the close fighting of the rival ships alongside each other, they would fire down on the enemy crews, maiming and killing them, but seldom doing any harm to the tough hulls. King Henry was keenly interested in the big bronze-case guns that came from the foundry of Hans Poppenruyter at Mechelen (Malines) in Flanders. He ordered some for his navy and tried them out by flattening the houses of the London suburb of Hounsditch. The great change in warships resulting from this innovation was that they became "ship-killers" from the blows of the new guns in the hull. Earlier sea fights had been virtually infantry fights at sea with the rivals close alongside; now it became possible to stay off at some distance to pound the enemy.

The *Henri Grace à Dieu*, popularly known as the *Great Harry*, was started at Woolwich in October 1512 and launched in June 1514. She would seem to have been some 165-feet long and to have measured 1000 to 1500 tons. The shipwrights had objected to cutting holes in the side for the great guns, but the king was insistent. There was a risk in this; the other great gun ship built at this time, the *Mary Rose*, suddenly heeled over and sank when the water came through her lower gunports. The *Great Harry* still had some of the awkward features of the old medieval round ship, with high forecastle and poop, but these were less extreme than in the earlier ships and their light "man-killing" guns were reduced in number.

The *Great Harry* saw relatively little action—she was not involved with the French when they came over in 1545. She was luxuriously fitted out as a showpiece. One painting showed her setting out for the Field of the Cloth of Gold, but some claim that she was not in that expedition. She finally came to an end in 1553 when she caught fire at Woolwich, but she had served importantly as the example of the new heavy guns, firing through portholes cut in the hull.

(See M. A. Lewis, *The History of the British Navy*, 1957.)

Victoria (Vittoria)

In September 1522 the little 85-ton *Victoria* limped up the river from Sanlúcar de Barrameda to Seville in Spain, whence she had sailed three years before. In the meantime, she had become the first vessel in history to circumnavigate the world. This extraordinary feat not only confirmed the theory that the earth was round, but also revealed the unsuspectedly huge size of the Pacific Ocean. The *Victoria* was now alone of the five ships that had sailed under Ferdinand Magellan in 1519; less than one-tenth of the men had survived, and Magellan's body lay in the Philippines where he had been killed.

The *Victoria's* arrival rounded out the most important 30 years in the history of exploration. In 1492 Columbus had discovered America, and in 1497–1499 da Gama had sailed around the tip of Africa and on to India, laying the foundations of the European empire in the East. There would be more exploring in the future, but none of it would compare in significance to those 30 years in the High Renaissance period.

Magellan's story goes back to 1513 when Vasco Núñez de Balboa, from a hill near Panama, first looked upon the Pacific Ocean and waded out to take possession of it for the king of Spain. Columbus had died, apparently believing that he had reached the "Indies." Now it was clear that much ocean lay to the westward of America.

It was Ferdinand Magellan's project to explore that sea. He came from a noble Portuguese family of French descent, and had been brought up as a page at the royal court—a rather rugged page. He went out to India with Francisco d'Almeida, the first viceroy, and took part in the Portuguese seizure of Malacca, getting out to the edge of the Spice Islands. Next, he went on an expedition to Morocco where, fairly or unfairly, he was charged with graft. At any rate, it was clear that he had no future in the Portuguese service—in their final interview the king would not let Magellan kiss his hand.

But there was another king not far away. Magellan went at once to young Charles of Spain, soon to be known as the Emperor Charles V. Magellan pointed out the possibility of claiming the rich Spice Islands, by projecting the line of demarcation around the world. Pope Alexander VI in 1493 had decreed that the newly discovered lands should be divided between Portugal (all those in Asia and Africa) and Spain (America); the demarcation was slightly modified in 1494, giving Portugal a claim to Brazil. Magellan now suggested that the demarcation line, originally an Atlantic matter, be projected around the world to the edge of the Portuguese coast.

The *Victoria*, or *Vittoria*, would be the only one of Magellan's five ships to survive the voyage. She was also the only ship whose antecedents are known. Like Columbus' *Santa Maria*, she was a Basque product, built at the little port of Guizpiziozm, which was also the home of Juan Sebastian de Elcano, her final master. She was one of the smaller vessels; the flagship *Trinidad* measured 100 tons; the *San Antonio*, 120 tons; the *Concepción*, 90 tons; and the caravel *Santiago*, 75 tons. That was about the average tonnage of Columbus' three ships and of various other exploring squadrons of those early days. The crews numbered somewhat over 200 men; there were numerous junior officers, which was fortunate because the mortality among commanders was going to be heavy.

King Charles commissioned Magellan to find his way through or around America and across the Pacific to the rich islands which he already knew from the approach around the Cape of Good Hope. One of his closest friends was already located on Ternate, the leading source of cloves. A cause of latent trouble was the fact that Magellan, like Columbus, was a foreigner in an expedition manned largely by Spaniards. The captains of three of the ships began conspiring very early.

The story moves from one dramatic episode to another—the mutiny at Port St. Julian in Patagonia; the passage of the famous strait; the near starvation in the Pacific crossing; the death of Magellan and the massacre in the Philippines; the purchase of cloves and division of forces at Ternate; and finally the grueling home voyage in the *Victoria*.

The expedition crossed the Atlantic and had pleasant shore liberty in Rio de Janeiro. But the atmosphere grew more somber as they moved south and spent time in sheltered Port St. Julian in Patagonia. By that time, mutiny was taking form under three of the Spanish captains, with a plot to kill Magellan and sail back to Spain. On Palm Sunday, the bad captains refused Magellan's invitation to dine with him. Thus forewarned, he moved fast. He sent a boat over to the *Victoria*; when her captain laughed at Magellan's letter, he was stabbed to death. When the *Concepción* tried to escape, the flagship spouted broadsides and musketry into her and the captain was taken prisoner. The captain of the *San Antonio*, seeing how things were going, gave himself up without a fight. Having quickly gained control of the situation, Magellan established a court-martial which condemned all the mutineers; he pardoned most of them, including Elcano, who would bring the *Victoria* home. The three bad captains, however, received spectacular drastic treatment. A gallows was set up for the execution of the *Concepción*'s captain, with the body of the *Victoria*'s captain placed alongside. (This was the spot where Drake, a half century later, would have a prominent troublemaker beheaded.) Magellan had the third captain marooned, along with a troublemaking chaplain. They were howling as the fleet sailed away, leaving them to their fate. There was one more mutiny, which meant the loss of a ship; in Magellan's temporary absence, the crew of the *San Antonio* deposed their captain and sailed back to Spain. The little caravel *Santiago* had already been wrecked while searching for provisions on the coast. So now, only three ships headed for the Pacific.

According to the chronicler of the voyage, Magellan had seen a map in the treasury of the king, showing a well-defined strait at the south end of South America. Apparently a big antarctic continent lay below it—the existence of Cape Horn would not be known until the voyage of the *Unitie* in 1616.

The entrance to the 334-mile strait, which would ever after bear the name Magellan, was discovered on October 21, 1520. The scenery was magnificent and the peril constant. Even for steamers in modern times it involves hazardous navigation. The modern official sailing directions describe it as "both difficult and dangerous because of incomplete soundings, lack of aids to navigation, the great distances between anchorages, the strong current, and the meager limits for maneuvering of vessels." As late as 1974 a 200,000-ton tanker hit a rock in the strait, producing a 60-mile oil slick up the coast of Chile. However, Magellan seems to have lived a charmed life. His ships missed the worst rocks and the most vicious squalls.

On November 28, after a 38-day passage, the ships sailed out into the open sea. It was so calm that he named it Pacific, a name that would crowd out Balboa's "South Sea," a phrase now employed largely in travel literature.

Emerging from the ordeal of the strait, the *Trinidad, Concepción,* and *Victoria* were shortly to be involved in an even more grueling one. Neither they nor anyone else had any conception of the size of the newly discovered ocean. They sailed northward to about the latitude of the future Valparaiso, then headed westward. So far as weather went, they sailed for three months without encountering a storm. What is more remarkable, considering how thickly the Pacific is studded with islands and atolls, they missed them all except one which was uninhabited and had no food or water. That produced a desperate logistical situation, with an ever increasing danger of starvation. This was partly the fault of cheating ship chandlers in Seville and partly because no one had any idea of such a long voyage. As supplies ran out, rats sold at a ducat apiece; and the crew ate the leather chafing gear on the yards.

Finally, on March 6, 1521, nearly 100 days out from the strait, they came upon the lush island of Guam; after a short fight with the natives Magellan persuaded the islanders to give the crews food and water. But the natives were such shameless thieves that Guam came to be known as the Ladrones' (or Thieves') Island.

Magellan then moved on to the Philippines, in the central area where the battle of Leyte Gulf, greatest of sea actions, would be fought in 1944. Stops were made at various islands, but Magellan's strange ideas caused a crisis at Cebu, where Sultan Humabon was most hospitable. There was a round of banqueting and lively trading, but Magellan's main enthusiasm was for making converts to Christianity. The sultan himself became a convert, so did his sultana and ultimately 1000 others. Magellan even offered recruiting inducements: he said that if the girls were baptized, his men "could have intercourse with their women without committing a very great sin." In summing up the visit, Morison wrote: "Up to a point, the stay at Cebu was the most delightful of the entire voyage, even better than Rio de Janeiro. The men had plenty to eat and drink, the women were kind both before and after conversion. Magellan felt very proud of being the means of saving a thousand souls and acquiring a new province for Spain. Alas, if he could only have left well enough alone!"

This tranquil, pleasant scene suddenly erupted into tragedy. Magellan offered the support of his armed soldiers to attack any enemy of the sultan. Humabon accepted the offer to attack a troublesome rajah on a nearby island. On April 27, 1521, Magellan made a bungled amphibious attack on Mactan with 60 soldiers; 1500 of the enemy returned the attack and drove them back toward the boats. Magellan tried to cover their retreat. Wounded, he fought for an hour, but finally fell down in the water and was slashed to death.

A second tragedy followed closely. Upon being told that the Spaniards were plotting against him, the king invited all the Spaniards to a state banquet, then had three of the captains massacred and the others of lesser rank either killed or sold as slaves to the Chinese. "Cebu immediately relapsed into paganism," remarked Morison, "and every evidence of the brief experiment with Christianity was destroyed."

The survivors, who had drawn their ships out of range, now took stock of their shattered condition. Three captains had been lost in the Port St. Julian mutiny, and now three more, plus Magellan, were dead. Only 111 men were left, less than half those who set out from Spain. It was decided to burn the *Concepción* and move everyone and everything into the surviving *Trinidad* and *Victoria*.

The two ships then moved on toward the East Indies, where the men spent a delightful month of "rest and recreation" at Palawan. Finally, they arrived at the original target of the voyage, the rich clove island of Ternate in the Spice Islands. Magellan's closest friend had been there, but had recently been killed. There was also the possibility that the line of demarcation might be stretched to include these islands in the Spanish sphere. The Spaniards were greeted hospitably and acquired a generous amount of cloves.

Then came the question of getting back home. It was decided that the *Victoria* now under the command of Juan Sebastian de Elcano, who had been pardoned as a St. Julian mutineer, would go home through the Portuguese East Indies and around Good Hope. The *Trinidad* under Gomez de Espinosa would try the Pacific route to Mexico. She struggled out into the Pacific storms, not knowing of the smoother route to the northward, only to be captured by the Portuguese. After several years of captivity, Espinosa returned to Spain, where Charles V honored him generously.

In the meantime, the little *Victoria* began to thread her way through the hostile waters of the Portuguese Indies. Elcano was an expert navigator but of somewhat doubtful character. The ship began her final share of the great voyage on December 21, 1521, with 47 Europeans and 13 natives. She dodged the more prominent places until she reached Timor for a pleasant month in that island of sandalwood. After a long battle with headwinds and scurvy, developed during the crossing of the Indian Ocean, the *Victoria* finally rounded the Cape of Good Hope. More hardship followed as the ship came up the west coast of Africa. In the Cape Verde Islands, the suspicious Portuguese tried to detain them. Elcano was forced to leave some of his crew ashore and escape with the remaining 18, who had grueling work at the pumps to keep the ship afloat. After a rugged passage, she finally reached Sanlúcar at the mouth of the Guadalquivir River; two boats towed her up the river to Seville, where she anchored on September 8, three years after setting out.

Charles V received Elcano graciously, awarding him a generous pension and a coat of arms showing cloves and other spices and two Malay chiefs. The 26 tons of cloves from Ternate brought the equivalent of some $22,680, and the other spices $1800 more. Despite all losses, the voyage showed a good profit.

The *Victoria,* after extensive repairs, made one round voyage to the West Indies and then disappeared with all hands. Elcano received high honors in the Basque country, splurged in new finery, fathered bastards in two Spanish cities, and then set out as pilot of another Spanish Pacific expedition, on which he died.

(See C. M. Parr, *Ferdinand Magellan Circumnavigator,* 1964.)

Jesus of Lubeck

The *Jesus of Lubeck* was an old-fashioned "high-charged" warship which Henry VIII had purchased for the navy from the Hanseatic League in 1544. Queen Elizabeth loaned her to a reluctant John Hawkins for his African-West Indian slaving voyages in 1564 and 1567. The old 700-ton tub had so deteriorated in the intervening 20 years that she was a constant liability, but her very worthlessness had its usefulness in turning Hawkins' mind toward the smaller and more efficient *Revenge* type.

The older ships had been designed for defense in close action. If the enemy swarmed into the waist, he still had to attack the two veritable forts of the forecastle and poop. In the meantime the little "man-killer" guns could play down upon the enemy. Such a ship, like the others of the earlier days, might carry a few heavy guns, following the *Great Harry* example, but most of the action was at close range. The old tubs were slow and difficult to maneuver.

The queen gave her permission for the slaving voyages but exacted a price. She bestowed the old *Jesus of Lubeck* on Hawkins on the condition that she would get a generous percentage of the expedition's profits. Hawkins found the vessel something of a nuisance on his first 1564–1565 voyage, but a very serious liability on the second in 1567–1568. One of her company described her condition after a Caribbean storm:

> The *Jesus* was brought in such a case that she was not able to bear the sea longer, for in her stern on either side of the sternpost the planks did open and shut with every sea . . . the leaks so big as the thickness of a man's arm, the living fish did swim upon the ballasts as in the sea. Our general, seeing this, did his utmost to stop her leaks, as divers times before he had. And truly, without his great experience, we had been sunk in the sea in her within six days after we came out of England. . . .

Hawkins came to the unwelcome conclusion that before heading in to the Atlantic for home, he would have to put in for repairs. The one available place, before entering the Florida Strait, was the Mexican port of San Juan de Ulloa, near Veracruz, the port at which the annual plate fleets called. Although Spain technically allowed no trade with foreigners, Hawkins felt that help to a vessel in distress might be permitted. He had hardly landed at San Juan, however, when the annual plate fleet arrived in full force, with the new viceroy aboard. Permission was granted for the repairs, but on September 23, 1567, the Spaniards suddenly went back on their word and attacked. The *Jesus* was in too helpless a condition to move, but some of the smaller vessels escaped, including those with Hawkins and Francis Drake, who was also on the expedition. Many of the English crews were imprisoned and some were killed by the Inquisition. One wonders whether, in naming his important new-style ship the *Revenge* nine years later, Hawkins may not have had San Juan de Ulloa in mind.

(See R. V. B. Blackman, *Ships of the Royal Navy*, 1973.)

San Pablo

For nearly 250 years, from 1567 to 1815, an annual lone Spanish ship, richly laden, crossed the Pacific between Acapulco in Mexico and the Philippines. This so-called Manila Galleon helped to make Manila a rich entrepôt, exchanging Mexican silver for Chinese silks, porcelain, and other products normally very difficult to export from China.

The inauguration of this service dated from an east-bound Pacific passage in the *San Pablo* under the direction of Andres de Urdaneta, one of the most skillful Spanish navigators and maritime leaders in the Pacific area, where he had first gone as a youth with Magellan. Urdaneta eventually became an Augustinian friar, and therefore was not eligible for a top command, but was actually in general charge under a nominal leader.

Urdaneta's big discovery, which would make the Manila Galleon operation possible, was a practicable route from Asia to America. Because of the Pacific wind pattern, it had been relatively simple for Magellan to sail westward to Asia with following winds, but the eastward passage was a different matter. One of Magellan's ships had tried the eastward route only to be driven back by fierce gales. Urdaneta found that the answer lay in sailing very far to the northward—so far north that the Manila Galleons never discovered Hawaii.

Philip II of Spain, for whom the Philippines were named, decided to bring those islands more securely into the Spanish fold, and ordered an expedition to be sent out for that purpose. Because of Urdaneta's high reputation, the king wrote him personally, inviting him to go as chief pilot and allowing him to nominate the captain general. Urdaneta chose Miguel de Legazpi as commander. The fleet sailed from Mexico on November 24, 1564, and established a temporary capital at Cebu, before moving to Manila in 1571.

It was decided to send the second largest ship, the *San Pablo*, of more than 300 tons, back to Mexico at once with Urdaneta in real charge. Instead of sailing directly eastward, he went northward to latitude 39°50′ N. There he picked up the westerlies, which carried the ship for almost three months without even sighting land. The *San Pablo* reached

California near Santa Barbara and then moved south to the Mexican port of Acapulco. That would thereafter be the route of the Manila Galleons.

With the voyage in 1566 to show what could be done, the annual voyages started the next year, to continue uninterrupted until 1815. The name Manila Galleon came into use with the shift of the capital from Cebu to Manila in 1571. The trade developed to such an extent that, when the English sea dog Thomas Cavendish captured the 1587 galleon *Santa Ana,* her cargo of gold, pearls, silks, and the like was estimated as worth a million pesos in Manila and twice as much in Europe. The English and other nationals kept hunting for another such tempting prize, but only three other galleons were ever captured.

(See W. L. Schurz, *The Manila Galleon,* 1959.)

Golden Hind

In historical aspect glamorous events are not always significant, while routine, dull affairs may be important. The bold Elizabethan seamen, however, stand high in both categories. They engaged in all sorts of lively exploits against the Spaniards, even when England was neutral. The Spaniards called them pirates, but the English begged the question by calling them "sea dogs," patting them on the back, and remaining proud of them ever since as clever rascals. These sea dogs were highly important because they opened the way to England's remarkable expansion on the seas and overseas.

One of these sea dogs, Francis Drake (later Sir Francis) has been called (like King Arthur and Lord Nelson) one of England's leading "father images," highly popular with successive generations of enthusiastic Englishmen. In his sea-dog role, Drake is associated with three different vessels. First, in the little *Judith* he raided the Spanish Main and was nearly captured at San Juan de Ulloa. Later, the *Revenge,* one of the crack new fast sea-dog galleons, carried Drake's flag as vice admiral of the fleet that wrecked the Spanish Armada. But between them, and best loved of the three, was the *Golden Hind,* in which he made the second circumnavigation of the earth after profitably raiding the Spanish colonies on the west coast of America.

Just as Balboa on looking down from the peak in Darien had sighted the Pacific for the first time, Drake, after raiding the Isthmus of Panama, looked down on the great western ocean and had an inspiration. He

knew that his Caribbean raiding had aroused the Spaniards to such fear
of "El Draque" that they were guarding everything so well that further
surprise would be quite difficult. But his glimpse of the Pacific
reminded him that a generous share of Spain's treasure came from
mines of Peru and was brought up the coast by ship from Callao to
Panama without any apparent need for special precautions. An expedition through the Strait of Magellan, therefore, might catch those ships
and the entire Spanish west coast settlements unguarded.

Back in England, he went after support for such a bold project.
England was neutral—a useful status when Europe was caught in the
religious wars of the counterreformation—and Elizabeth's chief adviser,
William Cecil, did not want to jeopardize that neutrality. His ardent
younger colleague, Francis Walsingham, however, was ready to take a
chance in the Protestant cause, as were some of the other Elizabethan
advisers. Elizabeth inclined toward Walsingham's views.

As a result, a group was secretly formed to back the exploit. The
"Pious Pirates," as a later writer called them, could strike a blow for
England and Protestantism, but at the same time could probably take
loot which would make the expedition highly profitable.

Over at the sea-dog base in Plymouth in southwest England, Drake
began to assemble a flotilla. This expedition was a sort of temporary
syndicate, with the capital contributed by a number of wealthy men
who would receive appropriate shares of any profits which might
result. Queen Elizabeth may have given some sort of informal permission. At any rate, she would get a good share of the profits.

Drake's flagship was the *Pelican,* which, when he entered the Strait of
Magellan he would rename the *Golden Hind,* the symbol on the crest of
Drake's wealthy principal supporter, Sir Christopher Hatton. The
Golden Hind was a good sturdy ship of 100 to 120 tons, belonging to the
Hawkins family and presumably originally a French Huguenot priva-
teer. There were two other large vessels, also a "flyboat" and two small
pinnaces, but shortly after leaving the Strait of Magellan, the *Golden
Hind* would be alone.

Drake sailed on December 13, 1577, from Plymouth. In January he
was at the Cape Verde Islands and picked up some small prizes in that
area. He skirted the Brazilian coast, explored briefly the River Plate, and
in June reached Magellan's stopping place of Port St. Julian in Patagonia. There a grim coincidence occured. Drake had given a high
position to his brilliant friend Thomas Doughty, but became convinced
that Doughty was plotting against him. A fleet court-martial voted that
"it would be unsafe to let him live." After dining and receiving com-
munion with Doughty, Drake had him beheaded on the spot where
Magellan had gibbeted his two mutinous captains.

The passage of the Strait of Magellan was unusually easy with a helpful following wind. In 16 days Drake reached the Pacific, but found it anything but pacific. A gale drove him south to within 60 miles of Cape Horn before the winds changed. One vessel was lost, another put back to England, and the *Golden Hind* went on alone.

Then began the great raiding of the west coast. The Spaniards had spread far south since the days of Pizarro and had established numerous little communities, at many of which silver from the interior reached the coast. Drake was thorough in his looting, but he did not believe in unnecessary roughness and countenanced no killing or raping. The marauders once found a Spaniard asleep with 13 barrels of silver, a flock of sheep, and some jerked beef. They appropriated his property but left him uninjured, screaming with rage. At Valparaiso they looted the church and carried off all the Chilean wine they could find. Apparently the Spaniards had not spread the alarm up the coast, hoping their disgrace would not be advertised, so Drake continued to take places by surprise.

The richest booty came when the expedition overtook a treasure ship, nicknamed *Cacafuego*, which had just left Callao for Panama. Never suspecting an English ship in those seas, the commander let Drake come alongside after some preliminary shots. Three days were required to move the treasure to the *Golden Hind,* which by this time was heavily loaded. The haul was estimated at 337,000 pesos, or $500,000. Drake then played the "very proper caballero." He gave gifts to each of the Spanish crew and to the passengers before releasing the ship.

The Spaniards assumed Drake would probably return by the Strait of Magellan and established two lonesome posts there to catch him. But he headed north up the coast as far as Oregon and then returned to California. He had some idea of locating the western end of the North-west Passage but gave that up. He spent five weeks in June and July of 1579 at a bay he called New Albion—the classical name for England— partly because of its white cliffs. He careened the *Golden Hind* there and established friendly relations with the Indians. Even four centuries later strenuous feuding has continued over just where that bay was located. Some would say that Drake found San Francisco Bay, but the consensus seems to be that the bay was near Point Reyes, where the white cliffs lend some point to the name New Albion. One factor in the feuding has been a brass-on-lead plate picked up in 1936 near San Francisco Bay and supposedly inscribed by Drake. The burden of proof, however, seems to be strongly against its authenticity.

The rest of the voyage was without high adventure. For two months, the expedition sighted no land. They sailed along Mindanao in the Philippines and then put in at Ternate, where they spent several days

and talked of establishing an English trading post; finally they departed
with a good load of cloves. Later, on an uninhabited island, Drake
careened the ship for a necessary cleaning off of tropical growths. The
one cause for alarm came when the *Golden Hind* ran on a shelving reef
off Celebes. Jettisoning some cannon and cloves did not help, and it
looked as though the voyage might be lost. However, the ship floated
off and Drake sailed home by much the same course as Elcano's in the
Victoria, dodging enemy posts along the route. He put into a port on
Sierra Leone for water and sailed into Plymouth on September 26, 1580.
Like the *Victoria,* the *Golden Hind* had been absent about three years.

Drake's first question on arrival was whether or not Elizabeth was
still alive. He sailed the *Golden Hind,* with its treasure, over to London
in October. The exact amount of the booty is uncertain; some smuggling of silver bars is said to have taken place. One estimate of the total
treasure at the time was £332,000; another was £500,000. The queen
ordered £10,000 delivered to Drake personally. The investors of the
syndicate, who had fitted out the fleet for £4000, are said to have
received 1000% on their investment. Much of the rest went to the
government. The Spanish ambassador urged Elizabeth to repudiate
Drake and return the booty to Spain. Instead, in a ceremony aboard the
Golden Hind at Deptford below London, she knighted him as Sir Francis
Drake.

Drake purchased an estate at Buckland Abby in Devon, remarried,
and settled down briefly as a country gentleman. But eight years later,
in the Armada crisis, he was at sea again in the *Revenge* as vice admiral
in charge of operations. In 1595 he and Sir John Hawkins both died
while commanding an expedition against the Spaniards in the
Caribbean.

For the four-hundredth anniversary of the landing in Drake's Bay, the
British built a model of the *Golden Hind* and sent it to California. The
true location of the bay was still in so much doubt, however, that the
governor of California appointed a commission of experts to settle the
matter. Their conclusion was that the preponderance of evidence
pointed to the Point Reyes area as the location of Drake's bay (New
Albion Bay).

(See J. A. Williamson, *The Age of Drake,* 1965.)

Revenge

Drake's flagship, the *Revenge*, leading the critical attack on the Armada at Gravelines. *(National Maritime Museum, Greenwich)*

The *Revenge* was the most celebrated ship of the Elizabethan navy—in fact, she was one of the most celebrated ships in all British naval history. She had a triple claim to such fame. She was the first of a type which would revolutionize naval tactics for three centuries to come. Second, she was the flagship of Drake in the great fight against the Spanish Armada. Finally, she was the only Elizabethan warship to be captured after heroically standing off dozens of Spanish warships in an action that became legendary.

Early in the evolution of the British warship, three ships represented successive stages. The *Great Harry* of Henry VII in 1514 was the first (or second) to have holes cut in the hull for the discharge of great guns. The *Sovereign of the Seas* in 1637 was the first of the great three-decked ships of the line. Between them, and more important than either, was the *Revenge* of 1577. In place of the "high-charged" lofty earlier ships, which were virtually defensive fortresses, built to fight at close quarters with the enemy, the *Revenge* class were highly mobile gun platforms, maneuverable enough to stand off at a distance and blast the enemy with their broadsides.

The man usually credited with this innovation was John Hawkins of Plymouth (later Sir John) who ranks with or very close to Sir Francis

Drake at the top of the highly effective Elizabethan "sea dogs." Drake stood first as a fighter, but Hawkins, while a good fighter, was a genius in producing ships, a far-ranging trader, and a skillful "operator" in many fields of Elizabethan activity.

The earlier English warships had operated mostly on short runs, either over to France or up the coast to Scotland. Hawkins and Drake, like some other "sea dogs," took their ships off to distant sea lanes to Africa or America, where the stately old tubs were too slow and cumbersome. Moreover, they were running afoul of the Spaniards, whose ships often carried plenty of excellent infantry. Consequently, they began to think of a new type of vessel, smaller, faster, and more "weatherly," that is, the ability to sail up into the wind. Of course, no sailing vessel, as yachtsmen know even today, can sail directly into the wind—the test of a weatherly ship was to sail in a fairly sharp angle to windward, whereas the clumsy tubs could do little better than go sideways. Fleets and frigates used to jockey for the "weather gage"— the ship to windward had freedom of action around a wide circle, while the ship to leeward could not move up against her. That was why Hawkins and his colleagues wanted weatherly ships, and when the Armada came, they could stand off and send broadsides against the "floating batteries" full of Spanish infantry.

Hawkins had firsthand experience with the inadequacy of the old lofty ships in the sorry *Jesus of Lubeck,* captured by the Spaniards at San Juan de Ulloa on the Mexican coast in 1567. Returning home to various activities, he soon became concerned with the navy, where his father-in-law was treasurer. Hawkins was shocked by the inefficiency and corruption in the naval establishment and finally wrote a detailed exposé to the queen's chief minister, citing chapter and verse to show how ship maintenance, shipbuilding, timber, and much else were costing twice as much as they should. The next step was to offer to undertake contracts to do the work at a greatly reduced cost.

In 1577 Hawkins succeeded to the post of treasurer of the navy at the death of his father-in-law. This gave him a chance to put his theories into practice. That same year the *Revenge* was launched at Chatham, near the mouth of the Thames. It is probable that he had a great deal to say about her distinctive qualities. From that time on, he would have full charge of shipbuilding and the rebuilding of old ships along his ideas.

The *Revenge* was relatively small, measuring 500 tons or even less, only half the size of the *Great Harry.* Rated as a galleon, she carried 46 guns ranged along the two sides of her gun deck. She has been called the first "ship of the line," the "line" in which capital ships sailed into action one after another. In the 11 years between her launching and the coming of the Spanish Armada, Hawkins turned out a whole class of sister ships on her lines and also rebuilt some old ships along similar lines. These new Hawkins vessels would be the backbone of the Elizabethan navy.

There would be ample need of these ships in the fateful year 1588. After years of standing by while Drake and others had raided his ships and shores, Philip II of Spain decided in 1587 to build a powerful Armada (the Spanish word for fleet) to invade England and restore the Roman Catholic religion there. But Drake swooped down on Cadiz in 1587 and destroyed many of the assembled ships as well as the lesser vessels assembling supplies. It was necessary, therefore, to postpone the attack for a year.

In early 1588 Drake shifted from the *Elizabeth Bonaventura* to the *Revenge,* which many considered the best of the new ships. He kept trying to persuade the queen and council to send him down again to repeat his 1587 performance. But many feared that while he was on the way to Spain, the Spaniards might fall upon undefended England.

Drake had command of the western squadron with his flag on the *Revenge* late in the spring; other units of the main fleet joined him there, under Lord Howard of Effingham, the Lord High Admiral, in the *Ark Royal;* Drake became vice admiral and Hawkins rear admiral. In that age, simple naval rank was not enough to ensure obedience from well-born admirals; social rank was needed in addition. Howard had the necessary social prestige; he belonged to the Protestant branch of the proudest house in English nobility (Henry VII had two Howard wives and beheaded them both). Howard and Drake made this system work—Drake deferred to Howard's rank and Howard respected Drake's ideas.

When navies later turned to steam, they were relieved of dependence on the winds; but in 1588 weather factors played an important role. Eventually, later that summer, Howard was permitted to sail against Spain but was only part way down when the wind suddenly shifted strongly from north to south. With their own way thus made most difficult, Howard and Drake turned back, knowing that the Spaniards could now easily reach England.

The English were barely back in Plymouth when they faced their worst crisis. Drake and the other captains were playing at bowls on Plymouth Hoe, according to the legend, when a scouting vessel hurried in with word that the Armada was barely 90 miles away. The same wind that favored the Armada was holding the English warships windbound in the harbor. But Drake said easily, "Time to finish the game and then beat the Spaniards." A whole grueling night at the oars and pulleys followed, to get the *Revenge* and the other ships clear of the harbor. The crisis was over, for when the Spaniards came up next morning they found that the English ships were now to windward of them with the desired weather gage.

The great Armada fight, from July 28 to August 12, fell into two distinct parts. During the first nine days, the rival fleets, with a strong following wind, swept along the whole south coast of England, expending much of their ammunition but inflicting relatively little damage. The Spaniards were disappointed at not being able to capture a single English vessel. They had brought along some 80,000 of their crack infantry for the time-honored practice of swarming over enemy decks. The English were likewise disappointed that their ships' guns had not had a more smashing effect on the Spaniards. Both sides came through the initial encounters relatively intact. But then came the "Protestant winds" with quite different results.

The Spaniards were under a stupid strategic handicap, which precluded almost any chance of success. To Philip II, the Armada was only a subordinate part of his plan to bring over the Spanish troops of the Duke of Parma from the Netherlands to invade England. Some of his advisers tried to point out that this was impracticable—the heavy Spanish warships could not get close to the shallow waters, and the Dutch "sea beggars" could offset the small boats. Also, communications with Parma were a most difficult matter. Philip nevertheless insisted. The Armada might have landed troops along the south coast of England but that was not permitted.

On Saturday, July 27, after a week in the English Channel, both fleets arrived in Calais Roads. This was an area of prime importance—within a 20-mile radius were the shores of three nations, each with its seaport. Calais, after more than two centuries of English rule, had been seized from "Bloody Mary" by the French. Twenty-odd miles to the north was the English port of Dover, and a similar distance to the northeast was Dunkirk in Spanish Flanders. Parma had his troops there, but the Flemish sandbanks were too shallow for the big Armada ships. Medina Sidonia realized that Calais, though a neutral port, was the only port capable of accommodating his ships. The Armada quickly anchored there. The English, reinforced now by their Squadron of the Narrow Seas, anchored close behind them. Both fleets stayed there on Sunday, while Medina Sidonia desperately tried to get into communication with Philip's Italian viceroy, Parma. Parma knew that it was out of the question to get his troops over to England, but he could not openly flout Philip's orders.

Sunday night, the untoward situation became violent. It was clear to the English that, with strong gales blowing straight into Calais, the situation called for fireships. Eight good-sized vessels, one of them furnished by Drake, were loaded with combustibles and, with their cannon doubleshotted, were let loose in the gale against the anchored Armada—the ships all vulnerable to the flames. The Spaniards reacted in the only possible way. They cut the cables and straggled out of the harbor, their orderly formation broken for the first time. The English quietly watched them.

On Monday, July 29, came the Battle of Gravelines (named for a Flemish town close to Calais), one of the fiercest and most decisive naval battles ever fought. The Spaniards had two serious handicaps. They were in danger of being driven by the gale onto the Flemish sandbanks. Moreover, they were desperately short of ammunition. The past week had seen an expenditure of ammunition far beyond anything in previous experience. They still had plenty of powder, but the big cannon balls were almost all gone. The English had also shot away a great deal of ammunition, but they had been able to draw extra supplies along the Channel.

With the start of the Battle of Gravelines, the *Revenge* came into her own. In the fighting of the previous week, there had been little account of particular ships; one only knew that wherever Drake went, there would be action. But now he was given a major assignment. Lord Howard in the *Ark Royal* had ordered Drake to lead the attack on the Spaniards, huddled where they had taken refuge from the fireships. His target was the *San Martin,* the great flagship of Medina Sidonia. In this action, Drake established an all-important step in naval tactics. He descended on the *San Martin,* followed closely in line by several of the largest ships. Each ship, as she passed by the target, let go with a crashing broadside. The fleet then followed around to come up again and again, with devastating effect. The *Revenge,* of course, was the first ship of the line. The *San Martin* took terrific punishment—the decks were piled high with dead and wounded, and casualities were in the hundreds—while the *Revenge* lost relatively few, only 60 in the whole nine days' fighting. The ship, however, showed signs of wear and tear; two cannon balls had gone through Drake's cabin.

The fight became a general melee; the Spanish ships gathered together in a group for protection, but the English kept pounding mercilessly at the battered and leaking ships. For a while during that terrible Monday, it looked as though a large number of them would be driven onto the sands, but the wind shifted just enough to save them, as it would do again later. For all that, it became known as the "Protestant wind." It blew the galleons straight up the North Sea. When the English also ran out of ammunition, they simply followed the Spaniards northward until, up on a level with Edinburgh and the Firth of Forth, the English decided that further chasing was unnecessary and headed for home, leaving the shattered Armada to struggle up around Scotland and down past Ireland.

In 1589 the *Revenge* put to sea again as Drake's flagship in what would prove an anticlimax. In conjunction with a large army force under Sir John Norris, Drake promoted an expedition against Portugal, which at that time belonged to Spain. It was technically a private expedition in the sea-dog tradition of receiving a few warships and permission from the queen, in anticipation of the profits. But there were no profits—the affair was badly bungled. The army landed some 50 miles above Lisbon, while the navy went down to capture the forts, but the army was not on hand to hold them. They called off the Lisbon attack and set out for the Azores to catch incoming treasure ships, but that too fell through, so they returned to England, with the *Revenge* in very battered condition. With no victory and no loot, and with a great loss of face, Drake was in deep disfavor with Elizabeth and was kept ashore until 1594.

The *Revenge* came to her end in a glorious but bizarre episode that has become a legend. To slow down Spanish naval recovery after the Armada, Hawkins proposed to cut down the supply of treasure from America by a constant naval patrol designed to intercept the convoys. The logical place for these patrols would be around the Azores—with the winds blowing as they did on the Atlantic, outward bound vessels stopped at the Canaries, as Columbus had done, and inward bound convoys at the Azores, well to the northward. Hawkins' plan was put into effect on a rather spasmodic basis, and most of the treasure slipped through.

Our concern here is with one of the intercepting patrols in the summer of 1591, and what would make it go down in history was its vice admiral, Sir Richard Grenville, in his flagship, the *Revenge*. He came from the upper social level of the Elizabethan sea dogs, a cousin of Sir Walter Raleigh, looking down on middle-class Drake and Hawkins. The Grenville family had lived for generations on the border of Devon and Cornwall and had held positions of some prominence. They were able and energetic, but were proud, harsh, and domineering. He had headed Raleigh's pioneer colonial effort in Virginia and had played an active role in Ireland. He had been off on the sidelines in the Armada year, partly because he refused to serve under Drake.

Grenville suddenly received orders for the number two role in the Azores expedition. It had originally been intended for Raleigh, but he was not permitted to go and probably recommended his cousin, Grenville. Later he would write a stirring account of "the last fight of the *Revenge*." The number one job went to the not overly brilliant Sir Thomas Howard. The expedition had several ships of the *Revenge* class, but, as they lay in wait for the flotilla from America, up at Flores in the northern Azores, nearly half their men were laid low by a fever epidemic. While they were laying for the ships from America, Spain was sending out a still stronger force of some 40 ships, half of them major warships, under the able commander Alonso de Bazan, to capture the English from the rear.

On September 7 Bazan came upon the English while many were ashore, filling water casks, repairing the ships, and nursing the invalids. Most of them, under Howard, managed to slip out to sea, but the *Revenge* was still in harbor. Grenville might have escaped, as the master advised, but, as Raleigh wrote:

> Sir Richard utterly refused to turn from the enemy, alleging that he chose to die than to dishonor his self, his country, and Majesty's ship. . . . Notwithstanding the greatness of his mind, he could not be persuaded.

He refused to take advantage of the last chance to escape. The whole of Bazan's command, an overwhelming force, was immediately upon the *Revenge,* which put up a magnificent resistence. The great *San Philip,* three times her size, tried to board her, but was shaken off, while the *San Barnabe* clung to her persistently while other ships, one after another, came up but were driven off and two of them sunk. The Spaniards had soldiers in large numbers while the English had only their marines but they repulsed the efforts to board. That fighting went on all through the night and into the next day, the situation becoming steadily more hopeless. Sir Richard himself was seriously wounded.

In his desperate mood, as Raleigh stated:

> Sir Richard finding himself in this distress, commanded the master gunner, whom he knew to be a most resolute man, to split and sink the ship that thereby nothing might remain of glory or victory to the Spaniards. . . . The master gunner condescended with divers others. But the Captain and the Master were of another opinion, and besought Sir Richard to have care of them . . . there being divers efficient and valiant men yet living, and whose wounds were not mortal, that might [give] to their country and prince acceptable service hereafter.

With six feet of water in the hold and three shotholes underwater, and with the Spaniards having had enough of the sanguinary work, that sensible decision overruled Grenville's mad objections. After receiving assurances of proper treatment, the *Revenge* surrendered—the only English ship captured by the Spaniards in the whole long war. The wounded Grenville was taken aboard the flagship and treated with the greatest honor until his death two or three days later. The captured *Revenge* never reached port; with scores of Spanish ships she succumbed to a terrific gale in the Azores. She was cast upon a cliff next to the island of Terceira, where she broke up completely. Few ships had achieved so much in so few years.

(See G. Mattingly, *The Armada*, 1959; A. L. Rowse, *Sir Richard Grenville of the Revenge*, 1949.)

Virginia of Sagadahoc

The *Virginia of Sagadahoc*, a conjectural painting by John P. Leavitt. *(Peabody Museum)*

This little 30-ton pinnace, built on the Sagadahoc (Kennebec) River in Maine in 1607, was the first vessel built by Europeans in America, north of the Spanish colonies.

England sent over two colonizing expeditions in 1607. One went to Jamestown and became the first permanent colony. The other, known as the Popham Colony, settled in Maine on the lower Kennebec, several miles below the site of Bath, which eventually became the nation's leading shipbuilding center. After a rugged winter and the death of a leader, the Popham colonists went back to England.

It was the Popham group which built the *Virginia*. The colonists had come over in two small vessels. One of the well-connected captains was George Popham, nephew of the Lord Chief Justice; the other was Ralph Gilbert, a son of the late Humphrey Gilbert. They set to work at once in building a storehouse, fort, and other buildings, as well as the *Virginia*.

The nearest we can come to conjecture about how the *Virginia* looked comes from "the draught of St. George fort erected by Captayne George Popham Esquire on the entry of the famous river of Sagadahoc in Virginia." It shows "a craft with a single deck, a square stern, and a single-masted fore and aft rig. Her sails are a sprit mainsail and what we today would call a jib." On the three-hundred-fiftieth anniversary of the settling of the colony in 1957, this sketch was the basis of a model built by the Bath Iron Works Corporation, and also of a United States postage stamp issued to celebrate the occasion. Investigations indicate the following possible dimensions: length over all, 51 feet 6 inches; length of keel, 38 feet 6 inches; maximum breadth inside of the planking, 13 feet; depth for tonnage, 5 feet. "The Popham colonists were well aware of the vessel characteristics necessary for successful trading operations on the coast and rivers of New England," says the document previously mentioned. The *Virginia* apparently accompanied the discouraged colonists when they decided to return to England.

Next to the *Virginia* in time, came the *Onrust*, or *Restless*, a small Dutch vessel built at Manhattan, the future New Amsterdam. Its construction was superintended by Adrian Block, after his ship, the *Tiger*, burned. In the *Onrust* he discovered Block Island. In 1631 the colonists of Massachusetts Bay constructed the *Blessing of the Bay*, about the size of the *Virginia* and forerunner of much further shipbuilding.

It is difficult to distinguish this *Virginia* from the numerous others of the same name, but it seems likely that she was involved when Jamestown almost lost its status as the first permanent colony. In company with three other vessels she started out for home with the discouraged colonists, only to encounter Lord De La Warr's incoming squadron, to which the others joined to keep Jamestown going.

(See W. A. Baker; *A Maritime History of Bath*, 1973.)

Half Moon

The *Half Moon,*
a twentieth-century
replica of the Dutch
"yacht."
(U.S. Naval Institute)

Much of Henry Hudson's life is a mystery, but in the course of two years (1609–1611) he left his name prominently and permanently on the map with the Hudson River and Hudson's Bay. He had an ambivalent record so far as nationality went; the river was discovered in the *Half Moon* under the Dutch flag and the bay in the *Discovery* under the English. In later days, the Hudson River Bay Line named one of its big steamers the *Hendrick Hudson,* but Hudson was definitely English, probably a native of London, and his relationship with Holland lasted barely a year.

The date and place of his birth are not known, nor is his education or the maiden name of his wife, Katherine. It is conjectured that he had early connections with the Muscovy Company, with whom he first sailed, and his close connection with prominent geographers indicates a good background in that field. His big achievements came just at the heyday of international geographic expansion following the defeat of the Spanish Armada. Willem Barents and Jan Huyghen van Linschoten were active in the approaches to the Arctic, and Bartholomew Gosnold, Weymouth, John Smith, and Popham along the Atlantic coast. Quebec was established in 1608, a year after Jamestown in Virginia.

In 1607–1608 Hudson had made a name for himself, exploring in the icy regions to the north of Europe for the Muscovy Company around

Spitzbergen and Novaya Zemlya. His success had not been complete, however, and question arose of future employment. This was the period of Holland's most active overseas expansion, and the Dutch consul was able to get him in touch with the Dutch East India Company. The result was that he entered into a contract on January 8, 1609, to engage in exploration to the northeastward, for the rather niggardly payment of 800 gulden. When negotiations had tended to flag, Hudson had applied pressure from the direction of Henry IV of France, who was actively promoting Champlain's colonizing ventures in America.

Hudson was not happy with the rather ordinary little vessel provided by the Dutch East India Company. The *Half Moon (Halve Maen)* was only 60 tons—a "yacht," but not in the pleasure sense—of old-fashioned lines, with high forecastle and poop and rather slender masts. He could get nothing better, however, and shipped a crew of 20, part English and part Dutch. The latter were fresh from the warm seas of the East Indies and suffered from the cold northern weather.

Hudson was rather shameless in his dealings with the Dutch East India Company. His contract called for sailing northeast, but he managed to persuade his crew to turn to the northwest, the region he wanted to explore. The crossing, which started from Texel on April 6, 1609, was a stormy one. After a stop at the Faroes they came to the Grand Banks, where they found plenty of cod and a few French fishermen. They reached the American coast around the region of the Penobscot River, cut a new topmast, and began frequent contacts with the Indians. They reached Cape Cod and ran south as far as North Carolina, deliberately not stopping at Jamestown. They looked into Chesapeake and Delaware Bays and, after skirting the New Jersey coast, reached New York Bay on September 2. Giovanni da Verrazano, sailing for the French, had already "discovered" New York Bay in 1524, but he had not gone farther.

Hudson was primarily interested in a strait through to the Pacific and this looked like a promising approach. He went on through the Narrows and then started up what would eventually be called the Hudson River. It was broad and navigable; hopes and enthusiasm ran high. At some of the broader expanses in the river, it looked almost as though China was just around the bend, just as the French, in the St. Lawrence above Montreal, had called out "Lachine! Lachine!" The wonder continued as they proceeded up through the Highlands. Finally on September 19 they reached almost to the future site of Albany. Since it seemed to be getting a bit shallow for the *Half Moon,* Hudson sent out a pinnace to explore. But the rapid contraction of the river dispelled the high hopes of a route to China, and Hudson reluctantly turned back down the river. He reached New York Bay on October 4 and then put out to

its 800 gulden. Thanks to this visit, New Amsterdam and New Nether-
land would be an important part of Holland's overseas empire until
1664.

Hudson's ambivalent national status created a crisis as soon as he
was back across the Atlantic. The *Half Moon* put into Dartmouth in
Devonshire on November 7. Adverse weather seriously slowed down
Hudson's report to the Dutch East India Company, but the English,
disturbed that an Englishman should have made what seemed like an
important discovery for the Dutch, stepped actively into the picture.
Hudson was picked up by authorities with an Order in Council, but
landed on his feet. His achievement stimulated Sir Thomas Smythe,
wealthy head of the East India and Virginia Companies, who arranged
to send Hudson back to America in a better vessel, the *Discovery*. He
sailed almost at once and never returned; he found Hudson's Bay, and
was set adrift by a mutinous crew. In 1610 the Dutch sent over to
Dartmouth for the *Half Moon* and a naval commander took her out to
the East Indies, where she lasted until 1617.

(See L. Powys, *Henry Hudson,* 1927.)

Unitie

Almost a century after Ferdinand Magellan discovered the strait which
bears his name, two Dutchmen discovered an alternate way of connecting the Atlantic and Pacific by way of Cape Horn around the southern
tip of South America. The Dutch East India Company, formed in 1602,
determined to prevent nonmembers from reaching their new trading
centers in Southeast Asia. They forbade all outsiders from trying to
reach Indonesia either by way of the Cape of Good Hope or by the Strait
of Magellan.

Two prominent Dutch nonmembers, Willem Cornelis Schouten, mariner of Hoorn (whence Cape Horn) and Jakob Le Maire, merchant of
Amsterdam, determined to find a third way of getting to Southeast
Asia. They set out from Texel on June 14, 1615, in two Hoorn ships. The
flagship and sole survivor was the good-sized 360-ton *Unitie* and a
smaller consort. These ships were substantially built with multiple
planking. They went out by way of Cape Verde, Sierra Leone, and the
Patagonia coast.

Passing beyond the Strait of Magellan, they skirted Tierra del Fuego and discovered a strait, which they named for Le Maire, separating "Staten Island" from the mainland. On January 29, 1616, on another island, they discovered "a high, hilly land, covered with snow, ending with a sharp point which we called Cape Horne." Nothing was said of the terrific westerly gales which would make "Cape Stiff" notorious. They proceeded on across the Pacific with the loss of the consort and the death of Le Maire.

When the *Unitie* finally arrived at Bantam, she and her cargo were confiscated because of the irregular route. The officers and crew were sent back to Amsterdam to stand trial; Schouten sued Governor Coen for damages and recovered the whole value of the *Unitie*.

Gradually, despite the extra mileage around Tierra del Fuego and the wild westerlies off the Cape, the Cape Horn route gained ascendancy over the Magellan run during the days of sail. The California clippers, racing to San Francisco, found that they could make better time around Cape Horn than in the tricky and sometimes forbidding Magellan passage. The Dutch themselves generally used the Good Hope route.

Mayflower

The *Mayflower*, a replica designed by William A. Baker and sailed to America by Captain Alan Villiers. *(U.S. Coast Guard)*

The little *Mayflower*, which brought 100 Pilgrims to Massachusetts in 1620, is one of the best-known and most warmly regarded ships in American history. There were other ships that brought settlers; the *Susan Constant* was flagship of the squadron that brought colonists to Jamestown in 1607, and the flagship *Arabella* headed the "Winthrop Fleet" that brought some 3000 colonists in 1630. But the *Mayflower* came alone and after a stormy passage landed her God-fearing passengers on a bleak coast at the beginning of winter. Those who survived the first winter told their story well, and there is still a flourishing Society of Mayflower Descendants.

The *Mayflower* was a "tramp," chartered for the voyage. She had had a varied experience. In 1609 she was apparently trading with Norway and, like so many English freighters, engaged in the busy wine trade between Bordeaux and London. She may have visited Hamburg and the Baltic, and perhaps the Greenland fishery. She belonged in part to her master, Captain Christopher Jones of Rotherhithe on the Thames, from whom she was chartered. She was a somewhat tubby ship of 180 tons, with three masts. Her most distinctive feature was a very high narrow poop. No pictures or plans have survived, but an excellent replica, the *Mayflower II*, designed by the naval architect and historian William A. Baker, was built at Brixham in 1957 as a gift of the English people to the Americans and was sailed over by Alan Villiers, the mariner and author, and now lies at Plymouth, Massachusetts.

If the ship was fairly conventional, the passengers were not. Most of them were left-wing English Puritans, known as Separatists to signify their break from the Church of England. In 1609 they had moved from their homes in East Anglia to Leyden in Holland to escape the intolerant attitude at home. By 1620, however, they decided to migrate to America. Sir Edwin Sandys, a prominent sympathetic Puritan, arranged with the Virginia Company to permit them to settle in the territories. They received the necessary financial support from a group of English merchants, with the understanding that they would repay the debt with fish and other overseas products.

The Leyden group purchased a small ship, rather inappropriately named the *Speedwell*, and sailed in her from Delft to Southampton Water, where they rendezvoused with the *Mayflower*, which Jones had brought around from the Thames. The Pilgrims, as they came to be called, were divided between the two ships. They sailed from Southampton on August 5 (15 New Style, or NS), but that was only the first of three farewells. The *Speedwell* soon signaled that she was in trouble, so the two ships put into Dartmouth for repairs on August 23–September 2, but once out on the open sea, the *Speedwell* was in such dangerously leaky condition that they put into Plymouth, where the smaller vessel was declared unfit for an ocean voyage. She returned to London with 20 of the passengers, who decided that they had had enough. The other Pilgrims crowded into the *Mayflower*, 100 of them in addition to the crew. Besides 15 male servants, there were 41 men and 44 women. On the voyage there was one death, the wife of John Carver, and two births, so that the *Mayflower* arrived with 101 passengers. The final departure was on September 6 (NS 16).

Those two delays at Dartmouth and Plymouth were unfortunate because they meant encountering the turbulent weather of the equinoctial "line storms" through which the *Mayflower* had to make her westward passage. One of the main beams cracked and had to be locked back into position, while conditions between decks meant real hardship for the passengers.

The landfall finally came on November 9 (NS 19) near Nauset on the back side of Cape Cod, in "one of the most dangerous strips of coast anywhere in the world." Pollock Rip and its other hazards made it a nightmare to traverse—those waters would claim wrecks for three centuries—in 1924 the *Wyoming*, largest of all wooden ships, would sink in a gale. Captain Jones showed his skill as a navigator in getting his ship safely around the tip of the cape to anchor in the harbor of what would be Provincetown.

At this point questions, which would last until long afterward, arose as to why the *Mayflower* had landed so far north, beyond the limits of the Virginia Company toward which she was supposedly headed. Some claimed that pressure had been brought on Jones to keep the new settlers away from the regions to the southward, but he has been cleared on that charge.

Before anyone went ashore at Provincetown, the Pilgrims produced an important constitutional document. Governor William Bradford, Elder William Brewster, and a few of the leaders were concerned about control of some of the restless settlers. So long as they were aboard ship, the captain had authority, but once ashore there was no authoritative body; the group was beyond the limits of Virginia Company authority. Stephen Hopkins was a troublemaker, and not the only one. Accordingly, the leaders drew up the famous "Mayflower Compact" on November 21, 1620, which every adult male signed. It read, in part:

> We whose names are underwritten . . . do, by these presents, solemnly and mutually, in the presence of God and of one another, covenant and combine ourselves together into a civil body politic for our better ordering and preservation, and furthermore of the ends aforesaid; and by virtue hereof to enact, constitute and frame just and equal laws, ordinances, acts, constitutions and offices from time to time, as shall be thought most mete and convenient for the general good of the colony; unto which we promise all due submission and obedience.

This Compact, drawn up in the cabin of the *Mayflower*, not only met the immediate need for a form of government since the Pilgrims had no charter, but would serve as the constitution of the "Old Colony" until 1691. Self-government would be one of the unique aspects of the English colonists, the Mayflower Compact of 1620 ranks with the creation of the first Virginia legislature at Jamestown the year before.

The *Mayflower* stayed on at Provincetown, at the tip of Cape Cod, for several weeks. The Pilgrims took advantage of the opportunity to lay in wood and water, to repair their small shallop, and to wash clothes and perform other chores. In the meantime they used the shallop to explore adjacent waters for a better place, and on December 11 (NS 21) they chose Plymouth harbor, a few miles to the northeast. Five days later, the *Mayflower* moved over there and the little settlement quickly began to take form. It happened that most of the local Indians had been killed off by a pestilence; the colony owed much at the beginning to one

Indian, Squanto, who was helpful in teaching them the best methods for planting corn and fishing. During the harsh winter nearly half of the colonists died, but when Captain Jones started back to England on March 26 (NS April 5) 1621, no one chose to return with him. The later career of the *Mayflower* is not clear; there were rumors that her timbers were built into a barn.

(See W. A. Baker, *The New Mayflower*, 1958.)

Vasa

The Swedish warship *Vasa* has had two periods of prominence, separated by more than three centuries during which she lay at the bottom of Stockholm's harbor. In 1628 she capsized during her first hours of active service. In 1961, she was raised from the depths. Still in sound condition, she has become a remarkable example of original conditions in great detail.

A powerful ship of the line, she was constructed at the order of King Gustavus Adolphus, greatest of the Vasa line of Swedish rulers. She was expected to strengthen Sweden's command of the Baltic. The *Vasa* was 162 feet in length and 39 feet in beam, and had a displacement of 1300 tons. On her three decks, she mounted 64 bronze cannon, 48 of which were big 24-pounders. She was built by a Dutchman and commanded by a Dane. She had much in common with England's three-decked great ship *Sovereign of the Seas,* built in 1637. The big difference was that the *Sovereign* had an active career of more than half a century, while the *Vasa* had only a few hours.

On August 10, 1628, the *Vasa* set sail for the first time to move to another part of Stockholm harbor. A sudden gust of wind caused her to list sharply to port, so that the water poured in through the lowest tier of open gun ports. She sank quickly in 100 feet of water. Incidentally, England's *Mary Rose* had sunk in the same manner in 1545. A few of the bronze guns were rescued but thereafter she lay forgotten.

As for responsibility, the Dutch shipbuilder and Danish captain were cleared. An embarrassing factor in the investigation was that the king, a soldier rather than a sailor, had dictated just what the basic dimensions should be. Apparently, the heavy weights were not properly distributed through the ship.

In 1956 Anders Franzén, a local resident long interested in marine archeology, located the sunken hull after extensive research. He interested the Swedish Navy in raising the wreck; deep sea divers dug a series of tunnels under the hull; wires were passed through, followed

by heavy cables which could transmit adequate lifting power from the surface. By 1960 the hull began to reach the surface.

Most wooden vessels, submerged for even much briefer lengths of time, tend to disintegrate. This is due in no small degree to the ravages of the *Teredo navalis,* or sea worm. The water of the Baltic, however, is distasteful to the sea worm, and the whole wreck remained intact. A museum has been developed in Stockholm harbor enabling the public to visualize just what a seventeenth-century ship was like.

(See A. Franzén, *The Warship Vasa,* 1960.)

Sovereign of the Seas

The *Sovereign of the Seas,* a three-decked first-rate ship of the line.
(From an original painting by William Vandevelde)

Even before she ever gained a fighting reputation, the English took great pride in the *Sovereign of the Seas,* designed and built by their outstanding naval architect Peter Pett in 1637. She came after a period of serious post-Armada neglect and was financed by the dubious ship money. Also, in retrospect, she stood out as a major step in the development of the sailing warship as the first three-decked "first rate," a predecessor of Nelson's *Victory.*

When James I had come down from Scotland in 1603, he let the navy, which had accomplished wonders under Elizabeth, go to pot. Things grew so bad under the early Stuarts that Barbary pirates raided the shores of the British Isles, carrying off men and women to slavery. This naval slump played into the hands of the Dutch, who were rapidly strengthening themselves, going so far as to wipe out an English settlement in the East Indies.

One reason for the continued slump was financial. Navies cost money and in the continuing friction between the Crown and the Puritans in Parliament there was a stalemate in which the Stuarts tried to keep things going without submitting to Parliament. From 1629 to 1640 no sessions of Parliament were held, and the Crown had to resort to all sorts of strange devices to raise money.

Charles I realized the need for a good navy and he and his henchmen finally hit upon a new device. It had long been a custom to call on the "Cinque Ports" of the southeast coast to furnish ships in place of making the usual land-based demands. To build up the navy, it was decided to call upon the whole country for "ship money." A howl immediately arose from the Puritan-Parliament group that this was an illegal subterfuge to raise funds without recourse to Parliament. One prominent Puritan went to prison rather than pay ship money. This demand was one more of the factors which brought on the showdown between Crown and Parliament.

If one looks at the ship money from the naval rather than the constitutional angle, it did strengthen the navy. In particular, it produced the masterpiece of the mid-seventeenth century. The king sent for Peter Pett, foremost among the Petts who for years had been designing and building ships for the navy. The king wanted a combination of strength and beauty, and he got it. The 1141-ton, 100-gun *Sovereign of the Seas* was launched at Woolwich dockyard on October 13, 1637.

Her distinctive feature was having three separate gun decks. The *Revenge* had introduced the idea of a single deck devoted entirely to broadside guns. But from this time on, there would be a few first-rate three-deckers to serve as flagships. Although they were always a bit clumsy compared with the two-decked "seventy-fours," it was felt that the extra height gave them a certain advantage. The *Sovereign* (the shortened name) was herself cut down to two decks to remedy her cranky sailing habits. She was smaller than the *Naseby (Royal Charles)*, but she played her part through the three Dutch-English Wars and was even a participant in the outset of the war against Louis XIV, taking part in the defeat of Beachy Head and later in the victory of La Hogue-Barfleur when she was more than 50 years old. In 1696 she was burned by accident. Incidentally, one of Donald McKay's crack American clippers was also named *Sovereign of the Seas*.

(See R. V. B. Blackman, *Ships of the Royal Navy*, 1973.)

Naseby
(Royal Charles)

The *Royal Charles*, captured by the Dutch who set fire to English vessels laid up in the Medway. *(National Maritime Museum, Greenwich)*

During her 12-year career, this ship, pride of the English Navy, provided the nation with two emotional extremes. In 1660 she brought Charles II back from Holland for the restoration of royal authority after two decades of interregnum or time out. The tens of thousands who cheered his arrival at Dover and then at London were overjoyed that the grim Puritan repression was over. Seven years later, at the end of the Second Dutch-English War, national humiliation was at its lowest when a Dutch fleet hijacked her and carried her back in triumph to Holland, where her symbols are still on display in the national museum.

The *Naseby*, named for Oliver Cromwell's crushing victory over the royal forces in 1645, was launched at Woolwich dockyard in 1655. At 1230 tons, she was larger than the celebrated *Sovereign of the Seas*, first of the three-decked ships of the line. She appeared during an interval in the Dutch-English Wars, but she went south to the Spanish coast under Admiral Robert Blake, one of England's greatest naval officers even though he had no previous naval experience.

The *Naseby's* first prominence came in 1660, two years after the death of Oliver Cromwell. General George Monk brought his army down from Scotland and paved the way for the royal restoration. After Charles II was agreed upon for the crown, Captain Sir Edward Montagu, another army man who joined the navy, was ordered over to Holland with some 37 great ships to bring him back. The *Naseby* became the flagship of this force. The Dutch had been rather cool to Charles during his long exile, but now they feted him with banquets and lavish entertainment.

Fortunately, we have a firsthand account of this famous crossing from Samuel Pepys, who had just begun his *Diary* and was now entering on the duties which would make him one of the greatest naval administrators. He owed his start to Sir Edward Montagu, his first cousin once removed. The fleet left Scheveningen, close to the Hague, on May 22, 1660, and arrived at Dover on May 25. While aboard ship on May 23, the king changed the name of the *Naseby*, because of its unpleasant connotations, to *Royal Charles*. Some other ship names were changed at the same time. As Pepys tells the story of the trip:

> May 22nd. News brought that the two Dukes are coming on board, which, by and by, they did, in a Dutch boat. . . . My Lord went in a boat to meet them, the Captain, myself, and others standing in the entering port. So soon as they were entered we shot the guns off around the fleet. After that they went to view the ship all over, and were most exceedingly pleased with it. . . . Two guns given to every man while he was drinking the King's health, and so likewise to the Duke's health. . . .

> May 23rd. The King, with the two Dukes and Queen of Bohemia, Princess Royal, and Prince of Orange, came on board, where I on their coming in kissed the King's, Queen's and Princess's hands, having done the other before. Infinite shooting off of the guns. . . . All day nothing but Lords and persons of honor on board, that we were exceedingly full. Dined in a great deal of state, the Royal company by themselves in the coach, which was a blessed sight to see. . . . After dinner the King and the Duke altered the names of some of the ships. . . . This done, the Queen, Princess Royal and Prince of Orange took leave of the King, and the Duke of York went on board the *London,* and the Duke of Gloucester, the *Swiftsure.*

> Which done, we weighed anchor, and with a fresh gale and most happy weather, we set sail for England. All the afternoon the King walked here and there up and down (quite contrary to what I thought him to have been) very active and stirring. Upon the quarterdeck he fell into discourse of his escape from Worcester, where it made me ready to weep to hear the story that he told of his difficulties . . . . We have all the Lords Commissioners aboard us, and many others. Under sail all night and most glorious weather.

May 24th. Up and make myself as fine as I could. . . . Extraordinary press of noble company and great mirth all day. . . . Walking on the decks, were persons of honour all the afternoon. . . . I was called to write a pass for my Lord Mandeville to take up horses to London, which I wrote in the King's name and carried it to him to sign. . . . To bed, coming in sight of land a little before night.

May 25th. By the morning we were come close to the land, and every body made ready to get on shore. The King and two Dukes did eat their breakfast before they went, and there being set some ship's diet, they did eat of nothing else but pease and pork and boiled beef. . . . The King had given £50 to Mr. Shepley for my Lord's servants, and £500 among the officers and common men of the ship. . . . That night the Captain told me that my Lord had appointed me £30 out of the 1000 ducats which the King had given to the ship, at which my heart was very much joyed. To bed. . . .

Great expectation of the King's making some knights, but there was none. About noon (though the brigantine that Bale made ready to carry him) yet he would go in my Lord's barge with the two Dukes. Our Captain steered and my Lord went along with him. I went, and Mr. Mansell, and one of the King's footmen, with a dog that the King loved (which dirtied the boat, which made us laugh . . .) and so we got on shore when the King did, who was received by General Monk with all imaginable love and respect at his entrance upon the land of Dover. Infinite the crowd of people, and the horsemen, citizens, and noblemen of all sorts. . . .

In an elaborate ceremony aboard ship, Montagu and Monk had both been honored as Knights of the Garter. Later, Montagu became Earl of Sandwich and Monk, Earl of Albemarle.

One would-be passenger had not made the crossing on the flagship. The king had just begun what would be his perennial liaison with Barbara Palmer, soon to be Lady Castlemaine. He told her, however, that for appearance's sake it would be better if she crossed over on another ship, but he did keep his promise to have the first night in London with her.

The next five years saw a round of routine duties for the *Royal Charles*, but then, with the start of the Second Dutch-English War, came a series of battles. Both in quality and quantity, the Dutch were probably the toughest and most evenly matched of any of England's naval enemies. The battles were hard-fought, knockdown, drag-out affairs, and the rival commanders of fairly equal high quality.

One of her toughest fights came in the battle of Lowestoft in 1665 under the Duke of York as Lord High Admiral and Captain William Penn, father of the founder of Pennsylvania. In a tough duel with the flagship of Admiral Opdam, a chain shot killed two men standing alongside the future James II, but the Dutch flagship was sunk, with her admiral. In 1666 the *Royal Charles* was in two more strenuous actions, the Four Days' Battles and then the defeat of Admiral de Ruyter in the St. James Day action off North Foreland.

In 1667 the English maritime situation was in grave difficulties because the navy's money was fast running out. The seamen and the dockyard workers had not been paid for a year or so and were in a somewhat mutinous mood. At Chatham dockyard barely a dozen men, out of the usual 800, were still on hand. Under these circumstances, it was decided to pay off most of the navy. The *Royal Charles* and many other warships were deactivated, lacking repairs and with only a remnant of their crews, in the Medway, a curving tidal river which flowed into the south side of the Thames estuary. Part way up, alongside the sharp curves of the river, was Chatham dockyard, the navy's principal base. Below it, at the mouth of the river, was the embryo new base at Sheerness. Some preparation had been made against a possible attack; midway up the river was a fort at Upnor and a chain stretched across the river.

The laid-up fleet tempted the Dutch to attack. Jan de Witt, the Grand Pensionary, wanted a chance to curb English arrogance. In addition, the Anglo-Dutch peace negotiations were under way at Breda and the attack might be reflected in the peace terms. Accordingly, in mid-June, a Dutch fleet of some 50 major warships and numerous smaller ones, with many fireships, appeared in the Thames. They first blasted the fort at Sheerness and removed or destroyed the stores of the new dockyard. Then they proceeded up the winding river with its mudflats. One brave Dutch captain, with his own vessel and fireships, managed to break the chain, leaving the way free for the other to descend on the anchored, sparsely manned, laid-up English warships. The dockyard workers had run off, as had many of the seamen. Numerous high naval officials had come down from London and began issuing conflicting orders—it was a case of "all chiefs and no Indians." This was particularly serious in the case of the *Royal Charles,* which lay in an exposed position. Several times, orders were given to tow her up the river to greater safety, but each time some interfering official countermanded the order and sent the boat elsewhere.

Pepys, who could remember those happier days aboard the great ship, told of the shameful ease with which she was taken:

> They told me about the taking of the *Royal Charles* that nothing but carelessness lost the ship, for they might have saved her that very tide that the Dutch came up, if they would have but used means and had had but boats, and that the want of boats plainly lost all the other ships. That the Dutch did take her with a boat of nine men who found

not a man on board her (and her laying so near them was a main temptation to them to come on) and presently a man went up and struck her flag and Jacke, and a trumpeter sounded upon her "Joan's placket [petticoat] is torn." That they did carry her down at a time, both for tides and wind, when the best pilot in Chatham would not have undertaken it, they heeling her on one side to make her draw little water, and so carried her away safe.

The Dutch burned three of the large ships; a heavy pall of smoke hung over the whole area. The Earl of Albemarle finally gave vigorous defense leadership; guns were brought down from London; and the Dutch, afraid of being caught too far up the river, withdrew without destroying the Chatham dockyard. One can imagine Pepys' emotions when he wrote an oft-quoted remark in his *Diary:* "The Court is as mad as ever and that night the Dutch burned our ships, the King did sup with my Lady Castlemaine at the Duchess of Monmouth, and there were all mad in hunting of a poor moth."

The captive *Royal Charles* was escorted to Hellevoetsluis, where big crowds visited the huge prize. Apparently the Dutch did not consider taking her into their navy; she drew too much water for general use on the Dutch coast. She lay there for a year and then was sold at auction for breaking up. Her metal stern piece, showing the English coat of arms with lion and unicorn, was taken off and stored in a warehouse, along with a white ensign; two centuries later, these naval trophies were proudly displayed in the Ryjks Museum at Amsterdam.

The Medway affair came too late to affect seriously the Treaty of Breda, which ended the Second Dutch-English War a few weeks later. It may have modified some of the more extreme English demands, but they did gain New Amsterdam (New York) and much else. The Royal Navy built a new *Royal Charles* in 1673.

(See P. G. Rogers, *The Dutch in the Medway*, 1970.)

II

THE EIGHTEENTH CENTURY

(1728–1815)

St. Gabriel and St. Peter

Boudeuse

Dolphin

Endeavour

Resolution

Gaspée

Margaretta

Ranger

Bonhomme Richard

Grosvenor

Empress of China

Grand Turk

Boussole and Astrolabe

Sirius

Bounty

Discovery

Columbia

Bellerophon

Rajah

Hermione

Constellation

Constitution

United States

Lutine

Enterprise

Essex

Philadelphia

Intrepid

Victory

Chesapeake

Chasseur

II

THE EIGHTEENTH CENTURY
(1728–1815)

The eighteenth century saw surprisingly little innovation in ship design and construction compared to the periods that preceded and followed it. To be sure, warships increased both in size and firepower, the massive three-deck ship of the line *Victory* representing a high-point in the art of building such vessels. American shipbuilders, in the meantime, followed a different line by constructing superfrigates such as the *Constitution* or fast privateers such as the *Chasseur*. During the almost half-century of conflict which dominated the period numerous French, English, and American warships gained fame through the heat of battle.

As for merchant vessels, the only significant change, a gradual increase in size, resulted from the rapid expansion of European commercial interests, especially into the distant Pacific, A typical British East Indiaman such as the *Grosvenor,* for instance, measured at least 800 tons and carried heavy armament. Even the vessels that carried European explorers to every corner of that vast ocean became progressively larger throughout the period, from Bering's little *St. Gabriel* of 1728 to Captain James Cook's 462-ton ship *Resolution* (1772–1775). Before the end of the century the tide of British colonization reached the Australian continent, the flag of the new United States became a familiar sight in Asian ports, and Tahiti was well on its way to becoming a household word among European and American sailors.

St. Gabriel and St. Peter

Bering Sea and Bering Strait derive their names from the Danish-born, senior Russian naval officer, whom Czar Peter had ordered out in 1725 to discover what if any connection there was between Siberia and America. Although this duty continued for years, the actual seaborne exploration was confined to only a few summer months in the *St. Gabriel* in 1728–1729, and the *St. Peter,* with a consort in 1741, ending in Bering's death from scurvy. The rest of the time was taken up in administrative details, trudging across Siberia, and in logistical problems in a region which had few basic necessities.

The decision to explore this area was just about Peter's last official act. He signed the order early in January 1725 and was dead before the end of the month, but his successor, the Empress Catherine, had the order carried out to the letter. The choice for the command fell on Vitus Bering, a native of Horsens on the Danish peninsula of Jutland. He had gone to sea early and had visited the East Indies. In 1704 a Norwegian-born Russian admiral persuaded him to become a sublieutenant in the Russian navy. He fought against the Swedes, and his promotion up through the grades was steady, so by 1725 he was a captain of the first rank and served as fleet captain. Russia had recently been expanding into Kamchatka, and an expedition had explored the Kuriles. An earlier explorer, Simon Dezhnev, had discovered Bering Strait, but in the foggy area had not seen across to America.

In 1728, after difficulties and delays in gathering the essentials for an expedition, Bering reported:

> When I reached Lower Kamchatka Post the timber for our ship was largely ready. We went to work on her on April 4, 1728, and with the help of God had her completed by July 10. The timber was hauled on dog teams. Since we had not brought any with us and the natives had none on hand, as they did not know how to make it, we manufactured out of a tree known there as listvennik (larch). For lack of anything better to take along on the sea voyage, we distilled liquor from grass by a process known in that country; salt we boiled out of sea water; butter was made from fish oil; and in place of meat we ate salt fish. We had on board enough provisions to last 40 men a year. On July 14 we sailed from the mouth of the Kamchatka River out to sea following the course laid down by the instructions of His Imperial Majesty Peter the Great.

The explorers named the vessel *St. Gabriel;* they discovered in the Bering Sea an island which they called St. Lawrence, because it was his day. They passed through Bering Strait but saw nothing on the other side. All the way from Kamchatka Point the Siberian coast was mountainous, almost as straight as a wall, and covered with snow. On August 15, off East Cape in latitude 67°18′ N, they could see that there was nothing more to the northward, and so they turned back. The *St. Gabriel* wintered at lower Kamchatka Post and put to sea again briefly on June 5, 1729, heading eastward because some of the natives claimed that they had seen land in that direction, but after careful search they found nothing. At Okhotsk, Bering decided to turn the *St. Gabriel* homeward.

At St. Petersburg the official reaction was divided. Some praised him, but others felt that doubtful questions had not been answered and decided to send him out on a second expedition. There was a long wait, however, before he finally headed eastward. The advance units had not prepared the expected materials, and Bering began to growl at the protracted delays.

At Okhotsk, Bering prepared two new small exploring ships, named the *St. Peter* and *St. Paul*. They were brigs, 80 feet in length and 20 feet in beam, and carried four small guns. They were launched in June 1740 but were delayed by the inadequacy of the freight boats. In October, Bering moved the ships over to the new harbor, which one of his officers had surveyed and charted. Situated on Avach Bay on the east coast of Kamchatka, the harbor was called Petropavlosk (the harbor of St. Peter and St. Paul). The little squadron sailed southeast by east on June 4, 1741, from Petropavlosk. Bering commanded the *St. Peter* and Lieutenant Albert Chirikov the *St. Paul*.

Bering's first glimpse of America, the lofty snow-covered Mount Saint Elias, visible from 120 miles away, came on July 17. The two vessels had separated, and Chirikov in the *St. Paul* had sighted land farther to the southward on July 14; later that week two of his boats with 15 men disappeared completely. Both ships continued along the coast of Alaska and then the coast of the Aleutians which was beset with continual fog and gales.

By September, scurvy was taking a heavy toll. Bering himself was in a very weakened state and some of the crew were dying. By the time they had passed Kiska and Attu, the officers and men could barely drag themselves around deck. They sought a haven where they could anchor safely in the Komandorskie Islands. The very sick were taken ashore, but the crews had not enough strength to haul the vessel up to safety. She was completely wrecked by a gale on November 28. Bering, sick as he was, kept a clear mind and retained control; he died on December 8 and was interred on the island.

In order to get home from the island, the survivors salvaged enough wood from the wreckage to build a small "hooker," as they called it, 36

feet long and 12 feet in beam, with a single mast and bowsprit. She was
given the larger vessel's name, *St. Peter*. Under Lieutenant Waxl, who
succeeded to command, she sailed from Bering Island on August 13 and
despite serious leakage managed to make Petropavlosk on August 27,
1742. Of the 77 men who had sailed 14 months earlier, only 45 had
survived. The record on the *St. Paul*, which had had her own hardships
under Chirikov, was almost the same—54 survivors out of 76—but 15
of those who died were in the two boats that had disappeared.

(See F. A. Golder, *Russian Expansion on the Pacific, 1641–1850*, 1960.)

Boudeuse

Overlapping Captain Cook's first voyage in the *Endeavour*, a French
expedition under Louis Antoine de Bougainville in the frigate *Boudeuse*
was also making discoveries in the South Sea islands. Bougainville was
perhaps the most versatile of the major explorers. A brilliant mathema-
tician with a keen scientific interest, he joined the French army and
played an important role as aide to Montcalm during the British attack
on Quebec. He later attempted to establish a colony in the Falkland
Islands, but without success.

Bougainville shifted to the navy, and in 1766 set out in the *Boudeuse*
on what has been called the only one of France's five exploring efforts to
be really successful in those years. Going through the Straits of Magellan, he made for Tahiti where Captain Wallis in the *Dolphin* had first
discovered the warm Polynesian charms the year before. Bougainville
was fascinated with Tahiti and called it the New Cythera. Then he
moved on to Samoa and the New Hebrides and reached the edge of the
Great Barrier Reef, but did not see Australia beyond it. He came back to
the edge of the Solomon Islands, the largest of which still bears his
name, as does a strait in the New Hebrides. Worried by hints of scurvy,
he made for the Moluccas and then came home by Batavia and Good
Hope—arriving at Saint Malo in March 1769, just as Cook was reaching
Tahiti. His health record for the voyage was almost as good as Cook's,
with only seven deaths. Some of Cook's sailors picked up venereal
disease at Tahiti, and international recriminations arose as to whether
Wallis's British tars or Bougainville's Frenchmen were responsible.

Bougainville enhanced his reputation in 1772 by writing the highly
readable *A Voyage Around the World*, which was immediately translated
into English. It played its part in glamorizing the South Seas, with the

Polynesians fitting into Rousseau's picture of the natural man and woman.

Bougainville had now outgrown the little *Boudeuse* and was climbing the ladder of naval rank with important commands during the American Revolution. In de Grasse's defeat at the Battle of the Saints in 1782, however, Bougainville fell into disgrace and was barred from court. In 1791 he became a vice admiral but soon retired to his estate in Normandy.

His name has been preserved not only by the island and strait in the South Seas, but also by the brilliant flowering shrub which he brought back from the Pacific, widely known as bougainvillea.

(See J. C. Beaglehole, *The Exploration of the Pacific,* 1966.)

Dolphin

The officers and crew of H.M.S. *Dolphin* experienced a memorable and delightful time when they discovered the island of Tahiti in 1767. They were the first Europeans exposed to the amorous hospitality of the Polynesians in a generous expression of South Sea glamor. They made the most of the situation and, as word got around, ship after ship managed to find an excuse to examine the delightful atmosphere of Tahiti situated just midway between New Zealand and Panama.

At the close of the Seven Years War, British and French frigates began to explore the Pacific, partly out of scientific curiosity and partly to gratify nationalist ambitions. The *Dolphin* was one of the first of these exploring frigates. She had first gone out in 1765 under Captain John Byron, known as "Foul Weather Jack," and had cruised for a year without finding much of anything. On Byron's return in 1766, the Admiralty arranged to send the *Dolphin* out again under Captain Samuel Wallis, a 38-year-old Cornishman, in hope of locating the supposedly huge mass of *Terra Australis Incognita,* in which many believed until the ghost was finally laid to rest in the early 1770s by Captain Cook. The *Dolphin* was a new and very special frigate of 32 guns and 511 tons. Her particular distinction was that she was the second Royal Navy frigate to get copper sheathing in 1764, which had the dual advantage of extra speed and protection against marine worms. For a consort, she was given the 30-year-old sloop *Swallow,* a wretchedly slow and erratic sailer.

These two ships, plus a storeship, sailed from Plymouth on August 21, 1766. From January 15 to April 11, 1767, the *Dolphin* was negotiating the Straits of Magellan and then headed out into the Pacific, leaving the slow old *Swallow* to go her own way under Captain Philip Carteret.

The discovery of Tahiti came as a surprise in mid-June 1767. Peaks, surmounted by clouds, had been sighted. In the words of George Robertson, master of the *Dolphin,* who kept an excellent journal, "We now supposed we saw the long wished for Southern Continent, which has often been talked of, but never before seen by any Europeans." Just when they realized that, instead of the nonexistent *Terra Australis*, they were closing in for the first time on the very delightful island of Tahiti is not certain. For the next five weeks (June 30–July 27, 1767) they would undergo a unique initiation into the glamor of the South Seas.

So far as the Tahitian men were concerned, emotional reactions shifted continually from good to bad. There was a fleet of a hundred war canoes on hand at their arrival, and there could never be any assurance that there would not be violence. On more than one occasion, volleys of stones were reciprocated by volleys of grapeshot. Guards were sent along with seamen who went ashore, and some natives even attempted to seize the *Dolphin.* Yet even in this atmosphere of mutual distrust, there was a continual barter, often under the most friendly circumstances. From the Tahitians, the ship drew a steady supply of pigs and fruit, and the payment most desired in exchange was iron, particularly in the form of nails or spikes.

That sort of barter occurred in various places where the Europeans landed, but on June 27, a week after the first contact, came an event which would place Tahiti in a unique position. Robertson recorded in his journal:

> But our young men seeing several very handsome young girls, they could not help feasting their eyes with so agreeable a sight; this as observed by some of the elderly men, and several of the girls were drawn out, some a light copper colour, others mulatto and some almost white. The old men made them stand in rank, and made signs for our people to take which they liked best, and as many as they liked, and for fear our men had been ignorant and not known how to use the poor young girls, the old men made signs how we should behave to the young women; this all the boat crews seemed to understand perfectly well, and begged the officer would receive a few of the young women aboard, at the same time they made signs to the young girls that they were not so ignorant as the old men supposed them; this seemed to please the old men greatly. When they saw our people merry, the poor young girls seemed a little afraid, but soon turned better acquainted.

The officer in the boat having no orders to bring out any of the natives, would not receive the young girls but made signs that he would see them afterwards. . . . When our boats returned on board the ship the sailors swore they had never seen handsomer made women in their lives and declared they would all to a man live on two thirds allowance, rather than lose so fine an opportunity of getting a girl apiece—this piece of news made all our men madly fond of the shore, even the sick, which had been on the Doctor's list for some weeks before now declared that they would be happy if they were permitted to go ashore, at the same time said a young girl would make an excellent nurse. . . .

This new situation had its economic consequences. The young girls began demanding nails as the price of their affections:

When I was ordering the liberty men into the boat the carpenter came, and told me that every cleat in the ship was drawn, and all the nails carried off. At the same time the Boatswain informed me that most of the hammock nails were drawed, and two thirds of the men obliged to lie on deck for want of nails to hang their hammocks. . . . Then some of the young gentlemen told me that the liberty men carried on a trade with the young girls, who had now rose their price for some days past from a twenty to thirty penny nail, to a forty penny, and some was so extravagent as to demand a seven or nine inch spick [spike]; this was plain proof of the way the large nails went.

This nail demand was hurting the existing barter in pork and other food. Captain Wallis complained of the inflation: "From this time, our market was very ill supplied, the Indians refusing to sell provisions at the usual price and making signs for larger nails." (Because of this situation, Cook, when he visited Tahiti two years later, gave flat orders that there was to be no bartering of nails for love.)

There were amorous alliances at a higher social level. "Queen" Purea, a somewhat inflated title, received Captain Wallis and the other officers at her home and was also received aboard ship. Richardson suggests that she tried strong persuasive methods to try to keep the English longer at Tahiti.

The island, now drawn into the European scheme of affairs, was quickly claimed by three powers. On June 26, 1767, the British formally claimed possession naming it King George III Island; the following year Bougainville claimed it for France, naming it "New Cythera"; and then the Viceroy of Peru, in one of the last bursts of Spanish imperial expansion, sent out three expeditions, culminating in claiming Tahiti for Spain. It was not until well into the next century that it was permanently annexed by France—perhaps an appropriate fate for the "amorous isle."

The *Dolphin* sailed away on July 27. She returned by way of Batavia and Cape Town, arriving in England on May 20, 1768. One direct result of the Tahiti episode was to ensure that the transit-of-Venus expedition under Cook would stop there for its observations.

(See N. A. Rose, *Voyage to the Amorous Isles*, 1955.)

Endeavour

The three voyages of Pacific discovery by Captain James Cook (1768–1779) were surpassed in geographical significance only by the 40 years of Renaissance voyaging by Columbus, da Gama, and Magellan (1492–1532). Cook's first voyage (1768–1771) in the *Endeavour* brought Australia and New Zealand actively into the world picture; they had been discovered but neglected by the Dutch. In his second voyage (1772–1775) in the *Resolution* he sailed back and forth across the Pacific to dispel the popular idea of a great southern continent. On the third voyage (1776–1779), again in the *Resolution*, he discovered Hawaii and the northwest corner of North America. Because the discoveries were so distinct in their nature, it seems best, in accordance with this study's emphasis on ships, to confine this article to the first voyage and to deal with the second and third separately under the name *Resolution*.

Cook's voyaging was part of a sudden interest in the Pacific. The French saw in Pacific exploration a chance to compensate for the loss of Canada and India in the recent Seven Years War. Both they and the British, in those years of Enlightenment, were definitely interested in scientific opportunities. The British were also desirous of charting the Pacific, and Cook was the prize hydrographer of the day. Finally, there was the possibility of snapping up an occasional colony or two.

Cook came from very modest circumstances on the east coast of England near Whitby, home port of many of the large fleet of colliers which carried coal to London. His father, a Scot, was a farm laborer who rose to be manager of a neighbor's farm. Cook served as apprentice in a country store, which bored him, and he managed to get an apprenticeship on a Whitby collier, the *Freelove*, where in due time he rose to mate. In 1755, with war impending, he took the then unusual step of volunteering for the navy as an able seaman on the *Eagle*. Within a month he was master's mate. Her next captain, an increasingly influential one, was so struck by Cook's ability that he secured for him a warrant as master. Cook developed a keen proficiency in hydrography and had charge of charting the tricky St. Lawrence for the attack on Quebec. It was done so well that not a ship grounded. For five years after the war Cook was in command of a little 70-ton schooner charged with the arduous task of surveying the rugged coast of Newfoundland. This experience put Cook in line for his great opportunity.

The prestigious Royal Society, leader in the scientific field, decided upon an expedition to the South Seas. Its avowed purpose was to observe the transit of Venus, an astronomical phenomenon which would not recur for another century. It was proposed to visit the Marquesas Islands for this, but when H.M.S. *Dolphin* arrived home with news of her amorous reception at Tahiti, it was decided to go there. Another motive for the voyage was to locate *Terra Australis Incognita,* a reputed great mid-Pacific landmass. Hopes for command of the expedition were entertained by Alexander Dalrymple, learned and arrogant hydrographer and believer in *Terra Australis.* The Admiralty, however, flatly refused to let a civilian command a naval expedition. That left the way clear for Cook, who, though only a warrant officer, had built up a high reputation for his scientific abilities.

The Navy Board was instructed to find a suitable ship and came up with an east coast collier of the very type with which Cook was familiar. The bark *Earl of Pembroke,* renamed *Endeavour,* was a 368-ton vessel, less than four years old; she was of a type known locally as a "cat." She was purchased for £2840. Cook explained the good qualities of these Whitby cats. They were strong with comparatively shallow draft, good carriers with plenty of room for men and stores. They could "safely sail near enough to land with time to turn away from warning sights, smells, and sounds; if at the worst they took the ground, they could sit on it a while without much fear of a fatal capsize." Cook's other three vessels in his later voyages were all Whitby cats.

A distinctive if bothersome addition to the *Endeavour's* personnel came with a note from the Admiralty that "Joseph Banks, Esq. and his Suite, comprising eight persons with their Baggage" would join the ship. Banks, who would become associated with Cook's voyaging, was no ordinary person. Still young, he had an inherited income of £6000 a year (the equivalent of more than £100,000 a year in the 1970s). After Eton and Harrow he studied at Christ Church, Oxford, diligently studying botany and other sciences. He had many influential friends. Even though Banks was something of a dilettante, he did much to sponsor scientific interests. The highly educated colleagues whom he brought aboard with their gear had impressive records. But they did take up room in a somewhat crowded vessel. Cook had to give up much of the privacy of his great cabin, while the other officers had to find quarters below. The question has been raised whether a traditional aristocratic captain would have been as accommodating. The senior scientist, closest to Cook, was Dr. Daniel Charles Solander, who had studied with the great Swedish botanist, Linnaeus.

On August 20, 1768, the *Endeavour* sailed from Plymouth with 94 persons crowded into her modest hull. She carried 10 carriage and 12 swivel guns, and had provisions and stores for 18 months. The passage down through the South Atlantic from Madeira was uneventful. At Rio de Janeiro, the *Endeavour* was denied warship privileges because she still looked like a collier. After five rugged weeks she finally rounded Cape Horn on January 31, 1769.

About 80 days from Cape Horn, she made her first and most glamorous landfall. Tahiti, long unknown, was coming into the European picture with a rush. Captain Wallis in the *Dolphin* had first experienced the Polynesian hospitality in 1767; Bougainville in the French *Boudeuse* had visited Tahiti in 1768; and now came the *Endeavour* in 1769. Out of these international contacts came a dispute as to which frigate had introduced venereal disease into the island society. Cook forbade the payment of nails and spikes for love. In accordance with his official mission, Cook established an observatory on appropriately named Venus Point. The social contacts were marred by constant thievery. Taking with him a Tahitian to act as interpreter with the Polynesians he might meet, Cook left Tahiti on July 13 and spent a month in the outlying islands, which he named the Society Islands in honor of the Royal Society which had helped to sponsor the expedition.

Cook headed westward for what would be the visits of greatest lasting importance, the big temperate islands discovered by Abel Janszoon Tasman in 1642. They were named for two Dutch provinces—New Zealand and New Holland; the latter would eventually be known as Australia. Because of their temperate climate and rich vegetation, Cook could foresee their future as "colonies of settlement" for the Europeans. The Dutch, having found nothing profitable in those regions "down under," had not followed up Tasman's findings—it remained for Cook to bring them into the pattern of European expansion.

After the delightful atmosphere of Tahiti, the *Endeavour* ran into much harsher conditions, for she was getting down into the "Roaring Forties," where westerly gales blew incessantly. On October 4 a young lookout won an extra gallon of rum for first sighting the North Island of New Zealand. During the next six months the *Endeavour* would completely circumnavigate the two islands, which Tasman had not done, and would in the process make 2500 miles of hydrographic surveys of lasting excellence. It was often rugged work, especially on the western side, with gales and hidden rocks. Contact with the natives was spasmodic. At times they met with Polynesian charm, more often with hostility. The New Zealand Maoris would prove to be among the most impressive natives encountered in European expansion, but they were enthusiastic cannibals.

According to his Admiralty instructions, Cook had his choice, after surveying New Zealand, of returning by Cape Horn or Good Hope. It was decided to do the latter and the *Endeavour* once again moved westward, traversing the Tasman Sea. Tasman had discovered the western coast of Australia and also Van Diemen's Land, now called Tasmania. In April 1771 Cook reached the southeastern corner of the island-continent, naming it New South Wales.

On May 6, 1770, he recorded an event which would have the greatest lasting effect of his whole voyage, making the name "Botany Bay" a familiar one. In his journal that day he wrote:

The great quantity of new plants &c Mr. Banks and Dr. Solander collected in this place occasioned my giving it the name of *Botany Bay* . . . it is capacious safe and commodious. It may be known by the land on the seacoast which is of pretty even and moderate height, rather higher than it is farther inland with steep rocky cliffs near the sea and looks like a long island lying close to the shore: the entrance of the harbour lies about the middle of this land, coming in from the southward it is discovered before you are abreast of it which you cannot do in coming from the northward. . . . There is shoal'd water a good way off from the South Shore. . . . We anchored near the south shore about a mile within the entrance for the convenience of sailing with a southerly wind and the getting of fresh water on the north shore in the first sandy cove within the island before which a ship might lie almost landlock'd and wood for fuel may be got every where.

Altho wood is here in great plenty yet there is very little variety, the largest trees are as large or larger than our oaks in England and grows a good deal like them . . . another sort grows tall and strait something like pines, the wood of this is hard and ponderous and something like the nature of American live oak, these are all the timber trees I met with. There are a few sorts of shrubs and several palm trees and mangroves about the head of the harbour. The country is woody low and flat as far inland as we could see and I believe that the soil is in general sandy, in the wood are a variety of very bootiful birds such as cockatoos, lorryqueets, parrots &c and crows exactly like those we have in England. Water fowl are less plenty about the head of the harbour where there are large flats of sand and mud. . . . On the sand and mud banks are oysters, muscles, cockles &c which I believe are the chief support of the inhabitants. . . .

During our stay in this harbour I caused the English colours to be displayed ashore every day and an inscription to be cut out upon one of the trees near the watering place setting forth the ship's name, date

&c. We steered along the shore NNE . . . about 2 or 3 miles from the land and abreast of the bay or harbour wherein there appeared to be safe anchorage which I called *Port Jackson*. It lies 3 leags to the northward of Botany Bay.

The enthusiasm of Banks seems to have "sold" Botany Bay to the English. However much they enthused over the flora and fauna, it is a safe bet that if Cook had gone three leagues north to the other bay which he named for Jackson, an Admiralty official, he would, as a seaman, have waxed lyrical over the future Sydney, one of the finest harbors in the world. As it was, when the British decided to transport their felons overseas in 1787, the choice fell on Botany Bay, and Captain Philip, commanding the first fleet of criminals in H.M.S. *Sirius*, had orders to dump them there. He took one look at Botany Bay and moved up to Port Jackson-Sydney. Because of the preliminary buildup, the name Botany Bay became associated with the convict settlement. Cook had at least done his part in directing attention to that area.

Proceeding up the eastern coast of Australia, the *Endeavour* almost ended her days on June 10 on the notorious Great Barrier Reef. This narrowing funnel between a jumble of coral formations stretches for some 1500 miles up the east coast. On that particular night, the ship seemed to be in safe waters; the last sounding showed 17 fathoms, when suddenly she struck a sharp coral reef and stuck fast at high tide. Cook and everyone else aboard rose to the occasion in magnificent fashion. Guns and other heavy equipment were thrown overboard and the pumps were steadily manned, but for some time the ship did not budge. Finally she was worked loose; a sail, with tufts of wool and oakum and spread with sheep dung, was dragged over the lead and she finally reached a river mouth, where repairs delayed her seven weeks. The coral rock has gone clear through her bottom, and part of her sheathing and false keel were gone. She ran into continual jeopardy from further reefs. She managed to get through to open sea and at the end of August discovered Endeavour Strait between Australia and New Guinea. The Great Barrier Reef came into prominence nearly two decades later following the *Bounty* mutiny. Captain Bligh, with expert seamanship, guided his small boat through it but the frigate *Pandora*, sent out to bring back the *Bounty* mutineers, was lost through her captain's ineptitude.

Cook now proceeded down to the Dutch East Indian capital, Batavia, for more thoroughgoing repairs. They were certainly needed—in one place the planking was worn down to one-eighth of an inch, and some of the timbers were in such a state that it was a wonder she stayed afloat. Those 10 weeks at Batavia improved the ship but had a disastrous effect on Cook's hitherto remarkable health record. Not a single man had died of scurvy, but now malaria, followed by dysentery, had disastrous consequences. Batavia had a notoriously deadly climate and the *Endeavour*'s death toll was very heavy, even after she put to sea on December 26, 1770. Cook said she was like a hospital ship with more than 40 men sick and the rest extremely weak. The ship returned by Cape Town and Ascension Island, and finally, in mid-July 1771, reached the Thames, ending her first voyage.

Cook was almost overlooked in the attention and honors given to Banks, who did nothing to check the impression that it was his voyage. Cook turned in a remarkably thorough report to the Admiralty who appreciated, as the public did not, all that he had done. He was promoted to commander, though some felt that he should have jumped to captain. (Though always referred to as Captain Cook, he had made this first voyage as lieutenant.) There was soon talk of a second voyage, which he would undertake in the *Resolution*.

(See J. C. Beaglehole, ed., *The Journals of Captain Cook,* 1955–1967.)

Resolution

The *Resolution* and *Discovery,* anchored in the Society Islands during Captain James Cook's third voyage. *(National Maritime Museum, Greenwich)*

Captain James Cook's first famous voyage to the Southwest Pacific had been made in H.M.S. *Endeavour,* a former coastal collier. She was then sent out on other duty and the Admiralty gave him another, larger Whitby collier, the *Marquis of Granby,* renamed the *Resolution,* in which he would make his second and third voyages. At 462 tons, she was considerably more roomy than the 368-ton *Endeavour.* Also, remembering those desperate days on the Great Barrier Reef and other close calls, the Admiralty gave him a consort so that the outside world could get word if anything went wrong out in those lonesome seas. The consort on the second voyage was another Whitby collier, the 360-ton *Adventure;* for the third voyage the consort would be the 337-ton *Discovery.*

In this and various other ways, the Admiralty went out of its way to provide Cook generously with whatever he might need. The one difficulty came in connection with the civilian scientists. Cook had accommodated himself to the wealthy and influential Joseph Banks on the first voyage, but now, his head swelled with the home-coming adulation, Banks began making outrageous demands, insisting on enlarging the ship's accommodations for the 15 on his staff and even for an orchestra in bright red uniforms. He talked as though he was going to be in general charge, and even tried to insist on a ship of the line or at least an old East Indiaman. These extravagant demands were enough to annoy the Admiralty, which included some powerful friends of Cook. The Admiralty ordered that Banks' structural additions be ripped out, as they were making the ship unseaworthy. Banks, in indignation, withdrew from the ship and set out for Iceland. Cook had his ship back as he wanted it, except for a new head scientist with an impossible personality. This "Scots-Prussian" was such a trial that Cook dispensed with scientists altogether for his third voyage and vigorously expressed his relief at being rid of the breed—"Damn and blast all scientists!" he exclaimed.

The second voyage (1772–1775) was in a class by itself. The first (1768–1771) had led to important new developments in the Southwest Pacific, particularly in Australia. The third (1776–1779) had a similar effect in the Northeast Pacific, with Hawaii, the American Northwest Coast, and Alaska. The second voyage aimed at negative findings and was highly successful at that. Its intention was to disprove, once and for all, the old idea of a *Terra Australis Incognita,* which the geographer Alexander Dalrymple had promoted so strongly. Cook was to traverse the whole south Pacific from Antarctica northward. He definitely proved that there was no such land. Even though the *Resolution* and *Adventure* were three years at sea, the story can be told quickly.

The ships sailed on July 13, 1772, exactly a year after arriving home from the first voyage. Lieutenant Tobias Furneaux, who had been with Wallis on the *Dolphin* in her celebrated Tahitian landfall, commanded the *Adventure.* The major pattern of the voyaging consisted of twice going down as far as possible to the very edge of Antarctica. With the seasons reversed in the Southern Hemisphere, this voyage would best be done in the winter months. After each Antarctica voyage came a withdrawal northward for a well-deserved rest and recreation in New Zealand and Tahiti, accompanied with lateral sweeps which would have caught the *Terra Australis* had there been one—but there was not.

A few episodes stood out in this voyaging. On the second visit to Antarctica when the farthest south latitude of 71°10′ was reached on January 31, 1774, and the ship was about to turn back, the teenage midshipman George Vancouver went out to the end of the jib boom and called out "Ne plus ultra"—nothing beyond this. For the rest of his life, even after leaving his name on the North American map, Vancouver could boast that he had been farther south than any other man. A rather grim affair occurred in New Zealand, when two midshipmen from the *Adventure* and the eight sailors of their boat's crew were killed and eaten by the Maoris. On approaching Tahiti and keenly anticipating its hospitality, the two ships ran into the gravest danger since the *Endeavour's* ordeal on the Great Barrier Reef; the wind went down completely and a strong current was pulling them toward the reefs and collision with each other—the wind came up just in time to save them. In their cruising among the mid-Pacific islands, they visited the Marquesas which had been discovered by the Spaniards two centuries before, and Cook discovered New Caledonia. Charting was an important part of Cook's voyages. Just as Commodore Preble's flagship was a valued training school for young American lieutenants, Cook's cruising was a similar training for some of the Royal Navy's best hydrographers, Vancouver and Bligh among them. Incidentally, navigating was greatly simplified on these two later voyages by the availability of Harrison's chronometer, which had been withheld from the first voyage through professional jealousy.

Cook was ashore for a year (July 10, 1775–July 12, 1776), just as the American Revolution was getting under way. He arrived three weeks after Bunker Hill and left a week after the Declaration of Independence. On his return to England Cook was received by the king and promoted to post-captain. To give Cook a chance for a well-deserved rest his friends at the Admiralty arranged for him a dignified and profitable sinecure at Greenwich Hospital. At age 47, with 30 years of fairly continuous service, the post looked attractive. He took the post with the provision that if something came up for which he was particularly fitted, he would be free to accept the offer. To no one's great surprise, something did come up.

Since Cook had so thoroughly covered the South Pacific, it was decided to shift him to the North Pacific with the particular charge to hunt for the Pacific end of the supposed Northwest Passage from the Atlantic. He returned to the *Resolution;* this time his consort was the *Discovery* under Captain Charles Clerke. Cook had a very able collection of officers, some of whom would rise to high places. It was an international tribute to his work that the French and Spanish governments gave orders that if his ships were encountered, they were to receive friendly treatment for being engaged in a mission for the general good, even though his ships belonged to the Royal Navy. Benjamin Franklin over in Paris saw to it that the American forces secured similar instructions.

The voyage started out along familiar lines—Cape Town, New Zealand, and Tahiti. Cook had brought out considerable livestock, which he distributed to island natives. Sailing almost due north from Tahiti, he made a most important surprise discovery on January 18, 1778. For the first time, European eyes looked upon the Hawaiian Islands. Somehow the Manila-Acapulco annual galleons had sailed to the north of the islands. The friendly Polynesians were quite similar to the Tahitians. Cook wondered how those two peoples and also the New Zealand Maoris had spread out over such great distances.

From Hawaii, Cook moved westward to the interminable stretch of mainland which Drake had called "New Albion," the poetic name of England. He reached the coast around Oregon and continued north to Nootka Sound—a name that would become widely familiar in the next few years—on the great island which would before long bear the name of Cook's "ne plus ultra" midshipman, Vancouver. The native Indians were fishermen, fur trappers, active traders, and pilferers par excellence. One of the chief results of Cook's visit to Nootka Sound was the acquisition of sea otter skins; they were not appreciated at the outset— it is said that the sailors spread them on their bunks for warmth. But when, after Cook's death, the *Resolution* reached China, the Chinese offered high prices for these choicest of furs. The result was a scramble to Nootka with keen rivalry among the Spaniards, British, Russians, and Americans.

Cook continued on up the sheltered Inside Passage toward Alaska, with constant vigilance for the possible outlet of the Northwest Passage. Naturally, none was found. On the northward searching they went up toward Bering Sea and then the narrow Bering Strait between America and Asia. They went briefly into the Arctic near Point Barrow until they ran into an impenetrable wall of ice, which meant turning around and exploring the Siberian side. There was a brief visit to Petropavlosk in Kamchatka. Remaining there longer might have meant being frozen in for months, so Cook decided to return to Hawaii—the islands that he had named for Lord Sandwich, First Lord of Admiralty, and inventor of the sandwich, and strong supporter of Cook—they would continue to be called the Sandwich Islands for years to come.

On his return to Hawaii in January 1779, Cook anchored in Kealakekua Bay on Hawaii, the major island. The *Resolution* was badly in need of repair. She had been in good shape on the second voyage, but the dockyard in England had done a shoddy repair job between voyages; the hull was chronically leaky and the rigging was in bad shape. While the refitting was going on, the Hawaiians engaged in constant manifestations of respect for Cook as almost divine. They prostrated themselves, staged elaborate processions, presented him with an elegant robe, and were ultragenerous to "Orono," as they called him.

Then Polynesian emotions suddenly went to the opposite extreme. Although the community was very generous, supplies were running low and some resentment developed at the continual drain. On February 4, 1779, Cook sailed away to do some surveying. A gale arose, tore some of the sails to shreds, and, particularly serious, "sprung" or cracked the foremast. Cook would have preferred some other bay for the repairs, but Kealakekua Bay was the only place available. On his return he sensed a general sullen withdrawal, quite the reverse of the former enthusiasm. Pilfering now became more widespread, and "incidents" kept recurring.

The climax came when the *Discovery's* cutter was stolen. Cook decided to take punitive steps, going ashore on February 14 with a lieutenant and a file of marines to seize the local chief as a hostage for the return of the boat. An angry crowd gathered and the chief did not appear. The marines were pelted with stones. As the marines fired some shots, Cook started to move down the shore to retire by boat; he never got there. A warrior struck him from behind and he fell on his knees, half in the water. The crowd roared angrily as Cook went down, stabbing and clubbing him and holding him under water. He raised his head once and looked at them and then fell insensible. They dragged his body ashore and continued the frenzied stabbing.

After Cook's death, the *Resolution* set out for home under the command of Clerke, who died en route. The *Resolution* returned to England by way of the Cape of Good Hope, completing one more circumnavigation. It is said that if Cook had not been killed, he would probably have been made a baronet. At any rate, he stands as the greatest of British explorers, admired for the wide variety of his achievements.

(See J. C. Beaglehole, ed., *The Journals of Captain James Cook on His Voyages of Discovery*, 1967.)

Gaspée

The *Gaspée*, a British revenue schooner attacked and burned by Providence mariners in June 1772. *(Naval Historical Center)*

In Providence and adjacent areas of Rhode Island one frequently runs across the name "Gaspée," commemorating the seizure and burning in 1772 of the British revenue cutter *Gaspée* near Newport by a group from Providence, a spectacular demonstration of colonial discontent with British maritime regulations on the eve of the Revolution.

The schooner *Gaspée*, named for the big peninsula in the lower St. Lawrence, had been purchased for customs regulation. Her commanding officer, Lieutenant William Duddingston, had been quite arrogant in his checking of American maritime movements. Rhode Island's geography put Providence (up the river) at a disadvantage compared with Newport, situated on an island at the entrance to Narragansett Bay. Newport was inclined to favor royal authority and was the base for the local warships; Providence favored the colonial side and found its shipping particularly liable to interference.

On this June day the Providence packet, *Hanna*, coming in from New York, was chased by the *Gaspée*. The packet captain deliberately lured the *Gaspée* through shoal water off Namquit Point, and, as anticipated, the heavier revenue cutter ran aground.

On reaching Providence, the packet captain reported this to John Brown, shipowner and magnate, of *the* family of Providence. Brown **69** instructed his senior captain, Abraham Whipple, to make ready eight longboats. Volunteers, summoned by drumbeat in the street, assembled at Sabin's Tavern and cast bullets while final plans were worked out. No special efforts at secrecy were made, except that actual names were to be avoided; Brown was to be "Head Sheriff" and Whipple "Captain." Around midnight the eight boats, with oars muffled, slipped down the river toward Newport.

As the boats approached the *Gaspée*, Lieutenant Duddingston came on deck in his nightshirt and demanded to know who was there. "The High Sheriff of this colony, damn you!" came the reply. One impetuous volunteer grabbed his musket and shot the lieutenant in the groin, the only casualty of the encounter. As the attackers swarmed over the rail, the crew of the *Gaspée* surrendered. They and the wounded Lieutenant were put ashore at Pawtucket, while the rest remained aboard to put the torch to the stranded cutter. The whole plan had worked out most smoothly.

While Providence celebrated, the outraged royal authorities at Newport determined to avenge the daring stroke. While a report was rushed off to the Admiralty, the governor offered a reward of £100 for information leading to the conviction of the leaders. Everyone in the area knew their identity, but not a soul informed the authorities, even after a royal proclamation in August raised the reward to £500 with amnesty to the informer. A special Board of Inquiry, headed by the chief justice, sat for 10 months, but could not get anyone to reveal the identity of the men who burned the *Gaspée*. That is one reason why the episode still ranks high in Rhode Island annals.

(See J. R. Bartlett, *The Destruction of the Gaspée in Naragansett Bay*, 1972.)

Margaretta

The *Margaretta* was only a small schooner, but she was one of the king's ships, flying the white ensign of the Royal Navy. Her claim to fame was that she was captured by the Americans on June 12, 1775, in the so-called "Lexington of the Seas," a fierce but quite informal action at Machias far up on the Maine coast.

The issue at stake was the furnishing of lumber to build barracks for the British redcoats at Boston and this issue came midway between Lexington-Concord and Bunker Hill. The ports nearer Boston had refused to furnish lumber for the British regiments. Machias was a new frontier community, with lumbering its chief occupation. The British sent up two sloops to gather pine boards and timber.

One of the more vigorous residents of Machias, Jeremiah O'Brien, was determined that no Machias lumber would go south for that unpopular purpose. The sloops had come up under the protection of the little H.M.S. *Margaretta* commanded by Midshipman John Moore. A crowd of Machias residents, armed with guns, swords, axes, and pikes swarmed aboard the sloops, and chased the *Margaretta*. There was an hour of most obstinate confrontation. Midshipman Moore was mortally wounded; Jeremiah O'Brien and his men boarded the *Margaretta* and she surrendered.

At the very same time, the New Englanders were putting an end to the furnishing of pine masts for the Royal Navy, which had started in 1652 with regular mast ships from Portsmouth, New Hampshire, and later also from Falmouth (Portland) Maine. When residents of the latter town refused to provide masts, a British squadron bombarded and burned a good part of the port in retaliation. The masts never reached England, which did not bother to lay in a new supply elsewhere; when France, with its good navy, entered the war in 1778, the lack of masts seriously handicapped the British naval efforts.

Ranger

The distinguished experience of John Paul Jones before he would gain fame in the fight of the *Bonhomme Richard* against the *Serapis* was his bold raiding of British waters in the sloop *Ranger* in the spring of 1778. Though the damage inflicted by the raid was small, the morale effect was tremendous. It was the first time since the Dutch raid on the Medway that an enemy had actually raided a British port. Militia assembled for defense and the Royal Navy swarmed out to catch the pirates. John Paul Jones suddenly had an impressive reputation along the British coasts.

Jones took command of the sloop-of-war *Ranger*, fresh from the builder at Portsmouth, New Hampshire, and sailed for France on November 1, 1777, one of the first to bring news of the victory of Saratoga, which would lead France to become an American ally. In Quiberon Bay he had the gratifying experience of being the first American to receive a French naval salute.

On the night of April 22–23, Jones raided the busy port of White-haven from which he had first gone to sea. The wind had gone down and his two vessels had to row three hours, not arriving until nearly dawn. To make matters worse, an Irish sailor slipped ashore and roused the town. More than 200 vessels were in port, but only one was set afire before Jones withdrew. A few hours later he engaged in a particularly fantastic farce. He decided to kidnap the Earl of Selkirk from his nearby estate and hold him, in order to exert pressure on the British to release their American naval prisoners. The Earl, however, was away. The sailors, disgusted that there was no prize money in the day's actions, insisted on some loot. Jones went ashore but stayed with the boats while two officers and some sailors presented a demand for the house-hold silver, which Lady Selkirk turned over. Jones later wrote her an extremely "corny" letter about his high principles and returned the silver. The third episode of the raid was a successful fight with H.M.S. *Drake,* a sloop of almost identical size as the *Ranger.* She was captured after an hour of hard fighting, in which her elderly captain was killed. The *Ranger* towed the *Drake* to Brest, where an enthusiastic welcome awaited him.

For eight months, however, Jones had a frustrating time in France, constantly pulling wires for an adequate command and constantly meeting disappointment. Finally, on the promise by the Minister of Marine of a large ship, Jones consented to have the *Ranger* sent home under the command of Lieutenant Thomas Simpson, a leader among those of the crew who had insisted upon taking loot in the raids of the *Ranger.*

(See S. E. Morison, *John Paul Jones, a Sailor's Biography,* 1959.)

Bonhomme Richard

The *Bonhomme Richard* (foreground), in which John Paul Jones defeated the *Serapis* on September 25, 1779. *(Naval Historical Center)*

Four fierce hours of frigate action gave John Paul Jones a lasting glamorous place in naval tradition. The performance of the other captains and ships of the little navy of the American Revolution offered little competition in that field. And yet in this famous battle, the ship, captain, and majority of the crew were not American. Jones, a Scot, had come to America just before the war. The *Bonhomme Richard,* a converted French East Indiaman, had never been within 3000 miles of America; and, of the 380 aboard, only 79 were Americans, including most of the officers. Manning this American warship were 137 French marines and 37 other French; 59 British; 29 Portuguese; 21 Irish; and men from six other countries. The battle itself was extremely unconventional: instead of exchanging broadsides at a distance, the ships grappled in a close embrace, and the crew of the victorious *Bonhomme Richard* swarmed aboard their British adversary and captured her before their own ship sank.

John Paul Jones himself was far from the pattern of the typical naval officer. He was superlative in action, but he had many less admirable characteristics. He was extremely egocentric, vain, and self-seeking. He scrambled constantly for rank and commands. His selfishness alienated his fellow officers many times, and his crews were often disgruntled. He was an habitual womanizer, usually on a "love them and leave them" basis, breaking off his affairs with a cruel brusqueness. Although he was the son of a gardener, he boasted constantly of his 73 gentlemanly sentiments, often in ridiculous manner. Even his name was assumed. He had started as John Paul, called himself John Jones for a while, and finally blossomed forth as John Paul Jones.

Jones was born on the very southern edge of Scotland on west coast waters of Solway Firth, not far from the active English port of Whitehaven, which he would later raid. His father was gardener on the estate of a Scottish laird. After he had had a few years of local schooling, his love of the sea led him at age 13 to apprenticeship aboard a Whitehaven brig, which for several years traded with Rappahannock in Virginia, where his brother was established as a tailor. It seems that he made several slaving voyages, which he found distasteful. His record in those early years is hazy and full of gaps, but it is known that in 1768 at age 21 he got his first command, the little 60-ton brig *John*, engaged in the West Indies trade. Some time afterward, he received a larger command, the ship *Betsey*, trading to Tobago. Things were prospering and he was looking forward to settling down comfortably as a gentleman farmer. But then in 1773 came what he called "the greatest misfortune of my life." At Tobago he refused to advance wages to the seamen. One burly ringleader swung a bludgeon at his head, whereupon Jones ran him through with his sword. That, at least, is what he later told Benjamin Franklin, but the story remains suspiciously hazy. To avoid legal action, he skipped the island, and for the next 20 months (1773–1775) his movements are almost a complete mystery—during that time he twice changed his name.

Then Jones joined the American navy and the record becomes clearer. On December 7, 1775, he was commissioned first lieutenant in the Continental Navy, which was just coming into being and was having a problem in securing adequate officers. Whereas the army had many experienced officers from the Seven Years War, the best the navy could do was to take a chance on merchant marine skippers, whose chief recommendation seemed to be the support of a member of the Continental Congress. The result was general mediocrity plus intense jealousy of rank. Jones had a supporter in Joseph Hewes of Edenton, North Carolina, who was a member of the Marine Committee, but that support had been only strong enough to get him rated eighteenth out of 24 when a seniority list was finally drawn up.

Jones saw various duty afloat, most notably his raiding of British waters in the *Ranger*. Following these exploits, he went to France, where he had a frustrating experience; in fact, much of the rest of his naval career was spent in Paris, negotiating for better things for himself. Decisions there depended partly upon Benjamin Franklin and the other American Commissioners, and partly upon the French Minister of Marine and his subordinates. Of these, only Franklin supported Jones completely, and some of the action came at the Parisian suburb of Passy, where Franklin had his headquarters, and where the wealthy French shipowner Le Roy de Chaumont was Jones' main contact for financial and logistical support. To complicate matters further, of Jones' many French mistresses, the leading one was Madame de Chaumont; they were often together during Chaumont's frequent travels.

The ship upon which Jones' heart was set was the very impressive frigate *L'Indien*, built in a private yard in Amsterdam, but international pressures finally kept her out of Jones' hands. The answer to his quest for an important command finally lay in an old French East Indiaman, the *Duc de Duras*, a rather tired old craft of some 850 to 900 tons, built in 1766. She was purchased by the Crown in February 1779 for $44,000; the Crown also assumed all other expenses, but the vessel was to fly the American flag. In honor of Benjamin Franklin and his *Poor Richard's Almanac*, she was named the *Bonhomme Richard*.

Jones immediately busied himself in fitting her out, which, next to fighting and making love, he enjoyed most. Four other ships were brought together for Jones' command, which gave him the courtesy title of "commodore," but seldom had there been a more uncoordinated squadron. The largest ship, even stronger than the *Richard*, was the frigate *Alliance*, built on the Merrimac and under the American flag but commanded by a half-mad French officer, Pierre Landais, who as a piece of especially bad management had been commissioned as a captain in the American navy. During the great fight the *Alliance* would actually fire into the *Richard*. In addition, the squadron had three smaller French vessels, only one of which, the *Pallas*, was of any help.

In the month before the famous action off Flamborough Head, Jones' squadron swept around the northern part of the British Isles, starting at the southwest corner of Ireland and going north to the islands above Scotland, turning south at the Shetlands, and then winding up at the Firth of Forth. There a shift in the wind spoiled his plan of demanding a heavy ransom from Leith as the alternative to burning it. Once again his presence spread terror all along the coast to Newcastle and beyond. Other ships of his fleet had gone their own way, paying scant attention to Jones' signals, while Landais repeatedly insulted him. Only a few prizes had been captured.

On the afternoon of September 25, 1779, the big Baltic convoy came in sight: 41 merchantmen laden with important naval stores, escorted by a new 44-gun frigate, the *Serapis*, under Captain Richard Pearson. Faster, stronger, and more heavily armed than the old *Richard*, she was supported by the 20-gun sloop *Countess of Scarbrough*. Pearson very properly signaled the merchantmen to take shelter close to the guns of Scarbrough Castle. Then he and Jones stood out to meet each other. It was three hours from their first sighting until they finally made contact about 6 o'clock, just as the sun was setting. The full moon came up shortly and the sea was calm as a millpond off the towering white cliffs of Flamborough Head.

Jones decided that, in view of his limitations, this was not a time for a conventional gun duel. His hope would lie in grappling for close encounter. Two of the *Richard's* big 18-pounders exploded with casualties; that cut down the American firepower. In the constant maneuvering, the *Serapis* tried to get in a position for raking, but the two ships stayed entangled. Pearson called out, "Has your ship struck?" to which Jones gave his immortal reply, "I have not yet begun to fight." (A favorite Marine Corps story is that one American marine, firing away from one of the fighting tops, said to his companion, "There's always some damned fool who doesn't get the word.")

Then came the long bloody "deadly embrace," holding the two ships at too close range for effective British gunnery. Below decks, the guns of the *Serapis* were tearing apart the interior of the old East Indiaman. But aloft, the *Richard's* marines in the tops swept the British decks clear of anyone who dared appear. The British powder boys had brought up cartridges but dropped them beside the abandoned guns. A Scottish sailor on the *Richard* went out on a yardarm with a handful of grenades and dropped them down on the *Serapis*, causing heavy casualties.

By 10 o'clock, the situation on the *Richard* seemed hopeless; the old ship was afire, the guns were nearly all useless, and morale was sinking fast. Then the mainmast of the *Serapis*, at which Jones had been concentrating his meager fire, fell. The Americans finally boarded and received Pearson' surrender. The *Bonhomme Richard* and the *Serapis* had been the principal actors in the fight; the other ships had done far less. The *Pallas*, to be sure, captured the *Countess of Scarbrough*, and two of the lesser ships did little but caused no damage. The scandal of the fight was that the mad Landais had actually fired into his commodore's ship, inflicting casualties.

Both the *Richard* and the *Serapis* were badly battered. It was finally possible to put the *Serapis* in condition of sorts, but the *Richard* was so far gone that she was abandoned to the deep. The casualties had been high, the *Richard* losing some 150 killed and wounded out of 322, and the *Serapis* about 100 killed out of 325. The convoy ships were all safe, and the Russia Company gave Pearson a magnificent silver vase for saving them; he was also later knighted.

France was understandably enthusiastic. John Adams wrote that "the cry of Versailles and the Clamour of Paris became as loud in the favour of Monsieur Jones as of Monsieur Franklin, and the inclination of the Ladies to embrace him almost as fashionable and as strong." However gratifying feminine appreciation may have been, Jones was experiencing a sharp anticlimax in other areas; he would not again recapture that high watermark of gratification. The *Serapis* had been taken into Dutch waters and question arose about her status. No further high command afloat came to Jones. There is no need to follow the unedifying story in detail. In 1788 he became a rear admiral in the navy of Catherine the Great of Russia and did considerable fighting against the Turks in the Black Sea region. He was dismissed in 1789, partly perhaps because of jealousy of British officers in the service and partly because of an alleged charge of rape. He lived three years longer, vainly trying to secure employment of some kind. His health deteriorated, and he died in Paris in 1792 in poverty. Many years later, in 1905, Jones' body was discovered in an unmarked grave and was transported with honors to Annapolis, where he was buried in elaborate fashion in the Naval Academy.

(See S. E. Morison, *John Paul Jones, a Sailor's Biography*, 1959.)

Grosvenor

One of the most dangerously stormy of the major sea lanes was the southeast coast of Africa which, until the Suez Canal was opened, had to be traversed by all shipping between the Atlantic and Asia. The very first European in those waters, Bartholomeu Dias, had been forced to turn back. Later, during the declining period of Portuguese power in India, an appalling number of shipwrecks were recorded among the galleons bound from India to Lisbon. Everyone with influence tried to smuggle cargo aboard, because it was worth so much more in Europe than in Asia. As a result, the overloaded ships were unable to survive the wild gales. Even as late as 1909, the modern liner *Waratah* succumbed to the gales east of Good Hope.

During the heyday of the English East India Company in the eighteenth century, the aristocrats on this run were that Company's ships. Protected by the Company's official monopoly of all British trade, they had no competition to fear, and could take their time. Though technically merchantmen, they were virtually warships in size and armament. In fact, John Paul Jones' *Bonhomme Richard* was just such a ship from the French East India Company's fleet. The command of such vessels was keenly sought and was given usually to those with influence; the profits from one or two voyages between London and India was enough to set one up for life.

The 800-ton *Grosvenor* sailed from Trincomalee in Ceylon on June 13, 1782, with some 20 passengers and their servants; a crew of 60 Europeans, plus some Indian "lascars," and an extremely valuable cargo—ever since Clive took over Bengal, large amounts of treasure, either taken as loot or received as bribes, had been carried off. The *Grosvenor*'s cargo is said to have included jewelry worth £517,000; 720 gold bars worth £420,000; and specie valued at £717,000. In addition, rumors arose that the invaluable Peacock Throne, originally from the palace of the Great Mogul at Delhi, was on board.

As the *Grosvenor* approached the African coast, a gale began to develop. The captain announced that they were at least 100 leagues from land, though actually they were much closer. Vessels had long been able to determine their north-south latitude, but east-west longitude, determined by the new chronometer, was not yet generally known. As a result, the *Grosvenor,* like so many other ships, bore down on a lee shore.

On August 4 the *Grosvenor* piled up on the inhospitable, rocky, stormy coast of Pondoland, just south of the present site of Durban, far north of the nearest settlement. Under the heavy pounding of the waves, the ship began to break up. By good luck, the afterportion drifted ashore, so that most of those aboard were able to reach safety. The whole group—men, women, and children—numbered some 135.

But their troubles had only just begun. The nearest European settlement was Cape Town far away over terribly rugged country. It soon became apparent that the women, children, and aged could not keep up. A handful of sailors started south on their own; after 117 days of extreme hardship a few of them staggered up to the home of a hospitable Boer. They were taken down to Cape Town, where the Dutch governor, although Holland and England were at war, organized an expedition of several hundred men to investigate. They ran into native hostility and came back with only two or three British and several Indians.

The fate of the main body of the expedition was shrouded in mystery. It was assumed that the men died of exhaustion or were killed by native Kaffirs, but the men rescued by the Dutch expedition brought back indications of the fate of the women. They reported that some of them had been captured in an attack by natives and carried off, and that another raid had yielded more captives. A Frenchman, visiting the area a few years later, was told by the natives that most of the men had been killed, but the women had been spared and were living in native kraals. This was confirmed by later reports, suggesting that some of the women had married and borne children to Kaffirs, and so preferred to remain where they were.

The *Grosvenor's* treasure, including the rumored Peacock Throne, was even longer a source of speculation and attempted recovery. If the ship had gone down in deeper water, divers might have been employed, but with the hull wedged in rocks fairly close to shore, the waves were too turbulent to allow successful salvage operations. The Admiralty made one unsuccessful attempt, and so did Captain Bligh of *Bounty* fame. Other attempts continued down through the years, induced by the thought of millions lying just out of reach. As late as the twentieth century, syndicates were formed to recover the treasure, but to no avail.

Recent research, however, indicates that both the story of the abduction of the women and the legend of vast treasure still aboard the *Grosvenor* have scant foundation in fact.

(See J. Burman, *Great Shipwrecks off the Coast of Southern Africa,* 1967.)

Empress of China

The close of the American Revolution brought a drastic change in the pattern of American overseas trade. The most profitable of all, employing the greatest number of vessels, was suddenly barred to the former colonies. This was the "sugar triangle," where colonial fish, flour, lumber, and meat were barred from the British West Indies, where they had been swapped for sugar, molasses, and rum. The little man who had loaded his sloop with domestic produce could no longer peddle it at Jamaica, Barbados, or Antigua.

Despite this negative action, rich new opportunities arose elsewhere with freedom from the old Navigation Act restrictions. Americans could now trade directly with the Baltic, Mediterranean, and elsewhere in Europe. They were, moreover, now free as well from the British East India Company's monopoly which had, since 1600, barred not only colonists but all nonmember Englishmen from trade with India, China, and other distant lands. So altogether, the poor became poorer and the rich, richer. For the big merchants with deep pockets and big privateers which served as merchantmen, there was a chance for high profit. Salem would make much of this, along with Boston, New York, and Philadelphia.

China, with its tea, was foremost among these new commercial opportunities. It was an ancient, proud empire which took its world position very seriously. In fact (just as Boston would call itself the "hub of the universe"), China called itself the "Middle Kingdom," in the center of the world, while the barbarians on the outer edge brought tribute to the emperor. The Chinese had scant interest in or desire for what the Westerners had to offer. They felt that if these outsiders wanted China's tea, they would trade on China's terms. Only one port was open to foreign trade—Canton, far down in the south, and it was rigorously regulated. A small group of officially appointed "hong merchants" were given full charge of all trading, while the foreigners were cooped up in their "factories." There were several of these factories for the various trading nations. Even the proud and powerful British East India Company was subject to these regulations.

Just four months after the British redcoats finally left New York late in 1783, the first American vessel sailed for Canton. This had been planned as a joint venture with capital furnished by Boston, New York, and Philadelphia, but Boston dropped out. The prime mover was Robert Morris of Philadelphia, a leader in official and private maritime activity. The French consul was one of the New York partners, as was Daniel Parker, who took charge of details. The captain, John Green, who had served in the Revolutionary Navy, was not a fortunate choice, but an able supercargo was found in Major Samuel Shaw, who would leave a good account of the voyage.

As in the case of Salem's *Grand Turk* that year, the choice of a ship fell on a now unemployed privateer, which was renamed the *Empress of China*.

Since the Chinese had little interest in American products, kegs of silver Spanish dollars—Mexican or Peruvian "pieces of eight"—were necessary unless someone could think of something better, and such hard cash was usually hard to come by. The one novelty was ginseng, a Chinese plant which commanded a good price as a geriatric aphrodisiac reputed to stimulate elderly men. Searches turned up a generous supply of ginseng; the *Empress of China* took out 242 casks, totaling about 30 tons. Unfortunately, the Canton market was glutted with newly arrived ginseng—the needs of the old men were amply met for some time to come. The Americans would soon do better with sea otter skins.

Captain Green's navigation needlessly prolonged the voyage, for he was unable to locate Sunda Strait and blundered around until a French ship of the line gave him guidance. Arriving finally near Canton, this first American ship received a rousing welcome from the ships of the Dutch, Danish, French and, even with the Revolution just over, the British East India Companies. They all replied to her 13-gun salute and extended personal courtesies.

The *Empress of China* returned home with some 200 tons of tea, plus the usual silks and chinaware; the chinaware was loaded in the bottom of the hold so that any leakage would not reach the tea. At Cape Town she met the Salem ship *Grand Turk,* the first New England ship to reach the Cape. The *Empress of China* returned to New York on May 11, 1785. The voyage had been only a modest financial success—Robert Morris' profit on his investment was about 30%—but it was enough to encourage further trading. The "Old China Trade" would go on with high profits for a few merchants, especially in New York and Boston, but it would have a more romantic appeal than some of the more extensive traffic in other routes.

(See F. R. Dulles, *The Old China Trade,* 1930.)

Grand Turk

The American Revolution fell with varying impact upon the American seaports. Some were burned and others were occupied by the British for months or years. But two ports experienced a spectacular rise to maritime success—Salem and Baltimore. In the case of Salem this was due in part to the construction of a considerable number of large, fast privateers. These contributed to the port's wealth by the sale of their prizes. When the war was over, these big ships and the accumulated capital enabled the port to take advantage of the newly opening sea lanes hitherto blocked by British commercial regulations.

Conspicuous in this category was the *Grand Turk,* owned by Elias Hasket Derby, Salem's foremost maritime magnate. A 300-ton ship with 22 guns, virtually the equivalent of a small frigate, she was built at Salem for Derby. Coming on the scene fairly late in the war, she quickly made up for lost time with her captures. She cruised for a while in the vicinity of England, sending her prizes into Bilbao; then she shifted to the West Indies and used Martinique. Her final capture was a big 400-ton ship, the *Pompey of London,* off St. Kitts. Her captain, despite the date, sent her into Salem, where on March 12, 1783, the court declared her a good prize because the news of peace had not yet reached Salem. Derby sold her to George Crowninshield, who used her in the pepper trade.

In November 1784 Derby sent the *Grand Turk* out to the Cape of Good Hope; she was too large for the nearer runs. As in the case of the *Empress of China,* American ships could now ignore the East India

Company's monopoly of all English trade between the Cape of Good Hope and the Straits of Magellan, a privilege which English nonmembers of the Company would not enjoy until 1813. The long voyages to the East emphasized the problem of "remote control" in the days of slow communication. A voyage was strictly a venture; in the months or even years off soundings, a captain was on his own, beyond the control of the owner, who could simply give general guidance. Unless there was a supercargo aboard to handle business details, the captain was responsible for the sale of the cargo, the acquisition of a return cargo, or making arrangements for carrying someone else's goods; he might even sell the ship if that seemed best. Fortunately, the Yankee captains were among the world's most skillful and resourceful, and Derby secured some of the best for his fast-expanding fleet.

The *Grand Turk* carried out a mixed cargo of rum, cheese, sugar, butter, salt, and ginseng; it was hoped that at Cape Town she could swap the ginseng for tea from China. However, when the captain arrived at that busy Dutch "tavern of the seas," he learned, to his disappointment, that the British East India Company's ships were not permitted to break bulk in that fashion. After some time, during which he conferred with the officers of the *Empress of China,* which was returning from her maiden voyage to Canton, the captain of a British East Indiaman made a special deal, in apparent violation of the break-bulk rule. He agreed to take all the *Grand Turk's* rum in exchange for tea, silks, and cotton nankeens, if the Salem ship would deliver the rum at the lonesome island of St. Helena. The *Grand Turk* delivered the rum and sold the tea at the neutral island of St. Eustatius in the West Indies. By that time, so much cargo had accumulated that it was divided with another Derby ship. The *Grand Turk* was back at Salem from her "tramping" in August 1785.

Four months later she sailed on a second voyage, which would be another major landmark in Salem trade. She had gone only as far as Cape Town the first time, but now she would lead the way, which scores of Salem vessels would follow, along the more distant sea routes beyond the Cape to India, China, and other remote places. Under Captain Ebenezer West, with William Vans as supercargo, she had an even more mixed outward cargo this time—rice, butter, flour, cheese, pork, beef, and fish, along with brandy, rum, wine, and beer, and some bar iron, earthenware, and candles. The markets were slow, and it took some time to dispose of the cargo, but eventually a break came at the Île de France (Mauritius), when a Frenchman offered a freighting cargo to Canton. The *Grand Turk* thus became the third American ship to reach Canton, and the first from New England. Pinqua, the official local hong merchant, loaded her with chinaware and tea. She stopped at Cape

Town to fill out her cargo with some hides, and was back at Salem in May 1787. The return cargo cost $23,000, but Derby is said to have sold it for more than double that amount.

For the third voyage, starting December 7, 1787, Derby picked his own son, Elias Hasket, Jr., fresh from Harvard, as master, a foretaste of the time when four of their Crowninshield cousins would command family ships beyond the Cape. The outward cargo this time, valued at $28,000, included barrels of beef and pork, boxes of cheese, firkins of butter, and 1200 gallons of rum, all from New England, in addition to flour, tobacco, chocolate, sugar, and French wine. They found a rich market at Île de France and then, being offered more than Derby anticipated her worth, the *Grand Turk* was sold for $13,000. That closes our story of the profitable pioneering of the *Grand Turk*, but the family activity in those waters continued. The *Grand Turk* had been so successful that the name seemed a good omen, and Derby brought up the crack shipbuilder from the North River to build a second ship of that name. She proved too big to be profitable. After her launching in May 1791, she made a voyage to Calcutta and one to Russia, then was sold at New York for $22,000 in 1795. A third *Grand Turk*, not of the same Derby family, was built as a privateer brig in 1812 and had fair success in that war.

(See J. D. Phillips, *Salem in the Eighteenth Century*, 1937.)

Boussole and Astrolabe

The most ambitious and most tragic of the post-Cook explorations in the Pacific was that of La Pérouse in the French frigates *Boussole* and *Astrolabe* (1785–1788). Planned to round out the Pacific story beyond what Cook had discovered, the French prepared the expedition generously and intelligently. It skirted the whole Pacific basin, made contacts on three continents, advanced the frontiers of knowledge, and then, after its second in command had been murdered in Samoa, it disappeared mysteriously, with nothing known of its fate for another four decades.

Whereas Bougainville, the other great French explorer, had a mixed army-navy career, Jean François de Galaup de La Pérouse was a full-time professional naval officer. He had had brilliant if lonesome duty during the American Revolution with a strong squadron up in Hudson's Bay, where he captured the two principal Hudson's Bay Company's posts. After the war La Pérouse, as one of the most promising of the regular officers, was appointed to follow up Cook's explorations. For this scientific mission he was given two substantial frigates, the *Boussole* and *Astrolabe,* and furnished not only with scientists but also with stores, equipment, and even a library. His royal instructions, which ran to 30-odd pages in printed form, unfolded an itinerary which would take him all over the periphery of the Pacific; he was also furnished with an almost bewildering array of scientific advice.

The expedition sailed from Brest on August 1, 1785, picking up ample wine at Tenerife. Touching at Chile, they proceeded to Easter Island and then to Hawaii. Running over to Mount Saint Elias in Alaska, they followed the American coast down as far as Monterey and, at the turn of the year, reached Macao and Manila. They explored the East Asian coast, the first European ships to visit the Sea of Japan, eventually discovering what became La Pérouse Strait between Sakhalin and Hokkaido. At Petropavlosk in September 1787, they ran into the warmest Russian hospitality and learned by mail that La Pérouse had been appointed to commodore. To preserve his story for posterity, La Pérouse sent his journals overland to Paris (a second installment would follow from Australia).

His next stop was Samoa, an unfortunate one. After receiving a most generous stock of supplies, de Langle, captain of the *Astrolabe,* was attacked by a Samoan mob, and he and 11 others were killed and 20 were seriously wounded.

At the turn of the year, La Pérouse visited Tonga and called at Botany Bay in Australia just after the British arrival with convicts to settle there. While the British were engaged in the move up the coast to Port Jackson (Sydney), Captain Hunter of the *Sirius* received them cordially. La Pérouse sent off a second installment of his journals and described to the Minister of Marine his further plans. On March 11, 1788, the *Boussole* and *Astrolabe* sailed, and that was the last that was heard of them.

The journals were subsequently published, but meantime the ships had completely disappeared from sight. Efforts to find them were long unsuccessful but in 1827, one Peter Dillon, commander of a British ship, ran down a succession of clues on the island of Vanikoro, or Mannicolo, in the Santa Cruz Islands. Various artifacts were found, including a plank inscribed with fleur de lis, a small millstone for grinding corn, and a copper boiler. An elderly native filled out the story with some recollections. The two ships had driven ashore in a fierce storm. One of them hit a reef and became a total loss; the other drove over a reef and considerable material was salvaged. The survivors built a smaller vessel from the wreckage and sailed away, leaving only a few survivors on

Vanikoro; one Frenchman had lived with a chief until fairly recently but had disappeared. Captain Dillon took his story and his findings back to England and then to France, where he was given a pension by the king. It has been pointed out that this was one of the only two exploring expeditions to disappear completely; the other was Sir John Franklin's in the *Erebus* and *Terror* in the Arctic.

(See J. C. Beaglehole, *The Exploration of the Pacific*, 1966.)

Sirius

H.M.S. *Sirius,*
lying in Botany Bay
in early 1788.
*(National Maritime
Museum,
Greenwich)*

The frigate *Sirius* (named for the Dog Star) was flagship of the first fleet which settled some 750 convicts in Australia in 1788 as the beginning of that British colony. Under the command of Captain Arthur Philip, the first governor, she was accompanied by a smaller naval vessel, five convict ships, and three victualing and storeships.

The motive for this settlement was the discovery in 1770 of "Botany Bay" by Captain James Cook in the *Endeavour*. His distinguished companion, Joseph Banks, was an amateur botanist and was so enthusiastic over the Bay's botanic richness plus its equable climate, that he made it sound very attractive at home. There is soon became a possible solution to Britain's penal problems after the American Revolution. England had long dumped—transported was the formal word—many of its convicted felons into the southern American colonies. That solution was no longer open and English prisons began to overflow; the old penal code had many savage punishments for some rather trifling offenses. At the same time, French explorers were beginning to prowl through the South Seas, and the fear that they might attempt colonization of Australia made action advisable. Someone, possibly Lord Sydney, the Home Secretary, suggested in 1786 that the convicts be sent down to settle Botany Bay.

Captain Arthur Philip was appointed Captain General and Governor in Chief, and was assigned, to his disgust, a quite unsatisfactory 20-gun frigate, the former storeship *Berwick,* which had been laid up for some time. She was patched up, and another smaller and faster vessel, the *Supply,* was added to his command. The convicts, some 568 males and 194 females, were put aboard six chartered merchantmen—the *Alexander, Lady Penrhyn, Charlotte, Edinburgh, Friendship,* and *Prince of Wales*—vessels between 274 and 452 tons. Two of them carried men only; one, females only; and the others carried both. Each ship was furnished with some 30 marines as guards. Philip had a valuable deputy in Captain John Hunter, who would take over the *Sirius* when Philip went ashore as governor. The expedition encountered few difficulties on the way; it stopped at Tenerife, Rio de Janeiro, and the Cape of Good Hope, where, incidentally, Philip moved to the faster, smaller *Supply.* The expedition had an excellent health record, with only 32 deaths.

They reached Botany Bay in January 1788, but whatever Joseph Banks may have said about its flora, Philip was not satisfied with it as a harbor. He explored up the coast and 15 miles to the northward found what he called the finest harbor in the world, where he moved the expedition. The new site was called Port Jackson, but he soon changed its name to Sydney. While this move was underway, two French frigates appeared on the scene—the exploring expedition of La Pérouse in the *Boussole* and *Astrolabe.* The Frenchman sent off the second installment of his journals and then sailed away, never to be heard of again until the wreck of his ships was found far to the northward in 1827.

Australia observed the centennial of its founding in January 1888; the first toast offered was, "We left our country for our country's good." The *Sirius* came to an end in 1789, running ashore at Norfolk Island where she was carrying convicts and marines.

(See C. Bateson, *The Convict Ships, Australia 1787–1888,* 2d ed. 1969.)

Bounty

The *Bounty*, from which Captain Bligh and his adherents were cast adrift on April 28, 1789. *(Peabody Museum)*

Shortly after World War I, two young veterans who did not want to settle down, went to a Boston publishing house with a proposition. If they were grub-staked with adequate advance royalties, they would go to Tahiti and produce a most interesting story. The publisher agreed, and out of this came the *Bounty* trilogy by Nordhoff and Hall—*Mutiny on the Bounty, Men Against the Sea,* and *Pitcairn's Island.* The success was tremendous; H. M. S. *Bounty* and Captain Bligh became household words. Until then, that uprising on April 28, 1789, had received only moderate attention. The mutiny on the *Hermione* had been much more bloody, and the uprisings at Spithead and Nore involved a whole fleet. But now Nordhoff and Hall's *Bounty* became *the* mutiny.

The mission of the *Bounty* to Tahiti had been a very special one. The American Revolution had broken up a profitable, longstanding triangular trade in which, among other things, Philadelphia, New York, and other North American ports sent flour to feed the slaves of Jamaica, Barbados, and other sugar islands, getting in exchange sugar and rum which could be exchanged for British manufactures. The British, at the close of the war, put an end to that arrangement, to the distress of the Americans and even more so to the sugar islands, where slaveholders found it difficult to feed their slaves.

From Captain James Cook's first Pacific voyage in the *Endeavour* came a suggestion of possible relief. Joseph Banks (later Sir Joseph), the **87** wealthy naturalist who went on the voyage, called attention to bread-fruit, a Tahiti palm tree bearing a fruit, the inside of which could be a good substitute for bread. He pulled governmental wires, at which he was most adept, and gained authorization for sending a naval vessel out to Tahiti to take a thousand or so young breadfruit plants to feed the West Indian slaves. The Navy Board procured a small three-masted ship, the *Bethia*, of 230 tons (this was smaller than any of Cook's ships) at barely half the price of the *Resolution*. She would be renamed and commissioned as H.M.S. *Bounty*. The crew of 47 would be severely cramped because a large part of the interior was transformed into a "floating green house," with a special gardener and assistant in charge. One result of the scant space was that no room was available for any marines, who had the duty of guarding the officers.

The command went to Lieutenant William Bligh, partly through the influence of Banks. Bligh had been sailing master under Cook in the *Resolution* and had done a great deal of charting—in fact he was rated as one of the best hydrographers. After Cook's death, Bligh helped to navigate the ship home and served in several actions during the remainder of the American Revolution. Then he was on half-pay for five years, commanding a large merchantman. His dual personality has been a matter for discussion ever since; he was a sort of Jekyll-and-Hyde. In addition to his navigating ability, he usually ran his ship well; he was thoughtful of his crew's health and morale when conditions were right; and he was level-headed in most crises. But he could lapse from the able, rational personality into the uptight, nagging behavior that could lead to mutiny; he was not a vicious sadist like Captain Pigot, who was chopped up on the *Hermione*, but could be an exasperating nagger. His whole naval record would be a mixture of high achievement and of serious mutinies—the *Bounty* was only one mutiny. Some people are called "accident-prone"; Bligh was certainly mutiny-prone.

Bligh was the only commissioned officer on the *Bounty*. There were several warrant officers including a troublesome master and a drunken surgeon; and there were several midshipmen, in addition to the gardener and his assistant, but the name that has always been associated with Bligh has been that of Fletcher Christian, master's mate. Like Bligh, he came from the west coast of England not far from John Paul Jones' early home, and both were from solid families. Christian attended grammar school and then entered the navy. He used family influence to meet Bligh and ask for a position on his ship—at the time he was 21 years old and Bligh, 10 years older. Just as there were sharply contrasting elements in Bligh's makeup, so were there in Christian's. Christian normally had a very cheerful disposition and made friends easily, but he was also subject to bad moods. For a long time Bligh and

Christian were extremely close—Christian was Bligh's protégé, dining
with him frequently and finally being promoted to acting lieutenant,
which made him second in command. The Bligh and Christian moods
would have much to do with the mutiny.

The *Bounty* sailed from Portsmouth on December 23, 1787. (Incidentally, six months earlier, the first convicts for Australia had set out for
Botany Bay—another Cook-Banks recommendation.) It was planned to
round Cape Horn but after a month of brutal freezing gales, Bligh
headed for Good Hope instead—he had done a remarkably successful
job in doing everything possible for the crew's well-being, and his
efforts were appreciated.

The *Bounty* was at Tahiti from October 26, 1788, to April 4, 1789.
Relations were unusually pleasant for the first two months. Loving was
more general than ever, accompanied by a rising venereal rate. Bligh
was in almost constant companionship with the local king and queen.
The potting of the breadfruit plants went on apace at Point Venus,
where the Cook observatory had been set up. It was now fortified.
Christian lived ashore, where he was in charge. He was becoming
rather indolent and was quite promiscuous among the native girls until
he took up with the tall and beautiful daughter of a chief; she was his
dutiful "wife" as long as they lived.

By the turn of the year, the happy, carefree situation was beginning
to go sour, both among the officers and the crew. "Such neglectful and
worthless petty officers I believe were never in a ship as are in this. If I
had any officers to supersede them, or was able to do without them,
considering them as common seamen, they should no longer occupy
their respective stations," wrote Bligh early in January. Punishments
and floggings increased. Miscreants were apprehended, flogged, and
placed in irons. Christian, so long the captain's particular pet, now
caught the heaviest of Bligh's ill humor, aroused by Christian's often
sloppy work. Violating all normal behavior, Bligh often criticized
Christian before the crew and even before the natives.

By the time the *Bounty* sailed from Tahiti on April 4, deterioration of
captain-crew relations was well under way. For the three weeks that she
pushed westward there was understandable resentment at the "paradise lost." The amorous time at Tahiti was an experience that they were
not likely to have again; and, in contrast, the life aboard ship was
becoming more unbearable—in particular the growing bitter antago-
nism between Captain Bligh and Christian. A recent author has suggested the possibility of a homosexual relationship turned sour.

The crisis came in the early hours of April 28, 1789, off the island of
Tofua in mid-Pacific. As a result of Bligh's nagging, Christian was in

such a desperately emotional state that he prepared a raft in which to escape from the ship. About 4 A.M. the mutiny pattern suddenly took form; yet the surprising thing is that, despite hours of confrontation on deck, there was no physical violence. One of the midshipmen, Edward Young, persuaded Christian to give up his idea of a raft escape and, instead, to depose Bligh and take over the ship; the temper of the crew, he argued, would make this possible. Christian finally agreed to head the movement, provided there would be no bloodshed.

Christian, cutlass in hand, invaded Bligh's cabin with four of the toughest members of the crew. Bligh was hauled out of his bed and began shouting "murder" at the top of his voice. The conspirators soon had the ship under their control. It had originally been planned to set Bligh and three or four others adrift in one of the smaller boats, but it soon became apparent that at least half the crew were "loyalists" who wanted to leave with Bligh, so the big launch was used. It could not hold all who wanted to go; three were persuaded to remain with the ship, but they made it clear that they were not mutineers. There was a long confrontation on deck, with a considerable number of men not sure what action to take. Occasionally, one of the "hard-core" sailors would yell, "Blow the bugger's brains out!" but went no further. Christian even gave Bligh his best chronometer. The two men stood together, talking in the gangway. "Consider what you are about, Mr. Christian," said Bligh. "For God's sake drop it. I'll gladly give my bond never to think of it again if you'll desist. I have a wife and four children in England, and you have danced your children on your knee." "It is too late. I have been in hell," said Christian. "It is not too late," said Bligh. The rope to the boat was finally thrown off, and the launch started on its own way.

With the bloodless mutiny over, the story divided into several distinct episodes: the remarkable open-boat passage under Bligh to Timor; the Admiralty's follow-up in sending the frigate *Pandora* to Tahiti to pick up the mutineers and her wreck on the return; the court martial at Portsmouth and the hanging of three mutineers. In the meantime the *Bounty* returned to Tahiti and continued on to Pitcairn's Island with the hard-core mutineers plus native men and women; later the ship was burned and still later all but two men were killed.

During those changes, the crew fell into several categories. More than half the crew were "loyalists" who went off with Bligh in the launch. But three loyalists, for whom there was no room, returned to Tahiti. There were the moderate mutineers who also returned to Tahiti, and finally the tough, hard-core group, some of whom were hanged.

Bligh partly redeemed his harsh reputation by taking the overloaded *Bounty* launch across the mid-Pacific, through the Great Barrier Reef and on to Timor, one of the longest single-boat trips to date. Even after his quartermaster was killed by island natives, there were 18 men, which left scant freeboard to keep the waves out. Food and water were desperately short; he put the men on a diet of two ounces of bread and a gill of water a day. And however irascible he might be at other times, his instant cheerfulness and solicitude for the well-being of the crew kept their morale high. The Great Barrier Reef, with its 1500 miles of treacherous coral, was a real test of his seamanship—Cook's *Endeavour* had almost been wrecked on it, and the frigate *Pandora,* sent out to get the mutineers, was lost on the reefs. Between April 28 and June 14, the boat had covered some 4000 miles. The exhausted men were scarcely able to walk, but Dutch hospitality at Coupang quickly revived them. Bligh proceeded on to London from Batavia in a Dutch ship, with the others following on.

Bligh was the hero of the hour; he was promoted to commander and then to post-captain. He was soon sent back to Tahiti for more bread-fruit plants, which he carried to Jamaica, but the slaves did not care for the flavor.

The Admiralty extended the long arm of the empire, sending out the frigate *Pandora* to round up the mutineers and bring them back to England for trial. She arrived at Tahiti on March 28 and remained there until May 8, during which time she rounded up 14 prisoners. Her captain, Edward Edwards, "a vicious martinet" with none of Bligh's better qualities, hunted down everyone who had been on the *Bounty*. Some of the nonmutineers, confident of their innocence, voluntarily reported to him and were locked up like the rest. To confine his 14 prisoners securely, he built a roundhouse on the quarterdeck; this ill-ventilated and unlighted cell became known as "Pandora's Box."

After searching the area for the *Bounty* without success, the *Pandora* was wrecked trying to get through the Great Barrier Reef on August 21. One bosun's mate, remembering the prisoners shut up in the "box," unbolted the scuttle (Captain Edwards had shown no concern for their safety), but four of them, fettered with leg irons, drowned.

The prisoners came before a general court martial at Portsmouth. Bligh, already out on his second breadfruit voyage, was absent, and the prosecution used a harsh memorandum which Bligh had left. A few were acquitted, but Midshipman Peter Haywood, amiable, well-connected, and innocent, was spared only after a strong lobby interceded for him. In the end, three mutineers were hanged, one from the starboard yardarm and two from the port.

In the meantime, there had been dramatic developments out in the far Pacific. After the mutiny, there was a question of, "What next?" The future seemed to depend to some extent upon whether Bligh and his boat crew ever reached safety; if they did, there seemed a very good chance that the Royal Navy would reach out for the mutineers. Under Christian's command and with discipline well enforced, the *Bounty,* after one or two stops, put into Tahiti temporarily. Some of the sailors resumed domestic relations with their "wives."

It was quickly decided, however, that if the *Bounty* was still at Tahiti or thereabouts, she would fall prey to a searching frigate. They hoped to find a place that was remote, uninhabited, and inaccessible. On September 23, five months after the mutiny, the *Bounty* sailed for the last time from Tahiti, loaded down with stores and provisions. There were passengers too, men and women, a biracial group. There were eight English mutineers, headed by Christian, and six Polynesian natives, brought along for labor. There were also 12 women: four of them were "wives" of the leaders, including "Isabella," the wife of Christian and daughter of a chief, a most admirable person. Some of the others were tricked aboard before the *Bounty* sailed.

After two more temporary inspections, Christian finally found the solution in a volume of Pacific voyages. In an account of Carteret's voyage in H.M.S. *Swallow* in 1767:

> We discovered land to the northward of us. Upon approaching it the next day, it appeared like a great rock rising out of the sea: it was not more than five miles in circumference, and seemed to be uninhabitable; it was, however, covered with trees, and we saw it at a distance of more than fifteen leagues, and having been discovered by a young gentleman, son to Major Pitcairn of the marines . . . we called it Pitcairn's Island. . . .

Major Pitcairn commanded the British troops at Lexington and was later killed at Bunker Hill. The island seemed to be a haven.

On January 15, 1790, they decided that this was the place and they landed in a bay of sorts, with a narrow beach. A week later, on January 23, the *Bounty* came to her end. There was a debate as to what to do with her because of the fear that another ship might sight her. It was decided to run her in on shore, but suddenly smoke was seen rising from her hull. One of the toughest of the hard-core sailors had gone below and set her afire. There was no longer any question of sailing home in her.

Three years later, the little colony almost disappeared because of friction over the women. Homes had been built for the families, with a fair amount of domesticity. There was one element of inequality from the start—only four native women for six native men. The situation was aggravated when the wife of Jack Williams, the colony's smith, died from a fall over a cliff. Williams, despondent for a while, finally demanded one of the other women, threatening to leave the island in the cutter otherwise. Christian called a meeting of the white settlers and it was decided to give him Nancy, wife of the native Tallaloo; Nancy was more than pleased, but her ex-husband went off to sulk. Under Nancy's leadership, he was pursued and his brains beaten out with a rock. The natives began to conspire to kill all the whites. On September 20, 1793, they killed Christian and four others. On October 4 all the remaining natives were killed, with the widows of the slain whites taking part. Two of the surviving whites took to the woods in alcoholic debauchery until finally killed in 1795 and 1799. The survivors soon developed their private harems.

After those two terrible days of slaughter, leadership fell to two men: John Adams, a tough, illiterate, former denizen of the London docks, and Edward Young, well-educated midshipman who was responsible for suggesting the general mutiny to Christian. Both leaders began to develop a strong religious atmosphere on Pitcairn. Knowing that he was slowly dying of asthma, Young did what he could to train Adams for leadership, teaching him to read and write and to understand religion. He succeeded remarkably well; Pitcairn saw the anomaly of Adams with his charming Tahitian harem exerting rigorous religious control over the population, who by now were expanding with numerous children of mixed parentage.

Pitcairn continued in splendid isolation, quite cut off from the world, until the whaler *Topaz* put in there in 1808; because of the War of 1812, England did not get word immediately. In 1817 there was temporary alarm when two British frigates called, but the contact was amiable. So it continued with occasional visits until in 1856, Britain moved most of the islanders to Norfolk Island. But many of them were unhappy at the change and returned to Pitcairn which, as time went on, became a formal part of the British Empire.

(See C. B. Nordhoff and J. N. Hall, *Bounty* trilogy: *Mutiny on the Bounty*, 1932; *Men Against the Sea*, 1934; *Pitcairn's Island*, 1934.)

Discovery

The discovery of fur seals by Cook in the *Resolution* led to a four-cornered scramble for the American Northwest Coast by the Spaniards, who made a last colonial stand there; by the Russians, who were finding their way down from Alaska; by the Americans, whose *Colum-*

bia discovered the river that bears her name; and by the British (after the initial discovery by Cook in 1778) in 1791 determined to complete the surveying of the Northwest Coast that Cook had begun. For this purpose, they sent out two warships, the sloop-of-war *Discovery* and the smaller brig *Chatham*. The command went to one of their most experienced surveyors, Captain George Vancouver, who had served with Cook. In the course of four years (1791–1795) he completed his immense surveying assignment, interspersed with diplomatic negotiations and various adventures. His name has a well-earned place on the map.

While this expedition was in the planning stage, a major international crisis arose over Spain's seizure of some British vessels at Nootka Sound, at the lower end of what is now Vancouver Island. To avenge the seizure, Britain prepared a powerful naval armament but Spain partially backed down. Vancouver would have lengthy negotiations to bring about a final settlement. His *Discovery* and the *Chatham*, under William R. Broughton, sailed from Falmouth on April 1, 1791. During the expedition they were together only part of the time, and when Broughton went to Madrid on diplomatic matters, the command of the *Chatham* went to Lieutenant Peter Puget, whose name is still attached to the sound that he discovered.

The ships went out to the Pacific by the Cape of Good Hope, first stopping for a surveying job on the Australian coast and at New Zealand, which Vancouver had already visited four times. Then came three delightful weeks at Tahiti—by this time everyone found an excuse to stop there. They moved on to the other Polynesian paradise that Cook had discovered, Hawaii, which was becoming a part of the new Northwest Coast complex; ships often ran over there in the winter. On a later visit to Hawaii, Vancouver became very intimate with the great King Kamehameha I; they exchanged rich presents and the king submitted the islands to Great Britain.

Then came Vancouver's main business, exploring and surveying the coasts of what would become Oregon, Washington, British Columbia, and Alaska, producing first-rate charts of the area. Interspersed with these important activities, various other matters commanded his attention. At a meeting with Captain Robert Gray of Boston, he learned an important item that he had missed: Gray in his ship *Columbia* had sailed in the fog past the great river named for his ship. This accident gave the United States a share in the new region. The *Discovery* ran aground, but Vancouver managed to get her free. A well-known picture shows her lying almost on her side with her topmasts down. Vancouver's supply ship, the *Daedalus*, joined the others at Nootka. Later, when her captain and an astronomer were killed in Hawaii, Vancouver ran down the culprits and had them shot. He took aboard two charming steadily.

The Nootka situation called for frequent diplomatic negotiations with Quadra, the Spanish governor, who was polite but stubborn. The distance from London and Madrid was a serious communications handicap, messages to and from the respective ministries taking months. Captain Broughton had been sent to Madrid to straighten things out. Just as Vancouver was about to start home, definite authority to cede Nootka to Britain reached Avala, the new governor. Vancouver's instructions had not come, but, on the strength of the Spanish documents, an amicable agreement was reached.

By September 2, 1794, with his surveying completed, Vancouver left for Monterey. The vessels rounded Cape Horn and took separate courses home. With the nation at war, Vancouver seized a Dutch East Indiaman at Saint Helena, then joined a big convoy homeward bound. He commenced work on his valuable Pacific observations, but died on May 10, 1798, before they were completed.

(See B. Anderson, *The Life and Voyages of Captain George Vancouver, Surveyor of the Seas,* 1966.)

Columbia

Explorers and other mariners sometimes left their names on the world map, but it was a very rare occasion when a ship achieved that prominence. One little Massachusetts-built vessel, the *Columbia,* in 1792 discovered the great river of the Pacific Northwest, and it has ever since borne her name. In addition, that discovery strengthened the United States claim to the Oregon region.

The little 212-ton *Columbia* was launched in 1773 on the North River in the Scituate area south of Boston. With the building of a thousand vessels, ranging from 30 to 470 tons, between 1678 and 1871, this tidal stream was a major shipbuilding area. The *Columbia,* built by James Briggs, became its most prominent product; another which helped to make history was the *Beaver,* which brought part of the tea dumped in the Boston Tea Party.

The *Columbia* was 15 years old when her chance for prominence came. Boston received word of Captain Cook's third voyage, in which the crew of the *Resolution* discovered the valuable pelts of the little sea otter on the American northwest coast and found that they commanded a high price at Canton.

The Boston merchant Joseph Barrell quickly sensed the potential profits in this Canton exchange. The *Empress of China* had already gone out to Canton and discovered that the Chinese wanted hard cash for their tea, having only slight interest in other American offerings. But here, as Barrell saw, the sea otter might come to the rescue. In exchange for cloth, hardware, and other items of relatively slight value, the Americans might secure these valuable furs to swap for tea in Canton.

Accordingly, with the backing of five other Bostonians, he fitted out two vessels for the trade. One was the 212-ton *Columbia* under a Cape Codder, John Kendrick. The other was far smaller and with a far abler skipper, the 90-ton sloop *Lady Washington* under Captain Robert Gray.

They sailed from Boston on September 30, 1787, and spent 40 days at the Cape Verdes, "thirty more than I thought necessary," wrote the impatient Gray. In April 1788 they rounded Cape Horn. Then, as Gray wrote again, "I had the good fortune to part company . . . and I made the Coast six weeks earlier by being alone." While Kendrick was pursuing his leisurely way northward, the energetic Gray had been exploring the coast all the way from Oregon up to what is now Vancouver Island, with its Nootka Sound, where Spaniards, Britons, and Indians were congregating, with sea otter as lure. The two captains and their crews wintered at Nootka, spending part of their time fashioning iron into chisels which were particularly desired by the Indians.

In July 1789 Kendrick engineered a swapping of the two commands: he would keep little *Lady Washington* and the *Columbia* would pass to the energetic Gray. Kendrick's motive for this was not clear—his mind was full of unreal projects. He instructed Gray to take the furs to Canton, swap them for tea, and then return to Boston, which Gray proceeded to do. At Canton his furs brought $21,000, but half of that was swallowed up in port charges. Gray arrived in Boston in August 1790 and received a lively welcome, with a 13-gun salute, a parade up State Street, and a celebration dinner for his command of the first American vessel to circumnavigate the earth.

Barrell lost no time in sending the *Columbia* back to the West Coast. Gray traded along the coast during the summer of 1791; they spent the winter in comfortable quarters and built a small schooner whose frames had been brought out from Boston. There were some peaceful Indians but also some violent ones. When his second mate went ashore with two sailors to fish, they were ambushed and killed. In revenge, Gray later sent in three boats to destroy the village.

On May 12, 1792, Gray discovered the great river which he named for the *Columbia*. Back in 1775, a Spanish captain, Hecate, had told of passing but not entering its mouth. It had then, and still has, a most dangerous bar. Gray maneuvered past two sandbars and through the surf to enter the river and, according to some reports, he took possession of it for the United States. The British naval explorer, George Vancouver, was making a thorough survey of the coast in his *Adventure* but had missed the mouth of the river. This was enough to give the Americans a share of the Oregon region. John Jacob Astor established his fur trading post, Astoria, there, and the American claims would be strengthened by the arrival of Lewis and Clark, sent overland by President Jefferson.

That October, Gray sailed for Canton with a goodly load of furs which he exchanged for tea and other Chinese goods. He completed his second circumnavigation, returning by Sumatra, Good Hope, and Saint Helena, and arrived at Boston on June 20, 1793. The *Columbia's* voyage opened up a new way of getting Canton tea without paying in silver; she had well earned her name on the map.

(See D. O. Johansen, *Empire of the Columbia: A History of the Pacific Northwest*, 1957.)

Bellerophon

The *Bellerophon*, on which Napoleon sought British protection after the Battle of Waterloo, 1815. *(Tate Gallery)*

The 74-gun ship-of-the-line *Bellerophon*, nicknamed "Billy Ruffian" by her crews, was perhaps the most distinguished of the some 100 ships of her class during the high tide of sailing warships in the French Revolutionary and Napoleonic Wars. In three of the major sea fights she received heavy blows, but inflicted far heavier ones on her opponents. And if that fighting record was not enough, she had the unique distinction of receiving Napoleon aboard when, after Waterloo, he threw himself on the mercy of the Royal Navy and the British people.

Like later battleships, ships of the line had two distinctive features. Their heavy broadsides could deal out punishing blows, and their tough hulls could stand up against similar enemy blows. These qualities were achieved at the cost of less speed than the lighter, faster frigates and cruisers. Although the various navies had a few larger, towering three-decked giants used as flagships, they were rather clumsy and the 74-gun ship was the largest warship that could sail well and fight well under most conditions. They were known as ships of the line because they normally operated in groups, sailing in line ahead, one after the other.

The *Bellerophon* was launched on October 26, 1786, at the yard of Graves and Nicolson on the River Medway near Chatham. She cost £30,232; her hull used up 2000 large oak trees, averaging 100 years old, at a time when such timber was becoming scarce. Her crew numbered some 600 but only a minority of them joined the ship of their own accord; the press gangs brought in most of the others.

During her quarter-century of service, the *Bellerophon* served in the Channel, Mediterranean, North Sea, and Baltic Fleets and on the West Indian and North American stations, often as a flagship. The first of her major encounters was the "Glorious First of June" in 1794 under Lord Howe, when the French fleet from Brest made a sacrifice play to save the grain ships from America. She fought three hours with the leading French ship, losing her foremast. The squadron admiral lost a leg, but the total casualties, four killed and 27 wounded, were lighter than they would be at the Nile and Trafalgar.

In the battle of the Nile on August 1, 1798, in a striking example of the "Nelson touch," the British came in on either side of the anchored French fleet, catching them two to one. It was the *Bellerophon*'s fate to be alongside the great French three-decker flagship *Orient*, which loosed two smashing broadsides, killing 70 men and causing much damage. The *Bellerophon*, however, poured her broadsides into the *Orient* with telling effect. The French flagship caught fire in several places, while the *Bellerophon* lost her masts and had to withdraw, just before the *Orient*'s magazine blew up in a devastating explosion. The log of the *Bellerophon* stated, "We had killed 3 lieutenants, 1 Master's Mate, 32 Sailors and 13 Marines . . . making in all 49 killed and 149 wounded." More sailors died of their wounds in the next few weeks. Jury masts were rigged and the damaged ships were escorted to Gibraltar, where the victory was celebrated. Admiral Lord St. Vincent declared that the *Bellerophon* was "more mauled than any ship I ever saw."

In her third major action, at Trafalgar on October 21, 1805, the *Bellerophon* was fifth of the 15 ships of the Port Division under Admiral Collingwood. The British tactics called for breaking through the enemy line, and when her turn came, the *Bellerophon* came under the heavy fire of five enemy ships, particularly the French seventy-four *l'Aigle,* with which she became closely entangled. The French ship had a large number of crack marksmen who swept the quarterdeck of the *Bellerophon* of most of her officers, finally killing the captain. (That, of course, was what was also happening to Nelson on the *Victory.*) Broadsides at close range below seriously damaged both ships, and a bomb almost reached the *Bellerophon's* magazine. By afternoon, the Franco-Spanish fleet was thoroughly routed in one of the most significant fights in naval history.

The battle had seriously damaged the *Bellerophon.* As one of her midshipmen wrote: "Our ship, as was to be expected from her situation suffered very considerably, having 28 killed outright, 127 badly and 40 slightly wounded, 23 since dead of their wounds. . . . The *Bellerophon* had her main mast and mizzen topmasts shot away, her fore topmast, three lower masts and most of her yards badly wounded, her standing rigging nearly cut to pieces. In hull also she was much injured, having had several knees and riders shot away, and part of her lower deck ripped up, besides other damage."

In company with the damaged *Victory,* which had Nelson's body aboard in a cask of spirits, the *Bellerophon* limped down to Gibraltar for temporary repairs and then up to England for major ones. The next 10 years saw her fairly steadily employed, part of the time up in the Baltic and then, during the War of 1812, in two convoy runs to Newfoundland, coupled with some blockade cruising on the coast. Early in 1815, with Napoleon at Elba and the American war ended, it looked as though the British economy measures would cause the *Bellerophon,* along with many others, to be laid up.

Then came the news of Napoleon's escape from Elba and the beginning of the Hundred Days. The *Bellerophon,* under an excellent new captain, Frederick Lewis Maitland, was ordered over to the blockade of the French coast in the vicinity of Rochefort, where Napoleon was expected following his defeat at Waterloo. To escape the clutches of the Prussians under Blücher, Napoleon had raced away from Waterloo to Paris by coach, and on June 22 he abdicated for the second time. The next day he asked the Minister of Marine to order two frigates to Rochefort in readiness to carry him and the members of his family to America. Several days of high-level negotiations followed. He had the amazingly naive belief that he might be able to settle in America, or even in England, not realizing the hostile emotions he had aroused.

Napoleon came aboard the *Bellerophon* on July 15, about a month after Waterloo. Captain Maitland, who had politely but dexterously avoided any commitment as to his future, described it:

> General Bertrand came first up the ship's side, and said to me "The Emperor is in the boat." He then ascended and when he came to the quarter-deck, pulled off his hat, and addressing me in a firm tone of voice, said "I am come to throw myself on the protection of your Prince and laws." When I showed him to his cabin, he looked around and said "Une belle chambre. This is a handsome cabin." I answered "Sir, it is at your service while you remain on board the ship I command. . . . "

Napoleon seemed to be going out of his way to impress everyone favorably, both that day and the next, when they went over to the flagship. But Admiral Hotham was not favorably impressed:

> . . . he was not natural, and he had very little the manners of what we should call a gentleman. He was civil, and under existing and very trying circumstances, good-humored, but not a gentleman.

The *Bellerophon* immediately set out for Torbay. The Admiralty ordered the ship to Plymouth, placing a rigid restriction against any communications of the French with the shore. On July 26, after much more high-level discussion, Captain Maitland received word that he might soon be relieved of his imperial burden. There had been constant injunctions to guard security to the limit; in addition, the ship was beginning to feel the burden of entertaining 30 guests of the Emperor's "family" who, incidentally, gave extremely meager tips.

Sir John Barrow, deputy secretary of the Admiralty, is credited with deciding what to do with Napoleon. This time there would be no nearby Elba—he picked a lonely, remote island far down in the South Atlantic. The First Lord wrote to Admiral Keith: "We have had a cabinet on the whole business . . . I can state for your *private* information that in all probability the ex-Emperor will be sent to some foreign colony, and in the meantime will not be allowed to land or to have any communication with the shore, and we shall not apprize him immediately of his future destination." The First Lord further wrote, "I think we shall send Bonaparte to St. Helena, and that Sir George Cockburn's appointment as Commander-in-Chief on the Cape Station which was suspended will now go forward and he will convey the prisoner to St. Helena and remain there for some time."

On July 26, the *Bellerophon*'s relief was mentioned by name: "The *Northumberland*, Sir George Cockburn's flagship, is in the Medway, and being fully manned is ready to proceed. . . . The sooner that Bonaparte is disposed of and dispatched to his destination, the better for all concerned." Napoleon's original graciousness turned to churlishness when he learned of the Saint Helena decision. On August 7, the *Northumberland* joined the *Bellerophon* and the flagship of Lord Keith, commander in chief of the Channel Fleet. Admiral Cockburn, who had burned Washington the year before, insisted on having the baggage of Napoleon and his family searched; this aroused Napoleon's indignation as did his being treated as a general rather than as Emperor. Before leaving the *Bellerophon*, Napoleon summoned Maitland to his cabin for a gracious farewell.

> I have requested to see you Captain to return my thanks for your kindness and attention to me whilst I have been on board the *Bellerophon* and likewise to beg you will convey them to the officers and ship's company you command. My reception in England has been very different from what I expected; but it gives me much satisfaction to assure you that I feel your conduct to me has been that of a gentleman and a man of honor.

Late in the forenoon, Lord Keith came over in the flagship's barge to convey Napoleon to the *Northumberland*; Napoleon kept the elderly admiral waiting nearly two hours before appearing on deck. Napoleon was the first to step into the barge, followed by General and Madame Bertrand and their children, Count and Countess Montholon and child, General Gourgaud, nine men and three women servants, and the surgeon O'Meara. Last came Lord Keith himself. The barge moved about 30 yards from the ship, and Napoleon stood up and bowed to the officers and men of the *Bellerophon*. The next day, the *Northumberland*, accompanied by two troop ships, a frigate, and several sloops of war, set out for Saint Helena.

That was the *Bellerophon*'s last commissioned service. Five weeks later, she was paid off and shortly afterward turned over to the Transport Board as a convict hulk, at first under her old name and then with the name appropriately changed to *Captivity*. In 1836, a half century after her launching, she was sold for £4030 to be broken up.

(See C. A. Pengelly, *The First Bellerophon*, 1966.)

Rajah

Salem's richest specialty during its golden age was pepper from Sumatra in the East Indies. Secrecy shrouded the beginnings of the trade. Young Captain Jonathan Carnes made the discovery in the early 1790s; he and his wealthy Peele relatives made a highly profitable start in the trade before the other Salem merchants and mariners, to say nothing of those in other ports, even knew where it came from.

Carnes, son of a former privateersman who had married the daughter of Jonathan Peele, had sailed out beyond Good Hope in 1788 and spent some time in the eastern seas engaged in mysterious exploration. He seems to have learned of the rich pepper supply at Bencoelen and other ports in western Sumatra.

In 1795 the 120-ton schooner *Rajah* cleared Salem for India; Carnes was captain and the Peeles were principal owners. Salem did not hear from her for 18 months but then came in for a dramatic surprise. The *Rajah* arrived with a whole cargo of bulk pepper—the first to reach America in quantity. The venture paid a profit of 700%. Salem was agog with curiosity but captain, owners, and crew gave no hint of where they had found the pepper. In 1798 the *Rajah*, now converted into a brig, made a second voyage, returning in 1799 with 158,000 pounds of pepper, paying customs duties of £9522. In mid-1801 a third voyage brought in 149,000 pounds of pepper. By that time the secret had leaked, and other Salem vessels began a long and profitable trade. Naturally, that was too much pepper for local consumption; much of it was shipped to other American ports or to Europe at further high profit. The trade, involving often treacherous Malays, had its occasional hazards—the *Friendship* of Salem would be overrun by natives; in reprisal the American frigate *Potomac* would bombard the port of Quallah Battoo.

Carnes, incidentally, laid the foundation of a distinguished museum. He brought back a quantity of various East Indian curiosities which he gave to the new East India Marine Society, where they became the nucleus of the Peabody Museum.

(See A. Laing, *Seafaring America*, 1974.)

Hermione

The mutiny on H.M.S. *Hermione* in September 1797 was perhaps the most lurid episode in British naval history. The captain who caused the mutiny was one of the most brutal officers in maritime history. The navy had had one spectacular mutiny on the *Bounty* 8 years earlier, but in 1797 harsh conditions aboard ship led to two fleet mutinies in home waters, and mutiny spread even to ships in South African waters.

The *Hermione* uprising, however, outdid all mutinies in sheer brutality. Nine of the officers, including the vicious captain, were thrown overboard; some of them were badly wounded. The aftermath of the uprising was also a fantastic story. The mutineers sailed the *Hermione* to Venezuela and turned her over to the enemy, the Spaniards, who were not sure what to do with her. Meanwhile, the British navy was searching for the ship and the mutineers. In nine years of searching, 33 of the mutineers were court-martialed and 24 hanged from the yardarm. As the third dramatic phase of the mutiny, boat crews from another British frigate boldly rowed into the Venezuelan port where she was anchored and "cut her out" after sharp fighting with her crew and being subjected to the fire of 200 guns from the Spanish forts. The full scope of all these activities was not appreciated until recent exhaustive research in British and Spanish naval archives disclosed the happenings.

The villain of the story of the *Hermione* was Captain Hugh Pigot, who embodied two potentially dangerous qualities of the eighteenth-century navy. One was "interest" and the other was unlimited authority. The armed services of that day were pretty much monopolized by the aristocracy; family influence was important not only in getting into the navy but also in being helped toward early promotion.

Pigot had a rich accumulation of interest. His father was a full admiral, even if not an especially bright one; one uncle was a lieutenant general and another had returned with a fortune from India. Consequently, from boyhood Hugh Pigot had grown up in an atmosphere of power and authority.

Related to these powerful interests was the complete control which a captain enjoyed over his crew. In the name of discipline, he could indulge his passion for authority to the limit. Pigot had a nasty disposition, including a violent objection to criticism of any sort. He had a sadistic nature which took special pleasure in the lashings that he dealt out freely. The principal instrument to enforce authority was the cat-o'-nine-tails, a whip with nine cords about the thickness of a pencil and very much more damaging than whips used in the army. Twelve lashes, Pigot's usual minimum, could lacerate severely the back of the poor devil stretched out against a grating. Some could take this punishment better than others. Three dozen lashes could kill one man; yet another man could survive 200 lashes. One of Pigot's victims, after receiving 12 lashes on three occasions, died as a result; so did another who had received 24 lashes and later 12.

The rank of post-captain, with a command of 20 guns or more, was an all-important goal in a naval officer's career—once achieved, rank, if not assignments, went on automatically until death. Thanks to the interest and influence of family and family friends, Pigot achieved captaincy in 1794 with the command of a medium-sized frigate, the *Success,* of 32 guns and 683 tons, down in the West Indies, where the commander in chief was a good friend, though Pigot had little experience to fit him for such a responsibility. This command was naturally very gratifying to Pigot, but not to the unlucky crew. Records state: "October marked the beginning of twenty-seven months of bullying, misery and dejection . . . many of the men were to be treated like criminals and driven to the limits—but for the time being not beyond— of mental and physical endurance." In one period of 38 weeks, the log shows that he inflicted 85 separate floggings, with a total of 1392 lashings.

On February 10, 1797, Pigot shifted to the command of the *Hermione,* a ship very similar to the *Success.* The surprising thing is that, whereas the crew of the *Success* endured those 27 months of hell, the crew of the *Hermione* broke out in bloody mutiny in seven months. That summer news reached the West Indies of the two great fleet mutinies in home waters. Closer at hand, the crew of the naval schooner *Marie Antoinette* had brutally murdered their two officers and taken her into an enemy port. In August the *Hermione* was ordered out for a seven-week patrol of the Mona Passage. Things went quietly for a while, but in mid-September Pigot committed three particularly vicious acts that foreshadowed his end. He was a stickler for speed and smartness. Casey, the best regarded of the midshipmen, was in charge of the maintop. He was about to come down when he noticed a carelessly dangling reefpoint, and waited while a sailor went out to secure it. On deck, Pigot was in a rage and began yelling insults at Casey in front of all the crew. Pigot demanded that Casey get down on his knees to apologize, which the midshipman refused to do. The next forenoon, Pigot had Casey stripped to the waist and a dozen lashes administered. This almost unheard-of treatment of a midshipman aroused widespread resentment.

Worse brutality was inflicted on the crew five days later. A sudden squall struck the ship and Pigot ordered the topsails to be reefed. He kept cursing at the men for not making better speed, especially the three teenagers on the mizzen-topsail yard. He yelled at them, "I'll flog the last man down." Suddenly the three scared youngsters lost their footing on the yard and fell screaming to their deaths on the deck below. Pigot looked at them and ordered, "Throw the lubbers overboard." The screams had aroused everyone on deck and aloft. The maintopmen began to murmur protests and stared down at him. Thereupon, Pigot ordered the bosun's mates to go up and lash at them in their precarious position, and to take their names. The next morning each also received a formal lashing.

It was this cruel and savage treatment, it has been remarked, that, "greatly increased the previous dislike of the captain and no doubt hastened, if not entirely decided the mutiny." During the night a hostile change came over many of the ship's company. One man remarked, "We're going to take over the ship." But there was no apparent definite planning and almost no clear-cut leadership.

At 11 P.M. on September 21, the ship seemed peaceful and quiet. Suddenly several men leaped on the marine guarding the captain's door: incidently, that is said to have been the earliest duty of marines—guarding the officers against the sailors. The guard was hit across the head with a cutlass before he could shout or shoot. As the group smashed down the door, Pigot leaped from his cot and grabbed his two-foot dirk. The invaders, with cutlasses or "tomahawks," crowded into the room and slashed at Pigot. He fought them off, but finally collapsed over the breech of the gun, his nightshirt soaked with blood. Slashed yet again, he called for mercy. "You yourself showed no mercy," shouted one sailor, "and therefore deserve none." One man ran Pigot through with the bayonet from the marine's gun. A cabin window was smashed; the men grasped the captain's bloody body and hurled it into the sea.

Two other attacks were nearly as bloody. The Third Lieutenant, who had the watch, was approached on the quarterdeck by a group of sailors. After slashing him, they saw him go over the rail. Somewhat later, they were amazed to see him reappear, like a ghost. He had fallen into the mizzen chains and had pulled himself up through a gunport. He begged to be spared because of his wife and children, but someone called, "Overboard he must go." In the course of this new slashing, one hand was severed at the wrist and then the shrieking officer was thrown overboard again.

A particular object of hatred was the Second Lieutenant, who had been very much a toady to Pigot. Aroused by the turmoil, he leaped naked from his cot, ran into the next cabin, and took refuge under the cot of the Marine Lieutenant, who was nearly dead with fever. The mutineers pulled him out from under the cot and slashed and stabbed him repeatedly, then pushed the bloody body out through a porthole. A midshipman whose testimony had caused a sailor to be flogged was bludgeoned and stabbed and thrown overboard.

After those first four bloody deaths there was a lull, reflecting the lack of planning and control. Rum was flowing freely and there were cries of, "Kill them all!" The mutineers found six more victims, all of whom were thrown overboard. These victims included the First Lieutenant, the surgeon, the Purser, the captain's clerk, the dying Marine Lieutenant, and the bosun. The only woman aboard was the bosun's wife. An enterprising ruffian carried the bosun out and threw him overboard; he then came back and appropriated the wife, who was heard to make no objections. Altogether nine officers, in addition to the midshipman, were killed. The fate of four others hung in the balance for a while, but eventually they were all spared—the carpenter, gunner, Master, and Midshipman Casey. The last two became prime witnesses at the courts-martial.

The mutineers compounded their felony by turning the *Hermione* over to the enemy at La Guaira on the Spanish Main. The initial contact was polite but cautious. The mutineers explained the absence of officers by their having been set adrift like Captain Bligh of the *Bounty*. Spanish administration was always a slow process, but here the unusual circumstances produced a reluctance to accept final responsibility. The governor at La Guaira constantly conferred with the captain general at nearby Caracas, but awaited a decision from the distant Crown. The *Hermione,* renamed the *Santa Cecelia,* was taken into the Spanish Navy and was moved up the coast to Puerto Cabello, but she became so tangled in red tape that she still lay at the port 26 months later.

The mutineers and other crew members presented numerous problems. The "loyal" members, including the quartet whose lives had been spared plus all the marines, were treated as regular prisoners of war and were soon exchanged with the British. The mutineers had expected to be treated as heroes; instead, they ran into contempt around La Guaira. The government gave them each $25 for expenses and they were housed in barracks. But when that money was gone, they were on their own; many of them earned a pittance hauling rock for the fortifications or working in the salt mines. The governor general had promised that they would not be turned over to the British; but on learning that the officers had been murdered, he regretted his promise. Gradually, the mutineers were allowed to sail away, for jobs afloat.

The British, in the meantime, were tireless in running down the *Hermione* crew. They posted announcements of generous rewards for information, and officers boarding ships at sea searched for mutineers. The marines, who were all loyal, were kept on hand to serve as witnesses, as were the Master and Midshipman Casey; the latter served again and again as witnesses in the long series of courts-martial. The first court-martial tried four men taken from a captured French privateer. All four were hanged from the yardarm and then hung in chains from the gibbets on Gallows Point at Jamaica. The long arm of the Royal Navy reached out as far as South Carolina, Denmark, and Yalta, and the mutineers went for years in dread of being recognized. By 1806, when the last mutineer was hanged, 33 of the *Hermione* crew had been brought to trial and 24 executed.

In the meantime the *Hermione* had come back into British hands through "one of the bravest, best planned, and most successful operations in British naval history." In October 1799 she was "cut out" where she lay in Puerto Cabello by boat crews from the frigate *Success*, led by Captain Edward Hamilton. It was a highly risky operation, for the *Hermione* had some 200 men aboard and the port was flanked by many fortress guns. Hamilton planned the stealthy approach and the role that each boat crew was to play. Some were to cut the anchor ropes, others to release the sails, while the rest were to handle the Spanish crew. The surprise was perfect; most of the Spaniards were between decks, firing the big guns at imaginary targets. There was some sharp fighting, but in an hour the ship was sailing out of the harbor to join the *Success*. The Spanish casualties included 119 killed, 97 seriously wounded, and the rest taken prisoner. The news was received with joy in England. Hamilton was knighted, and the payment for the captured ship was divided among the officers and men of the *Success*. The *Hermione* once more became a British frigate, renamed the *Retribution*.

(See D. Pope, *The Black Ship*, 1963.)

Constellation

The *Constellation* captures the French frigate *Insurgente* in the West Indies in February 1799. *(Naval Historical Center)*

There were just two matters of special interest in the long story of the 36-gun frigate *Constellation*. Her prime achievement at sea came at the very start of her career, in the quasi-war with France when she won the United States Navy's first two major frigate actions. The other matter was that of seniority among the navy's warships. The first three frigates were launched in 1797: the *United States* at Philadelphia on May 10, the *Constellation* at Baltimore on September 7, and the *Constitution* at Boston on October 21. Consequently, when the *United States* was burned at Norfolk in 1861, the *Constellation* gained historic credit as the oldest American warship afloat and was honored accordingly. In 1949, however, the leading historian of naval architecture claimed that the original 1797 ship had been broken up in 1854 and an entirely new *Constellation,* with different design and dimensions, had been built in her place. Not everyone agreed with this claim, and the ship is lovingly on display at Baltimore.

As for getting off to a quick start in the quasi-war, the *Constellation* became the flagship of the very able Commodore Thomas Truxtun. Hostilities had arisen from the depredations of semipiratical, quite irregular French craft, which were preying on American shipping. The regular French navy was in an extremely depleted state; Napoleon had been hard put to it to scrape up enough vessels for his Egyptian expedition in 1798, and they had been smashed by Nelson at Abukir. The *Constellation* would encounter two of the very few regular French frigates in American waters.

108

The first French frigate was the *Insurgente,* rated, like the *Constellation,* at 36 guns. They met near Nevis in February 1799. The French captain was not sure of the quasi-war status of belligerency, and a sudden squall carried away the ship's main-topmast. Truxtun took full advantage of the situation, pouring in broadsides from both sides and raking the *Insurgente* while crossing her bows. The American gunnery was excellent. After the *Insurgente* surrendered, one lieutenant who boarded her wrote enthusiastically of "seventy French pirates wallowing in their gore," while another lieutenant ran through a seaman who was fleeing his post and remarked, "We would put any man to death for looking pale on this ship."

Just about a year after the *Insurgente* action, the *Constellation* encountered a stronger French frigate, the *Vengeance,* not far from the site of the previous fight. This was a hard-fought action, with damage and casualties on both sides, and much of the fighting after dark. The French ship actually lowered its flag in surrender three times; since Truxtun could not see the French flag, he continued firing. Though badly damaged, the *Vengeance* managed to draw away and later turned up at Curaçao. That was Truxtun's last major action. His reputation was high, but he declined the command of the new Mediterranean Squadron because he was not allowed a flag captain to run his flagship.

In 1854 the *Constellation* ran afoul of a political practice which prevailed for years in naval construction. Congress would not vote for new ships but would pay to repair old ones. The navy got around this by doing away with the worn-out vessel and giving her name to an entirely new one, charging it up as a "great repair on the USS so-and-so." It became increasingly difficult to follow this practice in the records.

Just to add to the confusion, another practice prevailed to preserve the continuity of a famous ship. She would receive repair after repair until very few elements of the original ship remained. But at no time were the design and dimensions altered and spiritually she remained the original vessel—that was the case with two nations' most treasured veterans: Nelson's *Victory* and the *Constitution,* still on the official lists and flying the flag of the local admiral.

The *Constellation* had come down through the years enjoying similar status. She had served on various stations around the world, and during the Civil War had even cruised the Mediterranean looking for the Confederate raider *Alabama.* She later had several honorific posts as a receiving or training ship. In 1940 she was recommissioned as shore-based relief flagship of Atlantic commands, and flew the flag at Newport.

In 1949 her seniority as the oldest American warship afloat was questioned. Howard I. Chapelle, naval architect-historian, published his study of *The American Sailing Navy*, in which he pointed out that the old *Constellation* was broken up at Norfolk in 1854, and that her name was given to an entirely new first-class corvette built at the Norfolk Navy Yard. The new vessel differed in model and dimensions from the old and, according to Chapelle, neither was nor looked like the original frigate.

There was naturally a strong emotional reaction to this charge, especially in Baltimore. The *Constellation* was returned to Baltimore in July 1955, to be preserved as a national shrine by the Star Spangled Banner Flag House Association. Hours of devoted volunteer service have been given to her restoration, some of it financed by "coins" struck from her bronze spikes.

(See E. S. Ferguson, *Truxtun of the Constellation, The Life of Commodore Thomas Truxtun, U.S. Navy, 1755–1822*, 1956.)

Constitution

The *Constitution* demolished H.M.S. *Guerrière* on August 12, 1812. *(Naval Historical Center)*

The frigate *Constitution*, it has been remarked, is the oldest warship still afloat and in commission. The *Constellation* was launched six weeks earlier but is no longer in commission, while England's favorite war-

ship, the *Victory*, built in 1765, is preserved but no longer afloat at
Portsmouth Dockyard. Aside from these technicalities which make her actually the oldest, "Old Ironsides" has always been dearest of all ships to the American people, ever since she defeated two British frigates in the early months of the War of 1812, a victory which shocked the British who had been beating French frigates regularly for 20 years, and which was for Americans a cause for intense pride in their new navy. The *Constitution* has always been a Boston ship, enshrined there now as an historic national monument just across the harbor from the place where she was launched on October 21, 1797.

One of the men responsible for her success was Joshua Humphreys, a leading Philadelphia shipbuilder. When Congress in 1794 decided to build six frigates to chastise the Barbary pirates, Humphreys advised that some of them should be as strong as possible, since the United States could not afford many ships. Consequently, the navy built three supercruisers, stronger than the conventional British and French frigate classes and fast enough to run away from anything stronger. They were named *Constitution*, *United States*, and *President*. Nominally rated at 44 guns, they actually carried more. Their dimensions were fairly identical: 2200 tons, 175 feet in length and 42 feet in beam, normally carrying a crew of 450.

The *Constitution* first sailed from Boston on July 22, 1798, to participate in the quasi-war with France. Her first captain was undistinguished, and her performance fell well below that of the smaller *Constellation* under Thomas Truxtun.

One of the *Constitution*'s most valuable but not well-publicized services to the navy came in 1803–1804 during the Barbary Wars, while flagship of the Mediterranean Squadron under the dour Portlander Edward Preble. The squadron was in the Mediterranean from 1803 to 1807, but its role was significant only during the years in which Preble was commander of the *Constitution* off Tripoli. Some spectacular action followed the capture of the *Philadelphia*, especially in the heroic roles played by the little *Enterprise* and *Intrepid* with Preble exercising overall tactical direction. It later became apparent that something else of high value was going on aboard the flagship, for the *Constitution* during those years served somewhat as Naval Academy and Naval War College. Years later, Fletcher Pratt brought out a volume entitled *Preble's Boys*, which showed that nearly all the young American commanders who distinguished themselves so brilliantly during the War of 1812 had received thorough indoctrination under Preble's rigorous direction. Although the *Constitution* remained in the Mediterranean until 1807, the succeeding commanders were less effective.

The coming of the War of 1812 found the *Constitution* at her usual

Boston base. On July 12 she put to sea under Captain Isaac Hull with orders to join the squadron under Captain John Rodgers coming up the coast. However, she encountered a powerful five-ship British squadron off the New Jersey coast and had the narrowest escape of her career. As the wind died away, the enemy drew closer. For two days Captain Hull showed superb seamanship. The crew were kept busy in wetting the sails and in kedging—carrying an anchor well forward in a boat, dropping it overboard, and drawing the ship forward on it. The *Constitution* finally escaped.

Then came the high point of the *Constitution*'s career. Early in August she sailed from Boston just a few hours before a message arrived from the Secretary of the Navy replacing Hull by William Bainbridge. Hull sailed for the coast of Nova Scotia and on August 19 encountered the frigate *Guerrière*, originally captured from the French. She was well-hated for her actions off the New England coast, and her captain, the son of an admiral, was of the arrogant type. The first encounter came at 4:05 P.M., exchanging broadsides with little damage. For 45 minutes both ships maneuvered for an advantageous position. As they came closer together, Hull waited until they were 100 yards apart before returning a broadside. For 15 minutes there was an easy exchange of broadsides, each of the *Constitution*'s weighing about 100 pounds more than the British. It was at this stage that an American sailor, seeing some of the British shots fall into the sea, yelled, "Huzza! Her sides are made of iron," and "Old Ironsides" she was from that time on. At 6 P.M., the *Guerrière*'s mizzenmast fell over the side. Taking advantage of this mishap, Hull crossed her bow and poured a heavy broadside into her. The *Constitution*'s bowsprit fouled the enemy's mizzen rigging, and both sides prepared to board the enemy. However, the *Guerrière*'s foremast and mainmast fell into the sea and she became a helpless battered hulk. The British lost 78 killed and wounded; the Americans lost only 14. The *Guerrière* surrendered, and the wounded and prisoners were taken off with difficulty, because of the darkness and the heavy seas. The next day the *Guerrière* was blown up, and the victors made for Boston.

It would be some time before the British learned the shocking news, but the Americans immediately went into wild celebration. It was, however, a time of mixed emotions for the Hull family. Isaac's uncle, General William Hull, had ignominiously surrendered Detroit to a smaller force of British and Indians on July 12.

In the last week of the year the *Constitution*, now under William Bainbridge, won a second and very similar victory over the frigate *Java* off the coast of Brazil. (In the meantime, the *United States* had captured the *Macedonian*.) The *Java*, another former French frigate, known as the

Renomée in 1811, was on a very special mission to Bombay laden with stores for the British army, and with the newly appointed governor of India and his staff aboard. Her captain, Henry Lambert, commanded high respect.

The duel between the two frigates lasted nearly four hours. Although the *Java* held her own and managed to get in one raking broadside, the heavy fire and skillful maneuvering of the *Constitution* soon began to tell. The *Java*'s masts were all shot away, and she became an unmanageable hulk with her decks a shambles. Captain Bainbridge was injured early in the fight but remained in control; Captain Lambert was mortally wounded when trying to board the *Constitution.* By the time she finally surrendered, the *Java* had sustained 100 casualties, half of them fatal; once again the *Constitution*'s casualties were very much lower. The *Java* was too battered to bring home, so she was blown up and burned.

Those two four-hour periods of gunnery and ship-handling were enshrined in American legend. A century later we boys were familiar with the details, and Currier & Ives prints of the two dismasted British hulks were everywhere. British pride had suffered a blow, but the Royal Navy gradually recovered; it had over 100 more frigates which could be called in. By 1813 the British were beginning a blockade of the American coast, and by 1814 had almost hermetically sealed off the whole seaboard. The *United States* was up the river at New London with her topmasts down, and the *President* was captured by a British squadron while trying to escape from New York. For nine months the *Constitution* was blockaded in Boston, but in December 1814 she slipped to sea, captured two prizes, and then scored one last victory. Northward of Madeira, she encountered two small British frigates, the *Cyane* and the *Levant.* Old Ironsides was then under the command of Charles Stewart. With very deft ship-handling, Stewart got between the two ships, battling each separately, and they soon surrendered. Stewart started for home with his prizes but ran into three British frigates which recovered the *Levant.* On the way home, he learned that the peace treaty had been signed but that the *Cyane* was a fair prize. The *Constitution*'s war career ended with her arrival at New York. Not until 1821 did she put to sea again as flagship of the Mediterranean Squadron.

In mid-December 1830 Oliver Wendell Holmes was shocked to read in the local newspaper, copied from a New York journal:

> *Old Ironsides.* It has been affirmed on good authority that the Secretary of the Navy has recommended to the Board of Navy Commissioners to dispose of the frigate *Constitution.* . . . Such a national interest, so endeared to our national pride as Old Ironsides should never by any act of our government cease to belong to the Navy. . . .

Within two days, the *Boston Daily Advertiser* printed a poem which Holmes had dashed off; it became a classic of marine verse:

Ay tear her tattered ensign down!
  Long has it waved on high,
And many an eye has danced to see
  That banner in the sky.
Beneath it rung the battle shout,
  And burst the cannon's roar;
The meteor of the ocean air
  Shall sweep the clouds no more.

Her decks, once red with heroes' blood,
  Where knelt the vanquished foe,
When winds were carrying o'er the flood
  And waves were white below,
No more shall feel the victor's tread,
  Or know the conquered knee;
The harpies of the shore shall pluck
  The eagle of the sea!

Oh better that her shattered hulk
  Should sink beneath the wave
Her thunders shook the mighty deep
  And there should be her grave;
Nail to the mast her holy flag,
  Set every threadbare sail,
And give her to the god of storms,
  The lightning and the gale!

The protests were successful and the *Constitution* was saved. She was repaired at Boston and then began 20 years of active service in various stations. Between those repairs and others which followed, a question arose of just how much of the original timbers remained, as in the case of the *Victory*, but there was no time at which the ship lost her identity. This was in contrast to the *Constellation* where, according to Chapelle's claim, an entirely new and somewhat different ship was built.

During the Civil War the *Constitution* moved the Naval Academy from Annapolis up to Newport for the duration, where several important future admirals trained aboard her. After the war, she underwent further rebuilding and then served in various semiactive roles as training ship and receiving ship. In 1905 she again escaped destruction, and in 1929–1930 was thoroughly rebuilt, thanks to funds from private sources, including thousands of schoolchildren.

Recommissioned in 1931, the *Constitution* was sent on a triumphal tour of the Atlantic, Gulf, and Pacific Coasts. On May 7, 1934, she was returned to the Navy Yard at Boston as the oldest ship on the Navy List, flying the two-starred flag of the Commandant of the First Naval District. Even though the Boston Naval Shipyard was terminated in 1974, the *Constitution*, honored as a national historic monument, still remains there, visited by thousands.

(See T. P. Horgan, *Old Ironsides, the Story of USS Constitution*, 1963.)

United States

The *United States* engaged and defeated the British frigate *Macedonian* on October 25, 1812. *(Naval Historical Center)*

A sister ship of the *Constitution* and the *President*, the *United States* was one of the 44-gun superfrigates which did so much to enhance the prestige of the infant American navy. She was launched in the spring of 1797 at the Philadelphia yard of Joshua Humphreys, who had argued for this big class, saying that if the Americans could not afford a big navy, the few ships that they could afford should be the strongest possible. For some reason, despite the distinguished designer-constructor, the *United States* was the slowest of the "big three" and was often dubbed the "Old Wagon." Most of her naval career was routine and relatively uneventful, but in the autumn of 1812, by capturing the British frigate *Macedonian*, midway between the *Constitution*'s successes against the *Guerrière* and the *Java*, she won a lasting place among the navy's immortal ships and a thrilled admiration in the hearts of generations of schoolboys.

Her first operations in the quasi-war with France and in the Mediterranean were not spectacular. Her chance for glory came in 1812 under the command of Stephen Decatur, who had already won laurels at Tripoli. Breaking away from the other ships of the squadron, he sailed out into the Atlantic. On October 25, several hundred miles west of Madeira, he encountered a British warship, which crowded on so much sail that Decatur first thought her a ship of the line. She soon turned out to be the 38-gun frigate *Macedonian,* relatively new and in good shape, though somewhat short of men. She was commanded by Captain John S. Carden.

The two-hour fight started at 9:20 A.M. with good maneuvering on both sides, aiming at holding the weather gage to windward, and getting into position to rake the enemy from bow to stern. The *United States* had an advantage in its long 24-pounder guns, which had greater weight and range than the British 18-pounders, to say nothing of the short-range British carronade "smashers." In addition, the American gunnery was excellent. The *Macedonian* lost her mizzen topmast, which affected her maneuverability. The *United States* stood off at fairly long range and, among other things, dismounted the carronades. Within two hours, the *Macedonian* had lost her main- and fore-topmast as well, and casualties were mounting heavily. Decatur actually stood off for an hour to refill cartridges and repair rigging. When the *United States* returned and was in a position to rake again, the *Macedonian*'s colors came down. She had lost over 100 killed and wounded, the *United States* only 14.

Carden offered his sword, but Decatur declined it. The British captain was mortified at the possibility of being the first to surrender to another frigate and was much relieved to learn of the capture months before of the *Guerrière,* which Hull had had to sink. To be one-up on Hull, Decatur determined to bring the *Macedonian* into port despite her battered condition. The two ships made port together. Decatur was honored with parades in New York and got a generous share of the $200,000 prize money. The *Macedonian* was taken into the United States Navy under the same name.

The rest of the war was rather ignominious for the *United States* and *Macedonian.* With the expanding British blockade, they remained cooped up in the Thames River at New London, closly watched by a blockading squadron off Montauk Point under Admiral Thomas Hardy, in whose arms Nelson had died at Trafalgar. On occasion, when Decatur tried to slip out to sea, some mysterious characters touched off blue lights to warn the British. Decatur finally went down to New York to command the *President,* in which he was captured by another blockading squadron.

The later story of the *United States* furnishes little excitement, as she served in one distant station after another. About the only time she attracted attention was in 1835 at Toulon, as she fired a 21-gun salute in honor of the French king's birthday. Careless gunners had left solid shot in three guns, which fired into a harbor fortification and a warship, killing three French sailors.

The *United States* was laid up at Norfolk Navy Yard in 1861 when 10 of the old ships were burned to prevent their falling into Confederate hands—one of the ships, of course, was raised to become the ironclad *Virginia*. At the close of the war in 1865, the hulk of the *United States* was broken up, a very difficult process in view of the toughness of the old live oak timbers.

(See L. F. Guttridge, *The Commodores*, 1969.)

Lutine

The bell from H.M.S.
Lutine at Lloyds
in London.
(Mariners Museum)

From time to time, an old ship's bell clangs at the great marine insurance center of Lloyd's in London and all listen intently for the somber news of some ship lost or long overdue. That "*Lutine* bell" has a long tradition, going back to 1799, when the British frigate *Lutine* sank with all hands and much treasure on the coast of Holland, representing a heavy loss to those who had underwritten her valuable cargo. Lloyd's has sustained even heavier losses in its long history, as, for instance, when the Spaniards captured a whole Jamaica convoy in 1779, but the facts and rumors concerning the unlucky *Lutine* have held a special place in Lloyd's tradition.

She had been a 36-gun French frigate, launched at Brest in 1785, and was one of the 16 French warships captured by Admiral Hood at the Toulon base in 1795. In due time she became H.M.S. *Lutine,* and after repairs was assigned to duty in the North Sea Fleet. On October 9, 1799, after a ball aboard the ship, she sailed from Yarmouth on the English east coast, under Captain Lancelot Skynner, on what was to be her last voyage. She encountered a heavy gale and piled up on a shifting sandbank on the edge of the Zuider Zee and sank with all hands.

What made the *Lutine* a Lloyd's tradition was that she was credited with carrying a very heavy load of gold and silver. Warships were often used for that in those days, with the treasure sometimes on government account, especially for the payment of troops, and sometimes on private account, with her commander receiving a fee for the service. A whole crop of conflicting rumors arose as to just what the *Lutine*'s treasure was. Older accounts said that she was carrying pay for the British army in the Netherlands, but it now appears that another warship had that responsibility. It would seem that the *Lutine*'s treasure was on private account, chiefly for the bankers of Amsterdam or Hamburg. Whatever it was, the Lloyd's underwriters paid immediately for the insured loss.

Then came more than half a century of dispute over salvage from the wreck which, for a while, was partly exposed at low water. Under normal conditions, the salvage would go to the English underwriters, but this case was complicated by the fact that at the time of the wreck England and Holland were at war. That kept the situation open for years, although during that period occasional amounts were salvaged. The situation was improved after 1815 when Holland was once more under the House of Orange instead of the former French control. In 1857 an Anglo-Dutch arrangement provided that half the proceeds would go to the Lloyd's committee. Later, when Lloyd's was incorporated, it was provided that, since the original underwriters were unknown, the amount received from salvage would be used for the general benefit.

In the meantime Lloyd's received the *Lutine*'s 106-pound bell, which was in a state of excellent preservation. It became Lloyd's "best known relic" and has been used ever since to call attention to bad news. In addition, the ship's rudder was converted into a chair for the Lloyd's president, and a table at which he occasionally presides.

(See C. Wright and C. E. Fayle, *A History of Lloyd's from the Founding of Lloyd's Coffee House to the Present Day*, 1928.)

Enterprise

The *Enterprise* engaged and defeated H.M.S. *Boxer* off the Maine coast on September 5, 1813. *(Naval Historical Center)*

Few if any small vessels ever had as long-continued a record of successful operation as that of the little *Enterprise*, first a schooner and later a brig, between her launching in 1799 and her final wreck in 1823. Built on the eastern shore of Chesapeake Bay by Henry Spencer, she had some of the speedy qualities of the so-called Baltimore clippers. Also, being too small for a stuffy post-captain, her command fell to a series of ambitious, energetic lieutenants with reputations to make. In view of her continued success, she was continually repaired to carry on the name.

Originally, she was a schooner of 135 tons, with twelve 12-pounder guns; after her rebuilding in 1813, she was a brig with fourteen 18-pounder carronades and two long 9-pounders. Her success was such that on several occasions orders were given to build new vessels along her lines.

The *Enterprise* was immediately ordered into the Caribbean service, under Lieutenant John Shaw, in the quasi-war with France. Within a year she captured eight French privateers and freed 11 American vessels from captivity, with the result that when the navy was drastically cut down in 1801, popular demand insisted that she be among the 14 vessels retained.

In 1801 she was in the first Mediterranean Squadron under Commodore Dale. The only tangible success of that first squadron was the defeat under Lieutenant Andrew Sterrett of the "poleaxer" *Tripoli* in a three-hour action which left half the Tripolitan crew dead without a single American injury. The *Enterprise* continued active, carrying dis-   **119** patches, convoying merchantmen, and capturing one Barbary ship. In 1803, still on Mediterranean service, the *Enterprise,* under the command of Stephen Decatur, captured the Tripolitan ketch which, renamed the *Intrepid,* took part in two very daring exploits at Tripoli. In July 1804 the *Enterprise* participated in the major American attacks on Tripoli. She was virtually rebuilt at Venice in the winter of 1804–1805 and stayed on, with occasional encounters, in the Mediterranean until 1807, when she returned to the United States for the one relatively inactive period of her career.

In 1811 she was hauled out to the Washington Navy Yard and underwent major repairs, including conversion from schooner to brig and an increase in her battery. She cruised the American coast during the first year of the War of 1812.

On September 5, 1813, under the command of Lieutenant William Burrowes, she fought and won her major action with the British gun brig *Boxer* just east of Portland, Maine. It was a sharp fight, but the American gunnery won the victory. The London *Times* declared that "Americans have some superior mode of firing." Both Lieutenant Burrowes and Captain Blythe of the *Boxer* were killed. New England at that time was not enthusiastic about the War of 1812, and Portland gave equal funeral honors to the two dead captains. They are buried in Eastern Cemetery with the Stars and Stripes and Union Jack painted on their respective tombs. The reason for the *Boxer's* being in those waters was revealed when the effects of the British captain were examined. In the permissive spirit of war in those days, the British were shipping woolens for American uniforms in neutral ships by way of Halifax. The shippers in Halifax knew that this was understood officially on both sides, but were not sure that privateers would be so understanding. They consequently gave Captain Blythe a draft for £100 to accompany the neutral cargo. When his executors found this in his effects, they substituted the same amount in gold so as not to reveal the arrangement.

The *Enterprise* sailed for the Caribbean in company with another brig and took three prizes but, encountering a powerful enemy in February 1814, she jettisoned most of her guns and managed to outsail her opponent. She served as guardship at Charleston until the end of the war. In mid-1815 she returned once more to the Mediterranean, with Commodore Bainbridge's squadron, without adventure, then returned for two years on the American coast. In 1817 she went south to the Caribbean and Gulf of Mexico in pursuit of pirates, smugglers, and other wrongdoers. Her 24-year active career came to an end on July 9, 1823, when she grounded and broke up on little Curaçao Island in the Caribbean.

The performance of the *Enterprise* gave her such a high place in naval tradition that five more ships successively bore the name. The fourth was one of the outstanding carriers of World War II, and the fifth, the first atomic-powered carrier.

(See S. Picking, *Sea Fight Off Monhegan, Enterprise and Boxer*, 1941.)

Essex

The *Essex* in the naval operating base at Nuku Hiva in the Marquesas. *(Naval Historical Center)*

The Salem-built frigate *Essex* carried the War of 1812 to the Pacific. There she captured 12 British whalers but was finally captured herself by two British warships at Valparaiso in violation of its neutral status.

Measuring 860 tons, she was built in the Salem yard of Enos Briggs at a cost of $139,362, which was raised by the citizens of Salem and the rest of Essex County. She was launched in September 1799, and 10 weeks later was presented to the United States Navy and accepted by Captain Edward Preble, her first commander. Her armament consisted of forty 32-pounder carronades and only 6 long 12-pounders. Those carronades, useful as they were for "smashing" at close range, would be the cause of her undoing when the enemy stayed beyond their range.

In 1800 the *Essex* went on a successful convoy expedition past the Cape of Good Hope to the Dutch East Indies. Then in 1801 she was one of the ships of the first Mediterranean Squadron, spending a year in convoying and blockading. She returned to the Mediterranean in 1804 and in 1805 took part in the attack on Derna. With the outbreak of the War of 1812, the *Essex*, now under the command of Captain David

Porter, captured the sloop *Alert* and took nine other prizes before she returned to New York in September.

The *Essex* had hardly returned from that cruise when she was ordered to sea again, this time on her memorable mission. She was to be one of a squadron, with the *Constitution* and the sloop *Hornet,* under Commodore William Bainbridge, to raid British shipping in the Pacific and Indian Oceans. Sailing from different ports, the ships were to rendezvous off Bahia in Brazil. But that rendezvous never came off. The *Constitution* had encountered the British frigate *Java* and sank her after a fierce and famous action, so Bainbridge decided to take her home for repairs, accompanied by the *Hornet.*

Nothing could have pleased Porter more. He was definitely a loner who preferred cruising on his own. Like his son, David Dixon Porter, "the second admiral," he had marked ability but a very difficult disposition. So he grasped the opportunity to carry out the original squadron plans in the *Essex* alone. By March 1813 he had reached Valparaiso after rounding Cape Horn and capturing a British packet.

He captured a dozen British whalers, one of which, the *Atlantic,* he took over as a satellite, renamed her the *Essex Junior,* and armed her with 20 guns. On another whaler he installed his foster son, David Glasgow Farragut, the future First Admiral. As a center for all this activity, he set up a veritable naval operating base, 5000 miles out in the Pacific on the island of Nuku Hiva in the Marquesas. It had many of the features that made Tahiti such a favorite with visiting sailors down through the years. It was there that Herman Melville would jump ship from the whaler *Acushnet,* and that Admiral Graf Spee would give the crew of the *Scharnhorst* a brief spell of rest and recreation just before Coronel and the Falkland Islands.

Some refitting and repair work was done at Nuku Hiva but there was time, too, for the girls who swarmed out to the frigate by the hundreds. Porter was in a permissive mood and allowed the men every fourth night ashore. He wrote of the girls that "they attach no shame to a proceeding which is considered as natural, an innocent and harmless amusement. With common sailors and their girls, all was helter-skelter and promiscuous intercourse, every girl the wife of every man in the mess and frequently of every man in the ship. Their only asking price was quantities of whale teeth." And better still, there was no trace of veneral disease. Captain Porter himself was smitten with the charms of Pitanee, the chief's granddaughter, but he said, "She received my advances with the coldness and hauteur of a princess." One of the junior officers, however, had better luck.

That pleasant existence came to an end in mid-December 1813, when the *Essex* and *Essex Junior* made for Valparaiso, arriving there on February 3. At Valaraiso, Porter ran afoul of H.M.S. *Phoebe* and H.M.S.

Cherub under the command of Captain James Hillyar, an old acquaintance, who had been sent out by the Admiralty for the express purpose of checking the raiding of the *Essex*. The initial contact was friendly on the surface with thinly veiled undertones. As reported by a midshipman who was on the quarterdeck, Hillyar inquired for the health of Porter, who returned the compliment but added, "If the *Phoebe* touches the *Essex*, there will be serious consequences." Hillyar then made a statement he would not live up to: "Upon my honor, I do not mean to touch you. I respect the neutrality of the port. . . . I thought you knew me better, Sir, than to think I would break my word—you have no occasion to be alarmed."

During the next six weeks Porter did have cause for alarm, despite the neutral status of Chilean waters. He knew that he would be outgunned in case of a showdown. He had not been happy about his short-ranged carronades; he had told the Secretary of the Navy that a ship "armed with long guns could take a position beyond the range of our carronades and cut us to pieces." But the Secretary had not agreed to the expense of changing the guns, so the vessels had carried on in "a whimsical war of nerves." Porter contemplated slipping out of Valparaiso, but Hillyar always seemed to be in the way.

A series of violent gusts thwarted his efforts at escape, one of them carrying away his main-topmast on March 28. Porter headed into shore, well within the three-mile limit. There was a brief exchange of broadsides and then the *Phoebe* and *Cherub*, out of range of his carronades, began raking the *Essex* with their long guns, to which he could not reply. Between 4:00 and 6:20 P.M. the *Essex* took terrific punishment, finally catching fire below decks.

Captain Porter gave up his sword amid a scene of horror. Casualties were high, including dead and wounded. Many bodies had been thrown overboard, and numerous amputations had been done during the night. A considerable number of sailors had been seen jumping over the side; they were British seamen who had joined from the whalers and feared punishment as deserters if they fell into British hands. The accounts differ as to the actual number of casualties, but there were only 130 survivors, who were paroled by Captain Hillyar and sent home on the *Essex Junior*.

The battered *Essex* was taken into the Royal Navy and eventually became a convict ship; she was sold in 1823. Porter became a member of the new Board of Naval Commissioners, commanded the West Indian antipiratical squadron, was disciplined for undue harshness against alleged pirates at Puerto Rico, and resigned in anger to become, for a while, head of the Mexican navy.

(See C. S. Forester, *The Age of Fighting Sail: The Story of the Naval War of 1812*, 1956.)

Philadelphia

The Tripolitan prize, the *Philadelphia*, burned in the harbor by Stephen Decatur in the *Intrepid* on February 16, 1804. *(Naval Historical Center)*

The 38-gun frigate *Philadelphia* terminated her four-year career when she was burned by the Americans after running aground off Tripoli. Designed by Josiah Fox and built by Samuel Humphreys, she was one of the frigates financed for the government by popular subscription. She was laid down late in 1798, launched late in 1799, and commissioned in April 1800, with the senior Stephen Decatur as her first commanding officer. On her maiden cruise, during the quasi-war with France, she captured five French vessels and recaptured six American merchantmen.

In 1801 she joined the first Mediterranean Squadron under Commodore Richard Dale, and cruised in the Gibraltar area without adventure. After a year at home, she returned to the Mediterranean in 1803 under the command of Captain William Bainbridge, and in August she captured a 28-gun Moroccan warship and recovered a captured American merchantman.

Then her luck turned. On October 31, 1803, while chasing a Tripolitan vessel near the entrance to Tripoli, she struck an uncharted rock. After an ineffectual attempt at scuttling, Bainbridge surrendered to the Tripolitans, to the disgust of many of the crew. The 307 officers and men were carried ashore for a long imprisonment. Two days later a strong wind freed the *Philadelphia* from the rock, leaving the Tripolitans with a fine frigate. Commodore Preble, off shore in the *Constitution*, wrote to

the Secretary of the Navy, "Would to God that the officers and crew had
one and all determined to prefer death to slavery."

The imprisoned officers, in the former American consular building,
were relatively well off, thanks to the efforts of the Danish consul,
though Bainbridge was filled with remorse at not having done more to
salvage the situation. The enlisted personnel, however, suffered by
being thrown into a warehouse already crowded with 600 slaves. They
were shackled, with the unskilled put to work on the harbor ramparts,
while the skilled carpenters, sailmakers, and blacksmiths were com-
pelled to assist in maintaining the bashaw's fleet.

But while Preble deplored the lack of valor shown aboard the *Philadelphia,* he found plenty of spirit among the others in the fleet. The little
captured ketch *Intrepid* under Stephen Decatur boldly sailed into the
harbor, boarded the frigate, and after vicious hand-to-hand fighting,
set her afire, and managed to sail away. By this bold action the *Philadelphia* at least was prevented from augmenting the Algerian fleet.

In 1804 a weak treaty with Algiers secured the release of the imprisoned officers and crew for a payment of $60,000.

(See *Dictionary of American Naval Fighting Ships,* 1959.)

Intrepid

The ketch *Intrepid* at harbor of Tripoli in 1804. *(Naval Historical Center)*

The little 64-ton "bomb" ketch *Intrepid* in the course of 1804 provided the United States with two of the boldest exploits of the whole "Heroic Age." Originally built in France in 1798 for Napoleon's Egyptian expedition, she was later sold to the Tripolitans as the *Mastico*. She was one of the Tripolitan small craft which forced the surrender of the *Philadelphia* after she ran aground at the entrance to the harbor at Tripoli on October 31, 1803. Two months later, on December 23, while sailing for Constantinople, the *Mastico* was captured by the little American cruiser *Enterprise* under Stephen Decatur, and was taken into the United States Navy as the *Intrepid*, a highly appropriate name.

Commodore Edward Preble, by far the most capable leader of the Mediterranean Squadron, decided that the *Philadelphia,* now floating free as a powerful addition to the Tripolitan fleet, should be burned. This was obviously a highly risky undertaking, as the frigate lay under the numerous guns of the shore batteries, with many Tripolitan warships close at hand.

For the command of this hazardous operation, Preble selected young Stephen Decatur, who was a man of spirit. The *Intrepid* was the obvious candidate for the job, as her rig would not arouse Tripolitan suspicions.

Preble ordered Decatur to slip into the harbor at night, board and burn the frigate, and make good his escape.

The attack was made on February 16, 1804, after a week's delay because of a storm. Some 75 officers and men were crowded into the little vessel, along with necessary combustibles. The *Syren* as a backup relief ship remained just outside the harbor for rescue work if necessary. To deceive the enemy, a few of the men were on deck in Moorish clothes; the others lay hidden. There were no pistols in the whole party; to avoid alarming the port, it would be a matter of cold steel.

The Americans made a line fast to the frigate's rigging. Short sharp fighting followed; at one point Decatur was ready to strike down one of his midshipmen when the man identified himself. The Tripolitan crew were quickly driven overboard. Consideration was given to taking the captured ship out to sea, but the pilot vetoed that idea because the channel was so tricky. The combustibles were placed on the *Philadelphia* where they would do the most damage, and the ship was soon in flames; some of the Americans barely got off in time. Despite falling debris and shots from the shore batteries, only one of the *Intrepid*'s men was even injured. When the ship crossed the Mediterranean to report to Preble's flagship, the *Constitution*, enthusiasm knew no bounds, not only in the fleet but also ashore. To the navy, Decatur became the embodiment of audacity. Preble urged immediate promotion and Decatur became a captain, which annoyed some of his seniors and contemporaries. Nelson called the feat "one of the most bold and daring acts of our age."

That autumn the *Intrepid* was called upon for a second raid in the harbor. This time neither she nor the men aboard her survived. Preble's plan had been to explode a "floating volcano" or infernal bomb in the midst of the main body of enemy vessels close to the harbor walls. The *Intrepid* was loaded with 100 barrels of gunpowder and one-hundred and fifty 13-inch and 9-inch shells, connected by a fuse to the combustibles in a room aft. The fuse was expected to burn for 15 minutes, giving time for the crew to get away before the explosion. The command went to Lieutenant Richard Somers. His second in command was Lieutenant Henry Wadsworth, for whom his sister's son, born in 1807, was named Henry Wadsworth Longfellow. There were to have been 10 others, but Midshipman Henry Israel, arriving with last minute orders from Preble, insisted on going also. Somers gave everyone a chance to withdraw but none accepted, though apparently they had no illusions about the suicidal mission. One midshipman recorded how they went over the side into the *Intrepid:* "All took their leave in the most cheerful manner with a shake of the hands, and one another, as they passed over the side to take their post in the ketch, might be heard, in their own peculiar manner, to cry out, 'Sam Jones, I leave you my blue jacket and duck trousers, stowed in my bag,' and 'Bill Cursit, you may have the tarpaulin hat, the Guernsey frock, and them petticoat trousers I got in Malta— and mind, boys, when you get home, give a good account of us.'''

Two signal guns were heard as the *Intrepid* entered the harbor, then at 9:47 P.M., before she would have had time to reach her objective, a terrific explosion rocked the whole area. No one knows just what caused that premature blast. It might have been a shot from a gunboat or a shore battery, but Commodore Preble preferred a more romantic alternative. He deduced that the *Intrepid* had been intercepted and boarded by the Tripolitans, and in contrast to the speedy surrender of the *Philadelphia* by Bainbridge, "the gallant Somers and heroes of his party determined at once to preferring death to slavery, put a match to the train leading directly to the magazine."

Somers won a lasting place in the navy's Valhalla of heroes. The first of the vessels named for him was the fast little *Somers,* in which three men would be hanged for conspiring at mutiny.

Two weeks after that second *Intrepid* episode came a change of command in the Mediterranean. Commodore Samuel Barron arrived with orders to take over from Preble. It was indeed unfortunate that the Navy Department had not departed from its rigid rotation policy to give Preble another year or two. One is reminded of Lord Fisher's later remark, "I'll be damned if I will jeopardize the safety of the country just because it's Juggins' turn to command the fleet." It was bad enough to lose Preble, but it was extra misfortune to get a Barron in his place. The Tripolitan situation soon deteriorated. Ever since 1804, teenagers and some of their elders have thrilled at the colorful exploits of Decatur, Somers, and the rest of "Preble's boys." Preble indoctrinated them thoroughly in qualities which would bring great results in 1812.

(See *Dictionary of American Naval Fighting Ships,* 1959.)

Victory

The deck of the *Victory* at the Battle of Trafalgar on October 21, 1805; Admiral Lord Nelson lies mortally wounded at the right. *(National Maritime Museum, Greenwich)*

Just as "Old Ironsides" is preseved at Boston, so Britain's *Victory* is enshrined at Portsmouth as Britain's most honored warship. Her reputation was bound up with Lord Nelson, Britain's most honored admiral. It was on her deck that Nelson was mortally wounded in winning Britain's most decisive naval victory at Trafalgar on October 21, 1805.

The *Victory* was already an aging ship at that time. Her keel had been laid at the Chatham dockyard near the mouth of the Thames in 1759, that *annus mirabilis* when it "rained victories" at Quebec and elsewhere. Her leisurely construction lasted until 1765, when she was launched. By that time the Seven Years' War was over and she swung idly at anchor for several years.

Like the *Sovereign of the Seas,* she was a three-decked "first rate" with 100 guns. The navy had only a few ships that size; they were rather slow and clumsy but because of their height they had a certain battle usefulness as flagships. The 74-gun "third rates," which could sail well and fight well, made up the bulk of the battle fleet. The *Victory*, measuring some 2164 tons, was of very solid appearance, her "tumble-home" sides curving inward as they rose above the water.

The *Victory*'s first important action came against the French in 1778 during the American Revolution. Their indecisive action at Ushant **129** arose in part from the failure of Admiral Keppel's next in command to participate properly, reflecting the political intriguing of the Sandwich administration. Several other admirals commanded the *Victory* in the Channel Fleet during the rest of the war. Among them was Admiral Kempenfelt, pioneer developer of signaling, who drowned in 1782 when the bottom dropped out of his rotten flagship, the *Royal George,* off Spithead.

Activity arrived with the outbreak of the French Revolutionary War and the Napoleonic Wars. Admiral Hood in the *Victory* led the fleet in the capture of the great French Mediterranean naval base at Toulon in 1793. The British had not taken advantage of the chance to destroy or carry off the bulk of the French fleet when young Bonaparte drove them out.

Late in 1795 Sir John Jervis (later Lord St. Vincent) took over as commander in chief in the Mediterranean, with the *Victory* as his flagship. He was a stickler on obedience and discipline, but he brought the Mediterranean fleet to a high state of efficiency. He won his title in the victory over the Spanish fleet off Cape St. Vincent in 1797. The most conspicuous action in that battle was Nelson's spectacular boarding and capturing two Spanish ships of the line. Nelson then had an autonomous command under St. Vincent with special duties off Toulon, which led into the Battle of the Nile. During all that time, St. Vincent's cabin on the *Victory* remained the center of authority until he became first Lord of Admiralty.

With the resumption of hostilities in 1803, England was faced with the possibility of invasion, as Napoleon's fleet was now greatly increased. Blockading forces were established, particularly under Cornwallis off Brest and under Nelson, now in the *Victory,* off Toulon. The navy was at the mercy of a group of selfish timber merchants who held up all supply of oak, gravely needed for repairs, until St. Vincent would relax his inspection. Nelson wrote desperate dispatches, telling how ship after ship was falling apart. A change in ministry finally yielded enough timber to patch up the ships.

By 1805 England was beginning to approach a crisis. Napoleon, who had an army poised across the Channel for an invasion of England, wanted his Mediterranean fleet under Villeneuve to come around, join the Channel fleet, and clear the way to England. The trouble was that his admirals were not of the caliber of his marshals. At Toulon, Villeneuve broke loose from Nelson, who did not know which way Villeneuve had gone. In the *Victory* Nelson gambled on the likelihood of the West Indies, and chased the French there and then back. Villeneuve took refuge in Cadiz and joined forces with his Spanish allies. Nelson, after a brief final stop in England, went south to meet him. He arrived off Cadiz on September 28, where "a sort of general joy was the consequence of his arrival." Nelson enjoyed an unusually warm and intimate association with his well-picked group of captains, whom he termed "a band of brothers." The *Victory* was the scene of warm social reunion, and this was one of the happiest times in Nelson's life.

Nelson took advantage of the situation to explain his tactical plans for the coming action. Throughout the eighteenth century the standard fleet battle had been a very stereotyped affair, with the two fleets sailing parallel to each other and each ship picking out an opponent. Admiral Rodney had abandoned that tradition at the Battle of the Saints in the West Indies in 1782, when he broke the enemy line by sailing through it and wrecking the French fleet that had recently forced the British surrender at Yorktown.

Nelson, with 27 ships of the line to the Franco-Spanish 31, planned a double breaking of the line which would isolate the leading enemy ships. He would lead one division in the *Victory* while Admiral Collingwood would lead the other in a parallel approach in the three-decker *Royal Sovereign*. The enemy had straggled out of Cadiz in a single crescent-shaped line. Nelson planned to hit it around the twelfth ship, which would bring him close to Villeneuve's flagship, the *Bucentaure*. The Spanish admiral, Gravina, would be nearer the rear. Nelson talked this plan over with his captains, so that each would know what was expected of him.

On the morning of October 21, 1805, Nelson put his plan into operation at Trafalgar with only a lazy one- or two-knot breeze—before the days of steam, sailing vessels were at the mercy of the wind's whims. Nelson had the signal run up on the *Victory*'s flags: "England expects every man to do his duty."

The action started around noon, with Collingwood's ships first in contact with the enemy, Nelson's coming into action later. The danger in the breaking-the-line approach was that the British attackers were exposed to the enemy's broadsides to which they could not respond. With the lack of a strong breeze, they suffered badly during this slow approach. The *Victory*, in the lead, took heavy punishment—one cannon ball killed eight marines drawn up on the poop; another just missed Nelson and smashed his secretary, while more than 50 were killed elsewhere in the ship. Finally, followed by the three-decker *Téméraire* (of which Turner later painted a celebrated painting), Nelson's division broke the line and for three hours was engaged in a terrific melee with ships appearing and disappearing in the heavy smoke. The *Victory* during most of that time remained entangled with the French *Redoubtable*, which put up a very stubborn and costly fight. Out of her crew of less than 600 men, 491 were killed and 81 wounded.

But the *Redoubtable* had her revenge—one of her sharpshooters mortally wounded Nelson. Over the objections of his officers, he had gone into action wearing his four big decorations which, of course, as he knew, marked him out as a target. The *Redoubtable* was so close that the marksmen in her fighting tops were almost overhead. One of them hit Nelson, the ball going down through his body. "They have done for me at last, Hardy," he exclaimed, "my back-bone is shot through." He was carried below to the bloody shambles of the cockpit, but lived on in agony for three hours. At one crashing broadside, he was heard to exclaim, "Oh, *Victory, Victory*, nor you distract my poor brain!" His flag captain, Hardy, came down and reported that 14 or 15 of the enemy ships had surrendered. Nelson exclaimed, "That is well, but I had bargained for twenty." The flagship's log finally recorded: "Partial victory, firing continued until 4:30 when victory having been reported to the Rt. Hon. Lord Viscount Nelson, K.B. and Commander-in-Chief, he died of his wounds."

All the ships were in a sorry state, many with masts shot away, leaks in their hulls, and chaos inside. The British suffered some 450 killed and 1240 wounded. The enemy had some 4700 killed and 2000 wounded, plus losing some 20,000 prisoners. Heavy as that toll was, it was much lower than in Waterloo and the other big land battles. Napoleon's sea forces had received such a drubbing that they no longer constituted a full-dress threat. There would still be plenty for the smaller cruisers to do in connection with commerce. With the danger of invasion apparently over, Britain's long mastery of the seas would begin.

It took two weeks (October 21–November 4) for the news to reach England. Collingwood's dispatches were brought up by a lieutenant in a naval cutter. When he delivered them to the Secretary of the Admiralty, his words reflected the mixed emotions of the nation: "Sir, we have won a great victory, but we have lost Lord Nelson." The battered *Victory*, after temporary repairs at Gibraltar, brought Nelson's body home, preserved in a cask of spirits. After reaching the mouth of the Thames, he was carried up the river by boat to London. There on December 9 a tremendous parade with 10,000 regular troops, plus dignitaries of every sort, and a group of four dozen seamen from the *Victory*, escorted the body to St. Paul's Cathedral. Later a statue of Nelson was set up atop a high column in the heart of London, ever since known as Trafalgar Square.

The rest of the *Victory*'s career was relatively uneventful. She remained in commission, and there is mention of her as head of an escort for 1000 ships from the Baltic. In 1824 she was assigned to harbor services and ultimately wound up at Portsmouth, a shrine for thou-

the pumps. A year later, the *Victory* was berthed in permanent quarters
in a drydock at Portsmouth.

(See A. R. Bugler, *H.M.S. Victory: Building, Restoration, and Repair,*
1966.)

Chesapeake

The *Chesapeake,*
captured by H.M.S.
Shannon, with the
British flag above the
American.
*(Naval Historical
Center)*

The 36-gun frigate *Chesapeake* had truly the extremely hard luck story
of the early American navy. She was the loser in two humiliating
encounters with British frigates—the *Leopard* in 1807 and the *Shannon*
in 1813—and in each case she was in a serious condition of unpreparedness for action.

She was built at Norfolk and launched on June 20, 1799. She measured 1244 tons, about the same as the 1278-ton *Constellation,* and had a
normal crew of 340. Except for one uneventful cruise as flagship in the
Mediterranean, she did little of note until 1807.

Then the *Chesapeake* ran afoul of the difficult problem of "impress-
ment." Until World War I, the British never had formal conscription for
either the army or navy, but for many years the navy had been authorized to impress or seize men for service aboard the warships. Crews of
incoming merchantmen and young men in the taverns or brothels of the
seaports were in constant danger of such seizure. The British never

claimed the right to impress Americans or other foreigners, but they did claim the right to recover alleged deserters from their service. And they were sometimes right. The difficulty at this particular period was that both the Royal Navy and the American merchant marine were expanding rapidly and were in need of good topmast hands. Service on the American merchantmen was much pleasanter and more profitable than in a British ship, so many Britishers did jump ship and, in the absence of foolproof identification cards, it was hard to know the truth.

The British cruisers had been rather arrogantly exercising the right of search and, if a boarding lieutenant claimed that a sailor was a British deserter, off he went. The British minister at Washington made a formal claim that three of the *Chesapeake*'s crew were British deserters; the Americans countered that the three men had previously been impressed from American vessels.

The *Chesapeake* was setting out to take over as flagship of the Mediterranean station under Commodore James Barron, the sorriest of the American captains, even worse than his rather ineffectual brother Samuel. Stores for a whole year's cruise were set aboard at Washington and there were several minor mischances as she headed down the bay. At Hampton Roads she arrived with her decks cluttered with everything under the sun and with a crew far below normal quality.

On Monday, June 22, 1807, the *Chesapeake* headed out to sea. At about 3:30 P.M., the British cruiser *Leopard,* with 44 guns to the *Chesapeake*'s 36, started out after her, about two miles offshore. The *Leopard* sent a boat over, with a lieutenant bearing the admiral's search order. Barron denied having any deserters and refused to muster the crew.

Then the voice of the *Leopard*'s captain came over the water: "Captain Barron, you must be aware of the necessity I am under of complying with orders." The *Leopard* soon opened fire—altogether five or six broadsides crashed into the American frigate at close range. The guns of the *Chesapeake* were in such disarray that there was no chance to return a single shot until an officer brought a hot coal. Barron was wounded in the leg, three men were killed, and several men were wounded. (Barron showed his quality by viciously blaming his officers.) He ordered the colors to be lowered in surrender; the boarding lieutenant refused to accept the surrender but took off four prisoners, one of whom was hanged. A wave of indignation swept up and down the coast. Barron was removed from command, and a court-martial later suspended him from service for five years. Stephen Decatur replaced him in command of the *Chesapeake;* because of this Barron resented Decatur and years later killed Decatur in a duel.

The *Chesapeake*'s other ordeal came six years later up on the New England coast. She was fitting out at Boston, with new officers, new crew, and a general need of shakedown. Plans had been made for her to go north to raid British shipping in Canadian waters. Her new commander, James Lawrence, fresh from an encounter in which his *Hornet* had crushed the *Peacock* in 15 minutes, had hoped for a better command than the *Chesapeake*.

His ego at a high point, Lawrence was "sucked in" to a challenge which he should not have accepted. Off Boston were two British frigates, one of them the *Shannon*, long regarded as the best gunnery ship in the Royal Navy. Her captain, Philip Bowes Vere Broke, had for seven years been tireless in whipping his ship into superlative gunnery ability. Broke managed to lure Lawrence into a fight by means of a formal challenge. Those were the days when naval officers, especially in the new American navy, took their "honor" very seriously and duels were common. But it was one thing to risk one's own life in a duel and quite another to risk one of the nation's few frigates, needed for an important mission.

Although the *Chesapeake* was in a state of unreadiness and had a green crew and officers who scarcely knew each other, Lawrence took on the best prepared frigate in the Royal Navy off Cape Ann just north of Boston. In 15 minutes all was over and the *Chesapeake* was a captive of the Royal Navy. A broadside from the *Shannon* had swept the American quarterdeck, killing or wounding most of the officers. Captain Broke suffered a serious scalp wound when he led a force of British invaders aboard the *Chesapeake* as the ships swung together. Down below, the mortally wounded Lawrence murmured, "Don't give up the ship," words that became "immortal" in the United States Navy. A later report said that he added, "Blow her up instead." Of course, they did give up the ship, very quickly. Lawrence became a hero. In New Jersey, when a plan was made in 1813 to start a boys' school in the long-established town of Maidenhead, the residents persuaded the legislature to name the town Lawrenceville for the gallant Lawrence.

The British were delighted to learn that one of their frigates could handle an American of similar size. The *Chesapeake* was taken into Halifax with the British flag above the American. Broke, severely wounded, was knighted; he did not go to sea again. The H.M.S. *Chesapeake* was sold out of the British service in 1819.

(See C. B. Cross, *The Chesapeake: A Biography of a Ship,* 1968.)

Chasseur

When Thomas Boyle took command of the Baltimore privateer *Chasseur* late in 1814, double superlatives were involved. An expert navigator, fearless and aggressive in action, Boyle was often rated as the best of the War of 1812 privateersmen, while the Baltimore clipper *Chasseur* was rated as the fastest and most successful of the 1812 privateers. Baltimore, morever, had the largest number of privateers. The city was in a unique position, some 185 miles up Chesapeake Bay, and consequently very vulnerable to the blockade which the British began to impose early in the war. The answer to that was the "Baltimore clipper," which Baltimore had already begun to develop on Jamaican or Bermudan lines. These fast little vessels had nothing in common with the later much larger China and California clippers, except that all were streamlined to produce speed even though it severely reduced cargo capacity.

The *Chasseur* was built at the Kemp yard in Baltimore and measured 356 tons, 115 feet in length and 26 feet in beam, quite large for a Baltimore clipper. Her war career got off to a slow start. She was launched on December 12, 1813, and began as a "letter of marque" rather than as a privateer proper. This meant that she cleared for a foreign port with a regular commercial cargo, but had a government license, also called letter of marque, authorizing her to capture any enemy vessels which she might encounter on her voyage. Her first captain, Pearl Durkee, was not a man of spirit and never got beyond Annapolis, where nearly three dozen vessels were tied up by the blockade. He returned to Baltimore until late September, then was blockaded again in Annapolis, where his crew mutinied at his inaction.

The *Chasseur* was sold at auction to a new syndicate of 17 men who decided to use her as a privateer proper, with her crew increased from 52 to 148. The command went to Captain William Wade, who had served as second officer under Boyle. Wade had a moderately successful cruise, capturing 11 vessels in the next six months. On June 13, 1814, the ship was sold again at Baltimore, with delivery at New York.

At last came the coming together of superlative ship and superlative captain when Thomas Boyle became the third commander of the *Chasseur*. He had already made a high reputation in another Baltimore clipper, the 187-ton *Comet,* built at Baltimore in 1810, which he commanded for two years, from the beginning of the war in August 1812 until the autumn of 1814. During that time he took 35 prizes; in the *Chassuer* he would take 25 in seven months. She sailed from New York on July 24, since the Chesapeake blockade was so tight that the Baltimore privateers were having to use other ports.

Boyle's main purpose was to carry the war into enemy waters, especially around Britain, as John Paul Jones and Gustavus Conyngham had done in the Revolution. This could serve several useful purposes: the American waters were swarming with British warships and the enemy could be made to tire of the war. British warships, moreover, could be withdrawn from other duties to protect local commerce, even access to the Irish Sea. With her speed, the *Chasseur* could take long chances with enemy cruisers, and she could easily keep changing her rig to avoid identification.

Boyle gained an international reputation for his impudent psychological warfare when he sarcastically parodied the blockade pronouncement of British Admiral Warren, who had declared the whole American coast under blockade. In international law a vessel cannot be properly seized for violating a blockade unless the blockade is so tight that a vessel runs a very real risk in trying to evade it. The Americans claimed that Admiral Warren did not have enough warships to warrant the whole Atlantic coast under blockade. Boyle consequently drew up his own proclamation of the British Isles under blockade by the *Chasseur*. He sent it by one of his released ships requesting that it be posted at Lloyd's in London:

BY THOMAS BOYLE, ESQUIRE

Commander of the Private Armed Brig Chasseur

Whereas it has been customary with the admirals of Great Britain commanding small forces on the coast of the United States, particularly with Sir John Borlase Warren and Sir Alexander Cochrane, to declare the coast of the said United States in a state of strict and rigorous blockade, without possessing the power to justify such a declaration, or stationing an adequate force to command such a blockade.

I, therefore by the power and authority in me vested (possessing sufficient force) declare all the ports, harbors, bays, creeks, rivers, inlets, outlets, and sea coasts of the United Kingdom of Great Britain and Ireland in a state of strict and rigorous blockade, and I do further declare that I consider the forces under my command adequate to maintain strictly, rigorously and effectively the said blockade.

And, I do hereby require the respective officers, whether captains or commanding officers, under my command, employed at or to be employed on the coast of England, Ireland and Scotland, to pay strict attention to this my proclamation.

And I hereby caution and forbid the ships of all and every nation, in amity and peace with the United States, from entering or attempting to enter or from coming or attempting to come out of any of the said ports, bays, creeks, rivers, inlets, islands or sea coasts, on or under any pretence whatever; and that no person may plead ignorance of this my proclamation, I have ordered the same to be made public in England.

Given under my hand on board the *Chasseur,*

Thomas Boyle

By Command of the Commanding Officer,

J. B. Stansbury,
Secretary

Boyle was immediately immersed in action. The next day, August 23, 1814, he captured two valuable prizes and then sent in a small sloop as a cartel to spread the news of his proclamation. Later that day came a shooting affray with a British frigate and then other battles, one after another. After two months out, the *Chasseur* had cargo in her hold worth $100,000, and also 48 prisoners. At New York, Boyle arranged to have repairs made.

On December 24, 1814, Boyle put to sea from New York on his second voyage. Although that same day, over in Ghent, commissioners had drawn up a treaty of peace between the United States and Britain, there would be a month of grace, in which prizes in the Caribbean would be lawful.

His final encounter was one of the hardest fought, for he had "caught a tiger." Off the coast of Cuba he began pursuit of a topsail schooner which looked harmless with only a few sailors on deck. Suddenly, when they were quite close, large numbers of men rose from behind the schooner's bulwarks; two gun ports were opened up and a terrific broadside which staggered the *Chasseur* was let loose. Instead of an innocent coaster, the vessel was an enemy cruiser. The Americans were quick to respond and the fight was hot and bloody, each vessel punishing the other heavily. Just as the *Chasseur*'s men stood by to board, the enemy flag came down. She was the schooner H.M.S. *St. Lawrence,* formerly the privateer *Atlas* of Philadelphia, a Chesapeake-built vessel herself. The British had lost six killed and 17 wounded; the *Chasseur* lost five killed and eight wounded.

The interesting thing about the encounter was that it was just what a privateer was supposed to avoid. Naval vessels were bound to fight an enemy, but the privateer was expected to get away without fighting— there was no percentage in a battle. And so, in his lengthy report to the owners' agent, Boyle closed with a virtual apology:

> I should not willingly perhaps have sought a contest with a king's vessel knowing it was not our object, but my expectations were at first a valuable vessel and a valuable cargo. When I found myself deceived, the honor of the flag left with me was not to be disgraced by flight.

Boyle had learned that the war was over, and when he reached Baltimore the *Chasseur* was received with cheers. In 1816 he made a commercial voyage to China in the *Chasseur* and made a record run back from Canton. He continued in the merchant service and is said to have beaten off a pirate attack on the brig *Panopea* in 1824 and to have died at sea a year later. His privateering prizes were reputed to have been worth more than $1,000,000.

(See J. P. Cranwell, *Crane, Men of Marque,* 1940.)

III

STEAM CHALLENGES SAIL

(1807–1860)

Clermont

New Orleans

Demologos
(Fulton)

Medusa

Cleopatra's Barge

James Monroe

Elizabeth

Beagle

Pilgrim and Alert

Sirius

Great Western

Britannia

Acushnet

Charles W. Morgan

Mississippi

Somers

Princeton

Michigan
(Wolverine)

Great Britain

Sea Witch

California

Flying Cloud

Challenge

America

Birkenhead

Great Republic

Red Jacket

Arctic

Andrew Jackson

Central America

Great Eastern

III

STEAM CHALLENGES SAIL
(1807–1860)

The year 1807 brought the first major breakthrough in marine technology in more than two centuries with the successful operation of *The North River Steamboat of Clermont,* better known simply as the *Clermont.* Less than 40 years later came the first transatlantic passages by steam power alone—the *Sirius* and the *Great Western* (1838); the first large steam vessel to be propeller-driven—the *Princeton* (1843); and the first screw-propelled, iron-hulled steamer—the *Great Britain* (1843).

The advocates of sail, however, responded to the challenge of steam with vigor. Indeed, the first vessel to ply the North Atlantic on regular schedule was the sailing packet *James Monroe* (1818) of the famed Black Ball Line. Not until the 1850s would steam packets take the lead in North Atlantic passenger service. With the appearance of the clipper ship at mid-century, the sailing vessel reached a high point in its development. Donald McKay's *Flying Cloud* was setting records for the California run, which other fast clippers plied the distant seas to Asia. Meanwhile, the sailing vessel continued to dominate such important maritime activities as exploration and whaling. And when the merchant princes of New England and New York took to the seas for pleasure, they turned to sailing yachts like *Cleopatra's Barge* (1817) and the famed *America* (1851). At mid-century, then, sail managed to stave off the threat of steam in most aspects of maritime activity.

Clermont

The steamboat *Clermont,* on the Hudson River. *(Mariners Museum)*

Successful steam navigation dates from the voyage of Robert Fulton's *Clermont* (dubbed "Fulton's Folly" by skeptics) up the Hudson from New York to Albany and back in August 1807. To be sure, earlier steamboats of sorts had run briefly but did not continue in operation; two decades earlier, for instance, "Poor John Fitch" built steamers that plied the Delaware River between Philadelphia and Trenton, but lacking financial backing, he quit shipbuilding and went west. Fulton did not actually invent the steamboat, but he brought together the ideas of others and promoted them with marked success.

Fulton, a Pennsylvanian, started as a portrait painter and went to England to study under the artist Benjamin West. Fulton made some influential friends, including James Watt, who did most to develop the steam engine. Fulton's interest shifted to engineering and for a while he engaged in canal construction. Later, he went to France, where he developed a close and lasting contact with the wealthy and influential Robert R. Livingston, United States minister to France. Livingston fancied himself as an inventor in steam; Fulton took his money but did not take his ideas. With the war between Britain and Napoleon at its peak, Fulton tried to sell the French his submarine with torpedoes. He also developed a steamboat which might tow Napoleon's flatboats over to England, but the demonstration failed when the weak hull parted and dropped the engine into the Seine.

In 1806 Fulton returned to New York determined to build a steamboat, leaving an order for the machinery with the English firm of Boulton & Watt. The engine was brought over in a sailing vessel. In the meantime, early in 1807, Fulton had Charles Browne, one of the crack East River shipbuilders, build a hull for the new vessel. It was 140 feet long with a 16-foot beam and very shallow draft. Then the engines from England were inserted—with a 24-inch cylinder and 4-foot stroke of piston. She burned pine wood for fuel. The side wheels were 15 feet in diameter. When she was enrolled at the New York custom house, she was called *The North River Steamboat of Clermont*. North River was the local name for the Hudson and Clermont was Livingston's estate up the river.

Amidst widespread skepticism and jesting, the *Clermont* set out on her momentous voyage on the morning of August 17. With wind and tide against her, she moved right along up the river. As a New Yorker described it shortly afterward:

> She had a most terrific appearance from other vessels which were navigating the river when she was making the passage. . . . They saw with astonishment that it was rapidly coming towards them and when it came so near that the noise of the machinery and paddles were heard, the crews—if what was said in the newspapers of the time be true—in some instances shrunk beneath the decks from the terrific sight. . . .

Even after the initial shock was over, there would be trouble from the crews of the sloops who saw the potential threat to their business, and time and again they rammed the steamer, hoping to disable her.

Fulton himself described the voyage on his return:

> I left New York Monday at 1 o'clock and arrived at Clermont, the country seat of Chancellor Livingston at 1 o'clock on Tuesday—time, 24 hours; distance, one hundred and ten miles. On Wednesday I departed from the Chancellor's at 8 o'clock in the morning and arrived at Albany, at 5 o'clock in the afternoon—distance, 40 miles; time, 8 hours. The sum is one hundred and fifty miles in thirty two hours, equal to nearly five miles an hour. . . . Throughout my whole way, both going and returning, the wind was ahead—no advantage could be derived from my sails—the whole has, therefore, been performed by the power of steam alone.

Two weeks later the *Clermont* was advertised to sail again on a regular schedule, leaving New York every Saturday afternoon, and Albany every Wednesday morning. The fare was $2.50 to West Point, $3.50 to Poughkeepsie, and $7.00 to Albany. "Passengers will breakfast before they come aboard. Dinner will be served up exactly at 1 o'clock; tea, with meats, which is also supper at 8 o'clock in the evening. . . . No one has a claim on the steward for victuals at any other time. . . . Every passenger paying full price is allowed 60 pounds of baggage. . . . Servants, who pay full price, are entitled to a berth."

The *Clermont* continued to give passenger service until July 1814, when she was retired; the new steamer *Richmond* took her place. Three other steamers, the *Car of Neptune, Paragon,* and *Firefly,* had also been added to the service. Chancellor Livingston's political influence had secured a series of charters which gave him and Fulton a tight monopoly of all service in the State of New York. That was why Colonel John Stevens of Hoboken, whose *Phoenix* was completed just after the *Clermont,* had to shift her down to the Delaware. Fulton died early in 1815, soon after his *Demologos* (subsequently known as the *Fulton*), the first of all steam warships, was completed, just too late for the War of 1812 blockade. With the end of the blockade, the Livingston-Fulton steamers started to move out into Long Island Sound. The monopoly lasted until 1824, when Chief Justice John Marshall of the United States Supreme Court, in the case of *Gibbons* v. *Ogden,* declared it abolished, with freedom for everyone to operate steamers.

(See J. T. Flexner, *Steamboats Come True,* 1944.)

New Orleans

It was on the Mississippi and its tributaries that steam navigation would be most appreciated and utilized. In the harbor services of ferries and tugs, steam would be useful in relieving dependence on winds and tides, but elsewhere on the seven seas its advantages were less obvious. Sloops could still operate on the Hudson and square-riggers on the high seas—and winds were free. In fact, it was almost 1900 before steam tonnage caught up with sail tonnage in the American merchant marine.

But the swift flow of the Mississippi made up-river traffic a serious problem. Rafts could bring down the commodities of the interior, but it was simplest to break them up at New Orleans. For up-river cargoes, keel boats could be laboriously poled upstream against the current, but it was backbreaking work.

The pioneer steamboat men back at New York were quick to realize a commercial advantage. The central figure was Nicholas J. Roosevelt, a competent mechanic who had operated a machine shop in New Jersey. He was closely associated with Livingston, Fulton, and Colonel Stevens in their early experimenting. They devised plans for a steamboat suitable for the western waters, to be built at Pittsburgh under the immediate direction of Roosevelt.

The resultant *New Orleans,* as she was named, was built on the banks of the Monongahela River in 1811 at a cost of about $38,000. She was 116 feet in length and 20 feet in beam, and was fitted with a low-pressure engine and side wheels. She had two cabins with berths and two masts with sails.

In September 1811, after a short trial spin, she was ready for her momentous run down river to New Orleans. On board was a captain, an engineer, a pilot, six hands, two women servants, a waiter, a cook, and a huge Newfoundland dog. Roosevelt and his spirited wife, daughter of Benjamin Latrobe from Baltimore, assistant designer of the United States Capitol, were the only passengers; their friends were alarmed because she was in an advanced state of pregnancy. She had accompanied him two years earlier when he had explored the river in a flatboat.

Enthusiastic crowds saw them off at Pittsburgh and greeted them at Cincinnati, but they implied that, while the progress down river was good, they doubted if it would be possible to make headway up river against the current. At Louisville they entertained some of their hosts at dinner aboard ship. In the midst of the meal they felt the steamer in motion and found that she was headed up the river at top speed. This demonstration of the most important capability of the boat was impressive and convincing.

Progressing up river, they found that the water was too low to clear the local falls, so they had to wait; during this time Mrs. Roosevelt became a mother but insisted on staying with the boat. The weather became more and more murky. At last it was reported that there would be but five inches beneath the keel to clear the shallowest place in the falls. They took the scary chance and made it clear. Unfortunately, they encountered a rare disturbance—the comet of 1811 coincided with a major earthquake.

Some of the Indians were inclined to blame the steamer for the phenomenon. The river was filled with toppled trees and debris; on one occasion they tied up to an island for the night; they heard a lot of scratching and bumping alongside the steamer and next morning the island had disappeared. They arrived safely at Natchez and the rest of the trip was uneventful; they reached New Orleans on January 12, 1812.

The *New Orleans* was quickly placed in service from New Orleans to Natchez, for both passengers and cargo—the all-important up-river service that had been so difficult in the presteam era. She lasted two years; in July 1814 she ran onto a stump at low water, sprang a leak, and sank. A few months earlier, the Fulton-Livingston yard at Pittsburgh turned out a larger steamer, the *Vesuvius*, and others were to follow. The most spectacular addition to the river fleet was the *Washington*, a two-decked steamer with high-pressure boilers, built under the direction of Captain Henry M. Shreve, a pioneer developer of river navigation. The need for steam navigation led to a constant increase of the river boats, particularly after the termination of the Livingston-Fulton monopoly.

(See J. H. Morrison, *History of American Steam Navigation*, 1903.)

Demologos
(Fulton)

The *Demologos*, the first steam warship. *(Naval Historical Center)*

Seven years after his *Clermont* chugged up the Hudson to begin steam navigation, Robert Fulton developed the first steam warship, during the War of 1812. By 1813 the British were blockading the coast and one of their strongest squadrons was patrolling the Sandy Hook entrance to New York harbor. One evening late in 1813, Fulton invited a group of prominent New York civilian, military, and naval leaders to his home and proposed a floating battery to break the British blockade.

The vessel which he proposed was specifically intended for local work against the Sandy Hook squadron at a time when it might be immobilized by lack of wind—it was not intended for deep-sea cruising. It had a double hull—a sort of catamaran type—with the paddle wheel protected between the two hulls. The hulls were protected by five feet of oak—a virtually impenetrable armor, guarding the machinery and the heavy battery of twenty 32-pounder guns.

Fulton's guests were enthusiastic about the project, and sent one of the commodores to Washington to present it to the government. In contrast to the usual official conservatism, the commodore found approval by everyone: the President, the naval authorities, and the naval affairs committees of Senate and House. Congress quickly authorized the vessel; the one drawback was that there was not enough money in the Treasury to keep the work going quickly.

Fulton called her the *Demologos,* or voice of the people; the navy later named her *Fulton,* and as other *Fultons* came along, she became known as *Fulton the First.* The hulls were built in the crack East River yards, then towed across the Hudson to receive boilers and machinery from the ironworks. The *Demologos* was launched at the yard of Adam and Noah Brown in October 1814 and then taken to Fulton's own plant. In the meantime, the crews of the blockading squadron were worrying about the news that had come via England about the new ship. It was rumored that she had steam-operated knives along her gunwales to cut boarders to pieces, and hoses that could spray boiling water.

Had there been funds on hand to get the *Demologos* finished that year, there might have been a Battle of Sandy Hook that would have put the Battle of Hampton Roads in the shade. As it was, she was not completed until the spring of 1815, by which time the war was over and Robert Fulton was dead. She made a few runs around the harbor and bay, and then was laid up at the Brooklyn Navy Yard as a sort of station ship. There, in 1829, she was ripped apart by an explosion in which a considerable number of people were killed or injured.

The Navy did, however, send a smaller steam vessel, the *Sea Gull,* into action. During the 1820s an armed river steamer was used by Commodore David Porter to chase the bold West Indian pirates. A more substantial steamer, the *Karteria,* was used by the Greek navy, under British command, in the revolution against Turkey.

(See F. M. Bennett, *The Steam Navy of the United States,* 1896.)

Medusa

"Raft of the Medusa." (Painting by Jean Louis André Théodore Géricault)

The loss of the *Medusa* was called by a noted author one of the most horrible shipwrecks in nautical history. A 44-gun French frigate, she sailed in 1816 to take over the colony of Senegal in West Africa. Her loss was an amazing instance of callous abandonment of command responsibility by her captain and the governor-designate, both of whom escaped in safety while more than 100 men died during 17 nightmare days and nights aboard a makeshift raft.

The colony of Senegal at the western tip of Africa was restored by Britain to the French at the Congress of Vienna in 1814. The *Medusa* and three smaller naval vessels sailed from Rochefort for Cape Verde on June 17, 1816. Part of the blame for the ensuing tragedy should fall on the restored Bourbon king who appointed a worthless favorite to the command. The Vicomte de Chaumarays had fled to England where he remained during most of the Napoleonic period. Arrogant and haughty, he was an incompetent leader with only scant seagoing experience. He was much more interested in his mistress, whom he brought along, than in the navigation of the ship. Little more worthy was Colonel Julien Schmaltz, another ex-émigré and governor-designate of Senegal.

The rest of the 400 aboard the *Medusa* were a mixed lot. The junior officers of the frigate were not consulted by Chaumarays and played **149** almost no part in the subsequent trouble; only one midshipman sought to uphold the honor of the French navy. There were some civilians, including a civil servant and a naturalist. The most numerous group consisted of 250 black soldiers under French officers.

The immediate cause of the trouble was Richefort, a civilian member of the Cape Verde Philosophical Society, who claimed knowledge of the coast and flattered Captain Chaumarays into abdicating to him the entire navigation of the ship, to the complete neglect of the regular junior officers. The consequent course of the ship was erratic—she was more than 100 miles off course before reaching Madeira. Those who knew the coast became apprehensive when Richefort failed to clear the Arguin bank, a well-known hazard which protruded far out from the coast.

On July 2 he piled the frigate up on the Arguin bank. For the moment, the situation was not serious. With good ship-handling the *Medusa* could have been gotten off, but the governor-designate refused to have any of the flour cargo thrown overboard, and the captain vetoed the other obvious step of jettisoning some of the heavy guns and ammunition. Soon it was too late; the wind came up and the dislocated rudder smashed the stern. At the time, the ship was 50 or 60 miles off the coast and about 300 miles north of Senegal. There were enough boats to have taken everyone off in a few trips. But two of the boats were preempted, one for the captain and his mistress and the other for the governor and his family. A disorderly scramble quickly filled the remaining boats. It was decided to carry off the rest of those aboard on a big raft, which was hastily put together. The commanders solemnly agreed that the boats would tow the raft to shore. Shamefully, the boats soon dropped their tow lines, made for shore themselves, and left the raft to do what it could.

Without any means of propulsion, the raft could simply drift. It had 147 aboard, of whom only 15 survived. The poor wretches were jammed tightly aboard, many of them knee-deep in water and some were washed overboard. The command devolved upon Midshipman Coudin, who, despite a serious leg injury, did what he could to give some guidance in that desperate situation. Aside from the perils of the sea, bitter fighting broke out. A number of mutinous black soldiers wanted to kill the officers and some of the leaders. In the bloody fighting that followed, both sides threw opponents overboard. A woman who had been a camp-follower of the French army was thrown overboard with her husband three times—twice they were pulled back aboard, but not the third time.

On top of all these ordeals came hunger and thirst; the very meager supplies dwindled away, and then came the horror of cannibalism. Day after day the number diminished, the survivors existing in a daze.

Finally, on the seventeenth day, the 15 exhausted survivors, including Midshipman Coudin, were rescued by the naval brig *Argus* and carried into St. Louis, the Senegal capital.

One other inexcusable sequel to the wreck occurred. Seventeen of the original complement had stayed aboard the *Medusa*. Not until they had been 52 days on the abandoned frigate did the governor remember that some specie was aboard. He sent a schooner out, which found only three survivors of the 17; two of the survivors died soon after reaching Senegal, and the third was assassinated just as he was leaving for France.

The captain and the governor were recalled in disgrace; many felt that they had escaped too easily. Two of the raft's survivors, the surgeon and a scientist, each wrote a detailed play-by-play account of the tragedy, which thoroughly shocked the French people. Even more widespread and longer lasting was the effect of *The Raft of the Medusa*, a grimly realistic painting by Géricault, which hangs in the Louvre.

(See L. Eitner, *Géricault's Raft of the Medusa*, 1972.)

Cleopatra's Barge

The brig *Cleopatra's Barge*, built in 1817. *(Peabody Museum, Salem)*

American yachting began in the grand manner when George Crowninshield, Jr., a short, stocky bachelor, in 1816 decided that he had had enough of the family countinghouse and that it was time to have some fun in a boat of his own. He was the eldest of the five sons of George Crowninshield and his Derby wife, a joining of the two families that stood at the head of Salem's remarkable maritime activity. He and his brothers had all commanded big Salem ships around the Cape of Good Hope, and George had later handled the business end of the family activity. One of his brothers was Secretary of the Navy, a post declined by another brother, who had sat in Congress, and on a trip had brought the first elephant to the states from India. George had shown a good public spirit; after severe storms he went out in his sloop to aid vessels in distress, and he had gone up to Halifax in 1813 to bring back the body of Captain Lawrence of the *Chesapeake.*

After his father died, Crowninshield closed up the family business. He began talking of acquiring a yacht, a vessel that was virtually unknown in Salem. He went to the Becket shipyard and said that he wanted a fast vessel and hang the expense. The resultant *Cleopatra's Barge* was an hermaphrodite brig of moderate size, square-rigged on the foremast and fore-and-aft on the main. In finishing her off and furnishing her, Crowninshield did things in lavish style even to a big four-poster bed with a canopy.

Cleopatra's Barge sailed on March 30, 1817, under the command of a Crowninshield nephew. The ship's company included a crony, a philosopher, two mates, nine foremast hands, a cook, a steward, a steward's mate, three boys, and the cat Pompey. Included also were ample stores and 300 letters of introduction.

Stopping a couple of weeks at both the Azores and Madeira en route to the Mediterranean, they raced the frigate *United States* off the Spanish coast, then, in the Mediterranean, commenced a round of social activity which Crowninshield enjoyed thoroughly. His letters of introduction brought invitations which he repaid with enthusiastic hospitality. His young nephew and captain did not share his enthusiasm:

> They began to crowd on board at daybreak and continue to press upon us till night. They must see the saloon, examine the buffet . . . take some wine . . . and what with seasickness among the ladies, the strong and offensive odors of friars, beggars and garlic, the company below is compelled to undergo a regular inquisition.

Rumors that Crowninshield planned to spirit Napoleon away from St. Helena caused the Bourbons to regard him with suspicion and on one occasion to have a frigate follow him for a while. He did, however, visit Elba and came home with some Napoleonic souvenirs. He returned to Salem in October 1817, after an absence of nearly seven months. He planned another cruise but died of a heart attack in November. The yacht, which had cost some $50,000, was sold at auction for $15,400. She soon fell into the appreciative hands of Hawaii's playboy king, Kamehameha II, but in 1824 was wrecked on a reef. The Peabody Museum at Salem contains a well-executed reproduction of her cabin.

(See B. Crowninshield, *An Account of the Yacht Cleopatra's Barge, Built at Salem in 1816*, 1889.)

James Monroe

On January 5, 1818, the square-rigger *James Monroe*, sailing from New York to Liverpool, established a most important "first time" in maritime history. This "first liner," leaving on a scheduled date, marked the beginning of line service, with a coordinated group of ships sailing between two or three ports. The pattern would not only become an important service in the sailing ship era but would be continued when steam supplanted the square-riggers.

The nearest approach to such service came from the so-called "regular traders," which limited themselves to two or more ports but not on fixed dates. They usually belonged to merchants who filled the holds with their own cargoes; later, as common carriers, they took on cargo for others; these regular traders also carried passengers and mail. The difficulty in this arrangement was the uncertainty of the sailing date. If the hold was only partly filled on the announced date, the vessels might wait around for quite a while to pick up extra freight earnings, while cargo lay idle in the hold and passengers waited impatiently at the tavern.

This dilatory practice annoyed Jeremiah Thompson, who had come to New York to handle the sale of his family's Yorkshire woolens. He talked things over with two Yorkshiremen with whom he was closely associated and with a Long Island merchant and his son. All were Quakers.

Their discussions led to an advertisement in the New York papers on October 27, 1817, with figures of four little ships in a row. It said that beginning the first week in January 1818, four ships—the *Amity, Courier, Pacific,* and *James Monroe*—under "commanders of great experience and activity" would carry passengers, mail, and freight on a monthly schedule between New York and Liverpool. These sailings, moreover, would be made promptly at the specified date and hour. The most significant phrase was that they would sail "full or not full." That was what particularly distinguished them from regular traders, with their annoying habit of postponing sailing in order to get more freight revenue. There was a risk, of course, of sailing only partly full at times, but the owners had sufficiently deep pockets to absorb that risk; as it turned out, the holds were full most of the time and the line prospered from the start.

Another striking difference from the seasonal voyages made by the regular traders, which meant a spring and a fall trip only, being comfortably ensconced in port during the bitter Atlantic winter, was that the packets sailed in each of the winter months, though the captain often let the first mate take the command. This schedule was emphasized by the fact that the line started operations in the midst of a specially cold winter.

Unlike the word clipper, which designated a steamlined vessel, the word packet meant a ship sailing on schedule on a specified run and, until later at least, not a particular type of vessel. All four ships of the original service had been regular traders, and now and then in later days a clipper might be fitted into the packet schedule. This first quartet were of the conventional transatlantic type of square-rigger, around 400 tons. The *James Monroe,* the newest of the four, was built in 1817 and measured 424 tons and was 118 feet in length and 28 feet in beam. On her foretopsail was a big black circle as a distinguishing mark, which led to the name, quickly adopted, of Black Ball Line. She was built in the East River yard of Adam Brown; for the next 30 years, virtually all the transatlantic packets were built in one of the yards along that tidal strait separating Manhattan from Brooklyn. They were expensive; an ordinary freighter could be built in Maine more cheaply, but in services which called for quality, the East River yards had almost a monopoly.

One reason for special strength in the packets was the need to stand the westbound winter passages. The winds on that stormy 3000-mile run blow generally from the west. Consequently the eastbound passage to Europe was a fairly regular affair, taking about three weeks. But if that was going "downhill" the return was all "uphill," and the duration of the passage would depend upon how hard the winds were blowing. A tabulation of the arrivals at New York shows that in 1817, the year before the line started, the average length of passage was 49 days. With their harder driving, the packets between 1818 and 1832 cut that down to 37.9 days and from 1833 to 1847, to 34.3 days. The *James Monroe*'s passages, during her five years of service, averaged 37 days, with the quickest at 23 days and the longest at 54. The speediest Black Baller was the *Yorkshire,* which between 1844 and 1862 averaged 29 days, with a record westbound run of 16 days and the slowest at 58.

For the first 20 years, until steamship service started, the packets were the principal communications link between the Old World and the New World. The irony was that with the prevailing westerlies, Europe could learn relatively quickly and regularly about what was going on in America but was not particularly interested; while the Americans never knew how long those adverse winds might hold up their letters and newspapers from England. There was the case of a celebrated royal divorce trial, where the story was cut off at a very lively point and was not picked up again until the next packet arrived several weeks later. When a packet arrived, the dispatches of the owners were taken right up to New York while the ship was in quarantine, so that the owners would have a head start of several hours to take advantage of the latest business news.

The packets generally carried several socially prominent cabin passengers, at the rate of "twenty guineas, wines included." The *James Monroe,* in that first January sailing, had eight passengers—two each from New York and Philadelphia and one each from Baltimore, Boston, Quincy, and Montreal. One of the liveliest descriptions of Black Ball travel was made, somewhat later, by the Irish actor Tyrone Power.

There were sometimes steerage passengers, usually westbound, but that did not become common until the swarm of refugees from the potato famine in Ireland.

More important than passengers, from the owners' standpoint, were the cargoes, especially westbound. The packets reflected the importance of the Industrial Revolution thanks to which Liverpool and New York were expanding rapidly in a complementary rather than competitive relationship. There were broadcloths and woolens from Leeds, Bradford, and other centers in Yorkshire. Close behind came the muslins, calicoes, and sundry cotton goods from Manchester and other points in Lancashire. Also predominant were the iron and steel products from Birmingham and Sheffield. Those constituted by far the most valuable items in American commerce, and it was to bring them over that Jeremiah Thompson and his friends started the Black Ball Line.

But there was always an effort to build up a two-way commerce— vessels in ballast earned no freight money. This was a real problem at New York and New England, which had rather scant cash crops to offer as exports. On that first eastbound trip of the *James Monroe,* her meager cargo consisted of 860 barrels of flour, 200 barrels of pot and pearl ashes, 1148 barrels of apples, 14 bales of wool, and some cranberries and turpentine, in addition to 71 bales of cotton which would before long increase radically. To remedy the scanty export cargoes, Jeremiah Thompson had another inspiration. Cotton production was booming in the South, with a heavy demand from the mills of Lancashire. As the Southerners were neglecting the shipment of cotton, Thompson managed to have considerable amounts of it brought up from Charleston, Savannah, and New Orleans to be shipped as outward cargo for the packets. This led before long to the so-called "cotton triangle," with the imports from England being carried down the coast.

The Black Ball was so successful that it doubled its services to two runs monthly, while two rival lines each had a weekly sailing; by 1822 there was a sailing every week from New York to Liverpool and Liverpool to New York. In addition, there were two lines to London and two to Le Havre. New York had a virtual monopoly of the transatlantic service. Philadelphia had one rather average line, and several efforts from Boston failed because of the difficulty of return cargoes. In 1819 the Black Ball built its first new ship, the 434-ton *Albion,* from the yard of Sidney Wright, a relative of two of the owners. However, in 1822 on an eastbound passage, she was wrecked in a gale on the south coast of Ireland with heavy loss of life. On the whole, the packets had an excellent safety record.

The *James Monroe* lasted in service until 1823; then like many of the other packets she entered upon a new life. For nine years she was in the Cuban trade and then she became a whaler from 1832 to 1849, sailing

out of Hudson and then Fairhaven. With the '49 gold rush, she sailed
for San Francisco and, probably deserted by her crew, ended her days
there.

(See R. G. Albion, *Square-Riggers on Schedule*, 1938.)

Elizabeth

The merchant brig *Elizabeth* won the name "Liberian *Mayflower*" because she carried the first black settlers to West Africa in 1820 to establish a home for freedmen. This was the work of the American Colonization Society, which was formed in 1817 to help solve America's problem of what to do with freed slaves. It was centered in the middle states, had some affiliates in Virginia and Maryland, and none in the deep South. As distinct from the later abolitionists, its membership was socially very acceptable.

There had been a recent precedent for this project in Sierra Leone, adjacent to the future Liberia, which the British had established in 1787 as a refuge for its freed slaves. Its *"Mayflower"* carried down a group of blacks, many of them former American slaves, but also 50 white London prostitutes whom the British had rounded up to become mothers for the new colony. The colony population grew, as blacks released from slavers captured by the British navy settled there.

The sailing of the chartered *Elizabeth* from New York was delayed while supplies were gathered and colonists recruited. There were 30 families of colonists, totaling 88 men, women, and children, shepherded by Dr. Samuel Bacon and two other agents. An emotional farewell service was held at the Colored Methodist Church on January 3, 1820, but the *Elizabeth* was stuck in the frozen river for a month, and her naval escort for several more days. They were to rendezvous at Cape Mesurado, in the future Liberia, but the *Elizabeth* unfortunately did not wait, and moved on to Sierra Leone where the colonists met a chilly reception. Exhausted by a stormy crossing, they simply did not know how to get started. Moreover, the governor of Sierra Leone refused to allow them to disembark on the mainland, and they were forced to settle on swampy Sherbro Island. With the rainy season already started and with the inhabitants showing signs of hostility, the settlers were generally miserable.

The *Elizabeth,* merely chartered for the voyage, apparently drops from view and the maritime concern now centers on the 18-gun sloop *Cyane*, which the *Constitution* had captured from the Royal Navy, and on her first lieutenant, Matthew Calbraith Perry, the future "opener" of Japan, who would play a positive role in the beginnings of Liberia. Perry was strongly interested in the American Colonization Society's project and had deliberately asked for the post on the *Cyane*, the *Elizabeth*'s escort. Finding that she had not waited at the rendezvous, the *Cyane* proceeded to the sorry setup at Sherbro. Perry, however, moved on to Cape Mesurado and became enthusiastic about it, calling it the most eligible situation for a colony that he had seen: "The natives are pacific in their dispositions, engage but little in the slave trade and . . . express a willingness to admit our countrymen among them. . . . It is to be hoped that the advantages of the place will remove this colony thither." Perry discussed the matter with a friendly resident of Mesurado, who sent runners into the interior to sound out the kings and chiefs. When favorable replies came back, Perry sailed on to Sherbro to inform Dr. Bacon. Much of the success of Liberia may be attributed to Perry's choice of this site.

The *Cyane* had a double duty on this cruise. In addition to looking out for the Liberian settlers, she had the duty of chasing slavers along the West African coast. In the autumn of 1820 when she looked in at Sherbro, Perry was appalled at the toll disease had taken. Had Dr. Bacon moved the colony when Perry had first recommended it, many lives might have been saved. Bacon and all the whites but one had died, including the young midshipman and the sailors left there to help. The Guinea Coast was known as the "white man's grave," but here the blacks had also fallen victims. Every one of the 88 blacks had caught the fever and 23 of them had died. The survivors, without their leaders, were listless and depressed. The *Cyane* sailed for home on October 4 and arrived in New York on Christmas day.

Perry was back on the African coast in October 1821 at his own request, for despite the sorry start of the settlement he had faith in its future. He now had his first command, the schooner *Shark*, a speedy Baltimore clipper type. He found that conditions had indeed begun to look up. The colonists, having the governor's permission at last, had moved over to Freetown in Sierra Leone. Better still, Rev. Eli Ayers, who had come over in the *Shark* as United States commissioner, sailed up to Mesurado in another schooner and purchased the future site of Monrovia for an assortment of trade goods. The Sherbro survivors were moved up there, and from time to time more blacks arrived from America. In August 1821, just after Perry and the *Shark* had left for the West Indies, Rev. Jehudi Ashmun, the "Great White Father" of Liberia, arrived with 52 new settlers.

In 1824, when more than 100 free blacks arrived from Virginia, Ashmun named the colony Liberia and the capital Monrovia, after

President Monroe who was an active leader of the movement, as was
Chief Justice Marshall, who also had a town named for him. Twenty years later, Perry visited Liberia as commander in chief of the new African Squadron. He was delighted at the progress that was being made under Governor Joseph J. Roberts, a very remarkable black. Altogether, Perry could feel gratification at what had been achieved, partly through his own efforts, since he had first come out with the *Cyane,* escorting the *Elizabeth.*

(See S. E. Morison, *"Old Bruin": Commodore Matthew C. Perry,* 1967.)

Beagle

The brig H.M.S. *Beagle,* famous for its surveying voyages. *(National Maritime Museum, Greenwich)*

The Royal Navy had a long record of exploring expeditions sent out for scientific investigations and for charting distant shores. They were conducted on commissioned warships, commanded by regular officers accompanied by a group of scientists under a prominent senior. The three most important and fruitful of these expeditions, with their senior scientists, were undertaken on the *Endeavour* with Joseph Banks (1769–1771), the *Challenger* with Charles Wyville Thomson (1872–1875), and between them, perhaps the most important of all, the *Beagle* with Charles Darwin (1831–1836) which led to a revolutionary interpretation of the origin of species and to his theory of the formation of coral atolls and reefs.

Darwin, grandson of a very prominent physician and nephew of Josiah Wedgewood, who founded a great pottery, had just graduated in 1831 after several easygoing years at Christ's College, Cambridge. He had no definite future plans; he had turned from the family tradition of medicine and was toying with the idea of the Church. He was an enthusiastic amateur naturalist, interested in birds, flowers, bugs, rocks, and so on. While he was in that state of uncertainty, a message came from the Admiralty in connection with possible appointment as naturalist on the forthcoming expedition of H.M.S. *Beagle*; he was to consult her captain, Robert Fitz Roy.

Fitz Roy would be very closely linked with Darwin during the cruise. Fitz Roy was descended from one of the bastards of King Charles II by Barbara Villiers, Countess of Castlemaine; he was a grandson of the Duke of Grafton, and a cousin of the great statesman Castlereagh. Fitz Roy had attended the Royal Naval College and had already at age 23 attained a high reputation for efficiency, especially in the field of hydrography. He had already been on a surveying cruise in the *Beagle* and had succeeded to her command when her captain committed suicide.

Despite marked differences in temperament and background, the two young men immediately hit it off, and Fitz Roy offered to share his cabin with Darwin. Darwin's father opposed the cruise as a foolish idea, but said that if he could find anyone who approved of it, he would give his permission. His uncle, Josiah Wedgewood, gave his enthusiastic support, so the father withdrew his objection. Though Darwin had had no connection with the sea, he was eager to start.

The *Beagle* sailed on December 27, 1831, on a cruise that lasted nearly five years. Her orders indicated a dual purpose. The principal aim was to continue the charting of the coasts of South America, the one continent which had not yet received such hydrographic treatment. The other, a less exacting task, was to establish a more accurate fixing of longitude by carrying a chain of chronological reckonings around the world. Fitz Roy had dozens of chronometers in his cabin. The *Beagle* was a 241-ton, 10-gun brig, considerably smaller than Cook's ships; there were 74 people aboard. Darwin and Fitz Roy got along fairly well, though there were marked differences in personality—in contrast to the easygoing Darwin, Fitz Roy could be short-tempered and a bit arrogant, but their flare-ups were over quickly. Fitz Roy was interested in Darwin's naturalistic quests and Darwin soon fitted into the seagoing life. But he was violently seasick in crossing the Bay of Biscay, a malady from which he never entirely escaped.

In the pattern of their coexistence, Darwin spent considerable time ashore while routine surveying was going on. He had omnivorous interests, observing all that he could and bringing back into the ship great quantities of specimens, some of which were shipped back to England from various ports of call. The first major shore expedition, in April 1832, was from Rio de Janeiro to a coffee plantation 100 miles inland, through the luxurious growth of the rainforest. Darwin was ecstatic over all that he saw, noted the predatory attitude of different kinds of fauna, and was indignant at the cruelty inflicted on slaves. He spent some months at Rio sharing a cottage with the artist and a midshipman and collecting specimens. The *Beagle* had made a first-rate impression at Rio for her smartness; when she sailed, the British Squadron on the station gave her a rousing send-off; the sailors manned the yards and the band played "To Glory You Steer."

In the long way southward to the Straits of Magellan the amenities ceased. Except for Buenos Aires and Montevideo in the Plata, there was the long dreary stretch of the pampas of Patagonia with cowboy gauchos, and then Tierra del Fuego with its extremely primitive natives. While the Patagonian coast was being surveyed, Darwin undertook a long overland passage northward toward Buenos Aires. He had been warned of the risks, but wanted to see the pampas way of life. He ran into the undisciplined rough army of General Rosas, future dictator, and was shocked at the brutality of his virtual annihilation of a group of Indian raiders. There was even some shooting in the streets of Buenos Aires.

Rejoining the *Beagle,* he went southward to Tierra del Fuego. Fitz Roy had on board three young Fuegians whom he had taken to England on a previous cruise in the hope of civilizing and christianizing them. They took on a surface polish and were even presented to the king and queen. The Fuegians disembarked with an English supervisor, but were subjected to native hostility; when Fitz Roy returned later he was discouraged to find that the "christianized" Fuegians had lapsed into their former state. Darwin, in his journal, raised the question of whether the Fuegians or the Australian bushmen represented a lower stage of development.

The *Beagle* passed through the Straits of Magellan and started up the west coast. They were just in time to witness the terrific earthquake which devastated Concepción and Talcahuano in February 1835. Darwin had occasional trips inland to examine the Andes. He had a low opinion of the Peruvian port of Callao. Fitz Roy received word of his promotion to post-captain, jumping the grade of commander. This was a crucial step in a naval officer's career—he would thereafter automatically gain in seniority even though he did not get a command. Fitz Roy would end up as a vice admiral.

To Darwin, the most striking experience of the whole voyage came in the Galapagos Islands, well out at sea just below the equator. What he saw here more than anything else he had observed started him thinking about evolution. The islands abounded in strange creatures not to be found elsewhere. Most striking of all were the giant tortoises—the name Galapagos was the Spanish for those huge ugly creatures, which sometimes ran up to 500 pounds. Sailors from whalers and other ships stopped there to capture them for food. Darwin even got on the back of one and rode it. Also ugly and distinctive were the lizardlike iguanas— marine and land. Darwin counted some 27 different types of birds, often differing from island to island in a way that started him thinking about his eventual ideas of the "origin of species." Fitz Roy reacted in a negative way to the development of these new ideas. He was very religious in a conventional fundamentalist way, still believing that God created the world in six days. As time went on, the two men would draw farther apart.

After Galapagos and with the surveying attended to, the *Beagle*, to the general joy of officers and crew, started westward across the Pacific, heading for home. She could now attend to the second part of her mission, the accurate fixing of longitude by a chain of reckonings. These reckonings fell in pleasanter places than those they had just visited, starting with Tahiti on November 25, 1835. Darwin was charmed with the island and the people in general, but did not find the women attractive. Then came New Zealand, Port Jackson (Sydney), and Hobart in Tasmania. Australia left him cold: "Fairewell, Australia! you are a rising child . . . but you are too great and ambitious for affection, and not yet great enough for respect. I leave your shores without sorrow or regret." Crossing the Indian Ocean, he was delighted with the Cocos Islands, where the women danced in the moonlight on the beach and where he could study the growth of coral reefs. Then came Mauritius, Cape Town, St. Helena, Ascension, and finally England. Darwin left the ship at Falmouth and made for home in Shrewsbury at the beginning of October 1836, after nearly five years' absence.

The voyage was particularly fruitful for Darwin, exciting many new ideas, especially the origin of species. His account of the voyage was published in 1839. Darwin settled down, married his cousin Emma Wedgewood, and never left England again.

The *Origin of Species* appeared in 1859 and aroused vociferous religious opposition. There was a dramatic confrontation at the meeting of the British Association at Oxford in 1860. Bishop Wilberforce of Oxford launched a scurrilous attack which, strange to say, was supported by Vice Admiral Robert Fitz Roy, Darwin's erstwhile cabin mate on the *Beagle*. Fitz Roy had served as governor of New Zealand; suffering some mental aberration, he cut his throat in 1865. Darwin lived until

1882, defending his thesis and being strongly supported by T. H. Huxley. The *Origin of Species* was published in many editions and in many countries. Those tortoises on Galapagos had stirred up something that would not subside.

(See A. Moorhead, *Darwin and the Beagle,* 1969.)

Pilgrim and Alert

The brig *Pilgrim* of Boston won a lasting place in American sea literature because Richard Henry Dana, who shipped aboard her as a sailor in 1834–1835, embodied his experiences in the classic *Two Years Before the Mast.* Built at Medford near Boston in 1828 and measuring 180 tons, she was one of the vessels owned by the Boston firm of Bryant & Sturgis for their trade with California. Dana returned in another of their vessels, the *Alert.*

Born in Cambridge, Massachusetts, Dana came from a socially prominent family with strong legal traditions. He was a freshman at Harvard when he and numerous classmates were "rusticated," or suspended, for participating in a rebellion against a professor. During his suspension he contracted measles which left his eyes so weakened that, although he was readmitted, it seemed wisest to withdraw; he decided to go to sea. He signed up as a foremast hand on the *Pilgrim* and sailed from Boston on August 14, 1834—he would not return until September 22, 1836.

It was quite a shift, as he said, to change from "the tight dress coat, silk cap, and kid gloves of an undergraduate to the American merchant sailor's garb of those days." From the very start, he recorded his experiences and sensations as a basis of what would be his classic work. The captain of the ship was Francis A. Thompson, a native of Maine, toward whom Dana would develop an increasing antipathy. Dana had no respect for the first mate. The captain demoted the inadequate second mate.

By early November the *Pilgrim* started 10 days of struggling around Cape Horn, with seas breaking over the deck and the exhausting work of trying to handle "the ropes and rigging covered with snow and sleet. . . . Our clothes were all wet through, and the only change was from the wet to the more wet. There is no fire in the forecastle, and we cannot dry clothes in the gallery." Shortly after passing Cape Horn, a popular young English sailor was lost overboard, which had a very sobering effect upon the crew. "Yet," said Dana, "a sailor's life is at best but a mixture of a little good with much evil, and a little pleasure with much pain."

In mid-January the *Pilgrim* made Santa Barbara, 150 days out of Boston. This was the beginning of many tedious months of trading on the California coast. It was about 60 years since the Franciscans had built their string of missions, all the way from San Diego to San Francisco; California was now under Mexico, which had thrown off Spanish rule. Conditions were primitive; the principal economic activity was the exportation of hides and tallow from the cattle herds. That was why the *Pilgrim* and other vessels went out there. At each stop on the coast they set up shop to sell their trade goods—priced at about three times what they had cost in Boston. Then the hides were manhandled down to the shore and carried out to the ship in boats. This task fell largely upon the visiting crews, rather than upon the natives. When the holds were filled, the hides were taken down the coast to San Diego, where in company storehouses they were processed for shipment home. The ports of call included, in addition to Santa Barbara: San Pedro, with its dreary mudflats as the outlet for Los Angeles; San Juan Capistrano, where the hides had to be tumbled down bluffs some 400 feet high; and occasionally the colonial capital at Monterey and even farther north to San Francisco. It was hard and tedious work; Dana began to pull wires to get home quickly.

Dana made occasional remarks about the hard lot of the crew but the real climax came while the *Pilgrim* lay off San Pedro, when Captain Thompson indulged in a shocking sadistic outburst. As Dana told it:

> For several days the captain seemed very much out of humor. . . . His . . . displeasure was chiefly turned against a large, heavy-moulded fellow from the Middle states, who was called Sam. The man hesitated in his speech, and was rather slow in his motions, and was only a tolerably good sailor. . . . The captain was down in the hold . . . when he heard his voice raised in violent dispute. . . . "Will you ever be impudent to me again?" "I never have been, sir," said Sam. "Answer my question, or I'll make a spread eagle of you. I'll flog you, by G—d." "I'm no negro slave," said Sam. "Then, I'll make you one."

At that point, when one of the most mature, responsible members of the crew, John the Swede, asked, "What are you going to flog the man for, sir?" the captain ordered him put in irons.

> Sam was by this time seized up, as it was called, then placed against the shrouds with his wrists made fast to them, his jacket off and his back exposed. . . . The captain stood on the break of the deck, so as to have a good swing at him. . . . Swinging the rope over his head and

bending his body so as to give it full force, the captain brought it down on the poor fellow's back, once, twice, six times. The man writhed in pain. . . . "Now for you," said the captain, making up to John . . . when he was made fast, he asked him what he was to be flogged for. . . . "I flog you for your interference." "Can't a man ask questions without being flogged?" "No," shouted the captain, "nobody shall open his mouth aboard this vessel but myself. . . . If you want to know what I flog you for, I'll tell you. It's because I like to do it." . . . The man writhed under the pain until he could endure it no longer. When he called out. . . . "Oh Jesus Christ; Oh Jesus Christ!" "Don't call on Jesus Christ," shouted the captain. "He can't help you. Call on Frank Thompson! He's the man." At these words, which I shall never forget, my blood was cold. I could take it no longer. Disgusted, sick, I turned away. . . . I vowed that, if God should ever give me the means, I would do something to redress the grievances and relieve the sufferings of that class of beings with whom my lot had so long been set.

Not long afterward, relief was in sight with the arrival of another, larger Bryant & Sturgis ship, the *Alert*. Dana had written Boston, urging that he be permitted to return on her rather than have another dreary year in the *Pilgrim* on the coast. Although it would be eight months before she would set out for Boston, he transferred to her on September 8, 1835, for her coastal trading. He had been aboard the *Pilgrim* a year and 25 days—he would be with the *Alert* an almost equal time—a year and 17 days. However, they were happier days, for she was a roomy, comfortable ship, with a first-rate crew. The only fly in the ointment was that Captain Thompson also transferred to her but, aside from occasional churlishness to Dana, he did not repeat his extremely bad conduct. The *Alert*, at 389 tons, was double the size of the *Pilgrim*. She had been built in Boston in 1828 and had apparently been in the China trade.

The first months aboard the *Alert* were pretty much the same gathering of hides along the coast, with a few pleasant breaks. A third Bryant & Sturgis ship, the *California*, arrived from Boston with news and letters. "Monterey was the best place to go ashore on the whole coast, and we had no liberty-day for nearly three months, everyone was for going ashore. . . . Toward noon, we procured horses and rode out to Carmel Mission." Then, in mid-January, they all attended the wedding festivities at Santa Barbara, where the ship's agent was marrying the daughter of "the grandee of the place," and watched a fandango.

At last came six weeks of loading for home at San Diego "all the hides that had been collected since the *California* left the coast (a little more than two years), amounting to about forty thousand, had been cured, dried, and stowed away in the house, waiting for our good ship to take them to Boston." As usual, the crew had the laborious work of longshoremen. It was during this period that Dana observed: "arrived the brig *Pilgrim* from the windward. It was a sad sight for her crew to see us getting ready to go off the coast, while they, who had been longer on the coast than the *Alert* were condemned to another year's hard service." On May 8, 1836, the *Alert* finally sailed for home, but ran aground on leaving port which delayed her departure for a day. Over 40,000 hides and 30,000 horns, besides several barrels of beaver and otter skins, were stowed below.

The joy of leaving California was tempered by "the thought that we should be off Cape Horn in the very dead of winter . . . the prospect of meeting this in a ship half manned and loaded so deep that every sea must wash her fore and aft was by no means pleasant." The actual doubling of Cape Horn bore out those somber forebodings. It was a beastly experience, which lost nothing in Dana's vivid narrative, lasting from late June to late July. There were gales that meant hardship aloft; then would come temporary hopeful periods, followed by more gales. For a while, there was serious consideration of trying the Straits of Magellan, but then a new gale came in from the eastward. At one hopeful period, the crew were exasperated to find that the ship was lying hove to, inactive. Some said that Captain Thompson was frightened and afraid to make sail; others argued that in his scared condition he had "made a free use of brandy and opium, and was unfit for his duty. . . . It was proposed to take the ship from the captain and give the command of her to the mate." The carpenter prevented this near-mutiny by his diplomatic efforts with the captain, who finally came on deck and smoothed things over.

The *Alert* reached Boston on September 22, 1836. The hides went out to the shoe factories of Lynn and vicinity. Dana resumed his studies at Harvard and graduated at the head of his class. Captain Thompson was not reemployed by Bryant & Sturgis, and "got up a voyage to Sumatra for pepper." He had some bizarre difficulties with the natives and even bombarded their village; then he came down with fever and died on the way to Penang. The crew of the *Pilgrim* had planned to bring him to trial for those floggings, but he was gone before they returned to Boston. As for the *Pilgrim* herself, Dana wrote, "She was sold at the end of this voyage to a merchant in New Hampshire, who employed her on short voyages, and after a few years, I read of her total loss at sea, by fire, off the coast of North Carolina." The *Alert* made two more voyages to California, then was sold to Thomas W. Williams, the leading whale-ship owner of New London. In 19 years she had delivered at New London more than 25,000 barrels of whale and sperm oil. The Confederate raider *Alabama* burned her in 1862.

Dana worked over his book *Two Years Before the Mast,* called "the world's first masterpiece of life in a merchantman's forecastle," at leisure. Several publishers rejected the manuscript, but in 1840 Harper's gave him $250 and published it. Since then, the book has never been out of print and has been published in several foreign editions. His later work, *The Seaman's Manual,* published in 1841, gave useful advice about seamen's rights. This subject, about which he first became aware during his voyages on the *Pilgrim* and the *Alert,* became of increasing concern to him during his long and distinguished career as a Boston lawyer.

(See J. H. Kemble, ed., R. H. Dana, *Two Years Before the Mast,* 1941.)

Sirius

The *Sirius* slipped into a prominent niche in maritime history as the first regular steamship to cross the Atlantic. Chartered as a substitute for a larger, regular vessel, she arrived in New York on April 23, 1838, a few hours ahead of her rival, the *Great Western.* Together, they launched regular transatlantic steamship service.

There had been plans for a full-dress rivalry that spring between Brunel's *Great Western* and the *British Queen* of the British and American Steam Navigation Company, founded and headed by an ambitious American, Junius Smith. Smith's Scottish engine builder went bankrupt, however, and the delay in finding a new builder made it clear that the ship could not be finished before the *Great Western.*

To meet that emergency, Smith's company chartered the 703-ton *Sirius* of the St. George Steam Packet Company, recently built for service between London and Cork. Barely half the size of the *Great Western,* she was a wooden sidewheeler with some passenger accommodations.

Under the command of Lieutenant Roberts, the *Sirius* sailed from London on March 28, 1838. She stopped at Cork to take on passengers and coal, and sailed from there on April 4 with 19 cabin and 21 steerage passengers, and with 450 tons of coal, 58 casks of resin, and 20 tons of freshwater. With all this load, she had little freeboard and some of the crew were so concerned that there was talk of turning back. It was rumored that Lieutenant Roberts was even driven to facing the crew with drawn pistol. Toward the end of the voyage, the fuel supply began to run short, and to keep up steam, it was necessary to break up some woodwork and apply the resin. At any rate, she was within sight of land on the evening of April 22 and reached New York harbor the next morning, several hours before the arrival of the *Great Western* that afternoon. Her passage from Cork had been 18½ days.

The *Sirius* sailed back on May 1, reached Falmouth on May 19, and continued on to London. After another round voyage to New York, she was returned to her owners and to her Irish Sea service. She was wrecked near Ballycotton on June 1, 1847.

(See N. R. P. Bonsor, *The North Atlantic Seaway*, 1955.)

Great Western

One of the outstanding figures in mid-nineteenth-century British transportation reveled in the name of Isambard Kingdom Brunel; a versatile person, he had engineering skill, imagination, and promotional ability. Starting as chief engineer of the London-Bristol Great Western Railway, he backed the idea of extending its service across the Atlantic. From this project came three important steamships, each highly distinctive—the *Great Western, Great Britain,* and *Great Eastern.*

In the summer of 1836, a group of the railway's officials and prominent Bristol businessmen formed the Great Western Steamship Company. Construction started at once. The *Great Western* was laid down in July 1836 at Bristol by William Patterson. A year later she was launched and then towed around to London for her machinery, designed by Brunel. She was a wooden sidewheeler with a very sturdy hull. Her side-level engines, of 450 horsepower, took up 45% of her hull capacity and her bunkers could hold 800 tons of coal, more than enough to carry her across the Atlantic. Just before she sailed, rumors of a fire caused all but seven of her passengers to cancel reservations. She averaged 8.7 knots on her outward passage and 9.3 eastward. Her maiden passage from Bristol to New York, under the command of a Royal Navy lieutenant, was a thoroughly satisfactory affair and made a very good impression.

But when she arrived at New York on April 23, 1838, she found that a rival line had stolen a march on her. This was the British & American Steam Navigation Company, formed in 1836 by Junius Smith, an American layer resident in England, with the backing of John Laird of Birkenhead. They contracted for the *British Queen,* also a wooden sidewheeler and slightly larger than the *Great Western.* It was planned that she would sail for New York at about the same time as the *Great*

Western, but the Glasgow firm to whom her machinery was subcontracted went bankrupt, so she could not meet the sailing date. Thereupon Junius Smith chartered the 700-ton *Sirius* that was plying between England and Ireland to make the trip. She managed to reach New York on the morning of April 23, 18 days from Cork, just hours before the *Great Western*.

The arrival of these first two transatlantic steamships made April 23, 1838, one of the great days in the history of the port of New York. As one newspaper described it:

> The news of the arrival of the *Sirius* spread like wild fire through the city, and the river became literally dotted over with boats conveying the curious to and from the stranger. There seemed to be an universal voice of congratulations, and every visage was illuminated with delight. . . .

> While all this was going on, suddenly there was seen over Governors Island a dense black cloud of smoke, spreading itself upwards, and betokening another arrival. On it came with great rapidity, and about 3 o'clock its cause was made fully manifest to the multitudes. It was the steamship *Great Western*. . . . This immense moving mass was propelled at a rapid rate through the waters of the Bay; she passed swiftly and gracefully around the *Sirius*, exchanging salutes with her, and then proceeded to her destined anchorage in the East River. If the public was stimulated by the arrival of the *Sirius*, it became intoxicated with delight upon view of the superb *Great Western*.

But despite this brave start, neither Brunel nor Junius Smith was able to gain a permanent foothold in New York. The *Great Western* had made an impressive start, but she had no partner to keep up a regular schedule. Had Brunel immediately started a sister ship to the *Great Western*, he might have succeeded, but instead he lost both time and money in a more ambitious project, the *Great Britain*, with her iron hull and screw propeller. Both innovations were in the line of future development, but her running ashore, plus the capital involved, kept the Great Western Company from taking advantage of the Admiralty's subsidy project. For the time being, Junius Smith seemed to be better off—once going, his *British Queen* performed well and he had the *President* to provide alternative service. However, the *President* in 1841 "went missing" with all hands, while the third line, with its *Liverpool*, did not materialize. The *Great Western* made a considerable number of subsequent sailings, shifting her British base from Bristol to Liverpool, which was becoming an increasingly important commercial port. She finally withdrew from the transatlantic service, leaving the run to Boston and the Cunarders.

(See L. T. C. Rolt, *Isambard Kingdom Brunel, a Biography*, 1957.)

Britannia

The wooden sidewheeler *Britannia*, in frozen Boston Harbor, 1844. *(Peabody Museum, Salem)*

On July 4, 1840, the little wooden sidewheeler *Britannia* sailed from Liverpool for Halifax and Boston to inaugurate the most celebrated of steamship services—the Cunard Line. Two years earlier, transatlantic steam service had started at New York. The *Sirius* and *Great Western* had arrived a few hours apart on April 23, 1838, while later in the year a third rival, the *Liverpool,* had entered the competition; these rival services continued for a short time. But until more efficient engines were developed, coal and machinery took up so much room that there was not enough space for cargo to meet expenses.

This drawback led to the next step in those critical years about 1839–1840. The British government, convinced of the importance of regular communication with its far-flung interests, had for a century maintained regular service with its fast mail brigs on various runs out of Falmouth. It was now shown that steamships could offer quicker and more dependable service—the *Great Western* demonstrated that such service was possible. Samuel MacQueen persuaded Parliament that a guarantee of regular governmental subsidy payments was necessary to assure satisfactory results. And so, about 1839–1840, three very important lines received subsidies: P & O (Peninsular and Oriental) to India and the East, Royal Mail to the Caribbean, and Cunard to North America. Lines to other parts of the world would follow later.

When the question of the run to Halifax and Boston came up, it was expected that the companies that sent over the *Great Western* and the *Sirius* would show interest, but neither was in a position to guarantee

the frequency of service called for. However, wealthy Samuel Cunard,
from Halifax, took ship for England to look into financing and shipbuilding. He was put in touch with three Scots who responded with
enthusiasm: George Burns of Glasgow and the brothers David and
Charles MacIver of Liverpool. With their various friends, £270,000 was
raised; Cunard himself was the chief subscriber at £55,000. They
formed the North American Royal Mail Steam Packet Company, quickly
and generally known as the Cunard Line. As for vessels to meet the
contract terms, Cunard consulted Robert Napier who agreed to furnish
the boilers and machinery, with the hulls subcontracted to regular
shipbuilders. The Cunard Line started with four small wooden sidewheelers, about 1150 tons—*Britannia, Acadia, Caledonia,* and *Columbia*—thereafter all Cunard names would end in -ia, with names of
onetime Roman provinces fitting conveniently into the pattern. From
then on the funnels would be red with a black top.

Boston was particularly pleased with the new Cunard arrangement. It
was fighting a rearguard action against New York which was getting a
lion's share of the shipping and commerce—the sailing packets had
concentrated there and so had the first of the transatlantic steamships.
The British, however, had picked Boston as closest to Halifax, the other
port of call. When the *Britannia* arrived on her first voyage, Samuel
Cunard was the guest of honor at a dinner attended by 2000 enthusiastic guests. Four years later came another tangible appreciation of Boston's gratitude. An extremely cold spell, the worst in a half century,
froze the entire harbor solid. To prevent a delay in the mails, the
Bostonians sawed out a seven-mile channel through the ice (Currier &
Ives made a spectacular print of this). The British post office offered to
reimburse the Bostonians, but they declined with thanks. For the only
time since the Black Ball packets started in 1818, New York was not the
principal terminus of the crack ships of the Atlantic. But these halcyon
days for Boston were numbered. Because of the constantly increasing
business in New York, Cunard in 1847 started sending alternate ships
to New York, which soon became the main line from Liverpool.

The steamships ended the sailing packets' monopoly in carrying
passengers, mail, and fine freight. For a while, the "square-riggers on
schedule" of the Black Ball and other lines retained a fair share of the
passenger traffic because they were more comfortable. Some travelers
divided their crossings between the two services. Tyrone Power came
over in a Black Ball liner and left one of the most delightful descriptions
of that way of life. Then, in an unfortunate moment, he decided to
return on the new steamship *President*—she sailed from New York in
1841 and was never heard from again.

Charles Dickens made the crossing in the opposite order—coming over on the *Britannia* in 1842, when the January North Atlantic gales were at their worst, and returning much more comfortably on a packet. His *American Notes* reflect various aspects of conditions on the first Cunarder. Perhaps because he was an Englishman, he did not object to the cuisine as some Americans did, but on the discomforts he was very vocal, starting with coming out on the lighter to the liner in the stream:

> But we are made fast alongside the packet, whose huge red funnel is smoking bravely, giving rich promise of serious intentions. Packing cases, portmanteaus, carpet bags and boxes are already passed from hand to hand, and hauled on board with breathless rapidity. The officers, smartly dressed, are at the gangway, handing the passengers up the side and hurrying the men. . . .

> The waiting for the mail bags is worst of all. If we could have gone off in that last burst, we should have started triumphantly. . . . The captain appears on the paddle box with his speaking trumpet; the officers take their stations; the hands are on the alert; the flagging hopes of the passengers revive; the cooks pause in their savoury work, and look out with faces full of interest. The boat comes alongside. . . . Three cheers more, and as the first one rings upon our ears, the vessel throbs like a strong giant . . . the great wheels turn fiercely around for the first time. . . .

> My own two hands, and my feet likewise, being very cold . . . I crept below at midnight. It was not exactly comfortable below. . . . Two passengers' wives (one of them my own) lay already in silent agonies upon the sofa; and one lady's maid (my lady's) was a mere bundle on the floor, execrating her destiny. . . . Now every plank and timber creaked as if the ship were made of wickerwork. . . .

> I am awakened out of a sound sleep by a dismal shriek from my wife who demands to know if there is any danger. I rouse myself and look out of bed. The water jug is jumping and leaping like a lively dolphin. . . . Then I began to realize that the stateroom is standing on its head. . . . A steward passes, "Steward," "Sir?" "What is the matter? What do you call this?" Rather a heavy sea on, sir, and a head-wind." . . .

> The head engineer has distinctly said that there was never such a time—meaning weather—and four hands are ill and have given in, dead beat. Several berths are full of water and all the cabins are leaky. The ships cook secretly swigging damaged whiskey, has been found drunk; and had been played upon by the fire-engine until quite sober. All the stewards have fallen down stairs at various dinner times and go about with plasters in various places. The baker is ill and so is the pastry cook. . . .

It was with great relief that Mr. and Mrs. Dickens holed in at the Tremont House in Boston. The homeward trip on a square-rigged packet brought forth enthusiasm and almost no criticism.

The *Britannia*'s Cunard career ended in 1849 when she was sold to the North German Confederation's navy for the Schleswig-Holstein war with Denmark; she was transferred to the Prussian navy where she served until 1880 when, as a target ship, she was sunk.

In his initial instructions to Captain Woodruff for the *Britannia*'s first voyage, Cunard wrote, "It is of the first importance to the Partners that she attain a character for speed and safety." That speed and safety character became a cardinal point of Cunard policy, with safety even ahead of speed. With the threat of ice and fog on their run, safety was of the highest importance, as the competition with the Collins Line in the 1850s would illustrate. The *Britannia* would have Cunard successors down to the 1970s.

(See T. Hughes, *The Blue Riband of the Atlantic*, 1973.)

Acushnet

Twice in the course of six years a square-rigger went around Cape Horn with a foremast hand of good education who would produce important literature as a result of the voyage. The first was Richard Henry Dana in the brig *Pilgrim*, whose *Two Years Before the Mast* recorded his experiences. The second was Herman Melville in the whaler *Acushnet*; Melville's experiences in the South Seas led to *Typee*, *Moby Dick*, and other works.

Melville had already made a transatlantic voyage in the ship *Highlander* to Liverpool, recounted in his novel *Redburn*. On January 3, 1841, he sailed from Fairhaven, across the harbor from New Bedford, Massachusetts, as a foremast hand on the new 359-ton whaler *Acushnet*, commanded by Captain Valentine Pease.

Melville was aboard the *Acushnet* a year and a half before he jumped ship. In March the *Acushnet* stopped at Rio de Janeiro and in April rounded Cape Horn, where Melville saw his first albatross. In May there was a stop at Mas Afuera, Robinson Crusoe's old island. En route, Melville had a significant encounter with one of the sailors, William Henry Chase, whose father, Owen Chase, had been mate of the Nantucket whaler *Essex* and had written an account of her sinking in 1820 by a whale in the Pacific. Melville was fascinated with the story, which he had not heard before. Chase had a copy of his father's book in his bag, and Melville acknowledged that it had a strong effect upon him. *Moby Dick* would not appear for another 10 years, but the whale tale had probably initiated that book. Also, his descriptions of the *Pequod*

and the life aboard her would reflect his experiences aboard the
Acushnet.

In June the ship reached Nuku Hiva in the Marquesas Islands, where Melville got his first taste of South Seas charm. Becoming restless and wanting to explore more South Seas islands, he and his friend, Richard Tobin Green, jumped ship on July 9, 1842; this was the end of his connection with the *Acushnet.* After five days in the jungle they reached the lush Typee valley, which he described as an "earthly paradise," especially after he met the charming Fayawa. Ever restless, however, Melville shipped aboard another whaler, the *Lucy Ann* of Sydney. It was an exciting time in the islands because a French naval force was in those waters, snapping up Tahiti and other colonies. On August 17, 1843, Melville enlisted in Hawaii on the U.S.S. *United States;* he later recounted these experiences in *White Jacket.* Arriving at Boston in October 1844, he began writing the very popular *Typee,* published in 1846; *Omoo,* in 1847; the less popular *Mardi,* in 1849; *Redburn* on his Liverpool voyage, in 1849; *White Jacket* on his naval experience, in 1850; and his masterpiece, *Moby Dick,* in 1851. During those years of Melville's writing, the *Acushnet* had gone on whaling until August 1852, when she was wrecked.

(See L. Howard, *Herman Melville, a Biography,* 1951.)

Charles W. Morgan

The whaler
Charles W. Morgan,
at Mystic Seaport.
(Mystic Seaport)

One of the most celebrated survivors of America's age of sail is the veteran whaler *Charles W. Morgan,* enshrined at Mystic Seaport on the Connecticut coast, the prime attraction for millions of visitors. Built in July 1841, she made 37 voyages in 80 years, terminating in 1921; during that time she brought in 54,483 barrels of oil and 152,931 pounds of whalebone, worth more than $1,400,000—a record for American whalers. She voyaged farther than any other American whaler and in her wanderings visited almost every region, north, south, east, and west.

The *Morgan* was built in the Hillman yard on the Acushnet River at New Bedford, which by that time had overtaken Nantucket as a whaling port and was approaching the peak of its prosperity. She was a typical bluff-bowed type, 106 feet long and 27 feet in beam; she measured 351 tons by the old measurement, cut to 313 in the revised 1864 rates. Three-masted, she was part of the time a full-rigged ship, but spent many years as a bark without the square-rig yards on her mizzen. This arrangement required fewer men, and the whalers were in no hurry on their voyages of three years or so. She cost somewhat over $52,000, with half of her 64 shares owned by Charles W. Morgan, a Quaker, born in Philadelphia, who had come to New Bedford and married the granddaughter of the wealthy shipowner and whaling magnate, William Rotch. A few years later, Edward Mott Robinson, father of the famous Hetty Green, became the principal owner.

The records at Mystic Seaport and elsewhere make it possible to follow in detail most of the 37 voyages of the *Morgan*. The first voyage (1841–1845) produced cargo worth $56,000, a bit more than her whole original cost. The most profitable catch was on the sixth voyage (October 4, 1859–May 2, 1863) while the Civil War was in progress; it yielded $165,000. But whaling was a gamble, depending on the number of whales encountered, and some voyages had very meager results. That gambling aspect was reflected in the pay of the officers and crew. Instead of fixed wages, as in the normal merchant marine, the whalers, like the privateersmen, received a "lay" or share of the proceeds, ranging from a fairly generous amount for the master down to $\frac{1}{200}$ or so for the cabin boy. The earlier voyages were based at New Bedford and lasted an average of three years. However, in 1886 the *Morgan,* like many other whalers, shifted her base to San Francisco to avoid the lengthy passage around Cape Horn. The 18 voyages from 1886 to 1906 were across the Pacific and averaged only about a year apiece.

During her 80 years of cruising the *Morgan* had 18 different captains, 10 for one voyage only, six for two voyages, and one for three; James A. Earle, however, had nine voyages. Most of Earle's voyages were the short San Francisco runs between 1890 and 1906 when, because of troublesome mates, Earle resigned his command at Durban and came home by steamship. Earle was one of the six captains who took their wives to sea; his was a New Zealand schoolteacher who went up to Honolulu to marry him. Captain Charles St. Church's wife, Charlotte, served formally as assistant navigator.

Below the captains were the mates and the boatsteerer-harpooners. The whaler carried a mate for each of its whaleboats (usually four). The boatsteerer, who also served as harpooner, pulled the forward oar in the whaleboat and harpooned the whale. After the harpooning, he moved aft, changed places with the mate, and steered the boat while the mate killed the whale with a lance.

The longest record of service aboard the *Morgan* was that of George Parkin Christian of Norfolk Island (great grandson of Fletcher Christian, leader of the *Bounty* mutiny, and his charming "wife," daughter of a Tahitian chief). Christian made 13 voyages on the *Morgan* between 1893 and 1913, nine of them as second mate, one as first mate, and three as boatsteerer. At the outset, most of the foremast hands were native New Englanders, but as time went on an increasing proportion of Portuguese, either from the Azores or the Cape Verde Islands, were taken on.

About the closest the *Morgan* came to mutiny was on her thirtieth voyage (November 1904–June 1906), when she sailed from San Francisco for the last time, returning to New Bedford under Captain Edwin J. Reed. The forecastle contained a prime troublemaker, Charles King, who promoted a policy of disobedience. He was put in irons until he promised better behavior, as were several others for various infractions. The carpenter refused to repair a pump and later tried to attack the mate with an axe. At Tahiti several crewmen deserted but later returned to the ship. King and nine other men refused to man the boats to chase a whale and yielded only when Captain Reed threatened to keep them all in irons for the rest of the voyage. There were other causes of trouble in the next two voyages.

The *Morgan*'s last whaling voyage ended on May 28, 1921, when she returned from her thirty-seventh cruise with a $25,000 cargo. Her next assignment was in the film *Down to the Sea in Ships,* with Clara Bow among the supporting cast. Then in 1924 she sailed up to Salem for the film *Java Head.* Harry Neyland, a marine artist, strove valiantly to raise support for taking her over as a museum. He finally succeeded in arousing the interest of Colonel Edward H. R. Green, son of Hetty Green and grandson of Edward Robinson, who had been one of her original principal owners. The *Morgan* had a brief period of glory. Green provided an elaborate berth for her at his summer estate in South Dartmouth, a crew of whalers were put aboard, and she attracted thousands of visitors. Green later lost interest in the *Morgan* and made no provision for her in his will. Neyland tried again to raise support for her, and a group of men formed a corporation to help preserve her.

Carl Cutler, author of *Greyhounds of the Sea* and one of the three founders of the Marine Historical Association at Mystic, Connecticut, saved the situation with a promise to repair and maintain the vessel. On November 8, 1941, just a century after she was launched and just a month before the attack on Pearl Harbor, the *Morgan* was towed over to the Mystic River by a Coast Guard cutter. Her future was at last secure, but not until the war was over was it possible to do much for her restoration. Even then, there were problems.

At the time the *Morgan* came to Mystic Seaport, as it came to be called, the project was a modest affair, largely centered in a former warehouse. It grew rapidly, much of the new progress concentrating on the reproduction of a nineteenth-century maritime village with many appropriate activities. The *Morgan,* embedded in the sand in the middle of the waterfront, her lofty masts and delicate spars dominating the scene, was the focus of tourist attraction. During the early 1970s, visitors to the Seaport averaged 500,000 a year and almost all of them went aboard the whaler.

It was now evident that the *Morgan* was in need of a major overhaul, since it has always been difficult to keep ahead of decay in a wooden

vessel. To meet this need, an extensive "ship preservation facility" was
constructed, in part through the generosity of Henry B. Du Pont. The facility had two purposes: partly to serve the *Morgan* and other members of the growing collection of old vessels at Mystic, and partly to give the visitors to the Seaport an overall picture of the shipbuilding process under way. The *Morgan*, which had been declared a National Historic Landmark by the Secretary of the Interior in 1967, was the first to benefit. Included in the facility was a 375-ton lift dock extending into the Mystic River, capable of lifting out the *Morgan* for her overhaul. The bottom of her hull was found in good condition, and on June 21, 1974, she was once more afloat. With appropriate ceremonies she was towed up the river a short distance to her new resting place, where she continues to attract millions of visitors.

(See J. F. Leavitt, *The Charles W. Morgan*, 1974.)

Mississippi

The sidewheeler *Mississippi*, flagship of Commodore Perry. *(Naval Historical Center)*

In 1841, just before experimenting with the *Princeton*'s screw propeller, the United States built two excellent wooden side-wheel frigates: the *Missouri* and the *Mississippi*. To show her off to the Europeans, the *Missouri* was sent abroad as flagship of the Mediterranean Squadron.

At Gibraltar, as a result of a fire in her paint locker, she was burned to the water's edge.

The *Mississippi,* on the other hand, went on to a distinguished career of more than 20 years. She was laid down at the Philadelphia Navy Yard in 1839 and commissioned at the end of 1841. She had been built under the supervision of Commodore Matthew Calbraith Perry, one of the main proponents of steam in the navy. After several years in the Home Squadron, she was Perry's flagship in the Mexican War, taking an active part in operations along the Mexican Gulf Coast, and she was still his favorite when he went up to the Bay of Fundy to settle a fisheries dispute.

When Perry went on his celebrated expedition to open Japan in 1853–1855, he took the *Mississippi,* considering her the best man of war, though he later shifted his flag to the *Susquehanna.*

In 1859 the *Mississippi* was out on the China station when the British were running into heavy fire against the Chinese forts at Pei-ho. Disregarding considerations of neutrality, her commander, Josiah Tatnall, gave valuable assistance, explaining, "Blood is thicker than water."

In 1862 the *Mississippi* engaged in the operations against New Orleans under Farragut, with young George Dewey, later hero of Manila Bay, as her first lieutenant. In the attack on Port Hudson the pilot became confused in the heavy night firing and ran her aground; she caught fire and blew up. "She goes down magnificently, anyway," said Dewey, who loved the old ship.

(See S. E. Morison, *"Old Bruin": Commodore Matthew C. Perry,* 1967.)

Somers

The top-heavy gun brig *Somers.* *(Naval Historical Center)*

The United States Navy has claimed that it has never had a mutiny, but it came very close to one in 1842 aboard the brig *Somers,* when three men were hanged for plotting a mutiny. Matthew Calbraith Perry, who would set out to "open" Japan a decade later, was closely connected with the affair. The *Somers* was inaugurating Perry's new apprentice system; his brother-in-law was her commanding officer; and two of his sons and a nephew were aboard. In fact, James Fenimore Cooper sneered at the *Somers* as a "family yacht."

Perry also had a connection with the building of the *Somers* at the Brooklyn Navy Yard, where he was commandant. The little 239-ton brig, named for Lieutenant Richard Somers, who had died in the explosion of the ketch *Intrepid* at Tripoli, was built on very sharp lines and was rated as one of the fastest vessels in the navy, partly because she carried so much sail. Due to this top-heaviness, both she and her sister ship, the *Bainbridge,* were later capsized with heavy loss of life.

The *Somers*'s commanding officer, whose role in this unfortunate affair would be highly controversial, was Commander Alexander Slidell Mackenzie (he added the last name in honor of a Scottish uncle). His father was a successful New York merchant, his sister Jane married **181**

Perry, and one brother was later the Confederate diplomat taken off the *Trent* by a Union cruiser. Mackenzie was rated as a successful officer, but his career had been interrupted by furloughs during which he had written several books. He had a reputation for mild manners and thoughtfulness for his men.

The raison d'être for this particular cruise was the apprentice program which was close to Perry's heart. Instead of the unsatisfactory current recruiting system, the plan was to get hundreds of handpicked teen-agers and train them carefully aboard ship. The first contingent of 74 was now on board the *Somers*. All the personnel were unusually youthful. The first lieutenant, Guert Gainsvoort, of an old Knickerbocker family, was highly competent.

Despite the elite quality of many aboard, three prime troublemakers had been included in the ship's company. Two were petty officers: brutal, bearded Samuel Cromwell, about 35 years old, was boatswain's mate; and Elisha Small, about 30 years old, a shifty little fellow but an excellent sailor, was captain of the main top. Both men had apparently served on slavers. The third of this bad trio was Midshipman Philip Spencer, 19 years old, son of the Secretary of War in Tyler's Cabinet. Spencer had a long record as a juvenile delinquent; he was expelled from Hobart College and was a dropout at Union College. Through his father's influence, he had received a midshipman's warrant and had earned a long disciplinary record afloat. His favorite reading was *The Pirate's Own Book,* and he boasted that he would become a pirate.

On September 13, 1842, the *Somers* had received a lively send-off from New York, and headed for West Africa with dispatches for the *Vandalia*. The ship called pleasantly at Madeira, Tenerife, and Cape Verdes, and reached Monrovia on November 10 to find that the *Vandalia* had already left for home. Mackenzie thereupon set out for St. Thomas in the Danish West Indies.

The atmosphere on board had been good on the way over, but now began to change; there was a growing churlishness and moroseness among the crew. Spencer was hobnobbing with Cromwell and trying to curry favor with the crew. On November 25, taking advantage of the seeming disaffection between officers and crew, Spencer put his romantic notions to the test. He took James W. Wales, the purser's steward, out to where the boats were lashed down and unfolded a plan for mutiny. They would murder the officers, capture the ship, and turn her into piracy. Spencer had compiled a list of "certain" and "doubtful" crew members; keeping a nucleus to run the ship, they would dispose of the rest of the crew and the apprentices. They would then proceed to a pirate rendezvous off Cuba, known to Cromwell. From there they would cruise the trade routes, plundering and sinking the defenseless merchantmen and murdering the crews, but keeping the women for a while. Finally, they would put into Cuba, sell the *Somers*, and live in luxury. With the brig's high speed, it was not an impractical idea.

Spencer revealed the plan to Wales, thinking that he had a grudge against Mackenzie. But Wales was loyal and, shocked at the plan, managed to get word to the captain. Mackenzie summoned Spencer to the quarterdeck and confronted him with the story. Spencer said it was all a joke. "This joke may cost you your life," replied Mackenzie. He seated the midshipman on the starboard arms chest, chained him to the bulwarks, and handcuffed him. One of the other midshipmen, searching Spencer's effects, found the list of the 33 crew members marked "certain" or "doubtful" and indicating their mutiny stations. Cromwell and Small were locked up on the other side when their actions became suspicious. On November 30 four more were chained to the bulwarks.

Then came the very difficult command decision of what to do next. It would be several days before they could reach St. Thomas and perhaps turn the prisoners over to the *Vandalia*. The crucial question was whether it would be safe to delay a decision, in view of the doubtful behavior of the crew. Mackenzie could not set up a formal court-martial, but he did set up an informal counterpart. He ordered the four wardroom officers and three senior midshipmen to examine the evidence, deliberate, and give him their advice. They spent 13 or 14 hours on the question and reported on the morning of December 1, five days after the report from Wales, that they had come to a "cool, decided, and unanimous opinion" that the three ringleaders were "guilty of a full and determined intention to commit a mutiny" and that they were convinced "that it would be impossible to carry them to the United States. . . ." and that "they should be put to death, in the manner best calculated . . . to make a beneficial impression upon the disaffected."

Mackenzie, who agreed with the verdict, decided to put it immediately into effect. Spencer declared, "There are few crimes that I have not committed. I feel sincerely penitent." The other prisoners made appropriate remarks. Cromwell and Small were soon dangling from the starboard side of the main yardarm and Spencer from the port side. All went well on the rest of the way to Brooklyn Navy Yard, which they reached on December 14, after a brief stop at St. Thomas.

It was not surprising that all hell broke loose at New York. Secretary Spencer wanted to have Mackenzie tried for murder in a civil court. But the Secretary of the Navy convened a court of inquiry, which lasted from December 28 to January 19. It found that "the immediate execution of the prisoners was demanded by duty and justified by necessity" and that the conduct of Mackenzie and his officers "was prudent, calm and firm, and he and they honestly performed their duty in the service of their country." Things did not go quite so easily in the court-martial, which lasted from February 2 to April 1 aboard the *North Carolina* at the Brooklyn Navy Yard. The verdict was the equivocal "not proven." The board voted "to acquit Commander Alexander Slidell Mackenzie of the charges and specifications preferred by the Secretary of the Navy against him."

During the long period of inquiry and trial, the case provoked widespread interest and discussion throughout the country. Then and ever since, some have argued that the *Somers* could have reached port safely, with a chance for formal naval justice. Probably the one hit most heavily in the whole episode was Matthew Calbraith Perry, for, in addition to the involvement of his relatives aboard, this meant the end of his favored project for an apprentice system.

Herman Melville, who was related to one of the *Somers*'s officers, drew from the incident for his last work of fiction, *Billy Budd*.

As for the *Somers*, she lasted only four years longer. The top-heavy brig, under the command of Lieutenant Raphael Semmes, later commander of the *Alabama*, capsized in a sudden squall off Vera Cruz on December 8, 1846, while chasing a blockade runner, and sank in 10 minutes, losing 32 officers and men of her crew of 76.

(See S. E. Morison, *"Old Bruin": Commodore Matthew C. Perry*, 1967; F. F. Van de Water, *The Captain Called It Mutiny*, 1954.)

Princeton

Explosion of the Peace-maker on steam warship *Princeton,* 1844. *(Naval Historical Center)*

The United States Navy not only had the first steam warship—Fulton's *Demologos*—but also the first screw-propeller warship—Ericsson's *Princeton.* The various navies had tried a few sidewheelers but found them inadequate for combat duty. For one thing, the side-wheel mechanism broke up the long broadside rows of guns which had been an essential feature of warships ever since Elizabethan times. Then, too, the exposed paddle wheels were vulnerable to gunfire, as were the boilers and machinery lying above the waterline. With the screw propeller, both those faults could be avoided. Once the screw propeller had demonstrated its effectiveness, the conversion of navies to steam was rapid.

The major credit for the screw propeller is generally accorded to a Swedish engineer, John Ericsson, who moved to England which afforded a broader field for experimentation. His efforts attracted the attention of the American consul at Liverpool and he in turn conveyed his enthusiasm to Captain Robert Stockton, member of a prominent New Jersey family and one of the most progressive officers in the United States Navy.

The upshot was that Stockton persuaded the American navy to build a sloop of war equipped with a screw propeller. Named for Stockton's home town, Princeton, she was built at the Philadelphia Navy Yard; her novel machinery embodied Ericsson's ideas and was under Stockton's **185** supervision. In the propeller arrangement the power was transmitted inside the hull by a long iron shaft to the propeller, with its several blades, outside the stern. The *Princeton* was laid down on October 20, 1842, and launched on September 5, 1843. Those dates are important because the British were also experimenting. The *Princeton* measured 954 tons and was capable of seven knots. Stockton was her first commanding officer. She made a trial run to New York in October 1843 and then saw fairly routine service.

In February 1844 she attracted national attention, not because of her screw propeller but because of her two big guns. Ericsson had invented one of them, the "Oregon," with its breech strengthened with wrought iron. The other gun, the "Peace-maker," was a fairly similar type, designed under Stockton's direction. In February 1844 Stockton had the ship in the Potomac and was host at a trip down the river with President Tyler and about 200 prominent guests. Some of the crowd, in a happy mood, kept insisting that the Peace-maker be fired again. Against Stockton's better judgment, it was fired and exploded its breech, killing the Secretary of State, the Secretary of the Navy, and several others. President Tyler escaped injury, being below deck with his fiancée. This accident unfairly prejudiced the navy against Ericsson, though it does not seem to have affected the acceptance of the screw propeller.

In the meantime the British navy lost out on a narrow margin for the honor of the first screw propeller. The conservative Admiralty questioned whether the screw could develop adequate power. To find out, they prepared two small steamers of similar size and power: the paddle-wheel *Alecto* and the screw *Rattler*. Chained stern to stern, they tried full speed ahead and the screw *Rattler* towed the sidewheeler backwards.

The *Princeton* had two uneventful years with the Home Squadron and then two years in the Mediterranean; following a survey, she was condemned and broken up at the Boston Navy Yard in 1849. In the following five years the Navy built seven large screw ships and some smaller ones; the British were doing likewise.

(See *Dictionary of American Naval Fighting Ships*, 1959.)

Michigan
(Wolverine)

The iron-hulled sidewheeler *Michigan*. *(Naval Historical Center)*

The first iron-hulled, as distinct from armored, ship in the United States Navy was the *Michigan,* which showed the flag in the Great Lakes from 1843 to 1923. The decision to build her of iron came from Secretary of the Navy A. P. Upshur, who wanted "to use the immense resources of our country in that most valuable metal" and "to ascertain the practicality and utility of building vessels, at least for harbor defense, of so cheap and indestructible a material."

The British had placed two armed vessels on Lake Erie during the 1837 rebellion, and that was regarded as a precedent. The *Michigan* was built at Erie, Pennsylvania, and designed by naval constructor Samuel Hart. The iron parts were fashioned at Pittsburgh and carried overland to Erie, where they were assembled. In her attempted launching in December 1843, she stuck going down the ways and could not be budged, but the next morning was found floating comfortably offshore. She was a side-wheel steamer, measuring 685 tons, 168 feet long, with a beam of 27 feet and a draft of 9 feet. She carried one 18-pounder.

There were a few adventurous episodes in her long career of patrolling. In 1851 she assisted in the arrest of one James J. Strange, head of a dissident Mormon colony at the head of Lake Michigan. He was freed **187** but several years later was assassinated by two of his followers, who fled to the *Michigan* for sanctuary and were freed.

During the Civil War a group of Confederate naval officers planned to seize the *Michigan* and use her as a raider, but President Jefferson Davis did not approve the project. In 1864 Secretary of the Navy Welles warned the *Michigan* to be on guard against conspiracies. Some 20 Confederates, under an acting master, secured passage on the steamer *Philo Parsons,* seized her, and burned another steamer. There were ambitious plans to free some of the Confederate prisoners at Johnson's Island where the *Michigan* was standing guard, but her captain discovered the conspiracy, arrested the ringleader, and broke up the affair before the *Philo Parsons* got there.

Aside from that, the old *Michigan's* patrolling was useful but rather uneventful. In 1905, to give the name to one of the new battleships, the *Michigan* was renamed the *Wolverine*. She was decommissioned in 1912 and turned over to the Pennsylvania Naval Militia for training cruises until a machinery breakdown in 1923. Efforts to raise funds to preserve her were unsuccessful and in 1948 she was sold for scrap, but two parts of her, the bow and cutwater, were set up as memorials near the shipyard where she had been built.

(See *Dictionary of American Naval Fighting Ships,* 1959.)

Great Britain

The iron-hulled
steamship *Great
Britain.*
*(National Maritime
Museum, Greenwich)*

In 1968 a prominent British naval architect wrote to the London *Times* that "the most significant ship to be built in the last two or three centuries should be brought back to England and restored." He was referring to the *Great Britain,* launched in 1843, the brainchild of the brilliant and versatile Isambard Kingdom Brunel. She was indeed more significant than his other two "Great" masterpieces: the *Great Western* of 1838, pioneer in transatlantic steam navigation, and the tremendous "white elephant" *Great Eastern* of 1858, larger than any other ship for almost a half century, but whose history would be written in red ink. The *Great Britain* owed her prominence to two Brunel innovations in major shipbuilding: the iron hull and the screw propeller. That letter to the *Times,* consequently, started a movement to bring her long-neglected hull back from a cove in the Falkland Islands.

Originally, Brunel had planned another wooden paddlewheeler like the *Great Western,* which was performing successfully on the New York run. But two new vessels which had recently appeared caused him to diverge from that conventional plan. The first was a little iron paddle-wheel steamer which came to Bristol to load for Antwerp. Brunel had two of his colleagues make the trip on her. Their enthusiastic report led the Great Western Steamship Company to decide on an iron hull. Then the schooner *Archimedes,* with one of the earliest screw propellers, **189** visited Bristol, whereupon Brunel scrapped the work already started on paddle-wheel machinery and shifted to prepare for screw propulsion.

In the early 1840s, while the new ship was under construction, the Brunel family were completing achievements in two other fields. Stretched out over almost 20 years, Isambard Kingdom Brunel and his father, Marc Isambard, achieved an engineering first with a tunnel under the Thames below London, for which his father was knighted. In the meantime, since 1833, the younger Brunel had been engineer and general factotum of the new Great Western Railway to run between London and Bristol. He had been tireless in planning and supervising every step of that trunk line to the southwest, and, in addition to the vast array of minutiae, he had designed several beautiful major bridges and numerous lesser ones. Some of that railway activity would continue, but steamships were becoming his major interest.

The *Great Britain* was much larger than the other new steamships on the Atlantic, measuring some 3270 tons displacement, as compared with 2300 for the *Great Western*. She was 322 feet in length and 51 feet in beam. Her engines, built by the company itself, generated 1500 horsepower, just double the *Great Western*'s, and she had a 15-foot propeller. In contrast to conventional wooden shipbuilding, Brunel insisted on great longitudinal strength, starting with 10 big iron girders running the entire length of the ship. In addition, the *Great Britain* had five watertight transverse bulkheads, along with other strengthening. These innovations enabled her to survive 11 months on the rocks of the Irish coast. She was built in the basin of the William Patterson yard at Bristol and was floated out on July 19, 1843, with the Prince Consort christening her.

She left Liverpool (rather than Bristol) for New York on June 26, 1846, and the first two voyages went well. Then on September 22 fate struck one of the hardest of its many blows at Brunel. In thick weather, after dark, the *Great Britain* piled up on the rocks of Dundrum Bay in County Down in Ireland. There had been widespread doubt about the stability of iron ships, and it seemed as though this was definitely the end. She lay 11 months exposed to the pounding of the heavy seas. Brunel built a heavy shield of fagots to protect the stern, and finally on a high "spring" tide the ship was floated clear on August 27, 1847. It was a victory for Brunel and for iron, but it was a costly one. The repairs had placed too great a strain on the finances of the Great Western Steamship Company, which went under after just 10 years. Both the splendid Brunel ships were sold. The *Great Western* was purchased by the Royal Mail Steam Packet Company and served 10 years on the run between Southampton and the West Indies.

The *Great Britain* was sold to the firm of Gibbs, Bright & Company of Bristol and Liverpool, which placed her in the Australian trade after the discovery of gold there in 1851. In 1852 she sailed from Liverpool to Melbourne with 630 passengers. She continued in that trade, successful and popular, making 32 voyages by 1875, interrupted by service as a troopship during the Crimean War and the Indian Mutiny. She was laid up in 1875 and advertised for sale. In 1882 she was sold to E. Biggs, Sons & Company, which took out her machinery and converted her to a sailing vessel, sheathed with wood. She made two voyages from Britain to San Francisco with coal, but in 1886, setting out for Panama, she ran into a terrific gale off Cape Horn and put into Port Stanley in the Falkland Islands.

The hulk of the old *Great Britain* was sold to the Falkland Islands Company for storing wool and later coal, some of which was furnished in 1914 to the British squadron about to sink Graf Spee's ships. In 1933 the governor of the Falkland Islands made an appeal for the preservation of the famous ship, but the expense seemed excessive and in 1937 she was towed over to Sparrow Cove to end her days.

The project for her preservation was revived in 1966 with initiative from San Francisco, where a waterfront exhibit was planned. The Falkland Islands situation was examined and a bark was purchased and taken to San Francisco. It was generously agreed, however, that Bristol had a prior claim to the remains of the *Great Britain*. In 1967 Dr. Euan Corlett, a prominent British naval architect who had long been studying the ship's story, wrote the letter to the *Times* already cited. Various interests began to cooperate with his "Steamship *Great Britain* Project," and enough money was raised to make a start. After tons of silt and marine growth had been removed, she floated and was placed aboard a huge pontoon. On April 25, 1970, she left Port Stanley for Bristol by way of Montevideo, and on July 19—actually the one-hundred twenty-seventh anniversary of her being floated out of the Great Western Dock—she was edged into the same dock where she had been built. Naturally much remains to be done; a Repair and Restoration Committee was formed, and there is widespread hope that finances will permit carrying through the project.

(See L. T. C. Rolt, *Isambard Kingdom Brunel, a Biography*, 1957.)

Sea Witch

The clipper *Sea Witch*, built for the China trade. *(Mariners Museum)*

$\mathbf{F}$ollowing the opening of the Chinese treaty ports, two New York firms in the tea trade built a little group of "tea clippers" which presaged the great rush of "California clippers" in the 1850s. The New York yard of Smith & Dimon built for Howland & Aspinwall the 757-ton *Rainbow* in 1845 and the 907-ton *Sea Witch* in 1846; Brown & Bell, also of the East River, built the 581-ton *Houqua* in 1844, the 957-ton *Samuel Russell* in 1847, and the 1003-ton *Oriental* in 1849. These are rated among the real clippers because of their sophistication of design, although, like British tea clippers such as the *Ariel* and *Cutty Sark* of the 1860s, they were smaller than many of the California clippers. The clippers as a whole sacrificed almost a third of their cargo capacity in the interest of speed, but since tea was a valuable, compact cargo, that did not matter. Several of these China clippers had the very rich opportunity of engaging also in the California trade before the later California clippers came on the scene.

One particular innovative feature in the new ships, the *Sea Witch* among the first, was the participation of a specialist designer, John W. Griffiths, in addition to the builder. Howland & Aspinwall had found their *Rainbow* such a success that they ordered the somewhat larger *Sea Witch* in addition. Her remarkable speed record was attributable in part to the superlative captain they secured for her. Robert H. Waterman

192

had served as mate and master in the crack Black Ball packet line, but his special distinction came in the old New Orleans packet *Natchez* which, with his powerful driving and with a following wind, he brought from China to New York in record time. He then set up three record-breaking China runs in the *Sea Witch,* after which Howland & Aspinwall transferred him to his controversial command of their huge *Challenge.*

With the coming of the Gold Rush, these early China clippers were in a unique position to take advantage of the California opportunities. The "forty-niners" were pouring into San Francisco, where because of scarcity, normal articles of trade were selling for several times their cost. Ultimately, the new big clippers would be rushed to completion to meet that situation, but in the meantime the China clippers could reap a rich extra profit in carrying general cargo out to San Francisco before proceeding on across the Pacific for their normal China run. The *Samuel Russell* had sailed for San Francisco on January 5, 1850, and the *Sea Witch* followed on April 14. A ship could almost pay for itself in one of those expanded voyages.

George W. Frasee became captain of the *Sea Witch* after Waterman was shifted to the *Challenge.* Frasee made four voyages, but in 1855, while en route to San Francisco, he was murdered and his body was taken ashore at Rio de Janeiro. The ship continued on under a new captain. In China, however, she took on a cargo far less pleasant than tea, loading 500 Chinese coolies at Amoy for Havana. On March 28, 1856, when 18 miles from Havana, she struck a reef and became a total loss.

(See C. C. Cutler, *Greyhounds of the Sea,* 1930.)

California

The wooden sidewheeler *California,* in Pacific Mail service. (Peabody Museum, Salem)

During the Gold Rush years, travelers had a choice of three different ways to reach California from the East Coast. One could travel by covered wagon across the plains and mountains, with the danger of encountering Indians en route. That was doing it the hard way. The easiest, in contrast, was aboard a clipper or other sailing vessel, all the way from New York or Boston around Cape Horn to San Francisco. But that took several months—even the three fastest sailing passages took 89 days and many were twice that long. The quickest and most expensive way was by steamship from New York down the coast to the Isthmus of Panama, across the Isthmus by land, and then up the west coast to California; mail and troops went by that route and so did passengers who could afford it.

The 1057-ton wooden sidewheeler *California* made the first Pacific run on this "Panama route," encountering a rush of business not anticipated when she was built or even when she sailed on that first run. In 1847 the main objective of the new service was Oregon, which the United States had recently acquired by treaty. To provide passenger and mail service to the new region, which was very slowly filling up, Congress on March 3, 1847, voted to grant subsidies for this service. It was not expected that there would be sufficient business to break even without such help. The Navy made a contract with the New York firm of Howland & Aspinwall to undertake the new "Pacific Mail" service with three steamships.

The *California,* the first of these, was built in the crack East River shipyard of the versatile William H. Webb, and her side-lever engines,

194

capable of 250 horsepower, were the work of Stillman, Allen & Company. Her keel was laid on January 4, 1848, and she was launched on May 19 at a total cost of $200,000. Since it was not anticipated that travel to Oregon would be heavy, she had accommodations for only 50 or 60 cabin and 100 to 150 steerage passengers.

Her captain was Cleveland Forbes, who had commanded a steamer on New York Bay in the Camden & Amboy service. He was still ignorant of the gold discovery when the *California* sailed from New York for the West Coast on October 6, 1848, inaugurating the new service of the Pacific Mail Steamship Company. The ship stopped at Rio de Janeiro and, instead of the longer run around Cape Horn, traversed the treacherous Straits of Magellan and then proceeded up the west coast.

A tremendous surprise awaited her when she pulled in at Panama on January 17, 1849. Hundreds were eager to board her for San Francisco. Gold had been discovered at Sutter's Mill in northern California in mid-January 1848, almost exactly a year before her arrival in Panama and just before the United States received formal title to California by treaty on February 2. Although news of the discovery of gold had spread gradually after January 1848, the real Gold Rush is usually dated from President Polk's message of December 5, 1848. Because of the time lag between the discovery and that message, those who rushed to California became known as the "forty-niners."

On the waterfront of Panama considerable confusion and dissension arose when some 729 people tried to crowd into space that would hold scarcely half that number. Some had received tickets from the line, and they enjoyed a certain priority. Mass meetings were held, with feelings strongest against some 70 Peruvians who, having heard of the gold discovery, joined the ship as it came up the coast. Although the general designated to command in California informed them that aliens were by law barred from the gold fields and they would be liable to arrest if they tried to get there, they were finally given makeshift accommodations on deck. After a two-week stopover, the *California* sailed from Panama with about 350 passengers.

On her way north, she stopped at Acapulco, San Blas, Mazatlan, and Monterey. Cordwood was cut and put on board when it was thought that her 500 tons of coal were nearly exhausted, but later an extra stock of coal was discovered. At Acapulco a threat of mutiny developed when a stowaway was caught and put in irons. He was released when all the firemen swore that they would not work another hour unless the man was freed. Those stokers, incidentally, were among the first to rush ashore for the mines as soon as the ship reached San Francisco.

The *California*'s arrival was tumultuous. She was the first steamship to come in through the Golden Gate and the crowds were wildly enthusiastic. The warships of the Pacific Squadron all saluted her. The captain asked Commodore Jones to put guards aboard to prevent the crew from running away, but the commodore declined, saying that the marines would probably join in the rush. Very quickly the captain and the mate were the only ones left aboard the *California,* and it was necessary to offer high wages to get a crew for the return.

The *California* continued on the regular service between Panama and San Francisco until 1854, when she was placed on a relief status. Later she went to another coastal line, making her last trip as a steamer in November 1875. Two years later she was converted into a bark, carrying coal and lumber, at times as far as Australia. Her end came late in 1894 or early 1895, when she was wrecked on the rocks at Pasasmayo, Peru. Though she and her lumber cargo were a total loss, no lives were lost.

The Pacific Mail's service continued as the major link between Panama and San Francisco until 1869, when the first transcontinental railroad was completed. By that time, the Pacific Mail's main concern was with big transpacific sidewheelers to China and Japan.

(See J. H. Kemble, *The Panama Route, 1848–1869,* 1943.)

Flying Cloud

Of all the 100 or so vessels recognized as clippers, it is generally agreed that first place goes to the 1782-ton *Flying Cloud,* built in 1851 by Donald McKay at East Boston. It is also conceded that McKay deserves first place among the clipper-ship builders, on the basis of what several of his masterpieces, in addition to the *Flying Cloud,* achieved. The emphasis in that competition was primarily on speed, especially on the run around Cape Horn between New York and San Francisco. There was an element of luck in the racing—a ship might be running well ahead of schedule when wind could carry off a topmast, winds could die away completely, or fog could shut in at a critical time. But the *Flying Cloud*'s primacy rests on a solid basis. Of all the well-recorded runs, only three were completed in less than 90 days and two of those 89-day runs were made by the *Flying Cloud,* first in 1851 and again, a few hours faster, in 1854. The third was made by the *Andrew Jackson,* built at Mystic, Connecticut, in 1860.

McKay designed his ships with imagination and a sense of beauty, and also put them together with skill and meticulous care. He was born in Nova Scotia and came southward as an apprentice. He had part of his training in the East River yard of Isaac Webb who was also training his son, William H. Webb, who would be McKay's rival for superlative honors. His clippers would be almost up to McKay's and, in addition, Webb turned out packets, steamships, and even warships. McKay moved up to Newburyport, where he build some substantial packets. He won the warm support of Enoch Train, a wealthy Boston shipowner who persuaded him to move to East Boston and helped to start him there.

The *Flying Cloud* was 225 feet in length and 40 feet in beam, and at 1782 tons, it was about double the size of the China clippers already on the scene. Her entrance lines were slightly concave and very sharp. It was a coincidence that the two most celebrated sailing vessels in American history were built only a few miles apart, the frigate *Constitution* at the upper end of the harbor and the *Flying Cloud* across the harbor, further down, at East Boston. She was launched on April 15, 1851, and was originally owned by Enoch Train, who sold her to the distinguished New York firm of Grinnell, Minturn & Company for $90,000. For her master, the company picked Josiah Perkins Cressy from Marblehead, who had won a reputation as a successful "driver," especially in the ship *Oneida*. He commanded her in both the 1851 and 1854 voyages and played a strong part in the ship's success.

On her first famous voyage she left New York on June 2, 1851. The ship's original log, still preserved, gives the feel of some of the experiences on that great voyage. She started off with "moderate breezes, fine weather," but approaching Hatteras with "good breezes," she lost main and mizzen topgallant masts and mainsail yard. Clippers, of course, did not shorten sail except in extreme conditions. On June 4 in mid-Atlantic, in the latitude of Cuba, she "discovered main mast badly sprung 4 feet below the hounds." On June 25 she rounded Cape San Roque, the bulge of Brazil, and continued southward. Then on July 10, off the pampas of Argentina, she encountered fierce pamperos, "very heavy squalls with much & very severe thunder and lightning. Double reefed the topsails: latter part blowing hard gale—No observations." The next day was worse: "heavy gales, close-reefed topsails split fore staysail and main topmast staysail at 1 P.M. Discovered main topmast sprung (same time brig in company to leeward lost both fore and main topmast), sent down royal and topgallant yards & booms off lower and topsail yard to relieve the mast, very turbulent sea running. Ship laboring hard and shipping large quantities of water over lee rail." The next day two holes were found bored in the side by one of the crew, who was put in irons. Then on July 23, about 50 days out of New York: "Cape Horn N. 5 miles at 8 A.M. the whole coast covered with snow— wild ducks numerous."

On July 31, far off Valparaiso, the *Flying Cloud* reported: "Latter part high sea running, very wet, fore and aft." The distance run this day by observation was 374 miles, an average of 15.72 knots; during squalls 18 knots of line was not sufficient to measure her rate of speed. This was the fastest day's run yet made by a ship—nearly 40 miles better than any steamship traveled in a day up to the Civil War, though some of McKay's own creations would travel more than 400 miles a day during the next few years. All through August the *Flying Cloud* sped up the coast without event. On August 23, while she was well up the California coast, the yacht *America* was establishing her own great speed record by defeating all the British yachts at Cowes. Finally, just a month after rounding Cape Horn, the log states: "Light breezes and pleasant. Middle strong and squally at 2 A.M. Hove ship to for daylight at 6 A.M. Made South Farallon NE 2 degrees E 6 miles; at 7 took a pilot; at 11 hour, 30 mins came to anchor in five fathoms of water off North Beach, San Francisco Harbor." That record of 89 days and 21 hours stood for three years, when the *Flying Cloud* herself bettered it by 13 hours, a permanent record from anchor to anchor.

As pointed out in connection with the yacht *America,* the summer of 1851 was perhaps the most thrilling of maritime periods, because of the emphasis on speed. Just two weeks before the *Flying Cloud* had sailed, the Collins liner *Pacific* became the first to cross the Atlantic in 10 days.

Aside from the fourth voyage in 1854, the next few years for the *Flying Cloud* were relatively uneventful, except for breaking her own speed record within 89 days, 8 hours. Later that year she went on to China; a few days out from Whampoa she ran on a reef but got off, leaking 11 inches of water an hour. The pumps were kept going for the rest of the 115-day voyage and she arrived safely with her million-dollar cargo intact, for which Captain Cressy received a silver service and high commendation from the underwriters and owners. On the sixth voyage in 1856 Captain Cressy stayed at home to rest and the ship had an unpleasant outward passage, badly damaged in hull, spars, and rigging, but she made the fastest day's passage in her career—402 miles. Captain Cressy went to San Francisco and brought her home.

By that time the tide in clipper fortunes was turning—there were too many of them and not enough business. For almost three years the *Flying Cloud* lay idle at New York. But in 1860 she made a fast passage to London and then went out to China. Returning to England, she made a voyage to Australia and Hong Kong, then carried troops to London.

In 1862 she became involved in the "flight from the flag," when scores of the best American ships changed to British registry to avoid the high war-risk rates on American ships occasioned by the *Alabama* and other raiders. Her service under the Red Ensign was uneventful

and she wound up in the lowest of occupations, carrying lumber from
the Maritimes to England. She broke her back in a gale in 1874 and a
year later was burned for her copper and other fastenings.

(See C. C. Cutler, *Greyhounds of the Sea*, 1930.)

Challenge

Few clippers started off with higher hopes than the big 2006-ton *Challenge*, which put to sea from New York for San Francisco on July 13, 1851. One of the features of the passion for speed in those exciting years was the fact that shipowners, normally very tight in the matter of expenses, were ready not only to spend extravagantly but to wager still further amounts on the speed record. The major house of N. L. & G. G. ("No Loss and Great Gain") Griswold had a real spending spree in building a clipper aimed to be the fastest of the lot and appropriately named her the *Challenge*. The hull, spars, luxurious interior fittings, and everything else were the best available. For all that, she would prove a disappointment.

The choice for builder was William H. Webb, the closest runner-up to Donald McKay in the specialty of clippers, which were only one part of Webb's versatile scope. One of the red-letter days in East River construction was January 21, 1851, when the Webb yard launched, in close succession, the 1072-ton Le Havre packet *Isaac Bell*, the 1244-ton clipper *Gazell*, and the 2067-ton steamer *Golden Gate* for the Pacific Mail. The alcoholic enthusiasm for that triple christening was repeated four months later with the launching of the huge much-touted *Challenge*. Incidentally, in that most productive spring McKay had launched his *Flying Cloud* at East Boston and George Steers his yacht *America* on the East River.

The Griswold firm also tempted one of the ablest American captains to take the command. Robert H. Waterman, after three record-breaking China runs in the *Sea Witch*, had decided that he would retire as a gentleman farmer, but the Griswolds offered enough to lure him back. They thus secured top quality in command but were unlucky in getting a crew. With the sudden expansion of American shipping, good foremast hands were few and far between. Somehow or other a reasonably adequate crew had been brought together for the *Flying Cloud* that spring, but the 50 men assembled for the *Challenge* were a particularly sorry lot—all but two were foreigners and only six could even steer.

Furthermore, the winds did not blow for the Griswolds and Waterman as they had for the Grinnell, Minturn firm and Cressy. The *Challenge* ran into light winds and calms down the Atlantic coast and encountered 12 tough days off Cape Horn. She reached San Francisco on October 20, 1851, in 108 days, a respectable record but a disappointment to the owners and the optimists who had bet on her.

The distinctive part of the run, however, was the friction between Captain Waterman and his crew. Writing to a friend later, Waterman gave his account of the trouble:

> The truth is, when in the neighborhood of Rio, about fifty of the crew fell on the mate with the intention of killing him and afterwards me, by their own confession. I was on the poop taking observations while the mate stood forward at the gallery. They stabbed him and had beaten him shockingly before I could get to him. I struck down three of them, rescued the mate and quelled the mutiny. I flogged eight of them. Off Cape Horn, three men fell from the mizzentopsail yard and were killed and after a few weeks four more of the men died of dysentery.

When the *Challenge* reached San Francisco, that story of trouble had been distorted by drunken sailors into "hell ship" proportions. The *California Chronicle* gave a particularly lurid version:

> The account given of Captain Waterman by his crew, if true makes him one of the most inhuman masters of his age.
>
> If they are true, he should be burned alive—he should never leave the city a live man. Nine of his men are missing, and the sailors who are here declare that four were shaken down from the foretopsail yard into the sea where they were drowned, and five of them died from the effects of wounds and ill treatment.
>
> The scene at this time beggars all description. Five of them are mangled and bruised in the most shocking manner. One poor fellow died today and five others, it is expected, will soon be in the embrace of death. One of the men now lying on his deathbed had been severely injured in his genitals by a kick from this brute in human form. . . . The captain, the vile monster, has made his escape, and so has his brutal mate.

For a few hours Waterman was in real danger. A mob of some 2000 assembled and visited the premises of the ship's agents in search of him. The mayor saved the situation by calling the volunteer Vigilance Committee; in five minutes 600 of its members assembled and the mob quietly retreated.

When the matter came to trial, Waterman was cleared. Several of the crew and all the passengers testified in his behalf, and nine of the

seamen volunteered to go to China under him. The captain who
relieved Waterman, however, had to pay $200 in advance money to get even 40 men who would sign on for Shanghai. They were a tough lot, however, and it was necessary at Hong Kong to get the American commodore to send marines aboard to restore order. Instead of tea, the owners opted for the less desirable cargo of 553 Chinese coolies for San Francisco. On the Pacific run she made some good bursts of speed. Then came another run to Hong Kong and a return cargo of tea for England. The *Challenge* was sold to the British, who used her for trade with China and India; in 1876, with her name changed to *Golden City*, she was wrecked off the French coast.

(See C. C. Cutler, *Greyhounds of the Sea*, 1930.)

America

The racing yacht
America.
*(Peabody Museum,
Salem)*

The best-known of American yachts, with a wide international reputation, was the schooner *America*, which in 1851 swept to a clean-cut victory over all the competitors from the Royal Yacht Club. Her reputation has been kept fresh ever since by the periodic challenges for the silver "America's Cup," which remains in the possession of the New York Yacht Club. That victory was one of the reasons that the year 1851 has been called the *annus mirabilis,* the wonderful year of the American merchant marine. By a coincidence, the two most celebrated performances of speed by American sail occurred simultaneously. On August 23, while the *America* was speeding around the Isle of Wight, the *Flying Cloud* was racing up the West Coast on her unprecedented 89-day run from New York to San Francisco. The exuberant passion for speed permeated the whole maritime community.

The unique properties of the *America* have normally been ascribed to its designer, 31-year-old George Steers, who was making a name for himself with pilot boats and yachts. The yacht was built under Steers's supervision in the major East River shipyard of William H. Brown, who handled the business negotiations. On the social and financial side was a syndicate of wealthy aristocrats, members of the New York Yacht Club. Foremost among them was John Cox Stevens, who would handle the Anglo-American negotiations as commodore of the New York Yacht Club. He was the eldest of the remarkable sons of Colonel John Stevens of Hoboken, who together played important roles in the development of steamboats and railroads and grew wealthy from, among other things, their Camden & Amboy Railroad across the waist of New Jersey. John Cox Stevens was a rather haughty aristocrat. His brother, Edwin A., a future commodore of the New York Yacht Club, was another member of the syndicate, as were Colonel James Alexander Hamilton, Hamilton Wilkes, John W. Beekman Findlay, and George L. Schuyler.

The negotiations for the construction started in November 1850, and a pressure for speed resulted from an approach from the Royal Yacht Club, whose commodore, the Earl of Wilton, informed John Stevens that Sir Henry Bulwer, the British minister at Washington, had inspected the schooner yacht at New York and had been impressed by her radical but graceful lines. This was the beginning of a polite but cautious correspondence leading up to the invitation to Cowes.

The "radical but graceful lines" mentioned by Sir Henry were shown in pictures of her in frame during construction. The most striking feature was her quite shallow draft forward, with deep draft at the stern. Her particular characteristics were described by an English correspondent just after she won her famous race:

> The peculiarity of her build is the subject of general remark. When on the dock, on a dead level, her masts are perpendicular; but when afloat they have a rake of four and a half feet; she is thus wedge shaped both ways, the least resistance, both on her sides and under water, being at

the bows. Much has been said of her extreme sharpness, but this is more apparent than real. Near the waterline the bows assume a perfectly rounded form, and her model, when closely examined, approaches nearly as possible to that which nature, the great modeller, had given to the waterfowl. Her sides are equally round and full, and she is about one-half wider amid-ships than our vessels of the same tonnage. The result of this peculiar construction is that she floats over the water instead of having to plough her way through it, and an increase of speed does not, as in ordinary vessels, occasion an increase of resistance. This will account for the enormous spars she carries—lying flat as it were, on the water, her stern acting as a powerful rudder, where the resistance to her progress is the least. She stands upright in a gale which compels other yachts to heel over considerably.

She measured 170 tons, with a length of 101 feet and beam of 23 feet. Her enormous spars measured 79 and 81 feet and her main boom, 58 feet. Her frame was composed of oak, locust, cedar, chestnut, and hackmatack, supported by diagonal iron braces. Her outer planking was three-inch oak. She had four staterooms and a large fore cabin with 14 berths.

Launched on May 3 (18 days after the *Flying Cloud*), she sailed from New York for Le Havre. It was originally planned that some of the owners would cross by yacht, but John and Edward Stevens and Colonel and Mrs. Hamilton went by liner, and the staterooms on the *America* were offered to George Steers, his brother James, and the latter's two teen-age sons. They enjoyed the crossing and the race but were rather bitter about the snobbery which excluded them from the social amenities—Cowes was anything but democratic. They did not even have a chance to bet the funds they brought over for that purpose. The skipper of the yacht, both in the Atlantic crossing and in the race, was "Old Dick" Brown, veteran Sandy Hook pilot.

It was agreed that the race would be open to all rigs and nations; although a wide variety of schooners and cutters were among the 15 contenders, no foreign yacht except the *America* was entered. The Royal Yacht Club offered a "hundred guinea cup" as a prize. The course lay some 53 miles around the Isle of Wight, starting and ending at Cowes, the home of the club.

The morning of Friday, August 23, found Cowes in a state of excitement and high anticipation, occasioned principally by the presence of the long, low black hull and raking masts of the American yacht. In the words of the *Times* correspondent who wrote with great enthusiasm and detail:

In the memory of man, Cowes never presented such an appearance as upon last Friday. There must have been upwards of one hundred yachts laying at anchor in the roads; the beach crowded from Egypt to the piers—the esplanade in front of the club thronged with ladies and gentlemen, and with the people inland, who came over on shoals with wives, sons and daughters for the day. Booths were erected all along the quay, and the roadstead was alive with boats, while from the sea and shore arose an incessant buzz of voices, mingled with the splashing of oars, the flapping of sails and the hissing of steam from the excursion vessels preparing to accompany the race.

The yachts for the race lined up off Cowes Castle. The mist was carried off about 9 o'clock by a very gentle breeze from the westward, which veered around a little to the south. The 15 yachts lined up—seven were schooners and eight cutters. At 10 o'clock came the signal gun for sailing, and the whole of the beautiful fleet was under weigh. The only laggard was the *America,* which did not move for a second or so after the others.

In the late forenoon, "the *America* began to show a touch of her quality . . . she 'walked along' past cutter and schooner, and when off Brading had left every vessel in the squadron behind her . . . with the exception of the *Volante,* which she overtook at 11:30. At 3:30 the *Bacchante* and *Eclipse,* which had been working honestly and steadily, were about 2½ miles to leeward behind her. Further away still were visible five or six yachts, some hull down, some dipped further still."

About 5:30 near the Needles at the Western end of the island, the royal steam yacht *Victoria and Albert* came close and was properly saluted. There is a story that Queen Victoria asked her equerry what yacht was second. "Your majesty," was the alleged reply, "there is no second." The royal encounter, with the American yacht now alone among the contestants, was the climax of the race. Shortly afterward, the wind died down and the finish to Cowes was a mere formality.

From that point onward, the story falls into two distinct parts. One is the subsequent career of the yacht herself, continuing with various vicissitudes until destroyed in a blizzard at Annapolis Yacht Yard on March 29, 1942, when over 90 years old. The other half of the story is the long series of challenges, principally from England, for the "America's Cup," a competition still continuing in races at Newport. Both stories are interesting, but none of the subsequent action can compare with those amazing hours around the Isle of Wight.

(See E. Bradford, *The America's Cup,* 1964.)

Birkenhead

Wreck of H.M.S. *Birkenhead,* off Cape of Good Hope, 1852. *(National Maritime Museum, Greenwich)*

The British have always been extremely proud of their "Birkenhead Drill," when several hundred redcoats stood fast on the deck of their sinking transport in 1852 and went down with their ship off South Africa, rather than endanger the lives of their women and children. This call of "women and children first" stood in sharp contrast to the terrible behavior of the French crews of the *Medusa* and *Bourgogne* or even the firemen on the American *Arctic.*

The 1400-ton *Birkenhead* was launched in 1845 in the Liverpool suburb of Birkenhead as a paddle-wheel iron-hulled frigate. The Admiralty, however, decided against iron for combat purposes and converted her into a transport. At the time of her disaster she was bringing replacements for the British forces in the Kaffir war—480 officers and men from 10 different regiments. She was bound for Algoa Bay under Commander Robert Salmond, with Colonel Seton of the 74th Highlanders as senior military officer.

Arriving from Cork in Ireland, she put into Simons Bay just below Cape Town for two days. Then on February 25, 1852, she set out up the coast off Danger Point for Algoa Bay, keeping rather too close to the shore. About 1 A.M. she crunched into a sharp pinnacle of rock which opened her bow to an inrush of water, drowning some of the men in their hammocks. The captain unwisely ordered the engines reversed, and the ship backed off into deep water, with the water running in faster than ever.

The troops were brought up on deck; some of them engaged in the hopeless job of pumping, others tried to push horses overboard, still others worked desperately but with scant success to get some of the boats free and overboard. Although there were numerous boats, many of them were in bad condition. It was a special misfortune that the big pinnace had been crushed when the funnel fell over. As it was, three boats were put over and into one of them were put the 13 women and children on board.

Most of the troops were lined up on deck. As the ship broke apart, it was obvious that she could not stay afloat long. Captain Salmond finally called out, "All who can swim, jump overboard and make for the boats." But they were not given that choice. Colonel Seton over-ruled Salmond with the order, "Stand fast!" Seton feared that the men might endanger the women and children by swamping their boat. A recent author, however, has called it the "Birkenhead Blunder," a piece of army command stupidity, ranking with the "Charge of the Light Brigade" in the Crimea two years later. At any rate, the men stood fast and many went down with the ship. Some of them managed to get to shore two miles away despite the triple threat of sharks, entangling seaweed, and the surf on the rockbound shore. Altogether, some 491 lives were lost, including Commander Salmond and Colonel Seton. The handful of women and children were saved and a great tradition was born.

There was a repetition of this same fatal discipline in 1893 when the *Victoria* and *Camperdown* collided in the Mediterranean. For almost an hour, with sinking inevitable, the *Victoria*'s crew were drawn up on deck and half of them went down with the ship. The navy as well as the army had its discipline and its stupidity.

(See D. Bevan, *Drums of the Birkenhead*, 1972.)

Great Republic

The keenest blow suffered by Donald McKay in his remarkable clipper-building career was the accidental burning of his huge 4555-ton masterpiece, the *Great Republic*, in 1853, just as she was about to sail on her maiden voyage. Salvaged and cut down to 3356 tons, she sailed on various routes with occasional distinction until 1872.

McKay had planned her for the booming passenger and cargo service between London and Melbourne, Australia, in which several of his best ships were already engaged. McKay designed and built her at his own risk at his East Boston yard. The whole shipping world followed with the keenest interest every detail of her construction—her 335-foot length and 53-foot beam, her four decks, her four masts, her very elaborate passenger accommodations, and all the rest. Tremendous crowds gathered for her launching on October 4, 1853, following which she was towed to New York to load for Liverpool. On the night of December 26, a great fire started on Front Street and embers were carried by the wind to where the *Great Republic* lay. She was quickly ablaze; her masts were cut away and she was scuttled, but the water was too shallow to save her upper works, and she was burned to the water's edge. McKay gave her up to the underwriters—the insurance amounted to $180,000 on the ship and $275,000 on the cargo.

The wreck was raised and pumped out, and was purchased by A. A. Low & Brothers, the firm which had built the pioneer *Houqua* and *Samuel Russell.* Captain Nathaniel B. Palmer supervised the reconstruction. With three decks instead of four and with spars reduced, the *Great Republic* sailed for Liverpool on February 24, 1855, with a crew of 50, just half of the originally planned 100. Her draft was too much for entering the Liverpool docks. With the Crimean War in progress, she, like several other American clippers, was chartered as a transport by the French. Then she made some fast records on the traditional New York–San Francisco route, with one run in 92 days. She sailed for London with an odoriferous guano cargo from the Chincha Islands and was badly battered by a gale. She saw further service on the Cape Horn run, with brief Civil War logistical service to the Southern naval bases. After more guano and miscellaneous runs, she was sold in Yarmouth, Nova Scotia, in 1866. Three years later she was sold in Liverpool and renamed *Denmark.* Badly leaking in a March gale, she was abandoned at sea, all hands reaching Bermuda safely.

(See C. C. Cutler, *Greyhounds of the Sea,* 1930.)

Red Jacket

Most of the best clippers were built on New York's East River or around Boston, but one exception was the *Red Jacket,* built at Rockland, Maine, in 1853, which had some unique achievements. This 2305-ton clipper, designed by Samuel H. Pook and built in the Rockland yard of "Deacon" George Thomas, was 251 feet in length and 44 feet in beam, with very sharp lines. Beautiful and graceful, she was sometimes called the best looking of the clippers. She was named for a Seneca Indian chief, a pro-British leader in the American Revolution who wore a red coat given to him by a British officer. The *Red Jacket*'s first owners were Seacomb & Taylor of Boston. Her first captain was a versatile Cape Codder, Asa Eldridge, who had commanded the crack Collins Dramatic Line packet *Roscius* and who was later lost commanding the Collins Line *Pacific,* which went missing in 1855.

The *Red Jacket*'s particular reputation rested on an all-time record run of 13 days, 1 hour, and 25 minutes across the very stormy North Atlantic from New York to Liverpool in January 1854. Launched on November 2, 1853, she came on the scene relatively late and never participated in the conventional Cape Horn–San Francisco run.

Once arrived in England with that transatlantic record, her activities shifted to the London-Melbourne run, which was booming following the discovery of gold in Australia. Chartered by the White Star Line **208** (not to be confused with the later transatlantic service), she made the

13,880-mile run to Melbourne in 69 days. With passengers and gold dust, she came back by Cape Horn, with some dangerous ice experi- ences. The line purchased her for a reputed £ 30,000 and she became a favorite passenger liner. She held her own against the *Lightning, Chariot of Fame, Empress of the Seas,* and *James Baines* built by Donald McKay.

For a while after the passenger service to Australia fell off, she engaged in various trades, including during the 1870s the Quebec-Liverpool timber trade. Eventually, she wound up her career as a coal hulk in the Cape Verde Islands.

(See C. C. Cutler, *Greyhounds of the Sea,* 1930.)

Arctic

The wooden sidewheeler *Arctic,* after collision in mid-ocean, 1854. *(Peabody Museum, Salem)*

The climax of the old American merchant marine came from the mid-1840s to the mid-1850s. Various circumstances combined to produce it, particularly the China and California trade and the sudden inrush of Irish and German immigrants. American shipping increased in quantity until it almost reached that of the British, and in quality surpassed that of the British. In only one field were the British ahead: their Cunard liners since 1850 had developed the prime service across the Atlantic. As a matter of pride, therefore, the Americans decided to spend heavily to "beat the Cunarders." And for four glorious years well-subsidized American ships of the Collins Line regularly did beat the Cunarders into port. But the American emphasis was almost entirely on speed; as a result, two of its four liners were lost—the *Arctic* in 1854 with a heavy loss of life, and the *Pacific* two years later, disappearing without a trace. That, for a century, was the end of American effort to secure the "blue riband" of the Atlantic.

The matter of steamship subsidies had come to a head in Britain in 1839–1840. The British had appreciated that it was in the government interest to pay generously to offset the cost of coal, if they were to have regular service on overseas routes. As a result, subsidized lines were established by the P & O (Peninsular and Oriental) to India, by the Royal Mail to the West Indies, and by Cunard to Halifax and Boston. With American supremacy in clippers, yachting, and other fields, pride demanded that steps be taken to excel in transatlantic service as well.

Toward this end, Congress in 1847 voted to establish a line "far in excess of any of its predecessors on the North Atlantic." It was voted to build four ships for a monthly service at $385,000 a year; this was later increased. The prime mover in the new line was a persuasive, smooth Cape Cod extrovert, Edward Knight Collins. He had appropriate background for the task. His father had run a series of New York–Vera Cruz packets, and he himself had run a line of big New York–New Orleans packets, and then had branched out into the most successful of the New York–Liverpool square-rigged packets. He not only had fine ships, all named for great thespians—*Shakespeare, Roscius, Garrick, Siddons*—but he also developed the important art of cultivating traveler comfort.

The new Collins Line was formed with the financial backing of James Brown and his family, Brown Brothers & Company of Baltimore. The company's backing of more than $1,000,000 included $180,000 from Collins. In addition, Brown met the company's further needs with a loan. The company contracted for four wooden sidewheelers: the *Atlantic, Pacific, Arctic,* and *Baltic.* At some 2860 tons, they were more than double the size of the original Cunarders.

The ships were elaborate in every way; no expense was spared. They had straight stems instead of the usual clipper bows and generally elaborate fittings. The table and service were designed to appeal to first-class company.

The *Atlantic* had inaugurated the Collins service with a sailing from New York on April 17, 1850, exactly 10 years after the first Cunard sailing on April 17, 1840. Almost immediately the New York papers began to cover the Cunard-Collins crossings as a sporting event, with the Cunarders always in the rear.

The fateful voyage of the *Arctic* started from Liverpool on September 20, 1854, under the command of Captain James C. Luce, who had had a prominent career in packets. The liners of that day, and for a considerable time later, carried numerous V.I.P.s, but this time passengers of special significance were aboard. They included Collins's wife and two of their children, a daughter 19 and a son 13, and Mrs. Collins's brother and his wife. The Brown family was represented by James Brown's favorite daughter, Millie; her brother William and his French wife; her sister Grace and her husband George Allen (one of the ship's engine builders) and their two children. All would be victims of the disaster.

The ship had sailed on the dot on September 20, in time to settle down for a typical Collins repast. Even back in his Dramatic Line days, Collins had believed in feeding his passengers well. A good table would be a strong drawing card in contrast to the rather uninspired cuisine aboard the Cunarders. The luncheon menu on the *Arctic*, even in that pre-deep-freeze era, read:

Soups: Green Turtle Soup, Potage aux Chous

Boiled: Ham; Tongue; Cold Corned Beef; Turkey, Oyster Sauce; Fowl, Parsley Sauce; Leg of Mutton, Caper Sauce

Fish: Codfish, Stuffed and Baked; Boiled Bass, Hollandaise Sauce

Roast: Beef; Veal; Mutton; Lamb; Goose, Champagne Sauce; Duck; Pig; Turkey; Fowl

etc. etc.

And so the ship progressed—"paddles rhythmically slapping, the *Arctic* steamed confidently along at 13 knots. She had reached the Grand Banks of Newfoundland, the vast region notorious for its cold treacherous mists." In later days, a ship would have been blowing her whistle at regular intervals, but the *Arctic* had no whistle.

On September 27 the *Arctic* drove into a fog bank. And with that came an alarmed cry from the lookout, "There's a steamer ahead!" A bark-rigged steamer headed eastward under a full press of sail made a desperate last-minute effort but crashed into the *Arctic*. She was the *Vesta*, a small screw steamer bound for France with a large group of fishermen from the little colony of St. Pierre. For the moment, it looked as though the *Vesta* with her crumpled bow was in danger. There was one important feature, however: she was built of iron and was compart-mentalized. It soon became evident that the *Arctic* was the one in danger. Three holes had been cut below the waterline and water was pouring in. Her bow was sinking and had a list to starboard. Gradually, the water encroached on the engine room.

On deck the crucial question of the lifeboats had to be faced. Some excellent new Francis lifeboats were available, but only enough for a fraction of those aboard the sinking ship. It was becoming obvious that not everyone could be taken off. Unfortunately, the vigorous first officer had gone off in a boat to assist the *Vesta;* had he been aboard, his discipline might have improved the situation. As it was, stokers and some other men rushed the boats, crowding out the women and children. A group of engineers went off in their own boat.

While this was happening, some prominent passengers, including the Collins family and the Browns, were isolated at one side, crowded out by the stokers. They took a poll as to who should be saved, if anyone, and decided on Millie; but apparently she went down with the rest of them.

Efforts were made to put together a large raft to carry as many persons as possible; the ship's last lifeboat was attached to it to help in the work. "Luce and the few passengers who were attempting to keep the crowd back were having scant success. Then suddenly there was a premature alarm that the *Arctic* was about to go down. And once more decency and honor vanished before the mad selfish instinct of self-preservation. Another despicable rush was made for the last little lifeboat, coal heavers, firemen, waiters, and sailors precipitating themselves over the ship's bulwarks, crossing the raft, thrusting aside the dedicated few still trying to put it together, and rolling helter-skelter into the boat." One fireman, Patrick Tobin, was quite shameless about the matter, "It was every man for himself. No more attention was paid to the captain than to any other man on board. Life was as sweet to us as to others." And this was only two years after the redcoats had stayed in formation aboard the *Birkenhead* to save the women and children.

At 4:45 P.M., more than four hours after the collision, the *Arctic* finally sank, stern first. Those on deck were thrown into the icy waters or drawn under by the suction. Captain Luce had declared his intention to go down with his ship, and he did. But, like Captain Turner of the *Lusitania* 50 years later, he rose to the surface and was rescued. The big improvised raft started off with 76, including three women; but they kept dropping off, and only one man was saved. Others were on informal little rafts and some were picked up. Two of the lifeboats made a landing on a rugged Newfoundland beach, and the survivors made their way overland to St. John's, where the officials were very dilatory in sending out vessels to search for other survivors. As it was, some time elapsed before the rescuing vessels reached port to report survivors. One survivor turned out to be an "Enoch Arden" case. He was a New Orleans merchant named Fleury, who had been seen on deck as the ship went down. His attractive young widow remarried, had three children, and was living happily when in 1860 a letter arrived from Fleury. He had been rescued by a whaler just setting out on a long voyage. The whaler, in turn, had been wrecked and the survivors rescued by another whaler which had just reached port.

New York did not learn of the *Arctic*'s loss until October 11, 13 days after the sinking. The tragedy left the city in a state of profound shock; crowds of relatives besieged the newspaper offices to learn of any later possible rescue. The full reaction was summed up by Alexander Crosby Brown, some of whose relatives had gone down on the ship, in his book *Women and Children Last:* "Though instances of courage and heroism were reported, the details gleaned in the course of the newspaper interviews gradually confirmed the terrible story of such greed, inhumanity, and callous abandonment that people could hardly force themselves to believe it. Incredulity turned to dismay, then horror, and finally wrath. Of a total of around 400 persons on board the liner, the final tally disclosed that only 86 had been saved. Of these 70 per cent were crewmen, 30 per cent passengers. Of that whole company there was not a single woman or child."

The Collins Line survived the loss of the *Arctic*. The three remaining ships kept up the schedule, whereas the Cunard competition was slowed down by the demands of the Crimean War. The fatal blow came two years later, in 1856, with the loss of the *Pacific*. She left Liverpool on January 23 with a light midwinter passenger list of 46 and a crew of 141. She was never heard from again. The presumption was that she had struck an iceberg, since one had been sighted in the area. That news came while the Collins Line was having to fight to hold onto its subsidy; many of the Southerners had long resented paying so much to New York. Early in 1857 the subsidy was drastically cut to its original figure. The line's big new 3670-ton *Adriatic* came on the scene too late and made only one round trip. The last Collins voyage ended on February 18, 1858, with the arrival of the *Baltic*. Two months later, the *Atlantic, Baltic,* and *Adriatic* were auctioned off to satisfy creditors; the sole bidder acquired all three for $50,000. Collins moved west and engaged in various shore-based activities.

(See A. C. Brown, *Women and Children Last: The Loss of the Steamship Arctic*, 1961.)

Andrew Jackson

The clipper *Andrew Jackson* made one of the three fastest runs over the classic, clipper race track between New York and San Francisco—the other two 89-day runs were made by Donald McKay's *Flying Cloud*. In addition, the *Andrew Jackson* made an unbeaten westbound record of 15 days between Liverpool and New York. The surprising thing is that she made both those remarkable runs in 1860 at the very end of the clipper ship era. In fact, she had been built in 1855 after clipper construction was beginning to slow down sharply. Furthermore, she was not a product of the crack East River yards of New York or the yards of Boston, but of the quiet little outport of Mystic, Connecticut, midway between New York and Boston.

Measuring 1679 tons, just under the *Flying Cloud's* 1782, she was launched at the yard of Irons & Grinnell, and was originally named the *Belle Hoxie*—Hoxie was a prominent Mystic name and the yard had already produced a *Harriet Hoxie*. Soon after reaching New York, she was sold to John H. Brower & Company which renamed her *Andrew Jackson*.

In spite of her speed records, she was rated as a "medium clipper" rather than an "extreme clipper" such as the *Flying Cloud* and many others. She represented an approach to what would be called "Down Easters" after the Civil War. As Carl Cutler expressed it, this new modification "combined to a rare degree the beauty and speed of the extreme clipper with the huge stowage capacity of the packet ships." The vulnerable aspect of the extreme clipper was the sacrificing of a third of her carrying capacity in the quest for speed. By 1855, when the *Andrew Jackson* was built, the new compromise was evidently in the air. She was built with unusual strength—one of the most powerful clippers ever built—and with a reduction of the special gear aloft she could get by with a smaller crew. A ship's captain is an invaluable asset for speed, and she had Captain John E. (Jack) Williams, "with possibly one or two exceptions the hardest 'driver' that ever walked a quarterdeck."

The *Andrew Jackson* had a moderately successful record in her first four voyages and then came her record-breaking run (December 23, 1859–March 23, 1860), which ended in circumstances that have left the nit-pickers busy ever since over the question of the fastest of all the New York–San Francisco runs. She reached the pilot grounds off the Farallon Islands in 89 days and four hours. But then the wind went down and she had to wait until next morning for a pilot. The *Flying Cloud* in her second record voyage made it in 89 days and eight hours from anchor to anchor. The citizens of San Francisco gave high honors to Captain Williams for the fastest voyage, but the rival claims have continued. Carl Cutler in his *Greyhounds of the Sea* made a good case for the *Andrew Jackson*, saying that pilot to pilot was the real test of seamanship, and the remaining harbor run with a pilot was less significant. Cutler was a resident of Mystic, where he was the principal founder of Mystic Seaport; in addition, Captain Williams settled down in Mystic for the rest of his life. Cutler, in summing up, declared, "The honors are virtually even between the two ships. . . . Both were noble, good craft commanded by men who are entitled to be numbered among the first dozen of the hardest driving sailor men the world has produced."

Less widely appreciated was the *Andrew Jackson*'s unchallenged and unbroken record from Liverpool westward to New York later that same year in 15 days (November 3–18) under Captain Johnson.

Later, like so many of the best clippers, the *Andrew Jackson* was caught in the "flight from the flag" and sold to British registry in 1863 to avoid the high war-risk insurance rates on American flag ships. She made a voyage to Java in 1864. In 1868 she sailed from Shanghai for home but ran on a reef of Gasper Strait on December 4, 1868, and was a total loss.

(See O. T. Howe and F. C. Matthews, *American Clipper Ships, 1833–1858*, 1926–1927.)

Central America

For 20 years after the discovery of gold in California, the quickest way to the West from the East was by the two subsidized lines of steamships converging on the Isthmus of Panama from New York and San Francisco. The Pacific Mail, which went into operation in 1848–1849 with the *California*, had a long record of stability and good management under the distinguished firm of Howland & Aspinwall. The United States Mail, on the Atlantic side, was a different story. Under the partial direction of George Law, a rugged, colorful, and not altogether admirable character, it lacked clean-cut performance in finance, operation, and observance of subsidy contract terms. It started service with a small makeshift vessel because its regular ones were not ready.

The *Central America* had had the name for only two months when she met her end. She had been called the *George Law* until that character left the company. She was a wooden sidewheeler of 1214 tons, built by William H. Webb at his East River yard in 1852. Her two oscillating engines were built by the Morgan Iron Works at New York. Her dining room service left much to be desired. In fact, the United States Mail had a much poorer name with the public than did the Pacific Mail.

On September 8, 1857, at the height of the hurricane season, the *Central America* sailed from Havana, her midway stop between Aspinwall on the Isthmus and New York. She had a full passenger list of 474, many of whom were returning from California, a crew of 101, and about $2,000,000 in gold. Because of the subsidy arrangement with the Navy, the command of these liners went to naval officers—usually well-connected, promising men. Commander Herndon was appointed her captain. Matthew Fontaine Maury, "pathfinder of the seas," was Herndon's brother-in-law, and Herndon's daughter Ellen Lewis married (President) Chester Alan Arthur in 1859.

Two days out, the *Central America* ran into a northwest gale, which soon developed hurricane strength. Then her engines failed and could not be revived to keep her head into the wind. As she wallowed in the trough of the heavy seas, her seams began to open and she shipped water faster than the pumping could keep it down. It was generally conceded afterward that the fault lay not in the hull, but in the engines. Captain Herndon did all he could to rectify matters; the passengers joined in the pumping and in shifting the cargo to the windward side. Finally, when a Boston brig hove to, boats from the *Central America* began to make the dangerous passage through the heavy seas. There was no panic or efforts to rush the boats and no question that women and children came first. A hundred were saved but the second trip was the last.

With darkness coming on, Captain Herndon knew there was no further hope. He gave his watch to one of the passengers on the last trip to be given to his wife. He then went to his cabin, donned his full-dress uniform, and went back on deck, giving the picture of complete calmness. During the night the *Central America* went down with 475 of her passengers and crew, Captain Herndon, and the California gold. The news of the disaster aroused widespread popular indignation against the United States Mail Steamship Company.

By a grim coincidence, a similar wreck of a similar ship had occurred in 1852 in these same Atlantic waters. The Pacific Mail's *San Francisco,* like the *Central America,* had her hull by Webb and her engines by Morgan, and her engines were also blamed for the wreck. Sailing from New York on charter with some 750 troops aboard, she encountered a violent Christmas gale; her engines failed, and she fell into the trough. Some 550 of the 750 aboard were saved by other ships.

(See H. W. Baldwin, *Sea Fights and Ship Wrecks,* 1955.)

Great Eastern

The *Great Eastern,*
built in 1858.
*(National Maritime
Museum, Greenwich)*

The "Great Iron Ship," larger than any other vessel for a half century to come, was the result of a combination of bold imagination and engineering skill on the one hand and of economic miscalculation and hard luck on the other. Following the *Great Western* and *Great Britain,* she was the brainchild of Isambard Kingdom Brunel who, worn out with overexertion and worry, barely lived to see her afloat. The *Great Eastern* was well known to the world: on both sides of the Atlantic huge crowds turned out to see her and to tread her decks. But she never "paid," as her successive owners could testify.

By the 1850s Brunel was turning away from railway development which had commanded so much of his energy toward steamships. Special emphasis in the direction of ships came from news of the discovery of gold in Australia in 1851, just three years after the California discovery. It happened that his *Great Britain,* repaired after her serious wreck, was about to enter on more than 20 years of successful service between England and Australia. But Brunel conceived the idea of a vessel large enough to carry all the coal she would need for a nonstop run out to eastern seas. That was the purpose of the great 22,000-ton ship which could carry 15,000 tons of coal out to Trincomalee in Ceylon, whence her passengers and cargo could continue to India, China, or Australia. And that was the one thing she never had the opportunity to do.

217

The Eastern Steam Navigation Company, replacing the defunct earlier companies, sought to raise the £ 317,000 which Brunel optimistically estimated as the cost of hull and paddle engines. Brunel's most serious fault of judgment was in linking himself with W. Scott Russell, a brilliant shipbuilder but, as it turned out, unstable and apparently dishonest. Nearly all the initial capital outlay went through Russell's hands with very little to show for it, with the result that the great ship could not carry out the proposed service to Trincomalee. The ship was built under Russell's immediate direction in his Milwall yard on the dreary Isle of Dogs on the Thames, where it was decided that because of the cramped space, it would be necessary to build her parallel to the shore and to launch her sideways.

The construction was started in 1852 and went on for four years, with her gigantic hull towering 54 feet over the whole area. Many of Brunel's features, which were so satisfactory in the *Great Britain,* were incorporated and amplified in the giant ship. One feature, however, was unique and was seldom if ever copied thereafter. It was explained that it would not be possible to get a single paddle connection or a screw heavy enough to carry the whole strain of the ship's propulsion. During the construction 3,000,000 rivets were driven to pin down 3000 plates of iron, averaging about one-inch thick.

At length, on November 7, 1856, plans were made to launch her sideways, with a high spring tide. Unknown to Brunel, the directors had sold 3000 tickets for the ceremony, with the chairman's daughter presiding at the launching. When the day came, she christened the ship *Leviathan,* but later by popular acclaim the name was changed to *Great Eastern* to fit Brunel's other "Greats." When high tide came, the ship barely budged; never before had such heavy weight been concentrated in a single spot. That was the beginning of Brunel's crucial embarrassments, which would continue for months. At last, on January 31, 1858, her prospective master yelled, "The wedges are floating! She's afloat!" Brunel hurried aboard and directed her across the Thames to Deptford, while the bells of London began to peal.

The ship was finally afloat, but too much time and money had dribbled away to make the basic Trincomalee dream come true. In the past six years the ship had cost $4,000,000, and it was estimated that $600,000 more would be needed. The shareholders of the Eastern Steam Navigation Company had lost over $1,700,000. The question then arose of what to do next. Hopes of selling her to the Royal Navy failed, as did the efforts, after the Civil War started, to sell her to the Union Navy. Brunel then helped to found the Great Ship Company at $1,700,000, which bought the ship for $800,000. Disregarding Brunel's arguments for the long voyages to eastern seas, the company decided upon transatlantic runs.

Brunel did not live to see his great ship really in action. On September 9, 1858, the *Great Eastern,* in all her majesty, had put to sea from the mouth of the Thames, plowing through the waves at 13 knots. Suddenly, off Hastings on the south coast, came a terrific explosion from the "feedwater valves." The explosion demolished some of the cabin fixings and badly scalded a dozen of the engine room gang. Brunel had hoped to learn of her triumphal inaugural, but the report of this disaster was the last news that he heard. He died of Bright's disease on September 15, 1858.

Three decades of indecision as to what to do with the great ship followed. The original all-the-way-with-coal plan did not come up; there was no service to Trincomalee which, if capital had been available, might have justified the original plans at least until the Suez Canal was opened in 1869. The obvious answer was the transatlantic service, for which the *Great Eastern* was not particularly adapted, and which was already well served by Cunard and others. The *Great Eastern* made some trips to New York, attracting large crowds and developing a couple of "drunken cruises" down the coast. Then came one more misfortune to the "Greats." Near Montauk Point at the eastern end of Long Island, the *Great Eastern* ran into an uncharted pinnacle of rock which cut a great gash in her outer hull, though it did not penetrate the inner bottom. This disaster made another heavy inroad into any possible profits.

In 1865 the *Great Eastern* ran into her one major field of profit and usefulness, the laying of the Atlantic cable. A first attempt to complete the cable-laying project of Cyrus W. Field had been made in 1859, when a British warship and an American warship laid the cable between Ireland and Newfoundland. For a brief time, communication was established, then the line burned out. In 1865 the project was revived and the *Great Eastern* with her huge capacity undertook the job alone. All went well for a while, but the cable suddenly broke and could not be recovered. On a second attempt the *Great Eastern* triumphantly landed the cable in Heart's Content, Newfoundland, already connected by cable with the mainland. This completed permanent transatlantic cable connection.

Backed by this experience, the *Great Eastern* did considerable further cable laying, particularly going around Good Hope to Bombay, where she picked up a cable for Aden and carried it on up the Red Sea for a Mediterranean contact. But that good duty ended when the cable interests built a cable layer of their own, and the *Great Eastern* in 1874, then about 20 years old, had to find other employment. By that time she was really a drug on the market, a white elephant, capable only of attracting occasional crowds on barnstorming visits. Her most humiliating experience came when a Liverpool firm of textile merchants anchored her in the Mersey and put large advertisements on her sides and cheap carnival stunts aboard. In 1889–1890 she was finally broken up in the Mersey. The breaking up, however, did silence one longstanding rumor that the skeleton of a riveter was hidden in the double bottoms. Not until the *Lusitania* in 1906 was there another ship as large as the *Great Eastern*.

(See P. Beaver, *The Big Ship: Brunel's Great Eastern: A Pictorial History*, 1969; J. Dugan, *The Great Iron Ship*, 1953.)

IV

THE TRIUMPH OF
STEAM

(1859–1896)

Gloire

Warrior

Merrimack

Monitor

Hartford

Florida

Alabama

Kearsarge

H. L. Hunley

Shenandoah

Sultana

Ariel

Erzherzog Ferdinand
Maximilian

Agamemnon

Wampanoag

Cutty Sark

Mary Powell

Captain

Natchez and Robert E. Lee

Mary Celeste

Bear

Moewe

Glückauf

Trenton

Corsair
(Gloucester)

Victoria and Camperdown

Priscilla

Spray

Maine

Olympia

Oregon

La Bourgogne

Portland

IV

THE TRIUMPH OF STEAM
(1859–1896)

The last half of the nineteenth century marked the virtual end to the era of sail. At the beginning of the period major warships such as the *Hartford* (1862) and the *Ferdinand Maximilian* (1866), although steam-powered, were full-rigged as well, for only under sail could they achieve a reasonable cruising range. By the end of the nineteenth century, however, warships like the *Oregon* (1898) relied entirely on improved steam propulsion and, except for a few training vessels, sail disappeared forever from the world's major navies. Meanwhile, other new developments pointed to the future. The first ironclad warships, France's *Gloire* and Britain's *Warrior*, appeared in 1859 and 1861, respectively, and the following year witnessed the first battle between two such vessels—the *Merrimack* and the *Monitor*. The *Monitor* was also the first warship to mount its primary guns in a revolving turret. In 1864 the Confederate Navy's *Hunley* became the first submarine to sink an active warship, the Union cruiser *Housatonic*. Within a short span of years, therefore, the principles of naval construction were revolutionized.

Among mercantile fleets, however, change came more gradually. The introduction of the more efficient compound steam engine, which required less coal than earlier types, gave such British vessels as the *Agamemnon* (1866) sufficient range and capacity ultimately to supplant the square-rigger as carrier of the world's goods. And along the coast of America and Great Britain steamers like the *Mary Powell* gave fast, regular service for passengers and light cargoes, although bulk commodities were still carried more cheaply by sail. Steam even challenged sail in yachting circles, with floating palaces like J. P. Morgan's *Corsair;* however, in the yachting set sail has maintained its popularity. By the end of the nineteenth century merchant sail too had all but disappeared from the deep seas.

Gloire

An event of paramount importance in naval history occurred on November 24, 1859, when the French launched at Toulon the *Gloire,* the first seagoing ironclad, ancestor of the later battleships. The story goes to 1822 when Colonel Paixhans, a Napoleonic veteran, brought out a little study entitled *The New Maritime Force.* He argued that the navy got off too easily in fighting. An army might lose 10,000 men even in winning a victory, whereas the British navy had lost only 500 in its great victory at Trafalgar. He proposed to make naval actions by substituting explosive shells for solid cannon balls. Naval officers could visualize the havoc such shells would cause in a wooden warship, so the cry went up, "For God's sake, keep out the shells!" It was a relatively simple matter to develop shell guns, but keeping the shells out took longer to achieve. For the next several years the French and British both experimented in attaching 4½-inch slabs of iron to the sides of wooden ships.

The Crimean War, in which Turkey and her allies England, France, and Sardinia fought against Russia from 1854 to 1856, brought the issue of shells to a head. First, a Russian squadron with shell guns wiped out a Turkish squadron in the Black Sea. Then the war concentrated in an allied attack on the powerful fortifications of Sebastopol. Since it seemed suicidal to bring the conventional wooden warships into close range of the Russian guns, the French, with British cooperation, built a group of small but heavily armored floating batteries which could safely approach the Russian guns. Their success paved the way for the next step, under the brilliant leadership of Stanislas C. H. Dupuy de Lôme, whom the Emperor Napoleon III now placed in charge of naval construction. Like Colonel Paixhans, he was a graduate of the École Polytechnique. He studied naval construction in the British shipyards, which were the most advanced in the field, and gave evidence of many original ideas.

Under his enthusiastic leadership and with the constant support of Napoleon III, he launched upon an ambitious plan to challenge Britain's naval supremacy. The French were already catching up in wooden steamships of the line; now he saw a chance to get well ahead of England with ironclads which could threaten the wooden ships. In 1858 the French started a program of four armored ships, to be followed by others.

The *Gloire* was the first of these at 5617 tons. Her 900-horsepower engines could drive her at 12 knots; she had 36 guns arranged in the conventional broadside pattern, and she cost about $1,000,000. At the time of her launching, she was more than a match for anything afloat, including the huge three-decked wooden ship of the line the British had launched that year. Nor was she alone—the *Invincible, Normandie,* and *Couronne* were coming along. The *Couronne* had an iron instead of a wooden hull. Incidentally, in this new development iron armor did not necessarily require an iron hull. The British had built some iron-hulled warships but had discarded them for major fighting purposes.

The *Gloire* behaved well in a run over to Algiers, and the French had high hopes of their bid for sea power.

(See J. P. Baxter, III, *The Introduction of the Ironclad Warship,* 1932.)

Warrior

The British had let the French take the lead in the initial development of the ironclads. But even before the *Gloire* was launched, the British had laid down the keel of the *Warrior* to offset her. It was pointed out that this was consistent with British policy. It would be foolish, they said, to undertake a movement which would render obsolete their powerful existing fleet. But once their leadership was threatened, as it was with the big *Gloire* program, no time was to be lost in offsetting the threat. Although there was a change in ministry that year, the British did some necessary experimenting and then got underway with their own ironclad, which was stronger than the *Gloire* and had an iron instead of a wooden hull. Because of her advanced industrial development, England was in a better position to make up for lost time than France, whose industry still lagged.

The *Warrior* was launched on December 29, 1860, and completed on October 24, 1861, at a cost of about $1,800,000. She had a belt of 4½-inch armor backed by 18 inches of teak. But instead of protecting her entire hull, it covered only the vital central section. She measured 9210 tons, as compared with 5617 tons for the French rival, and she was more heavily armed. To match the ambitious French ironclad program, the British radically increased theirs, and the "scare" abated.

It was remarked of the *Warrior* that "she should be able to overtake and overwhelm any other warship in existence." She was never called upon to exercise that power in the course of her service afloat. For almost a quarter century the British would keep experimenting to find just the type of ship they wanted, until they achieved the *Royal Sovereign* class about 1890. In the meantime there were some 20 different

classes, all of which possessed the quality of the capital ship in being
able to withstand the same sort of blows that their guns could deal out. These capital ships were referred to as ironclads until steel supplanted iron late in the century, at which time they became known as battleships.

(See J. P. Baxter, III, *The Introduction of the Ironclad Warship,* 1932.)

Merrimack

The sinking of the frigate *Cumberland* by the ironclad *Merrimack* in Hampton Roads, March 8, 1862. *(Naval Historical Center)*

The Confederate *Merrimack* and the Union *Monitor* fought the first battle of ironclad warships in Hampton Roads in Virginia on March 9, 1862. On the previous day the *Merrimack* had easily sunk two wooden Union sailing cruisers. The *Monitor-Merrimack* fight was long credited with having revolutionized naval warfare, but that overlooked the fact that France with its *Gloire* in 1859 and Britain with its *Warrior* in 1861 already had ironclads at sea and more were being built. They had not, however, been engaged in battle. The Hampton Roads action was fairly indecisive, but the *Monitor* could claim a tactical victory in having saved the rest of the wooden Union ships from destruction. A strategic victory has been claimed for the *Merrimack*, however, because her formidable presence prevented the Union army under McClellan from an easy James River attack on Richmond, forcing it to a land approach which was finally checked by the Confederates under Lee.

During the first part of the *Merrimack*'s dual career she was one of the navy's five crack, new, wooden steam frigates. Named for the northern Massachusetts river, she was launched at Boston Navy Yard in December 1855. (Incidentally, the terminal "k" in her name was finally restored after years of reference to the *Merrimac*.) She made one trip to Europe and then served as flagship on the Pacific station, returning to Norfolk Navy Yard early in 1860 for repairs, especially to her engines.

She was there when the approach of the Civil War produced a bizarre affair at Norfolk in April 1861. Virginia was about to join the Confederacy, and the Navy Department, concerned about the safety of the crack frigate, wanted to get her safely to sea. The energetic, young engineer-in-chief of the navy came down to get her engines in order. Then came one of the most unfortunate episodes in navy yard history. Then and later, the principal business of the yard was in the hands of the naval constructors and other staff officers with their mechanical ability, but the post of commandant, along with the best quarters, went to a senior line officer, with the argument that he was needed for command decisions. But the elderly, vacillating, indecisive commandant at Norfolk Navy Yard would not allow the *Merrimack* to be taken away. The whole yard fell into Confederate hands, with buildings and old ships set ablaze. The plan to blow up the big drydock miscarried, and the *Merrimack* was burned to the water's edge.

Stephen R. Mallory, the first and only Confederate Secretary of the Navy, grasped the possibilities in this situation. He had been chairman of the Senate Naval Affairs Committee and was one of the few who followed the ironclad programs in Europe, where France had launched the *Gloire* in 1859 and England the *Warrior* in 1860. Although the South was very weak in ironworks and other navy industry, he decided that the hulk of the *Merrimack* should be raised and taken into drydock. A naval officer and a constructor designed a protective case made of double layers of railroad iron. Plenty of big guns were on hand— Norfolk had been the principal depot for them, and they were a godsend to the Confederacy, both afloat and in coastal fortifications. Work started on the *Merrimack* several months before the North began to build the rival *Monitor*. The ship's engines were not improved by their weeks under water, but somehow moved her at six or seven knots. She consumed an inordinate amount of coal and was very clumsy in maneuvering. She also would be severely handicapped by her 21-foot draft in the rather shallow Hampton Roads. As noted later, she was unable to perform outside of local waters. She was formally launched on February 24, 1862, one day ahead of the rival *Monitor*, and was renamed the *Virginia*, but that name never fully supplanted the original *Merrimack*. The Southerners maintained good censorship over her progress and alarming rumors spread to the northward.

On March 8, 1862, the *Merrimack* was ready for action under the command of Franklin Buchanan, one of the ablest officers of the Old Navy. He had been first superintendent of the new Naval Academy at Annapolis and, at the outbreak of the war, was commandant of the Washington Navy Yard. Expecting that his native Maryland was joining the Confederacy, he submitted his resignation from the United States Navy. When Maryland did not secede, he tried unsuccessfully to return to the fold but was refused; he would ultimately become the first Confederate admiral.

The Hampton Roads area, adjoining the lower end of Chesapeake Bay, had long been the navy's principal rendezvous and numerous Union vessels were close at hand. The *Merrimack* came down the 10 miles of the Elizabeth River from the Navy Yard and then headed for her first two victims, the *Cumberland* and the *Congress,* both dependent on sail alone—two "sitting ducks" which did not have a chance.

After exchanging a broadside with the *Congress,* Buchanan headed for the *Cumberland.* Most of the Union shells simply rolled off the ironclad's sloping side, though one early salvo put two of the *Merrimack*'s guns out of order. Then broadsides ripped into the *Cumberland,* whose decks were soon running with blood. Finally, the *Merrimack* drew back for a running start and her two-pronged ram crashed into the frigate's side, opening a hole "wide enough to drive a horse and cart." Further broadsides were poured into the sinking ship, whose guns continued to fire as long as they could. Buchanan called on the *Cumberland* to surrender; Lieutenant Morris replied, "Never! We'll sink with our colors flying." And so it was; the *Cumberland* went down in 54 feet of water. In barely an hour, 121 of her crew of 376 were killed, wounded, or missing.

The turn of the *Congress* came next. At least she could not be rammed because the ironclad's ram had broken off in the *Cumberland.* The broadsides, however, did their deadly work. While the Union shells were making no impression on the *Merrimack*'s iron plating, the *Congress,* fast aground, had no shelter from the ironclad's fire. Dismembered bodies lay all over the decks and the frigate's young commander was killed. His successor ran up the white flag. But the Union troops ashore did not get the word; they continued firing and one shot wounded Buchanan in the thigh. Angry at the Union shooting, Buchanan ordered: "Pour hot shot into her and don't leave her until she's afire." The casualties on the *Congress* reached the same tragic proportions as those of the *Cumberland*—136 out of 434 killed, wounded, or missing. The burning *Congress* blew up about midnight.

The *Merrimack* had hopes of making a third victim of the big frigate *Minnesota,* sister ship of the original *Merrimack.* But she was aground and the ironclad could not get near enough to inflict any damage. The tide was running out fast and the pilots were urging a return, to which Buchanan's successor reluctantly agreed. The first day's fight was over. The Confederates were jubilant and the North was in panic.

The news of the *Merrimack*'s success created real gloom in the North. They did not know that Hampton Roads was pretty much the limit of her operations and that even there mudbanks would seriously cramp her style. The North could picture her smashing the blockade and attacking all the major ports. In the official conference at Washington, Secretary of War Stanton aroused the disgust of Secretary of the Navy Welles by constantly peering down the Potomac to see whether the monster was approaching the capital. There was talk of sinking barges loaded with stone to block her progress, and urgent warnings were sent all the way up the coast as far as Portland.

That alarm, of course, was due to be suddenly and miraculously dispelled, for the Ericsson *Monitor* was on her way southward. (The full account of the *Monitor-Merrimack* fight on March 9 is told under *Monitor*.)

The *Merrimack* lasted two months after that battle, but without further fighting. She and the *Monitor* were both present in the area, but apparently seemed evenly enough balanced not to desire another encounter. But while lying idle at the Norfolk Navy Yard up the Elizabeth River, the *Merrimack* was making her influence felt in the military field. She was what the naval strategists call a "fleet in being," that is, able to exercise her influence by her mere presence and without firing a shot.

At the beginning of the year, General McClellan had planned an easy way to capture Richmond. Instead of fighting overland across the 100 miles separating Washington and Richmond, he proposed to go by water—down Chesapeake Bay and up past Hampton Roads to the James River. The presence of the *Merrimack* made that too risky. Instead, the Union forces slogged their way up the peninsula between the York and James Rivers. They finally reached within five miles of Richmond where Lee defeated them in the Seven Days' Battles.

The *Merrimack* lasted only two months after the Hampton Roads battles. The Confederate forces finally withdrew from Norfolk and the adjacent area, leaving the *Merrimack* exposed. The pilots declared that she could not get up the James River, so, with great reluctance, she was run ashore and burned on May 11, 1862. The *Monitor* quickly slid into her mooring at the Norfolk Navy Yard.

(See R. W. Daly, *How the Merrimack Won*, 1957.)

Monitor

Battle of the *Monitor* and *Merrimack*, March 9, 1862. *(From the Franklin D. Roosevelt Library)*

Of the two ships that fought the first ironclad action in Hampton Roads in Virginia on March 9, 1862, the Union *Monitor* was a far less conventional type than her rival, the Confederate *Merrimack*. The *Merrimack* was built up on the hull of a prewar frigate, and she had the conventional broadside batteries. The *Monitor,* on the other hand, was the thoroughly novel conception of the Swedish-American inventor John Ericsson. With a turret imposed on a hull of extremely low freeboard, she was dubbed a "cheesebox on a raft" or "tin can on a shingle." Aside from what happened in Hampton Roads, the turret was a revolutionary "first" in warship construction, with Ericsson sharing inventive honors with naval Captain Christopher Coles and his unfortunate *Captain*.

The *Monitor* represented a race against time, finishing with a desperately narrow margin. The Confederates, thanks to their Secretary of the Navy Stephen Mallory, had gained a long head start in ironclad construction. As early as February 1861, he had advised the Confederates on the importance of ironclads. After the partial destruction of the Norfolk Navy Yard, he had approved the conversion of the sunken *Merrimack* into an ironclad. Her conversion was well under way before the North began countermeasures.

It was not until June that Northern Secretary of the Navy Gideon Welles memorialized Congress on the importance of ironclad warships and secured, three weeks later, an appropriation of $1,500,000 to investigate the possibilities. John Lenthall, chief of naval construction, was too busy turning out conventional wooden cruisers for the blockade to **229** bother with newfangled armor. Consequently, Welles created an iron-clad committee to which he appointed three other naval officers, and on September 3 advertised for "offers from parties for construction of one or more ironclad steam vessels of war." Out of the varying array of suggestions, the committee decided on two. One of the proposals materialized into the *New Ironsides,* a fairly conventional type of seago-ing ironclad, with high freeboard, along the general lines of the new European ironclads. It was unfortunate that her Philadelphia builders did not complete her earlier. She had an excellent performance during the war, and had she been ready in time for the Hampton Roads crisis, the navy might have started off with some generally useful ships along her lines. The other initial choice was developed by Cornelius S. Bushnell, a versatile and prosperous Connecticut industrialist. His proposed *Galena* was built at Mystic and did not turn out well under fire.

Bushnell, however, pushed ahead with a third choice. He consulted his friend John Ericsson who had already developed the navy's first screw propeller in the *Princeton.* When Bushnell called, Ericsson showed him a dusty model of an ironclad floating battery that he had offered to the French, without success, in the Crimean War. This model embodied many of the points that would be distinctive in the *Monitor.* Bushnell persuaded the reluctant Ericsson to take his model to Wash-ington, where President Lincoln approved it. After a stormy session in September, the ironclad committee gave grudging approval; the *Merri-mack* was already several months ahead.

It was agreed that the new ship was to be built in 100 days for $175,000. She was to have an iron hull (the *Merrimack*'s was wooden) with an iron-covered deck. In the middle of the deck would be a revolving turret—the daring new feature in naval architecture—with two big 11-inch guns protected by eight inches of armor. She had barely a foot of freeboard above the waterline. Forward on the deck was a small pilot house. The hull construction was assigned to T. F. Row-land's Continental Iron Works on the East River at Greenpoint and the engines to one of the New York ironworks. The turret was allotted to the Novelty Iron Works and various minor items were subcontracted to other firms, Ericsson in the meantime riding herd over all of them. As Rowland described it, "Mr. Ericsson was in every part of the vessel apparently at the same moment, skipping over planks and gangways, and up and down ladders like a boy of sixteen." On January 30 the *Monitor* was launched. Ericsson had chosen the name as a warning to wrongdoers. Lieutenant John L. Worden, an Annapolis graduate who had been a lieutenant for 20 years and had never commanded a ship, was the fortunate choice for commanding officer. The executive officer was young Samuel D. Greene, just three years out of Annapolis.

Time was running out fast, as the *Merrimack* was just about ready for action. On February 27 the *Monitor*'s first trial run was a failure because of faulty engine valves, but on March 6 she finally left New York under tow with two gunboats as escort. The first day went well, but on March 7 a rising gale created a near-havoc. Contrary to Ericsson's plans, someone had raised the turret and caulked the gap with oakum which washed out, allowing much water to leak into the hull. The ventilating system failed, and without a draft the boiler fires were dying down, filling the engine room with gas. The crew tried pumping by hand but the water gained on them. The situation seemed truly desperate. When the wind suddenly went down at sunset, the fires were lighted again, but the respite was short-lived and at midnight the gale returned in full force. The steering apparatus jammed and the ship's movements were out of control. A distress signal was run up and one of the escort vessels took the *Monitor* in tow, heading for calmer waters. When again the wind went down, some of the exhausted crew simply stretched out on deck.

By the afternoon of March 8, the *Monitor* rounded Cape Henry and entered Chesapeake Bay. From Hampton Roads, 20 miles beyond, a cloud of very black smoke appeared and the sound of distant gunfire could be heard—the *Merrimack,* after taking two hours to come down from the navy yard, was attacking the *Cumberland* at 3:00 P.M. and then would take on the *Congress.* By 10:00 P.M. the *Monitor* had reached Fort Monroe and received orders to proceed to the *Minnesota,* the probable next target of the *Merrimack.* The weary crew of the *Monitor* spent the rest of the night alongside the *Minnesota,* getting ready for action, removing the vessel's smokestacks, and making other adjustments.

The duel started about 8:00 A.M. as the *Merrimack,* belching her black smoke as usual, approached the *Monitor* which was guarding the *Minnesota.* The action seemed a sort of David and Goliath contest, since the *Merrimack* was four times as large as the *Monitor.* Their first solid shots, 165 pounds from the *Monitor* and 150 from the *Merrimack,* did no more than dent the opponent's iron plating, and that was the story for most of the fight. It has been claimed that if the *Monitor* could have used a full 50-pound powder charge, it might well have been enough to crush the *Merrimack*'s armor, but the navy, fearing an explosion, had limited the charge to 35 pounds. The two ships circled each other for two hours, with most of the shots bouncing off the opponent's armor. Each side hoped to find a vulnerable point—the *Monitor* tried for the *Merrimack*'s propeller and just missed but she riddled the *Merrimack*'s smokestack so that the diminished draft slowed down her speed. The *Merrimack* sought unsuccessfully to ram her opponent, but the *Monitor*'s shallower draft enabled her to keep out of the way. Then, near the end of the fight with the ships close together, the *Monitor*'s little pilot house, up in the bow, was hit by a Confederate gun barely 20 feet away. The shot temporarily blinded Lieutenant Worden and it took a while for Lieutenant Greene to go forward to take command. The *Merrimack* headed back to Norfolk and the *Monitor* stayed by the *Minnesota*, which she had saved. The honors for fighting were fairly even but, because of her mission in saving the *Minnesota*, the *Monitor* could be called the winner. In contrast to the bloody work of March 8, with the loss of the two frigates, the *Monitor* had demonstrated that armor could stand up against armor.

One lasting influence of the battle was the undue popularity of the *Monitor* as a type. It was regarded as capable of many things which more conventional ironclads, such as the *New Ironsides,* might have done better. For years after the war, monitor-type vessels found favor with Congress because they were tangible evidence of coastal defense and were not liable to be called away for service on distant sea lanes.

The *Monitor* herself lasted only seven months longer than the *Merrimack*. Heading southward under tow of the *Rhode Island* at the end of 1862, she foundered, with part of her crew, in a gale off Cape Hatteras, where her hulk was finally located in 1975. It was felt that rust had weakened the wreck too much for it to be raised.

(See W. C. White and R. White, *Tin Can on a Shingle,* 1957.)

Hartford

Admiral Farragut in the rigging of his flagship *Hartford*, in the Battle of Mobile Bay, August 5, 1864. *(Naval Historical Center)*

Because she bore the brunt of two of the bitterest Civil War battles, the *Hartford*, named for the capital of Connecticut, was preserved long after the normal span of years as a favorite war veteran. Built at the Boston Navy Yard in 1858, she was a good-looking square-rigger midway in size between cruisers such as the *Kearsarge* and the big frigates. It was predicted that such conventional wooden warships could not stand up against the new ironclads or against the powerful artillery of the new coastal forts. But David Glasgow Farragut, with whom the *Hartford* was intimately associated as flagship, much preferred wooden to iron hulls.

After initial service as flagship on the China station, she was hurriedly called home at the outbreak of war, and early in 1862 she became flagship of the new West Gulf Blockading Squadron. It was a more important assignment than the title implied. Catching blockade runners would be only a minor part of her duties; it was planned from the beginning that her major task would be the capture of New Orleans.

For such a project, it was necessary to find the right man for command. The choice fell upon a solid but unspectacular man who was, moreover, a Southerner. David Glasgow Farragut was born in Tennessee and later settled in Norfolk, his wife's home. In the War of 1812 he had served as a very young midshipman under the senior David Porter, who became more or less a guardian. Porter's brilliant, energetic son, **233**

David Dixon Porter, was closely associated with Farragut in the war years and, in fact, called the navy's attention to Farragut's suitability for the West Gulf command. When Virginia seceded, Farragut, whose loyalty to the Federal government was strong, quietly left Norfolk with his family and settled on the Hudson. Partly suspect as a Southerner for a while, he was given a desk job in the Navy Department until he secured the West Gulf command.

The navy was generous in the matter of ships and supplies, but there were serious problems. New Orleans lay 100 miles from the Gulf, with the passes at its mouth so clogged with mud that the larger ships could be pulled through them only with difficulty. Most serious of all were the pair of powerful forts some 20 miles above the passes, commanding the approaches at the last major bend in the river—Fort Jackson on the left and Fort St. Phillip across from it on the right—they would be Farragut's major concern. In addition, the Confederates were doing other things to make the approach more difficult. A heavy chain, supported by hulks, was stretched across the river just below the forts. Ironclads were still a novelty—the *Monitor-Merrimack* fight had occurred only two weeks before this New Orleans attack—but one big ironclad, the *Louisiana,* was partly completed and there was also a ram.

In organizing the attack, the first step was Porter's mortar fleet. Because the ships' guns could scarcely reach the forts, he gathered 20 schooners, each of which had a chunky mortar which could lob heavy shells into the forts. They were the first to go into action while Farragut was bringing his ships up into the river. One of the boldest episodes was the cutting of the chain, under heavy fire, opening a channel through which the fleet could pass.

The great event—the passing of the forts—came on April 24, 1862. It was arranged that the Union ships would attack in two columns, with small gunboats lashed alongside the *Hartford* and each big vessel. Farragut, who was as painstaking in preparation as he was bold in action, realized that many emergencies could occur. One potential source of danger was the ironclad *Louisiana,* but her incomplete condition kept her from becoming too grave a threat. More serious was the fireraft, loaded with pine chips, which a tug pushed against the *Hartford.* Her hull and rigging caught fire. Farragut was heard to murmur, "Oh, God, that it should end like this." The flames were quenched and soon the battle was won. Once past the forts, Farragut moved on up the river to occupy the sullen city of New Orleans.

That July the *Hartford* flew the first rear admiral's flag in American naval history. From the days of George Washington, Congress regularly created generals for the army, its members often benefitting by that practice, but they refused to create admirals, claiming that the title smacked of royalty. Recently, they had compromised with the title of flag officer but now, as a reward for New Orleans, Farragut became the first rear admiral—he would later become the first vice admiral and then the first four-star full admiral.

But Farragut was not happy that summer of 1862. He had hoped to move right over to Mobile, some 50 miles to the eastward, to close it as a major opening for blockade runners. But the authorities in Washington, from President Lincoln down, wanted above all to have the whole Mississippi opened, and so they persisted despite Farragut's constant pleas. This "war on the western waters" was a strange one, with forces of "tinclads" and other improvised vessels moving down to meet Farragut's square-riggers and other conventional vessels coming up from the South. Consequently, the *Hartford* and other vessels spent their time between New Orleans and Vicksburg. A special problem was that the naval guns could not reach the Confederate artillery on the very high bluffs. In an outburst of impatience, Farragut wrote, "They will use us in the river until the vessels break down. . . . The Government appears to think we can do anything. They expect us to navigate the Mississippi nine hundred miles in the face of batteries, ironclad rams, etc." At Port Hudson, where the Confederates had assembled considerable artillery, the *Hartford* managed to get past, but the other vessels were turned back and the old sidewheeler *Mississippi,* which had been Perry's flagship in opening Japan, was burned. On another occasion the *Hartford* by herself ran the Vicksburg batteries. This river warfare, which showed American naval versatility at its best, lasted until the combined army and navy forces captured Vicksburg on July 4, 1863, the day after the great Union victory at Gettysburg in the east. Lincoln could remark, "the father of waters flows unvexed to the sea," and Farragut could at last start planning for Mobile Bay.

Mobile presented a real problem, for the Confederates had been strengthening its defenses. A 40-mile gulf separated the port of Mobile from the sea, and the bottleneck to the gulf was guarded by Fort Morgan, one of the strongest forts on the coast. The Confederates put their faith in two things: mines (then called torpedoes) and the ironclad *Tennessee,* which was even stronger than the *Merrimack.* With mines and piling, they narrowed the entrance to force ships close to Fort Morgan. The mines were wooden casks filled with gunpowder, which were detonated by contact. Farragut's flag lieutenant made numerous nightly surveys to learn the location of the mines and render as many as possible harmless. Farragut used wooden ships again but reinforced his attack with monitors, whose importance he had finally come to realize.

After weeks of watchful waiting, the Battle of Mobile Bay finally came on August 5, 1864, with three hours of intensive fighting. While the

Tennessee and three small Confederate gunboats waited near Fort Morgan, Farragut attacked in a triple formation. In the center were the seven large wooden warships with the *Brooklyn* in the lead, followed by the flagship *Hartford*. Each of these vessels was accompanied on the port side by a wooden gunboat. Out on the right-hand side were four monitors—Farragut had waited impatiently for the arrival of the *Tecumseh*, one of the newest and strongest of the monitors.

The dramatic climax of the battle came with the sinking of the *Tecumseh* by a Confederate mine—she had moved outside the safe channel. Immediately there was confusion which threatened the whole Union attack. The *Brooklyn*, apparently worried by the torpedo threat, slowed down, blocking the whole approach. Farragut, who had climbed up into the shrouds, immediately took decisive action, shouting, "Damn the torpedoes! Full speed ahead!" The *Hartford* moved around to the head of the line and the day was saved. Despite the guns of Fort Morgan and the *Tennessee*, the Union fleet moved several miles down into the bay. There was a temporary lull but then the *Tennessee* fiercely renewed the attack, heading particularly for the *Hartford* and inflicting severe damage at close range. The whole Union fleet, however, kept up incessant attacks with gunfire and ramming until the big ironclad finally surrendered. The casualties in the Union fleet had been heavier than at New Orleans, where 44 were killed and 160 wounded. This time the score was 172 killed and 170 wounded, with the *Hartford* alone having 25 killed and 28 wounded.

That was the last of the fighting for Farragut and the *Hartford*. They parted company after she had carried him up to New York for a constant round of receptions and other honors, along with promotion to vice admiral, while she went to the navy yard for repairs.

For most of the next 20 years, the *Hartford* served as a flagship in the Pacific or on the Asiatic station. Because of her distinguished Civil War record, it was decided to preserve her and she received an extensive rebuilding at Mare Island. In 1899 she was transferred to the Atlantic and used as a training and cruise ship for Annapolis midshipmen until 1912, when she became a station ship at Charleston until 1926, but remained there until 1938. After seven years at Washington, she was towed to Norfolk Navy Yard and was classified as a relic. She sank at her berth in 1956 and was dismantled, and mementos were deposited in various museums.

(See V. C. Jones, *The Civil War at Sea*, 1960.)

Florida

Destruction of the New York clipper *Jacob Bell* by Confederate raider *Florida.* (Naval Historical Center)

The *Florida* ranked with the *Alabama* and the *Shenandoah* as one of the three British-built Confederate raiders. Ordered by Captain James D. Bulloch, she was built at the Liverpool yard of William G. Miller, not far from the Laird yard where the *Alabama* was being constructed. The two ships were fairly similar, but the *Florida* was slightly smaller and had two funnels instead of the usual one funnel. In order to conceal her true status, she was named the *Oreto,* implying Italian ownership, and on March 22, 1862, far ahead of the *Alabama,* cleared for the Mediterranean. Instead, she went to Nassau, where she took on guns and ammunition and on August 17, 1862, was commissioned as the C.S.S. *Florida,* with the jaunty John N. Maffit as her first commander. Despite her head start, her active raiding career was badly interrupted. Yellow fever carried off many of her crew and almost got Maffit, but she boldly ran the Federal blockade into Mobile, Alabama, lying there until January 1863, when she escaped.

Her principal raiding came in the first half of 1863, when with the *Alabama* she operated between the bulges of Brazil and West Africa, catching rich clippers on the Good Hope run to the East and the Cape Horn run to California. Then in mid-1863, the two raiders went their separate ways. While the *Alabama* headed for eastern seas, the *Florida* made for the riskier waters off New England, using captured vessels as satellites; when the Federal cruisers made things too hot for one ship, the raiders would shift to another. The height of impudence came when the schooner *Archer* made a raid on Portland, Maine, seizing the revenue cutter but, finding no ammunition, blew her up as the Federal forces were approaching in Boston and New York steamers with artillery.

In need of repairs, the *Florida* in August 1863 put into the big French dockyard at Brest, where she remained nearly six months. Maffit was in poor health and was replaced by Lieutenant Morris. Although closely watched by the *Kearsarge,* the *Florida* finally escaped to sea. After the *Alabama* was sunk, the *Florida* cruised for a while then put into the neutral port of Bahia in Brazil. But Captain Napoleon Collins of the *Wachusett,* a sister ship of the *Kearsarge,* weary of the Brazilian pro-Southern application of neutrality, rammed and captured the *Florida* while many of her officers and crew were ashore. Despite neutrality, the *Wachusett* towed her off as a prize. On November 24 at Newport News, the *Florida* was sunk in a collision. Captain Collins was court-martialed for the violation of neutrality, but later went on to high favor.

(See F. L. Owsley, *The C.S.S. Florida: Her Building and Operation,* 1965.)

Alabama

The British-built Confederate cruiser *Alabama* was probably the best-publicized commerce raider of all time. Burning Yankee square-riggers by the score, she terrorized Yankee shipping for almost two years. Britain was later called to account for her unneutral role in selling such a vessel to the South.

The story of the *Alabama* goes back to May 8, 1861, in the office of Stephen R. Mallory, the first and only Confederate Secretary of the Navy. He had a frustrating job, for the South had few ships, few seamen, and almost no shipbuilding or heavy industry. Under the circumstances, Mallory decided that at least the South might profitably raid Northern shipping. He was already converting the small steamer *Sumter* into a warship, but he hoped that British shipyards might produce more effective raiders, even though such production would skirt the edges of legitimate neutrality.

Mallory had expressed a desire to talk with Captain James D. Bulloch, a regular naval officer who was then commanding a major coastal steamer. Bulloch was a Georgian, and uncle of the infant Theodore Roosevelt. When Bulloch reported, Mallory said, "I am glad to see you. I want you to go to Europe. When can you start?" Bulloch replied that he

could start as soon as he knew what the Secretary wanted. Mallory
explained that he wanted to arrange with British yards to build two powerful first-class cruisers, equipped with both sail and steam; a London house would arrange payment. Bulloch started at once; to avoid interference from the new Federal blockade, he sailed from Montreal to Liverpool. He quickly made arrangements with two of the leading Liverpool yards for the ships which would become the *Alabama* and *Florida*. The *Alabama* at the Laird Yard was a "screw sloop" of about 1000 tons, 220 feet in length and 31 feet in beam. With the masts and yards of a bark rig, plus two engines of some 1000 horsepower, she could perform well under sail or steam; actually, to conserve precious coal, most of her cruising was under sail. Everything was up to the best British naval standards. She cost about $250,000, which was just about the same as that of her nemesis, the *Kearsarge,* one of the 14 new cruisers then under way in the American navy yards.

The situation would call for constant cloak-and-dagger work because of her irregular status—Bulloch, who proved most adept at this, would later write memoirs under the title *The Confederate Secret Service in Europe.* The British ministers Russell and Palmerston gave the runaround to United States Minister Charles Francis Adams, son of one president and grandson of another, who was continually informed by the consul at Liverpool what was going on with "No. 290," as the ship was called. Late in June 1862, Bulloch got word that it would not be safe to leave the ship at Liverpool another two days. She quickly sailed down the Mersey on an innocent-appearing trial run, with a party of ladies and gentlemen aboard. The party was sent back, and the "290" continued on to Terceira in the Azores; another ship carried the guns, ammunition, and supplies.

At this point, leaving the future *Alabama* in the Azores, we must digress to consider her celebrated commander, Raphael Semmes, who had been developing his raiding techniques in a vessel half the size of the *Alabama.* A native of Maryland, Semmes at age 52 was on the Lighthouse Board when in February 1861 he was summoned to the Confederate capital. He resigned his commission in the United States Navy to enter the Confederate States Navy. In April 1861 he was given command of a newly purchased New Orleans–Havana steam packet that was renamed *Sumter* for the fort which had just fallen. After two strenuous months refitting her as a raider, Semmes dropped down the Mississippi on June 18 and twelve days later narrowly escaped to sea, eluding a powerful Union blockader.

In the *Sumter* and later the *Alabama,* Semmes would be deprived of the chance for prize money, since the newly established Federal blockade shut off the Southern ports, and the Spaniards refused to sanction prize courts. The only alternative was to burn most of the captured vessels; those bonfires of Yankee square-riggers would mark Semmes's courses all the way from the Gulf of Mexico to the Strait of Sunda. In his memoirs, Semmes described the first burning, the *Golden Rocket:*

> The decks of the Maine-built ship were of pine, caulked the old-fashioned oakum, paid with pitch; the wood work of the cabin was like so much tinder. . . . The consequence was that the flames were not long in kindling, but leaped, full-grown, into the air in a very few minutes. . . . The indraught into the burning ship's holds and cabins added every minute new fury to the flames, and now they could be heard roaring like the fires of a hundred furnaces.

That scene would be repeated more than 50 times.

The *Sumter* continued down through the Caribbean, capturing a few more prizes and having a narrow escape from a Union cruiser at Martinique. She finally turned up at Gibraltar in a rundown condition. The British would not furnish coal, two Union cruisers blockaded her from nearby, and in April, Semmes and his officers left her, went to London and thence to Nassau where he received orders to take command of the new "290" in the Azores. Bulloch had hoped for the command, but it was felt that he could not be spared from his intricate negotiations in Europe. The *Sumter* was sold to the British and became a blockade runner.

Semmes took command of the C.S.S. *Alabama.* He persuaded 80 of the tough Liverpool sailors to stay with the ship, and they remained the major group in her heterogeneous crew. The guns, brought down in a separate ship, were transferred and mounted—one 110-pounder, one 68-pounder, and six 32-pounders—along with ammunition, stores, and coal.

The Azores had long been a favorite hunting ground for whalers, and they soon became victims of the *Alabama*'s first raiding. Then Semmes continued along the heavily used North Atlantic run, but he was careful not to get too close to the Northern ports where the telegraph could spread warnings up and down the coast. Out on the high seas, with no cables as yet, it was a different matter, resulting in a baffling game of hide and seek for the Federal cruisers. Down in the Gulf, he hoped to get one of the mail steamers with California gold, but the *Ariel*, which he caught, was headed the wrong way with troops and their families; in fact, the ladies snipped the gold buttons from the officers as souvenirs. He moved on out to Galveston which was under Union attack and sank the U.S.S. *Hatteras,* a converted excursion steamer, in a one-sided night action.

The next step was to lie in wait in the choicest of hunting grounds, down where the South Atlantic was narrowest between the bulges of Brazil and West Africa. Two of the richest clipper routes ran through there—headed around Cape Horn to California and around Good Hope for India and China. For a while the *Florida* was there too and both got rich prizes. That was the high watermark for the raiding; the tide would soon turn just as it did for the Confederates ashore at Gettysburg and Vicksburg.

The two raiders parted, the *Florida* heading for New England while Semmes set out for eastern seas. He captured a prize within sight of Cape Town and stayed there a while building such good will that more than a century later the Cape Malays at New Year's would sing, "Here Comes the *Alabama*." In November 1863 Semmes was in the waters around Java for some of his last seizures. One was particularly dramatic—the beautiful, speedy New York clipper *Contest*, bound from Japan. She actually outsailed the *Alabama* for several hours and seemed on the way to escape until the wind died down and then, with steam, the *Alabama* overtook and burned her.

The *Alabama* was a long way from port and in need of overhaul so Semmes headed back to Europe. He found refuge in the French port of Cherbourg, just across the channel from England. Of the many Union cruisers scattered in pursuit of the raiders, it fell to the *Kearsarge* to close in on her. On June 9, 1864, the two very similar vessels met outside the three-mile limit (see *Kearsarge* for details of the action). In less than two hours of exchanging fire, the *Alabama* sank. Semmes was picked up by an English yacht. The emotions of the Northerners were reflected on a souvenir plate showing the sinking raider: "The rebel pirate *Alabama*, built in an English yard of English oak, armed with English guns, manned by an English crew, and sunk in the English channel."

The real damage inflicted by the *Alabama* and other raiders was not so much in the actual sinkings as in the psychological fears. These fears raised the war-risk insurance rates so high that shippers avoided the Stars and Stripes. In mid-1863, at the high watermark, the rate to South America, the Pacific, and East Indies rose to 7½%; a merchant shipping a $10,000 cargo would have to pay $750 war risk on an American-flag ship, but nothing at all on a foreign-flag ship. The result was the "flight from the flag" with American vessels transferring to British or other foreign registry—with 1613 vessels, totalling 774,000 tons lost to the American merchant marine, for they were not allowed to return to American registry after the war.

The North kept protesting against the English violation of neutrality; international negotiations finally led to arbitration. England paid $15,-

000,000 for the damages inflicted by the *Alabama, Florida,* and *Shenandoah* in the so-called *Alabama* Claims. One other effect of the raiding was the fact that the pursuit of the raiders withdrew dozens of Yankee cruisers which might otherwise have tightened this blockade.

(See R. Semmes, *Memoirs of Service Afloat and Ashore during the Mexican War,* 1851.)

Kearsarge

Sinking of
Confederate raider
Alabama by Union
cruiser *Kearsarge,*
June 19, 1864.
*(From Franklin D.
Roosevelt Library)*

Two spectacular Civil War naval duels left the participants linked in the public mind—*Monitor-Merrimack* and *Kearsarge-Alabama.* The *Kearsarge,* built on the Maine–New Hampshire border, sank the celebrated Confederate raider in the English Channel. This victory gave her such a reputation that her name was given to the only American battleship not named for a state. She survived her great fight for 30 years, patrolling distant stations until finally wrecked in 1894, some years after the new steel navy was coming into being.

She was one of a highly successful class of 14 "screw sloops" built at the Northern navy yards during the first year of the war. Two of the others also won distinction: the *Wachusett* illegally captured the Confederate raider *Florida* in a neutral Brazilian port, while the *Housatonic* was sunk off Charleston by a pioneer Confederate submarine. All were fairly similar to the British-built *Alabama,* capable of operating under their square-rigged sails or engines. With their sleek black hulls and lofty spars, they were all conceded to be beautiful ships.

Named for a peak in the White Mountains, the *Kearsarge* was built at Portsmouth Navy Yard on the Maine side of the Piscataqua River. Her engines and boilers came from an ironworks at Hartford, Connecticut. Unlike the heterogeneous crew aboard the *Alabama,* most of the *Kearsarge* crew came from the Portsmouth region; in later years they would hold "alumni reunions" on the anniversary of the great fight.

Launched on September 11, 1861, barely five months after Fort Sumter, she was commissioned on January 24, 1862, and 12 days later set out for the west coast of Europe, where she would hunt most of the leading Southern raiders during the next two years. Her first contact was at Gibraltar, where for several months she and the *Tuscarora* would blockade Semmes's first command, the *Sumter,* until he gave her up. Then the *Kearsarge* moved down into the Azores hoping to encounter the *Alabama.*

In April 1863 the command passed from Captain Charles W. Pickering, a capable but not outstanding officer, to a dark horse who would become a prime hero. This was Captain John Ancrum Winslow who, despite his seniority, had gotten off to a slow start. In an unguarded moment he had exclaimed, "I wish they would bag old Abe." As a result, he had remained in command of a small Mississippi gunboat. Winslow was born in Wilmington, North Carolina, where his father was in business but the family background was Massachusetts from the first top Plymouth group; young Winslow was sent back there to school and received his midshipman appointment through Daniel Webster. He married and then made his home in Boston. When David D. Porter, his junior, was given the Mississippi command, Winslow asked for other duty and was ordered to the *Kearsarge,* joining her in April 1863.

With occasional distraction from two minor Confederate raiders, the main job of the *Kearsarge* was to blockade the *Florida* from September 1863 to February 1864, while she was wearing out her welcome undergoing very extensive refitting at Brest, the great French naval base. Winslow pointed out that one lone ship could not guard the two approaches 20 miles apart; on a dark and stormy winter night, the *Florida* broke loose. The persistent presence of the *Kearsarge* prevented a junction of the two lesser raiders.

Then came the great week. On June 12 the *Kearsarge* was at Flushing on the Scheldt when Winslow received a telegram from Drayton, American minister at Paris, that the *Alabama* had arrived at Cherbourg (see *Alabama*). He immediately started south; the crew responded with cheers at the prospect of a fight.

It has been remarked that seldom, if ever, have two ships been so evenly matched. The statistics were remarkably similar:

	Kearsarge	Alabama
Displacement, tons	1031	1011
Age, months	30	24
Guns	7	8
Broadside, pounds	366	296
Officers and men	163	149
Cost	$286,000	$250,000

In addition, their commanders during the Mexican War had been on the flagship as "shipmates, messmates, and roommates." Despite these statistical similarities, the Kearsarge did have two advantages, which Semmes would later cite as excuses. In her magazines the Kearsarge powder was fresh, whereas in the course of two years the Alabama powder had somewhat deteriorated in efficacy. Also, like some of the earlier Federal wooden ships, the Kearsarge was given an improvised armor protection by stringing heavy anchor chains along the sides, protecting vulnerable spots.

Semmes, disturbed by French delay in giving him repair facilities, issued a virtual challenge to Winslow and action was generally anticipated on Sunday, July 19. Spectators lined the shore; it is claimed that special trains ran down from Paris. To avoid any question of the three-mile limit, Winslow ran out twice that distance, while a French ironclad followed the Alabama out to see that she kept beyond neutral waters. As 11 o'clock approached, Captain Winslow was conducting Sunday service when the cry arose, "Here she comes." Immediately everyone rushed to stations.

The Alabama fired first—her 100-pound rifle had a somewhat longer range, but the Kearsarge quickly replied with the smashing impact of her 11-inch guns. The Kearsarge had one lucky escape—a 100-pound shell lodged at the head of her sternpost; had it exploded, it might have blown out her stern, but with the deteriorated powder it was a dud. Later, that shell with the top of the sternpost was sent to President Lincoln as a souvenir. Meanwhile, the Southerners were disturbed to see that some of their shots were bouncing back from the anchor chains; the Kearsarge was really another "Old Ironsides." All this time the ships were sailing around seven times in huge circles, a quarter or half mile apart. This pattern kept each of them from ramming or raking the opponent. During this maneuvering the heavy Union gunfire was causing severe damage and high casualties aboard the Alabama. At the

end of little more than an hour, two big 11-inch shells virtually ripped
the guts out of the *Alabama* and Semmes showed the white flag of
surrender. The great raider sank quickly with her bow in the air; most
of the boats on both ships had been smashed, and many, including the
wounded Semmes, were splashing around in the water. The yacht
Deerhound, owned by a wealthy Englishman, did some rescuing and
carried Semmes off to Southampton where he avoided capture. The
Alabama's casualties were fairly heavy, whereas the *Kearsarge* lost only
one man killed.

Northern joy was unrestrained at the news of victory. Winslow and
the crew were lionized at Boston and elsewhere, and Winslow was
immediately promoted to commodore and in 1870 became a rear admiral. The Confederacy also promoted Semmes to rear admiral.

The remaining three decades of the *Kearsage*'s career were an anticlimax so far as drama was concerned, for they constituted the dreary
"Dark Ages" of the United States Navy. It was natural that there would
be some reduction of force at the end of the war, but in 1869 Admiral
David D. Porter led a movement to revive sail at the expense of steam.
He hated steam and engineers, and secured a general order saying that
steam was to be used only in emergencies; such cases were to be
entered in the log and if the Navy Department didn't agree, the cost of
the coal would be deducted from the captain's pay. The cruiser *Wampanoag,* faster than any other ship, was laid up, never to go to sea again,
while the navy kept the seas with aging ships like the *Kearsarge,* "too
slow to run and too weak to fight." At a time when other navies were
going in for iron or steel hulls and rifled ordnance, these veterans were
patched up at heavy cost in the politics-ridden navy yards.

A ship would be commissioned for a cruise, usually three years, and
then be decommissioned for a long wait in the navy yard. The *Kearsarge*
served on most of the distant stations—European in 1865, South Pacific
in 1868, Asiatic in 1873, North Atlantic in 1879, European in 1883, and
West Indian in 1888. There were only occasional variations in the
routine. In 1866 a visit to Monrovia, Liberia, led to the deaths of seven
officers and seven seamen from yellow fever. In 1868 the *Kearsarge*
carried relief supplies for victims of an earthquake at Arica, Peru; and
in 1874 she carried a scientific party from Nagasaki to Vladivostok to
observe the transit of Venus. Partly for sentimental reasons, the old
ship outlasted most of her contemporaries, and by the late 1880s some
of the steel cruisers of the new navy were in service. Finally, on
February 2, 1894, en route from Haiti to Bluefields, Nicaragua, the
Kearsarge ended her career on Roncador Cay off the coast of Central
America, fortunately without loss of life. Six years later, a new pre-

dreadnought steel battleship was given the name *Kearsarge,* the only one of all the American battleships not named for a state.

(See J. M. Ellicott, *The Life of John Ancrum Winslow, Rear Admiral, United States Navy,* 1902.)

H. L. Hunley

Confederate
submarine *H. L.
Hunley,* built in 1863.
*(Naval Historical
Center)*

At the tip of the Battery in Charleston harbor is a thin, cigar-shaped hull commemorating the extraordinary heroism of the pioneer Confederate submariners. Six times their vessel, the *H. L. Hunley,* sank, carrying down most of her crew, a total of 45; yet after each sinking, there were volunteers to try again. On the positive side, she was the first submarine in history to sink an active warship—the big Union sloop-of-war *Housatonic,* sister ship of the famous *Kearsarge.*

The *H. L. Hunley* was not the first submarine—there had been various experimental ones, including the *Turtle* which was designed at Yale and failed to sink a British warship at New York during the American Revolution. Although the *Hunley* was the first to sink an active warship, the submarine proper would not be developed until the end of the century, with the *Holland* in 1897. The earlier subs depended upon manual labor for movement. An efficient sub could not be realized until the development of the internal combustion engine for movement on the surface and the electric battery for underwater movement.

The *Hunley's* name came from her inventor and promoter, Horace L. Hunley, a 40-year-old native of Tennessee who had become a New

Orleans lawyer and member of the Louisiana legislature. In 1861, with two associates, he had developed a two-man iron-plated submarine, the *Pioneer,* which was scuttled when Farragut approached New Orleans. Hunley moved his base of operations to Mobile Bay, where he built a second one which dived but failed to surface; her crew of seven men were the first victims.

Hunley decided that his latest sub, named for himself and paid for by him, would be most useful at Charleston, where a large assemblage of Union warships was in attendance—a promise of numerous targets. On September 19, 1863, Hunley wrote to General Beauregard, offering to bring the sub to Charleston. It arrived shortly by rail and was turned over to Lieutenant Payne and a crew of six men. The *Hunley* was some 20 feet long with side fins and tanks for water ballast. While she lay at her wharf, the wake of a passing freighter swamped and sank her; Payne escaped but the six crewmen drowned. A week later she sank again—her third time. Payne and two crewmen escaped.

Hunley went to Charleston to check the sub and to do some test diving. After some preliminary cruising, the *Hunley* dived and never came up—her bow was buried in the river mud. Hunley and all the crewmen died. Raised again, she made a practice run against a dummy ship but became tangled in the ship's anchor chain; the entire crew died.

Despite the almost suicidal prospects still another crew was assembled under the command of Lieutenant George F. Dixon. Equipped with a new spar torpedo, the *Hunley* started down the harbor on February 17, 1864, aiming for the big cruiser *Housatonic.* Although for some reason she was ordered to attack surfaced, her approach was not detected. She made a direct hit on the Union vessel, ripping a large hole in her side. The *Housatonic* went down in five minutes; only five of her crew were killed—the rest climbed onto the rigging which was still above water. But the poor *Hunley*—the first sub in history to sink a warship—was flooded by the backwash and went down with Lieutenant Dixon and the whole crew.

Oddly enough another submarine was prowling in Charleston harbor—the little *David,* similar in general features to the *Hunley,* but with a steam engine. Under Lieutenant T. W. Gassell she made for the *New Ironsides,* a powerful Union ironclad. The *David* hit her with a spar torpedo, inflicting only minor damage.

Shenandoah

The *Shenandoah* was the most reprehensible of the Confederate commerce raiders. In addition to participating in Britain's permissive violation of neutral obligations, she also destroyed a substantial portion of the Yankee whaling fleet in Bering Strait, despite having learned of Lee's surrender at Appomattox.

Unlike the *Alabama* and *Florida,* which were built to order as potential warships, she was purchased ready-made after a year of service as a British transport. Originally named the *Sea King,* she was built on the Clyde near Glasgow. She was about the same size as the other two raiders—1160 tons, 230 feet in length and 32 feet in beam, with her frames of iron instead of oak. She was a full-rigged ship with a screw propeller which could be raised when not in use, and with a collapsible funnel (for years afterward, when such a cruiser shifted from sail to steam, there was the command, "Up funnel and down screw."). Capable of some 13 knots under steam, she could make an exceptional 15 knots under sail.

The *Shenandoah* had already made a voyage to New Zealand with troops when Captain Bulloch purchased her for the Confederate Navy for £45,000 (about the same cost as the other two raiders). To disguise her purpose, she sailed from London on October 8, 1864, ostensibly on a trading voyage to Bombay. At the same time, with due secrecy, a smaller chartered steamer, the *Laurel,* left Liverpool with the officers, nucleus crew, guns, ammunition, and supplies. They rendezvoused at Madeira where the *Shenandoah* was converted for war service.

Her major difficulty was a shortage of crew—most of those who had come out from England on the two vessels refused to sign up; it would be necessary to get recruits from crews of captured ships. Her officers were a quite youthful group, including several who had served on the *Alabama,* among them the dandified but very competent navigator Irving Bulloch, brother to the Confederate naval factotum in Europe. To the surprise of some in the service, the command went to Lieutenant James Iredell Waddell of the Confederate States Navy, a native North Carolinian with a rich Maryland wife. Almost from the start, he failed to command the full respect of his officers. There were murmurs about his indecisiveness and occasional lack of competence. The *Alabama* veterans in particular felt that Waddell did not measure up to Raphael Semmes's crisp, competent authority.

Long before the *Shenandoah* sailed, it was planned at Richmond that she was to operate in the Pacific, with the whalers as her particular victims. The *Florida* had been heading for that service when she was captured in a Brazilian port. The *Shenandoah* captured several vessels while crossing the South Atlantic. Unfortunately, she had a bad crack in her propeller shaft bearings, so she sailed across the Pacific to Melbourne for repairs. Arriving there late in December, she spent three weeks in the colonial capital. The social hospitality was overwhelming, but the governor had cautious reservations because he was concerned about the neutral technicalities—it was a blow to the poor man when he learned that at the last minute 25 sailors had been smuggled aboard in violation of the Foreign Enlistments Act.

The *Shenandoah* then had a long, quite uneventful run northward all the way from Australia to Alaska. The one brief break came early in April (about the time of Lee's surrender) at Ponape in the Caroline Islands, where four whalers were caught and burned. They hoped for whaler victims in the bleak, foggy Sea of Okhotsk, but three weeks turned up only one New Bedford whaler, the bark *Abigail*, which happened to be very well stocked with liquor—"the whole crew fell into the most gorgeous and monumental spree ever witnessed. There were not a dozen sober men aboard the ship, except the prisoners."

The *Shenandoah* finally found the whalers in the waters around Bering Strait, on the international date line between Asia and America, and then came the grimmest and most bizarre week in the story of Confederate raiding. It was also one of the three terrific blows that virtually ruined American whaling—the discovery of petroleum in 1859, this deadly raid of the *Shenandoah* in 1865, and the wholesale crushing of much of what was left of the fleet in the Arctic ice in 1871.

Today, when Washington can have almost instant communication with forces anywhere around the seven seas, it is hard to realize how difficult it was to exercise remote control at that time. Even the Atlantic cable was not finally operative until 1866, while the Pacific islands were out of touch until the end of the century. On land, transmission of messages came more quickly. In 1860, for example, telegraph lines reached California from the East, supplanting the Pony Express.

As the *Shenandoah* made contact with the first of its whaler victims, she was greeted with amazing news. When her prize crew boarded the *William Thompson*, her captain protested, "My God, man, don't you know the war has ended?" "Did Grant surrender?" "No, the Army of Virginia surrendered. The war is over." "Sir, the war will not be over until the South is free."

There were similar remarks on some of the other whalers, but the news became more definite with the arrival of the bark *Susan Abigail* the next day, June 23. She had been loading in San Francisco when Lee surrendered on April 9, and had half-masted her flag on learning of

Lincoln's assassination. But as Waddell wrote in his journal, the papers contained a number of dispatches and among them was one that stated that the Southern government had removed to Danville and the greater part of the Army of Virginia had joined General Johnston's army in North Carolina, where an indecisive battle had been fought against General Sherman's army. At Danville a proclamation by President Davis announced that the war would be carried on with renewed vigor.

On such shaky evidence Waddell decided to carry out his mission, and his young officers, who could not visualize the fall of the South, upheld that unfortunate decision. Actually, Johnston's army had surrendered to Sherman in June, Jefferson Davis was imprisoned, and the Confederacy had ceased to exist.

As a result, 21 whalers were captured, of which 18 were burned. Three of them were lucky enough to be spared as cartels to carry the captive crews home. On one whaler the captain and owner had died; his young widow, aboard with her three children, had had his body preserved in a cask of whiskey so that he could be buried in New England. Waddell graciously agreed to spare the ship, saying that the South did not war on women and children. The final burnings came so fast that the crews were towed in whaleboats behind the *Shenandoah* until they could be taken aboard the cartels.

The rest of the whalers were quickly set ablaze—a few singly or in pairs at the outset and then, far down in Bering Strait, the final 11 in seven hours. The reactions of the captains varied. A few took it philosophically, one wept, some argued strenuously, and one, well-liquored up, refused to haul down his flag, drew up his armed crew along the rail, and threatened to use his bomb-gun, until the cruiser came alongside with her guns ready for a broadside.

One young Confederate officer described the wholesale burnings of that day:

> It was a scene never to be forgotten by anyone who beheld it. The red glare from the burning vessels shone far and wide over the drifting ice of these savage seas; the crackling of the fires made its devouring way through each doomed ship, fell on the still air like upbraiding voices. The sea was filled with boats drifting hither and thither with no hand to guide them, and with yards, sails and cordage, remnants of the stupendous ruin there progressing. In the distance, but where the light fell strong and red upon them, bringing out in bold relief each spar and line, were the ransomed vessels, the Noah's Arks that were to bear away the human life which in a few hours would be all that was left of the gallant whaling fleet.

With drifting ice threatening to close them in, the *Shenandoah* on June 29 headed for the open sea. This was the beginning of a 23,000-

mile nonstop flight to England, out of sight of land for 122 days. She was under sail most of the time—in view of her precarious status, she could not put into port for coal.

During the first part of the voyage, morale was still high. They all seemed to have full faith that Johnston's army would save the Confederate cause. There were high hopes of capturing one or more of the gold-laden steamships out of San Francisco. There was even talk of attacking San Francisco and laying it under tribute.

Then came the moment of truth. On August 2 the raider encountered a British bark, two weeks out of San Francisco, with newspapers which confirmed the fact that the war was over and the Confederacy ended. That news was a crushing blow, not unmixed with fear. There could be charges of piracy if they should encounter a Yankee cruiser. The remainder of the trip reflected these concerns, while friction between Waddell and his officers became acute. The officers wanted to seek relative safety in Cape Town, but Waddell insisted on pushing northward to Liverpool where they arrived on November 11. Their pilot told them, "Why, the war's been over so long people have stopped talking about it. The Southern armies have all surrendered long ago, and Jeff Davis is locked up in Fort Monroe. The Yankees have had a lot of cruisers out looking for you. They'll be wild when they find out you've outwitted them."

The next day Waddell threw himself on the mercy of the British, surrendering to the captain of H.M.S. *Donegal.* The officers and crew were confined until the official decision came from London. The British were by now weary of the whole raiding business; the decision was that the ship should be turned over to the Americans and the non-British members of the crew released. Even the British, who had violated the Foreign Enlistments Act, swore they were from Virginia, Georgia, Alabama, or elsewhere in the South. To the annoyance of Charles Francis Adams, all went free. Some of the officers went to Latin America. Waddell remained 10 years in England and then received command of a Pacific Mail liner which sank almost at once. The *Shenandoah* herself was purchased by the sultan of Zanzibar.

(See M. C. Morgan, *Dixie Raider: The Saga of the CSS Shenandoah,* 1948.)

Sultana

In what has been called "the greatest marine disaster of all time," the explosion and fire that sank the crack Mississippi River steamer *Sultana* on April 28, 1865, took at least 1585 lives and perhaps 1647. This toll exceeded the 1500 total for the liner *Titanic,* whose bottom was ripped open by an iceberg in 1912. Most of the *Sultana* victims were Union soldiers returning to their homes after incarceration at Andersonville and other Confederate prisons. A disaster of that magnitude would normally have attracted more attention, but it came while the newspapers were still full of Lincoln's assassination and funeral obsequies.

The *Sultana* was built at Cincinnati in 1863 at a cost of $60,000. A Cincinnati newspaper termed her "one of the largest and best business steamers ever constructed." She was licensed to carry 76 cabin passengers, who traveled in luxury, plus 300 deck passengers and crew. Her role as a military transport for soldiers was a sudden emergency development.

On her final fatal run, she left New Orleans on April 22 with a cabin passenger list of planters, businessman, a congressman, a naval officer, and so on; there were numerous ladies, few of whom would survive. The river was in a serious flood stage, overflowing its banks and slowing down progress. Just before reaching Vicksburg, the engineer reported to the captain that one of the boilers had sprung a leak and a trickle of water was oozing between two cracked plates. He insisted that the boilers be drawn so that the damaged boiler could be cooled and rivets driven into place. A riveter was called from town and after hasty repairs reported that although the patching was a good job, it was not perfect or permanent since he had not been allowed to remove the two plates.

In the meantime, the *Sultana* was called upon for a major emergency task. With the cessation of hostilities, Yankee prisoners by the thousands were being released at Andersonville and other stockades and were converging upon Vicksburg for parole and transportation home to the Midwest. Emaciated and sickly after their long ordeal, they were put in a temporary camp at Vicksburg with a major general, a colonel, and three captains charged with handling the complicated situation, in which there were disagreements and divided opinions. There were also charges that one rival steamboat line had been offering bribes to get as many of the prisoners as possible, since the government would pay $5 to carry each enlisted man up river and $10 for each officer. Naturally, this was a temptation to the steamboat men. Large numbers of soldiers, chiefly from Ohio and Indiana, were crowded aboard the *Sultana*. Her legal limit was only 376, but that restriction was evaded, despite objections from some of those in charge and despite the fact that a steamboat of the rival line, linked with the bribery charges, was alongside and could have comfortably taken aboard a large number to lighten the *Sultana*'s abnormal load. That offer was turned down. The weary ex-prisoners lay down on deck or wherever they could find a spot, while the crew put in extra stanchions to brace up the creaking decks. The exact number of persons who started up the river on the *Sultana* is not known. Estimates range from 2200 to 2400 soldiers, with 70 to 100 civilian passengers, and a crew of about 80, a total of about 2400 to 2600 aboard the vessel whose legal capacity was 376. And of that total, 1585 to 1647 would perish.

After coaling on the Arkansas side of the river, the *Sultana*, grievously overloaded and with her patched-up boiler, started north in the early hours of April 28. About seven miles above Memphis, while it was still dark, the boilers exploded with a tremendous roar and the ship was soon engulfed in flames. Those near the boiler area were terribly scalded, many were burned to death, and perhaps the greatest number of casualties drowned. James W. Elliott, whose grandfather, an Indiana captain, survived, has produced a "mosaic" account of scores of case histories of individual experiences in his *Transport to Disaster*. It makes gruesome reading but gives a vivid picture of that night of horror, with flames ashore and struggles to stay afloat in the dark river, now several miles beyond its normal banks. One of the few lighter touches was the story of the lady who donned her best hoopskirt when the explosion came, then jumped overboard, the skirt serving as a balloon to keep her afloat until rescued.

"By three-fifteen," it was reported, "seventy-five minutes after the explosion, there was no living person aboard the *Sultana*." Survivors dotted the river, many clinging to bits of wreckage and drifting among the hundreds who had drowned when they jumped overboard. Some 780 were eventually saved, but rescue came slowly. The steamer *Bostonia*, coming down the river, was the first to the rescue, picking up about 100 and rushing them down to Memphis. By the time some of the floating survivors and the bodies had reached the Memphis area, other boats put out to carry on the rescue work. Particularly effective was the work of a young ensign, executive officer of the gunboat *Essex*, who put out in the larger cutter, followed by the other boats, and made numerous rescues. In Memphis the survivors found a generous reception, with hospitals straining their facilities to help the Union unfortunates.

Elliott's chapter dealing with the question of responsibility for overloading the *Sultana* is entitled "The Old Army Game." The War Department tried to minimize the affair, while the officers involved in the critical decisions—the general, the colonel, and two of the captains—slid out from under. Captain Frederic Speed, adjutant general of the Department of Mississippi, was court-martialed, charged with neglect and carelessness, and sentenced to be dishonorably dismissed from the service. The judge advocate general, however, ruled that the sentence be disapproved and that Speed be publicly exonerated. He was accordingly mustered out honorable. Elliot termed this "one of the most effective whitewashings of all time."

(See J. W. Elliott, *Transport to Disaster*, 1962.)

Ariel

The flexible word "clipper" is applied properly to four distinct groups. First, in the early 1780s, were the little Baltimore clippers, of which the *Chasseur* was a prime example. Second, in the 1840s, after the Opium War, came the good-sized American China clippers such as the *Rainbow* and *Sea Witch*. Third, blending in with the first two groups but rather larger, were the California clippers of the early 1850s, the fastest, largest, and most impressive of all, with the *Flying Cloud* as the masterpiece. Fourth, in the 1860s and more lasting, came the British "tea clippers," about half the size of the American California clippers. The leaders in this group were the *Ariel, Cutty Sark, Taeping,* and *Thermopylae*. According to Captain Andrew Shewan, outstanding authority on the subject, the *Ariel* was the best, with the *Cutty Sark* following close behind.

The British had stood by while the California clippers had their day, and even bought some of them for their new Australian run. By the 1860s, however, they started to build their own, especially for the China tea trade. Since this was not bulky cargo, the vessels did not have to be as large as the California clippers, which carried a wide variety of cargo. The Scots of Aberdeen took the lead in this new construction for the British. One special new feature differentiated them from the all-wooden American clippers: this was composite construction, using iron for frames and reinforcement instead of wood. This innovation came about in part from the serious scarcity of ship timber in England, but there were also advantages in weight and added cargo space.

The *Ariel* was launched at the Robert Steele yard at Greenock, near Glasgow, on June 29, 1865, for a firm of London tea merchants. She was 197 feet long, 33 feet in beam, and measured 853 tons, just about half the tonnage of the American masterpiece *Flying Cloud*. She quickly showed her capacity for speed; it is said that only one ship ever passed her. Because of a strong, but perhaps not rational, emphasis on speed in the delivery of tea cargoes, the bill of lading contained a stipulation that an extra freight payment of 10 shillings a ton would be made for the first ship in dock with new tea from Foochow. It is easy to see what a difference of weeks en route might make, but a difference of a few hours seems immaterial. At any rate, the *Ariel* was involved in one of the most famous races of all with the *Taeping,* a similar ship, two years older and from the same yard. There is a celebrated painting of them racing up the Downs on September 5, 1866, at 14 knots—98 days, 22 hours out of Foochow. The *Ariel* was 10 minutes ahead, but the *Taeping* got the better tug and was docked 28 minutes earlier. The consignees, worried at so much tea arriving all at once, divided the premium between the two ships and abandoned the practice of paying premiums for extra speed in the delivery of tea.

With Australia supplanting China as the chief objective of the clippers after the opening of the Suez Canal, the *Ariel* sailed from London for Sydney on January 31, 1872, and was never heard from again. It is believed that she was probably "pooped" by a following sea.

(See D. R. MacGregor, *The Tea Clippers,* 1952.)

Erzherzog Ferdinand Maximilian

Named for the unfortunate Habsburg Archduke Maximilian who headed the Austrian navy before his tragic experience as Emperor of Mexico, this armored Austrian frigate rammed and sank the New York-built Italian *Re d'Italia* at Lissa on July 20, 1866. This had an effect on naval tactics by overemphasizing ramming: rams were now built into the bows of warships in various navies, resulting principally in the accidental sinking of their own ships. The torpedo, which came on the scene just a few years after Lissa, would make it too risky to attempt ramming.

The battle in 1866 was part of the Italian portion of the Austro-Prussian War which was a major step in Bismarck's buildup of Prussia. To assist in dividing Austria's forces, he made an alliance with the new kingdom of Italy, promising it the province of Venetia. And so it happened; the Italians were beaten both on land and sea, but they gained Venetia. When the rammed *Re d'Italia* was sinking at Lissa, her crew cheered, "Venice is ours."

The war in the Adriatic found both navies in a state of transition. They both followed the French and the British into armor, but a considerable part of their fleets were still wooden. The Italians were buying up ready-made ships abroad; their two proudest ones—the 5700-ton *Re d'Italia* and *Re di Portogallo*—being fresh from the New York yard of William M. Webb. The Austrian flagship, *Ferdinand Max,* of 5130 tons, was likewise armored. In almost all the categories of size and strength, the Italian fleet was much stronger on paper. But it was pointed out that the Austrians were ably commanded, whereas the Italians were hardly commanded at all.

Wilhelm von Tegetthoff, the 39-year-old Austrian commander, was a combination of all the qualities that make a good admiral: thorough in preparation, quick to size up a situation, and intelligently aggressive in action. Carlo Pellione de Persano, the 60-year-old Italian commander, had a good reputation, but was now excessively indecisive.

The fighting centered around the island of Lissa in the Adriatic, about 20 miles from the Dalmatian shore. It was held by the Austrians and the Italians planned to dislodge them. On land, the Prussian victory of Sadowa (or Königgrätz) on July 3 had ended the long contest between Austria and Prussia for the control of Germany. Now, on July 20, the rival fleets came together off Lissa, with Persano's indecisiveness offsetting the Italian strength.

The battle was a general melee, but the decisive event which impressed the outside world was the sinking of the *Re d'Italia*. Persano had for some reason just shifted his flag to a smaller turret ram, throwing the Italian line out of order. Tegetthoff, like Farragut at Mobile Bay, climbed up the shrouds to see above the smoke. The *Re d'Italia* was almost motionless when the *Ferdinand Max* at a speed of 11½ knots struck her amidships. Her bow, "with a terrible crunch," cut through both the iron armor and the wood backing. When the *Max* drew back, the Italian ironclad went down with her flags flying, carrying with her 381 officers and men; only 168 were saved. A smaller Italian ship exploded, with 231 killed. In the whole battle, only 38 Austrians were killed, just three of them on the armored ships. Persano was found guilty of negligence and incapacity, deprived of his rank, and dismissed from the service. Tegetthoff became a popular hero; he was promoted to vice admiral and soon became commander in chief.

The ram received undue prominence. It had already figured in the American Civil War, particularly in the sinking of the wooden *Cumberland* by the *Merrimack*. It was, of course, one of the consequences of the introduction of steam; sailing vessels could not strike so hard a blow. Various navies adopted the ram, Admiral Ammen being a particular devotee in the United States Navy, which built the ram *Katahdin*, one of the navy's most uncomfortable ships.

(See H. W. Wilson, *Battleships in Action*, 1926.)

Agamemnon

The *Agamemnon*, of the Blue Funnel Line. (*Peabody Museum, Salem*)

The *Agamemnon* and her two sister ships, the *Ajax* and the *Achilles*, of Holt's Blue Funnel Line, began a profound change in the carriage of heavy cargo by sea. Before these ships came on the scene in 1865, cotton, wheat, and other heavy items were carried in square-riggers. Mail and some fine freight had been moving by steamer, but the coal bunkers on these ships took up so much space that little room was left for heavier cargo. However, ten years after the launching of the *Agamemnon*, the carrying of heavy cargo on the Atlantic and other medium runs was shifting fast to iron-hulled steam freighters. The solution to the problem of lack of space lay in the new compound engine which used steam twice, once in a small cylinder and once in a large one, getting more than twice as much mileage out of a ton of coal as previously. That development was particularly bad for the American square-riggers.

The man who did most to bring about this change was Alfred Holt, son of a prosperous Liverpool textile merchant. Instead of seeking a conventional university education, Holt determined to gratify his desire to develop the power of steam in the transportation field. He worked for a while with railroad locomotives, then shifted to marine steam. His principal interest was to develop an engine that would get maximum mileage from a ton of coal, and ultimately he came up with the compound engine.

Alfred Holt, and indeed the Holt family, rank high among the ship **258** operators of history. In addition to the development of the compound engine, the Holts organized and operated very successfully a cargo line between Liverpool and the Orient, primarily for carrying tea. For some reason, the tea trade had always put a premium on the first cargoes to arrive from China. That need for speed had led, as in the case of the American clippers, to the development in England of smaller but very speedy tea clippers. The competition among these small, fast ships was keen. In 1865, the year the *Agamamnon* was launched, a memorable race took place between the clippers *Ariel* and *Taeping*. They left China together and 99 days later raced up the English Channel almost abreast. The *Ariel* won the 16,000-mile race by 10 minutes.

But that 99-day speed record proved to be well over the 62 days in which the new Blue Funnel liners could deliver the tea when they entered the trade. The *Agamemnon, Ajax,* and *Achilles* were built in the crack Scott yard at Greenock below Glasgow in Scotland. They had iron hulls and single propellers: they measured 2300 tons and had a speed of 10 knots. The *Agamemnon* first sailed for China on April 19, 1866, stopping at Mauritius, then Penang, Singapore, and Hong Kong. Her principal outward cargo was cloth; homeward bound it was tea—valuable cargo which paid well.

In the development of the compound engine, a main goal of the Holts had been to produce an engine that would be sufficiently economical with coal to make long, nonstop runs. There was consequently a worldwide sensation when the *Agamemnon* made an 8000-mile nonstop run from Liverpool to Mauritius. The impact of the long nonstop run was greatly increased with the opening of the Suez Canal in 1869, four years after the three Blue Funnel ships were built. The new route through the Suez Canal drastically reduced the mileage from Britain to the East. For sailing vessels, the Canal itself required some 100 miles of towing, only to reach the long, narrow Red Sea, where the winds were either nonexistent or were too baffling for passage by sail. This was a final blow to the prospects for the square-riggers on that run. Gradually, they began to be laid up and the little steam freighters took over.

The *Agamemnon* was given a new and more efficient compound engine in 1878. After more than 30 years of service, she was sold to a Dutch firm in 1897; she was broken up in Italy in 1907. The Blue Funnel Line has held its own against the prestigious P & O (Peninsular and Oriental) Line, which has been subsidized by the British government since 1840. It continues to operate successfully with all its ships bearing classical names.

(See F. E. Hyde and J. R. Harris, *Blue Funnell: A History of Alfred Holt and Company of Liverpool from 1865 to 1914,* 1956.)

Wampanoag

The U.S.S. Wampanoag, built in 1868. (Naval Historical Center)

During the Civil War the United States Navy decided to lay down a half dozen very fast cruisers, which might be a threat to the British or French should they enter the war on the Confederate side, or might also be useful in running down Southern raiders. When those needs became less critical later in the war, the cruisers remained unfinished. Not until about 1867 was it decided to complete their construction.

The vessels had different builders and designers of machinery. The two most distinctive vessels, the *Wampanoag* and the *Ammonusuc*, outstripped all the others. Their engines were designed by engineer-in-chief Benjamin F. Isherwood, who had designed most of the machinery for the Union Navy. The *Wampanoag* was a wooden, screw cruiser of 4215 tons and was 335 feet long. Her engines had a pair of cylinders 100 inches in diameter and a four-foot piston stroke. She had a surface condenser and eight vertical tubular boilers, with four superheaters and great wooden gear wheels which drove the propeller at two revolutions for each double-piston stroke. The *Ammonusuc* had similar equipment.

The important thing about the *Wampanoag* was her extraordinary speed. On her trials she maintained some 17 knots for 38 hours. Her captain declared that she was "faultless in her model and as a steamship the fastest in the world." She would remain so for at least 10 years. The other ship with Isherwood machinery had almost as fast a performance. But such speed came at high cost, for the vessels had a severely limited **260** cruising range and poor quarters below for the crew.

When Grant became president in 1869, he placed his friend Admiral David Porter in virtual charge of the navy. Porter had been a first-rate fighter afloat in the Civil War, but he was a troublesome intriguer ashore. He hated engineers in general and Isherwood in particular. He got out a series of general orders which, among other things, sought to restore the "spiritual value of sail" in contrast to steam. One of his general orders declared that sail was to be used wherever possible; if a captain used steam, he was to enter the reason in the ship's log, and if the Navy Department did not approve, the cost of the coal expended would be charged against his pay.

The most conspicuous victim of that policy was the *Wampanoag*, which never went to sea again. Disliking the Indian names bestowed during the war, Porter changed her name to *Florida*. She lay idle at Brooklyn Navy Yard until 1874 and then was sent to New London as a receiving and store ship; in 1885 she was sold for $41,000, 3% of her original cost. It was a vessel built before its time.

But if the Americans scorned speed, the British did not. It has been suggested that the speed of the *Wampanoag* encouraged the British to settle the *Alabama* Claims amicably. At the same time they laid down a new fast cruiser of their own, though not quite a match for the *Wampanoag*.

(See E. W. Sloan, *Benjamin Franklin Isherwood, Naval Engineer*, 1965.)

Cutty Sark

The British clipper *Cutty Sark*, built for the China trade. *(National Maritime Museum, Greenwich)*

Even before a popular whiskey was named for her, the British clipper *Cutty Sark* had a distinctive reputation, which was enhanced when she became the only clipper still preserved. The great American clippers lacking composite iron frames also slipped from view, but the *Cutty Sark* aroused such lasting admiration that she is now preserved in drydock at the National Maritime Museum at Greenwich.

Rated with the *Ariel, Thermopylae,* and *Taeping* as one of the fastest tea clippers, she came on the scene in 1869 just as the *Agamemnon,* with her compound engines, and the newly opened Suez Canal foretold the end of that glamorous tea traffic around Good Hope from Shanghai or Foochow to London. She tried it for a few years and then entered on the more distinctive performance of her career, carrying wool from Australia to England.

The *Cutty Sark* had been ordered by John Willis, "Old White Hat," wealthy shipowner and onetime sea captain, who wanted the best ship possible. For a builder he chose young Hercules Linton of Dumbarton, Scotland, a partner in the new shipbuilding firm of Scott and Linton. Linton was a superlative designer, but the rigid perfectionist demands of John Willis drove the firm out of business.

The *Cutty Sark,* like the other tea clippers, at 921 tons was barely half the size of the 1793-ton American clipper *Flying Cloud.* She had iron frames and the most expensive of perfect timbers and teak decks. Her name came from the "torn shirt" of the witch Nannie, represented in her figurehead, in Robert Burn's "Tam o'Shanter." Her maximum capacity was 1,375,000 pounds of tea, 5300 bales of wool, 1180 tons of coal, and 26,300 cases of case oil.

Launched on November 23, 1869, she had made eight tea voyages from China by 1877, her principal rival being the clipper *Thermopylae*, which beat her by five days on the first voyage. It became a boast of the *Cutty Sark* that no ship ever passed her, but the *Thermopylae* seemed to accomplish that at times. The time finally came when it was out of the question to compete with the Suez steamer route. During one year of shift she had a hectic voyage carrying Welsh steaming coal out to the United States Navy in China, with a below par captain and crew.

Then the *Cutty Sark* was on the Australian wool run by way of Cape Horn. Even though she was smaller than most other wool ships, she held her own until 1895. No small part of her success was due to her new captain, Richard Woodget. Alan Villiers says of him, "He was the obvious choice for the *Cutty Sark*. He was that rarity, the right man in the right place at the right time."

By mid-1890s she could no longer pay her way. She was sold to the Portuguese, who used her in various trades, but by 1922 she was no longer able to earn her way anywhere. A Captain Dowman, who had passed her at sea in the old days, spotted her at Falmouth, England, and did what he could to preserve her. His widow presented her to the Thames Nautical Training School and in 1952 the *Cutty Sark* Preservation Society was formed to take over, searching for a permanent berth for her as a national monument. She found such a berth in a drydock at the National Maritime Museum at Greenwich.

(See R. E. Brettle, *The Cutty Sark: Her Design and Builder,* 1969; D. R. MacGregor, *The Tea Clippers,* 1952.)

Mary Powell

The words "steamship" for the large vessels and "steamboat" for the small ones are useful for differentiation, but in borderline cases it is useful to call the medium-sized vessels "steamers." It happens that these middling steamers have aroused more emotional enthusiasm than any other means of transportation. Trains, planes, and buses lack individual identity. One might use the 5:15 train but it did not always have the same locomotive or cars; scheduled planes and buses often change personnel; however, some riders used to have favorite trolley cars. Even liners such as the *Mauretania* or *Queen Mary* may command popularity and respect, but few traveled on the same ship often enough to develop intimate affection. Earlier in the century affection was normally bestowed on vessels in local service for daytime commuter or excursion service. Those of us who grew up in Portland, Maine, developed such feeling for the old *Aucocisco* which, with her graceful lines and melodious whistle, plied down through Casco Bay for half a century. Farther down east in Penobscot Bay the *J. T. Morse* had its devotees. There was lasting love for the *Uncatena,* which for years linked Nantucket and Martha's Vineyard with the mainland. And at Nantasket the old white sidewheeler *Nantasket* was moved bodily to a bluff near the wharf. There were scores more of favorite vessels up and down the coasts; the Steamship Historical Society's journal tells of them with loving nostalgia.

A popular referendum of the steamboat buffs would probably give the palm to the *Mary Powell,* a wooden sidewheeler which plied the Hudson for more than 60 years, from 1860 to 1923, operating chiefly in commuter service between New York and mid-Hudson points. She was built by Michael S. Allison of Jersey City for Captain Absalom Anderson of Kingston, who designed her, and her engines were the work of

Fletcher, Harrison & Company. She was rebuilt in 1874 and in 1889, her later tonnage being 983.

In addition to her fine lines, she also had the distinction of being one of the fastest steamboats, and for a while the fastest, on the river. This was a reason for her success in commuter service, particularly to towns on the west side of the lower river, and it was such service with regular travelers which helped to build up her high reputation. Now and then, with a favorable tide and following wind, she made some special, carefully preserved records. On August 7, 1874, she made the run from her Vesey Street pier in New York to Newburgh in two hours and 47 minutes, including stops at three landings. Her pilot and engineer, to save time at landings, were able to put passengers ashore without even using lines to fasten her.

The *Mary Powell*'s long service was mostly uneventful, but in carrying General Custer's body from Poughkeepsie to West Point, the big crowd suddenly surged to the port side and nearly swamped her. On another occasion, a violent cyclone pushed her sideways for two miles and blew off both her funnels. During the winters, when the river was frozen over, she hibernated at Rondout. She was broken up at Kingston in 1923.

(See J. H. Morrison, *History of Steam Navigation,* 1903.)

Captain

In 1870 the *Captain,* a large new British ironclad, capsized at sea and went down with nearly all hands. Her victims included Captain Cowper Coles of the Royal Navy, often rated with John Ericsson as one of the two inventors of the turret which soon became an essential feature of all battleships. There was a difference in their turret experience. "If the story of how Ericsson introduced the turret into the U.S. Navy is the most dramatic in the history of warship construction, that of Coles' fight to get the turret accepted by the Admiralty is most tragic. . . . Coles fought year after year to get a seagoing turret ship built—only to be subjected to departmental obstruction and frustration." Coles was "finally fated to have the ship of his dreams built over-weight; so that under the stress of weather she was to shatter the hope of success her achievements seemed to justify."

The turret, a heavily armored rotating cupola containing two heavy guns, was a radical departure from conventional warship armament.

Almost from the time of the Armada, the capital ship depended upon its broadside battery—guns, sometimes by the dozens, side by side on wooden trucks, which when fired all together could deliver a shattering blast. Even the new ironclads *Gloire* and *Warrior* had some three dozen heavy guns, in keeping with tradition. They had scarcely put to sea, however, when in 1862 Ericsson's *Monitor* gave the turret world prominence. Described as a "cheesebox on a raft," it had a revolving armored turret containing two maximum size guns. In the spectacular action in Hampton Roads it held its own against the more conventional *Merrimack*.

Coles had already started agitating for turrets in the British ironclads but ran afoul of entrenched conservatism, especially in the chief constructor, backed by some of the Admiralty's sea lords—the civilian First Lord favored the idea. Coles wrote articles and gave lectures, whereby he won wide public support and had the newspapers on his side. The Admiralty, which had opposed Coles's plans, finally agreed to a compromise providing for two separate turret ships. One would be designed and built under Admiralty direction; this became the *Monarch*, built at Chatham dockyard. The other, the *Captain*, on Coles's design, was to be built by the private Laird yard near Liverpool, which had built the Confederate raider *Alabama*. The Admiralty pretty much kept its hands off the *Captain*.

As she approached completion, it became obvious that the *Captain* was considerably overweight and this in turn affected her stability. To make matters worse, Coles foolishly agreed to masts and sails of maximum size. She was laid down in January 1867, floated out in March 1869, and completed in January 1870. She had four 12-inch guns of maximum size in two turrets with heavy armor. The main cause for concern was that she lay low in the water with only seven or eight feet of freeboard. Her captain, however, felt confident.

Early in August 1870 she left for fleet maneuvers in the Mediterranean, with Coles aboard as a "privileged observer." On September 6, off the coast of Spain, she was feeling the effects of a gale and was listing badly, with water coming over the deck. By midnight, efforts were made to take in her sails but she was listing too much, and they were a grave source of danger. Shortly after midnight a blast of exceptional violence threw her over beyond her safety limits; she lay briefly on her beam ends and then sank, bottom upward. Coles and 472 officers and men were lost—her entire complement except for the gunner and 17 men who succeeded in getting ashore on the pinnace. It was a disaster unique in the Royal Navy for a ship of her size. Within a few years turrets became general, and the contribution of Coles was finally appreciated.

(See A. Hawkey, *H.M.S. Captain*, 1965.)

Natchez and Robert E. Lee

The Mississippi steamers *Robert E. Lee* and *Natchez*. *(Peabody Museum, Salem)*

One of the most widely publicized and longest remembered maritime sporting events in American history was the race of the steamers *Natchez* and *Robert E. Lee* up the Mississippi from New Orleans to St. Louis in mid-1870. Racing had long been popular on the inland rivers, particularly with boats leaving at the same time of day. It was a dangerous sport—scores of high-pressure boilers, often with someone sitting on the safety valve, blew up with fatal results. This particular race escaped that fate; coming as it did near the end of the great river boat era with its distinct way of life, it lent itself to the nostalgia which the South in 1870 was feeling about many things.

The steamers had reputations as two of the fastest on the river. The *Robert E. Lee* came from the upper river, based at St. Louis, and the *Natchez,* from down river, serving as a mail packet between Vicksburg, Natchez, and New Orleans. Backers of the two boats arranged the race, and the betting was said to have been heavy. Both boats were capable of 18 miles an hour upstream and 25 miles or so downstream.

They left New Orleans at 4:55 P.M. on June 30, 1870, and stayed almost neck and neck for several days. The thing that kept the race from becoming a clean-cut affair was that at Devil's Island the fog shut in so heavily that Captain Leathers of the *Natchez* tied up for six hours before continuing up the river. The *Robert E. Lee* continued on through the fog, arriving at St. Louis on July 4 at 11:25 A.M., with the *Natchez* **267** coming in at 4:35 P.M.. The *Lee* had taken three days, 18 hours, and 30 minutes for the 1210-mile run. The *Natchez* took six hours and 33 minutes longer, about the length of her "time out" at Devil's Island, which made the race just about a draw. It is assumed that the *Lee* backers collected their bets, but the *Natchez* backers remained loyal to their steamer.

It was not long after this famous race that the river-steamer passenger traffic succumbed to the competition of the Illinois Central and other railroads. The nostalgic feeling for the old way of life lasted on and about 1927 let to the building of the big sternwheel riverboat *Delta Queen*, on which many of the old amenities were re-created even to the calliope, or steam piano. Passengers came from far and wide. The various cruises went up the Ohio as far as Pittsburgh and up the Mississippi as far as Minneapolis; New Orleans was the natural southern terminal. The *Delta Queen* was honored by the government as a national historic monument. But being built of wood, albeit slow burning, it took a special act of Congress to keep her going. In 1976 a new fireproof consort, the *Mississippi Queen*, joined her on the river.

Mary Celeste

The brig *Mary Celeste*, shown as the *Amazon* of Parrsboro. (Peabody Museum, Salem)

The brigantine *Mary Celeste*, a modest little tramp trader, provided one of the most baffling mysteries in the history of the sea. Time and again, ships have gone "missing with all hands," but in this case "all hands" went missing but the ship remained intact. En route from New York to Genoa with a cargo of alcohol, she was discovered on December 4, 1872, in the eastern Atlantic without a soul aboard.

She was a Nova Scotia vessel, built in 1861 in John Dewes's yard on Spencer Isle in the Parrsboro district. Originally named the *Amazon*, she was about 100 feet long and 25 feet in beam, with a tonnage of 282. In 1868 she underwent a thorough overhauling and was renamed the *Mary Celeste,* shifting from British-Canadian to American registry, hailing from New York. She was one of the numerous vessels for which Captain James H. Winchester served as "ship's husband," or managing owner. Her captain, Benjamin H. Briggs, was originally from Wareham in the Cape Cod area and was the other principal owner. On this fatal trip, he was accompanied by his wife, Sarah, and their two-year-old daughter, Sophia; their seven-year-old son was left behind with his grandparents. Briggs was 38 years old and had a high reputation for character and competence. Also on board were two mates, a cook-steward, and four sailors, apparently from northern Europe. The ship sailed from New York early in November 1872, chartered to the New York firm of Meissner, Ackerman & Company and was carrying 1700 barrels of alcohol, valued at $36,000, to a consignee in Genoa. Up to that point, the record is clear but then the mystery shut down.

On December 4 contact was suddenly made ·by the brigantine *Dei Gratia* on her way from New York to the Mediterranean with oil and mixed cargo. Her captain, David Read Morehouse, was a longstanding friend of Captain Briggs. She was sailing along some 600 miles west of Portugal when the lookout sighted another brigantine yawing and falling off as if no one were at the wheel. Captain Morehouse signaled, then hailed. When no response came, he sent over a boat under his mate, Oliver Deveau. To their amazement, they found not only no helmsman but no one else. The *Mary Celeste*—they had noted the name on the stern—was a derelict.

Aside from a fair amount of water sloshing around below decks, she was in a surprisingly normal condition, with things very much in their proper places and no indication of why everyone had left. The yawl was missing; the other boat had been smashed during the loading in East River and had not been replaced. In later days when imaginations were producing fantastic additions to the story, it was reported that there was still a hot meal on the table—thoroughly impossible since the ship had been abandoned 10 days earlier. This information had been ascertained by the ship's log up to noon of November 24, and the temporary "slate log" to 8 A.M. on November 25, at which time she was a few miles off Santa Maria in the Azores. In the intervening days, without anyone at the helm, she coursed several hundred miles to where the *Dei Gratia* found her. Aside from the logs, the only other last minute writing was an incomplete note from Albert Richardson, the Nova Scotian mate, to "Frances my own dear wife, Frances N.R." That was all.

Mate Oliver Deveau took the derelict *Mary Celeste* into Gibraltar following the *Dei Gratia*, where officialdom took over in the primary matter of salvage and beyond that in a search into the background of the whole baffling situation. The American consul, Horatio J. Sprague, was very helpful and Captain R. W. Shubrick of the U.S.S. *Plymouth* offered useful suggestions. But the British authorities, a rather stuffy lot, took general charge of matters, especially J. Solly Flood who reveled in the title "Her Majesty's Advocate General and Proctor for the Queen in her Office of Admiralty." He seems to have been a tireless legal blood-hound who worked hard to try to prove that there had been violence aboard. Spots of rust were scraped up and given to a doctor for analysis. The doctor found nothing, but the United States State Department did not receive a copy of his report until 1887. The ship was examined with a fine-toothed comb—topside, inside, and below the waterline by a diver—but nothing incriminating was found. J. Solly Flood however still stuck to his theory of violence:

> My own opinion is that the crew got at the alcohol and in the fury of drunkenness murdered the Mate . . . his wife and child and the chief mate . . . and that they did, some time between the 25th of November and the 5th December escape on some vessel bound for North or South American ports or the West Indies.

For some time after December 4 there was the hope that the yawl with the Briggs family might have been picked up, but that hope gradually receded. On March 14, 1873, the Gibraltar Vice-Admiralty Court, concerned only with the salvage aspect, awarded £ 1700 to the officers and crew of the *Dei Gratia*, about one-fifth of the value of the vessel and cargo. The *Mary Celeste* was driven ashore, with all sails set, on a Haitian reef in 1885; her master was charged with barratry but died before the trial came off.

In addition to honest research, the *Mary Celeste* story inspired a fantastic crop of writings which wandered far from the truth into a "gargantuan monstrosity." Arthur Conan Doyle, creator of Sherlock Holmes, wrote an utterly wild "J. Habbakuk Josephson's Statement," and articles appeared in journals at late as 1931 and 1933, while the wholly imaginative *The Great Mary Celeste Hoax* achieved book form.

Dr. Oliver Cobb, a nephew of the Briggs family (Mrs. Briggs was a Cobb), devoted years to research in the case and came up with what seems to be a logical explanation:

> My theory is that Captain Briggs in the afternoon of November 24, 1872, fearing an explosion of the cargo of alcohol, put his wife and

child in a boat with Mr. Richardson and one sailor to care for them. Another sailor would hold the boat clear of the vessel. Mr. Gilling (the 2nd mate) with a sailor unrove the main-peak halliard as a tow rope. The fourth sailor would be at the wheel. The captain went below and got the chronometer, sextant and ship's papers. The cook was getting supplies to take in the boat. The cook evidently gathered up what food was available as no cooked food was found on the *Mary Celeste*. Probably at this time came a minor explosion which landed the hatch upside down on deck. They made haste to get away. . . .

The halliards were available for a tow rope and were probably bent on the ship's painter. The boat was hastily pushed away from the brigantine. Just at this time a breeze came from the north . . . the rope . . . parted at the rail leaving the boat adrift and about 400 feet away. . . . A piece of rope, maybe fifteen feet long might have been the key to this whole matter.

(See G. Bradford, *The Secret of Mary Celeste and Other Sea Fare*, 1967.)

Bear

The *Bear* on Greely relief mission in Greenland. *(Naval Historical Center)*

For 40 years of her frigid existence, the *Bear* was a revenue cutter patrolling Alaskan waters, chasing illicit sealers, engaged on errands of mercy, and often serving as almost the sole representative of United States authority in that bleak region. Except among the persistent malefactors, she built up a lasting, widespread affection. Those strenuous 40 years were less than half her long 89-year career of widely varied adventure. Built in Scotland as a tough, ice-resistant, oaken steam sealer, she spent nine years in that occupation before her brief service in the United States Navy, engaged in successful quest of a missing Arctic expedition before becoming a revenue cutter. Then going to the opposite frigid extreme, she participated in two expeditions to the Antarctic. Finally, headed south in a March gale to become a restaurant-museum, she went down in the Atlantic south of stormy Cape Sable in 1963.

The *Bear* was built at Dundee in Scotland in 1874, with oak frame and six-inch planking, sheathed with tough Australian ironwood, and braced in her bows to withstand the ice with which she would become all too well acquainted. She was a barkentine, with her lesser masts of Norway pine and her big mainmast a hollow iron tube. She was 190 feet long and her displacement was 1675 tons. For her first nine years she moved north each March from St. John's, Newfoundland, into the Labrador sealing grounds. It was almost ironic that her later long career would be spent in efforts to protect the helpless seals which she was now pursuing.

In 1884 the *Bear* was taken temporarily into the United States Navy on an errand of mercy to rescue a missing exploring group. As part of an International Polar Year project, a party of some two dozen men under Lieutenant Adolphus Greely of the army were stranded, more than a year overdue, up in Baffin Bay. The *Bear's* sister ship, sent up to bring them out, had been crushed in the ice. The Secretary of the Navy purchased the *Bear* and another ship to go to the rescue. After fitting her out with a strengthened hull at Brooklyn Navy Yard, she and her companion sailed for Baffin Bay in April 1884; the expedition moved with all possible speed because it was known that the explorers' supplies were exhausted. Two months later a lone, ragged figure was spotted on a ridge near Cape Sabine, in an extremely emaciated condition. He led the way to a half-buried tent with six more survivors, including Lieutenant Greely, almost dead of starvation—one unfortunate had his hands and feet frozen, and later died. The *Bear* put back to Portsmouth Navy Yard for full navy honors.

The navy, just receiving its first steel vessels, had no further use for the wooden *Bear*, but the Revenue Marine, faced with extensive new responsibilities in the freezing North Pacific, could see real value in the old icebreaker and received her by transfer in 1885. After further fitting out, she sailed from New York for the Pacific, arriving at San Francisco on February 23, 1886, 106 days out, ready for her 40 years of Revenue Marine (Coast Guard) duties in the new Bering Sea Patrol.

When in 1867 Secretary Seward purchased Alaska from Russia for

wide, and not fully realized, responsibilities for a huge portion of the
Pacific and Arctic Oceans. A few troops and officials were sent up, but
they could scarcely move about. Communications generally had to be
by water and the responsibility for many things fell on three small
cutters of the Revenue Marine—the *Bear, Rush,* and *Corwin.* Because of
her special ice protection, the *Bear* was given the rugged northern
sector from Norton Sound up through Bering Strait to Point Barrow, but
she would also have to spend much time in the "Seal Islands" to the
southward.

The United States inherited from the Russians the protection of the
seals on its own territory, but that was only part of the picture. Like the
salmon, the fur seal followed a wide-ranging migratory pattern each
year. The female would resort to a particular place to bring forth her
young and to become fertilized for the next crop. The efforts to preserve
the seals from destruction centered on the females—both when they
were ashore and when swimming around in pelagic fishing. Males
were generally fair game, and the government would allow the killing
of a specific quota—a multimillion dollar business. The most serious
complications were of international scope—long, difficult diplomatic
relations with the British and Canadians, and less easily regulated
relations with the Russians, Japanese, and others.

The most critical locale in this migratory setup was on St. Paul and St.
George, the so-called "Seal Islands" in the Pribilof group, in the Bering
Sea about 250 miles north of Unalaska in the Aleutians. Unless protected, the helpless females could be slaughtered by the tens of thousands and their little ones left to starve. Even with steady cruising, it
was most difficult to prevent hit-and-run raids, and there were frequent
suggestions that armed forces of sailors or soldiers be left ashore on the
islands. Further complications came from search and seizure of vessels
suspected of smuggling. Altogether, the life of a cutter captain was not a
happy one. That general pattern lasted through much of the *Bear*'s years
on those northern waters. During part of that time her skipper was the
rugged and very effective Captain M. A. Healy, whose personality
accounted for no small part of the *Bear*'s success.

While the sealing operations were a specialty of that wild region,
some of the *Bear*'s other duties were of the general revenue cutter
pattern. With her ice-breaking strength, she often released whalers
from the ice and otherwise served them. She contributed to the social
life of the Eskimos and at times helped to save them from starvation
when they were in distress. On one occasion when the *Bear* visited St.
Lawrence Island, every Eskimo inhabitant had died. She even moved
large numbers of reindeer across from Siberia to Alaska to ensure a

more adequate food supply. Her doctor's visits at Eskimo villages were most useful public health services.

Along with those beneficent roles, she was at times almost the only representative of Federal law and order. Her vigilance in matters of smuggling reflected the original reason for establishing the Revenue Marine. In the forecastle of a schooner, they once found 20 gallons of whiskey and 8000 cartridges. Captain Healy ordered the whiskey thrown overboard and gave a receipt for the ammunition. With no jails to hold prisoners, it was necessary to improvise punishment. Boarding a mutinous ship, Healy had 22 of the crew handcuffed to a line, so that their toes were barely touching the deck. That sufficiently softened the mutinous spirit so that before long they returned to their duties. And so it went, year after year.

The Bering Sea duties ended in 1926 when the *Bear* was replaced by a new steel icebreaker. There was a question of what to do with the old ship and for a while she was a floating museum at the municipal dock in Oakland. She also had a brief period of activity in the filming of Jack London's *The Sea Wolf*.

In 1932 the *Bear* had a new lease on life under the aegis of Rear Admiral Richard Byrd, who wanted an "ice ship" for his Antarctic operations. He purchased her at a bargain rate, had her fitted out at Boston, and sent her south in company with an old steel freighter renamed the *Jacob Ruppert* in honor of one of her backers. On September 25, 1933, she sailed for "Little America" by way of the Panama Canal and Dunedin, New Zealand. The activity in the Antarctic centered on the construction of Little America on the Bay of Whales and the Ross Ice Shelf. It was essential to get things unloaded before the long Antarctic night set in, with ice shutting off outer communications. It was necessary to get the *Jacob Ruppert* back to New Zealand before the ice should crush her fragile hull. The *Bear,* however, stayed on and explored the eastern portion of Ross Sea as far as she could go. Then the doctor had to go home in poor health, and the *Bear* fought her way out to pick up a replacement. Back at the Bay of Whales there was a question of whether she could escape being iced in for the winter, but again she managed to get out of the bay through blinding "sea smoke." Then on March 2, 1934, she encountered the most violent hurricane of her long career:

> Ship bearing heavily in mountainous seas, rolling fifty degrees each side. Green water breaking aboard. Have lifelines stretched along weather deck in network pattern. . . . For three days no mess tables have been set. . . . Well deck completely submerged, galley waist deep in water at times. . . . So violent has been lurching of ship that men unable to stay in bunks. . . .

She survived both that hurricane and still another finally reaching Dunedin on March 12, 1934. After wintering there, she returned to the Bay of Whales for further exploration, especially in Marie Byrd Land. Finally, she made a last-minute getaway on February 6, 1935, and was back in Washington in May.

Byrd referred to the *Bear*'s gallant performance as her "last polar voyage," but then he brought her back to the Antarctic in 1939 in connection with the United States Antarctic Service Expedition to establish bases. She made two voyages, one in 1939–1940 and the other in 1940–1941. Even then the old ship had further service ahead, up in Greenland waters. Now painted white, she was one of three ships forming the Northeast Greenland Patrol under Coast Guard control. They were to watch for possible German activity in that frigid area. In September 1941 the patrol captured a Norwegian ship, the *Buskoe*, carrying communications equipment for the Germans. She was boarded and seized, and the *Bear* conducted the prize ship back to Boston. She continued on the Greenland Patrol until 1944, when she was decommissioned. In 1948 she was sold to a Halifax shipping operator who planned to return her to her original sealing role, but abandoned the project because of rising costs.

In 1962 a Philadelphia restaurant owner, Alfred Johnson, purchased the *Bear* for $12,000 for use as a restaurant-museum. Partly restored to proper condition, she left Halifax under tow for Philadelphia on March 17, 1963. Had Johnson waited until summer for that operation, the *Bear* might have gone on for a few more years. But a heavy gale, with snow and sleet, caught her, the towline snapped, some of her topmasts went by the board, and her seams loosened up. Planes went to the rescue, a raft was dropped, and the crew got to the tug in safety. The *Bear* remained afloat for a few hours, but at 9:30 P.M. she gave up the fight at the age of 89 years, and sank some 90 miles south of Cape Sable.

(See M. A. Ransom, *Sea of the Bear; Journal of a Voyage to Alaska and the Arctic,* 1964.)

Moewe

The little 848-ton German gunboat *Moewe* (Sea Gull) might be called the birthplace of Germany's West African colonial empire. During a single cruise in 1884 she had planted the flag and taken possession of Togoland, Cameroons, and German Southwest Africa as part of Germany's share in the "scramble for Africa."

Until 1884, Bismarck had withstood the pressure of German business interests to take such a step. Many German businessmen had been in West Africa for some time with their trading posts, sometimes on old hulks, swapping all sorts of European trade goods for the local supplies of palm oil, ivory, and so on. For a while the coast was wide open for such business, but after a while the French and later the British had staked off sections of the coast and hinterland to the exclusion of other nations. Bismarck had not wanted to annoy the British and kept German hands off the area. However, in 1884 he decided to act quickly and definitely. He placed matters in the capable hands of Gustav Nachtigal who, in addition to practical exploring experience in the Sahara, had been one of the most vociferous exponents of German colonialism.

This was the heyday of "gunboat diplomacy"—Britain and France had plenty of these little naval units engaged in showing the flag, chastising unruly natives, and trying without too great success to dodge yellow fever and malaria in that deadly "white man's grave." The *Moewe*'s cramped quarters had to accommodate two prominent civilians—Dr. Nachtigal and a colleague. One of the junior officers on the little vessel was Lieutenant Graf Maximilian von Spee, who would become a specialist in colonial expansion and 30 years later would command Germany's East Asiatic Squadron.

There had already been preparation among the native chiefs. One tongue-in-cheek explanation of the process told of preparing a pad of treaty forms ceding all animal, mineral, and vegetable rights, and then going up the river, stopping at every settlement with liquor for the chiefs and presents for their wives and getting each chief to sign his "X," and then returning to the coast, whistle for a gunboat to raise the flag. At any rate, the *Moewe* made rapid progress with treaties, first in narrow Togoland, between English Gold Coast and French Dahomey, and then down in the much larger Cameroons. The final phase was in the barren region of Southwest Africa, where the British had secured Walfish Bay but did not want to tie themselves down with anything more. So there the three colonies were—the titles were confirmed in international agreements and they would remain in German hands until World War I. Nachtigal did not survive the expedition; he died aboard the *Moewe* off Cape Palmas early in 1885; Spee had a bout of rheumatic fever which would trouble him throughout his life.

Glückauf

The *Glückauf* (Good Luck) was the first vessel to embody the essential features of the modern tanker. Her hull was subdivided by a longitudinal bulkhead, crossed by several transverse bulkheads, using the plating of the ship as the outer wall of each tank. The engines and crew quarters were aft of the tank area.

When American petroleum first came on the world market in the 1860s, it was carried in barrels. This was an expensive method, involving not only the cost of the containers but much waste space between them in the hold, and considerable longshoreman cost in loading and unloading. To obviate these costs, tanks were built into the holds of some sailing vessels—sail was considered safer than steam because of the danger of fire.

In 1884 a prominent German shipowner, Wilhelm A. Riedermann, had 72 tanks built into the hold of his sailing vessel *Andromeda* for carrying oil. He was so pleased with her performance that he took the next step of using the ship's plating as the outer wall of the tanks between the fore-and-aft bulkhead and the transverse bulkheads.

Riedermann immediately ran into hostile opposition because of fear of fire and also of leakage through rivet holes. No German yard would build his vessel, so he turned to the British yard of Armstrong-Mitchell at Newcastle-upon-Tyne, where the keel was laid on November 25, 1885. She was launched on June 16, 1886, and was named the *Glückauf*, which the skeptics twisted into *Fleigauf* (Blow Up).

This first tanker was 300 feet long and 37 feet in the beam and measured some 2300 gross and 3020 deadweight tons, with a capacity of about 13,000 barrels; she was barkentine-rigged.

The *Glückauf* sailed from Newcastle on July 13, 1886, on her first transatlantic voyage, arriving at New York on July 30, preparatory to loading at the Ocean Oil Company terminal at Williamsburg. But again she encountered conservative hostility. The longshoremen could foresee technological unemployment resulting from doing away with handling barrels, and police were stationed to prevent trouble. In sympathy, however, the coal merchants refused to furnish fuel, and she had to pick up enough coal at Newfoundland to get home. She was back in her home port in Germany on August 26, 1886, after a 20-day run—her normal speed was nine knots.

Once a start was made, she continued on the transatlantic run, having added enough bunker space to be independent of the New York coal dealers. The *Glückauf* was wrecked on the south shore of Long Island on March 4, 1893.

On some of the distant voyaging "case oil" was developed, with two five-gallon tanks in a case, which could be carried by a Chinese coolie or African porter, but on the major run to Europe the tankers caught on rapidly. In 1885, 99% of American oil exports was carried in barrels; by 1906, 99% was carried in bulk tankers.

Trenton

Wrecks of the
Trenton (left) and
other ships at Apia,
Samoa, after the
March 15, 1889,
typhoon.
(Mariners Museum)

The frigate *Trenton* came to an end at Samoa in the midst of an international crisis and a terrific typhoon which wrecked the entire American and German squadrons. She was flying the flag of Rear Admiral L. A. Kimberly, commander in chief on the Pacific station, and had been ordered down to protect American and native interests in the disputed Samoan islands.

A large frigate of 3900 tons, named for the capital of New Jersey, the *Trenton* had been the crack ship of the "Dark Ages" of the United States Navy following the Civil War. Built at New York Navy Yard in 1874, she was "for many years after her completion the most formidable cruising ship in our neglected navy and the only one that in type and armament at all approached the practice of other navies." She was said to have been the first warship equipped with electric lights but, in contrast to that modern touch, her eleven 8-inch guns were muzzleloaders at a time when breechloaders were becoming general. Her three-cylinder compound engine developed 3100 horsepower. In 1889 a few of the new American steel cruisers were afloat, but the *Trenton* was still a favorite flagship on distant stations.

When she arrived at Apia on March 10, 1889, the narrow harbor, with its coral reefs, was already crowded with six other warships, in addition to several merchantmen. Two American ships, the 2100-ton sloop *Vandalia* and the little 1375-ton gunboat *Nipsic,* rounded out Kimberly's squadron. The Germans had three warships of moderate size, the *Olga, Adler,* and *Eber.* The most impressive cruiser, and the only one to ride out the typhoon, was the 2765-ton five-year-old British cruiser *Calliope* with 16 modern breech-loading guns and powerful engines. Anchorages at Apia were assigned on a basis of first come, first served. The better locations at the inner end of the crowded harbor were already occupied when the two late-comers arrived: the *Vandalia* from San Francisco and the *Trenton* from Panama. They received exposed positions at the mouth of the harbor close to reefs and with a minimum of protection from the seas.

That international aggregation was occasioned by the rivalry which had disturbed Samoa for several years, with the consuls supported by cruisers. The Germans had been growing increasingly aggressive, hoping to annex the whole of Samoa. They had exiled the overall king of Samoa to a colony in West Africa, and were backing another Samoan, Tamatese, in his place. The British and Americans supported a rival, Mataffa, who had taken to the interior. There had been some shooting. Now the Germans declared martial law. At Washington, when the Republicans came into power early in 1889, Admiral Kimberly was ordered south, to give full protection and defense to United States citizens and property and to protect the native goverment of Samoa "against subjugation and displacement in violation of positive agreement and understanding between the treaty members." To complicate matters, there was as yet no cable communication with the outside world; messages to and from Washington, London, and Berlin had to go by ship to New Zealand.

By Friday, March 15, the weather began to deteriorate. Some of the commanders would have liked to move around to the safer and more commodious harbor of Pago Pago on the island of Tutuila, but fear that in their absence the rivals might take advantage of the situation deterred them. Instead of changing locations, they set out extra anchors and braced themselves for the ordeal, while the barometer rose and fell in a puzzling manner. By Friday night the storm was on them, and one of the *Trenton*'s anchors had broken away. From that time on until Sunday morning, the situation in the harbor was chaotic. More anchors broke loose, some of the engine rooms were flooded, and there was constant danger of collision. On the *Trenton,* the builders' bad judgment created a special hazard—the hawse holes in the bow had been placed too low. As the *Trenton* headed into the storm, water kept flooding in on the lower berth deck and continued to do so despite the constant stuffing of hammocks and blankets into the holes. The ship was awash below and the water flooded the engine rooms. Some of the crew were put to pumping, but even though the flagship band played steadily to cheer them, the water kept gaining on them. With the sail blown away, the whole crew on one occasion were sent aloft to form a sort of human sail in a vain effort to keep the ship off the reef.

The other ships had varying experiences. When a huge double tidal wave struck the harbor, the little *Eber* was swamped and went down. The five survivors owed their lives to the gesture of King Mataffa, who sent 300 of his anti-German Samoans over to assist in rescue work.

The *Adler* had been driven on top of the reef, where her remains would last for years. The heaviest American sufferer was the *Vandalia* in her exposed position. Broadside to the reef, she took a terrific pounding, losing four officers and 39 men before the *Trenton* pulled the rest to safety. Two of the ships managed to beach themselves with relative safety, the German *Olga* and the American *Nipsic,* and were later able to return home safely. The little *Nipsic,* however, was the only ship to display shoddy behavior during the raging storm. Many of her crew went aloft and refused to take part in rescue operations. When they were finally taken ashore, they put up a sorry picture of drunkenness and lack of discipline.

While the American and German squadrons were all run ashore, the English *Calliope* put on a magnificent performance. In view of the increasing possibilities of collision, her captain decided to take a chance and head out into the gale. His engineer, who would later be promoted for his accomplishment, put on every bit of power the engines could produce, so that the *Calliope* was able to make about one knot. As she passed the *Trenton,* fast ashore, she managed to clear the very narrow passage between the American flagship and the reef. The officers and men of the *Trenton* cheered the British ship, whose crew responded with cheers. The *Calliope* continued on outside in safety. The tradition of those cheers lasted on in Anglo-American relations.

The storm abated on Sunday morning, providing a chance to take stock of the damage. All six German and American ships were ashore, but the *Olga* and *Nipsic* would be able to go home under their own power. The *Eber* was sunk, while the *Vandalia* and *Adler* were wrecked beyond repair. Admiral Kimberly had hoped to save the *Trenton,* but a survey showed that it was hopeless. Her propeller was gone, the rudder was wrecked, her back was broken in two places, and the water, still rising, was up to her engine room platform. So while her band played "Hail Columbia" and other tunes, her stores were taken ashore. She had lost only one seaman in the crisis. The total death toll was 142—

four officers and 47 men for the Americans and five officers and 86 men for the Germans.

Bismarck, who had not yet been removed by William II, decided to discontinue German aggressiveness, and at a conference in Berlin the powers agreed to support Samoan independence. Recently, a book has been written entitled *The Typhoon That Stopped a War*. Whether things would have actually gone that far, those terrible hours in Apia harbor certainly relieved martial pressure.

(See E. P. Hoyt, *The Typhoon That Stopped a War*, 1968.)

Corsair
(Gloucester)

The *Corsair*
(Gloucester),
during the
Spanish-American
War.
*(Naval Historical
Center)*

During the Spanish-American War one of the nation's crack steam yachts, converted into a warship, played a distinguished role under a very able commander. At the turn of the century, steam yachts were at the peak of their popularity. They were luxuries but, as Cleveland Amory pointed out in his *The Last Resorts*, money flowed freely in the days before the income tax; wages were extremely low. There is a story that someone asked J. P. Morgan what it cost to operate a yacht like his *Corsair* and the alleged reply was, "If you have to ask, you can't afford it."

On the eve of the Spanish-American War, Morgan's 200-ton *Corsair* ranked fifth in size among the numerous American steam yachts. The only yachts ahead of her were William K. Vanderbilt's *Valiant*, Mrs.

Drexel Fell's *May*, H. F. Ballantine's *Eleanor*, and John Jacob Astor's *Nourmahal*. These yachtowners developed a special way of life, with their crusiing and coasting, but there was a question in the minds of their fellow members of the New York and Seewanhaka Yacht Clubs as to whether they were really yachtsmen. The *Corsair*, designed by J. B. Webb, was launched at the Philadelphia yard of Reanie, Neafie in 1891, and her graceful black hull became a familiar sight along the Atlantic coast.

With the coming of the Spanish-American War, as again in World War I, it became a common habit of the owners of such steam yachts to turn them over to the navy, sometimes for the token payment of $1.00.

The *Corsair* was acquired by the navy on April 23, 1898, converted into the gunboat *Gloucester*, and commissioned on May 16. No small part of her striking success was attributed to her commanding officer, Lieutenant Commander Richard Wainwright, one of the most brilliant younger officers of the day. She participated in the Battle of Santiago and then made a distinctive record in the conquest of Puerto Rico. At Guánica she arrived ahead of the fleet and single-handedly captured the city for the army. Then in company with the *Wasp*, she seized Arroyo a day ahead of the army, and raised the United States flag. She then cruised the northeast coast from New York to Cape Cod, waters familiar from her yachting days.

After the Spanish-American War, the *Gloucester* served three years as schoolship at the Naval Academy at Annapolis. Then came three years as tender to the commander in chief of the South Atlantic Fleet. From 1905 to 1917 she served with the naval militias of Massachusetts and New York. During World War I she patrolled the harbor waters of New York. In 1919 she was removed from the Navy List and was sold. By that time, J. P. Morgan had another *Corsair*.

(See *Dictionary of American Naval Fighting Ships*, 1959.)

Victoria and Camperdown

The *Victoria,* sinking after a collision with the *Camperdown.* (Mystic Seaport)

Stubbornness and stupidity on the part of the commander in chief produced a collision which sent a new battleship to the bottom of the Mediterranean with half her crew and the admiral who had admitted, "It was my fault." The amazing aspect of the affair was the fact that for an hour the likelihood of collision was evident on the bridges of both ships. The situation revealed a basic problem in naval and military discipline—if an order is obviously wrong, should subordinates take matters into their own hands, defying normal command authority?

The collision of the battleships *Victoria* and *Camperdown* occurred in the course of maneuvers of the British Mediterranean Fleet in July 1893, off the coast of Syria. The *Victoria,* a new single-turreted ship of 10,479 tons, was the flagship of Vice Admiral Sir George Tryon. She was a rather ugly-looking vessel with a pair of funnels side by side. Tryon was taking his 11 battleships in two columns up the coast from Beirut to Tripoli. The *Victoria* headed one division and the *Camperdown,* flagship of Rear Admiral Markham, the other.

In order to enter port in reverse direction, Tryon proposed to turn the two divisions in on each other. The trouble was that the two columns were only six cables (1200 feet) apart when Tryon gave the signal for the turn. The other officers knew that this would bring the ships together, since they needed at least eight cables. Those on the flagship remonstrated as strongly as they dared to the irascible admiral. For a moment he agreed to eight cables but then went back to six. When the reversal to 283 six cables was signaled to Markham's division, they could not believe it and wanted confirmation; Tryon asked what was holding them up, so they went into the fatal maneuver. With collision becoming more inevitable, neither flagship, until it was too late, ordered the watertight bulkheads closed or got out the collision nets.

The *Camperdown* struck the *Victoria* heavily, pushing her back some 70 feet. Her ram bow sliced deeply into the *Victoria,* just forward of the turret, and as the ships pulled apart the gash was enlarged so that water rushed in freely. Except for the poor men down in the firerooms, most of the crew were lined up in two long columns facing inward, maintaining perfect discipline, reminiscent of the soldiers on the *Birkenhead* 40 years before. When word to jump finally came, it was too late, because the ship quickly turned turtle and sank. Boats from the other ships saved about half of the crew, but 22 officers and 337 men went down with Admiral Tryon.

The court-martial declared that Admiral Tryon, "as the result of a temporary aberration, made a most inexplicable and fatal mistake." It expressed regret that Admiral Markham "had not protested against the fatal order" but "decided that it was not in the best interests of the Service to censure him for obeying the orders of his superior officer."

(See O. Parkes, *British Battleships*, *'Warrior'* 1860 to *'Vanguard'* 1950, 1957.)

Priscilla

The Long Island Sound steamer *Priscilla* long shared in double superlatives. She was the crack ship of the Fall River Line, which in turn was the most popular and successful of the American coastwise lines. The half century between the Civil War and World War I has been termed the "Dark Ages" of American deep-water merchant marine, when foreign-flag ships took over most of the imports and exports; however, the coastwide trade was protected against foreign competition and was very prosperous.

Of all the coastwise lines, the continually successful Fall River Line combined an overnight run from New York on Long Island Sound with a short train trip to Boston. It gradually surpassed the rival Long Island Sound lines to New London, Norwich, Stonington, and other ports, partly because the short rail run to Boston allowed passengers to sleep longer in the morning, and partly because of the line's superlative safety and service. It ran for 90 years, from 1848 to 1938, and its crack ship, the *Priscilla,* ran almost half that time, from 1894 to the end of service in 1938.

The Fall River steamers were all sidewheelers, even after the general adoption of propellers. It was argued that the sidewheelers were more maneuverable and could reverse more quickly, an important precaution against collisions in the fog. Aside from that, however, the line took the lead in modern features. The earlier steamers all had the usual wooden hulls, but a major landmark in the Fall River Line's history came in 1883 with the shift to iron, and later steel, hulls. During the next 11 years came its five celebrated "Ps"—the *Pilgrim, Puritan, Plymouth, Priscilla,* and *Providence.* They all embodied the same basic features: impressive, trim white hulls with two substantial black funnels and large passenger and cargo capacity. In 1908 the Fall River Line broke from the "P" arrangement with its new *Commonwealth,* a few tons larger than the *Priscilla* and a trifle faster, but the *Priscilla* remained the longstanding favorite.

The *Priscilla* was launched in Chester, Pennsylvania, in the yard of John Roach, who had built the first four steel cruisers of the "New Navy." Her machinery was the product of the Fletcher iron works in Hoboken, New Jersey. She measured 5339 tons displacement, just under the *Commonwealth*'s 5400, and had a speed of nearly 19 knots. She had a total of 296 staterooms and 11 bridal suites. Together with "free berths" she could accommodate 1100 passengers, plus 200 crew. The big interior public rooms were in impressive "steamboat gothic."

One of the Fall River Line's proudest achievements was its safety record. In all its 90 years of service, only one passenger lost his life by accident. That compares well with the Cunard Line's boast that in 75 years, up to the torpedoing of the *Lusitania,* it had never lost a passenger or a piece of mail. The Fall River Line record was the product of eternal vigilance and the most modern safety devices. Starting with the *Pilgrim* in 1883, the line took the lead in double bottoms. This paid off on one of her early trips when she struck an uncharted rock in New York Harbor. It tore a 100-foot gash in her outer hull, but the inner hull remained tight, and she reached safety under her own power. It was claimed that no other vessel of the day could have remained afloat under such conditions. In addition, she had a series of watertight bulkheads and her whole engine and boiler area was enclosed in iron. She was also probably the first to have automatic fire alarms—fire was always a major cause of apprehension. Long before the general regulations on such safety devices, she had lifeboat capacity for the 1300 passenger and crew total. Because of the too-common unpreparedness in connection with lifeboats, specially trained lifeboat crews were quartered near their boats.

Accompanying these precautions in equipment, the high quality of the officers and crew contributed to the safety record—the traveler was impressed by the display of keen, alert vigilance. The line had a consistent policy of "promotion from within"—men worked up through the ranks; no officers were hired from outside. The captains averaged at least 30 years of experience and the other senior officers almost as much. Altogether, the equipment and personnel policies were in extreme contrast to those in the New York–Havana Ware Line, where the sorry state of affairs did much to account for the heavy loss of life on the *Morro Castle* in 1934.

It was not until the opening of the Cape Cod Canal in 1914 that through steamer service between New York and Boston could compete successfully with the traditional steamer and rail arrangement, though the *Harvard* and *Yale* began direct service in 1907. A boat train left Boston at 5 P.M., reaching Fall River in ample time for dinner and a comfortable night on board the steamer, arriving in New York at a reasonable morning hour. Things were not so comfortable in the opposite direction. The first part of the trip was all right, leaving East River at 5 P.M. and progressing up through Hell Gate into the sheltered waters of Long Island Sound. Only when the ship proceeded on past Point Judith into Narragansett Bay was there apt to be rough going. On the pier at Fall River passengers transferred in the cold gray dawn for the train ride to Boston.

By the turn of the century, mergers and consolidations among the steamship lines and in conjunction with the railroads caused the system to become more complicated than simply the New York–Fall River run. Eventually, the New York, New Haven & Hartford acquired general control, including services to Stonington and Providence as well as Newport, which became a center of operations. There were occasional independent services, often with secondhand ships; the ill-fated *Larchmont*, which sank with heavy loss of life after a collision, was formerly the *Cumberland* on the Maine coast. Another independent service, not as tautly managed as the Fall River, became popularly known as the "Bedbug Line."

The public image of the Fall River Line was enhanced by writings and by a song. Roger McAdam wrote five popular volumes about the line, including one on *Priscilla of Fall River*. There was also a widely popular song:

> On the Old Fall River Line
> On the Old Fall River Line
> I fell for Susie's line of talk
> And Susie fell for mine

So I took her to the parson
   And he tied it tight as twine
And I wished, O Lord, I'd fell overboard
   On the Old Fall River Line.

The Fall River Line, while still operating with a fair amount of business, suddenly terminated service in 1938 because of a stubborn labor strike. Maritime labor, rather quiescent until the National Maritime Union started its aggressive career in 1936, began making demands which the management, under New Haven control, refused to accept, and the grand old line became a tradition.

(See R. W. McAdam, *Priscilla of Fall River*, 1947.)

Spray

Captain J. Slocum in the yawl *Spray.* (Peabody Museum, Salem)

Captain Joshua Slocum sailed alone around the world in his 12-ton sloop *Spray*, claiming that he was the first to perform that feat. The voyage covered 41,000 miles and took three years and two months (1895–1898). In addition to his love of adventure and his seamanship, Slocum had a flair for showmanship; his volume *Sailing Alone Around the World,* full of well-told yarns, gave him a widespread reputation, which was amplified by frequent performances on the lecture platform.

Slocum was a native of the Bay of Fundy region of Nova Scotia and took early to the sea. He was 20 years a shipmaster and was well acquainted with distant seas. His principal commands were the ship *Northern Light* and then his own bark *Aquidneck,* which was wrecked on the coast of Brazil. He and his family returned to New York in a canoe.

Slocum had been scouting around for a vessel when, in 1892, a friend told him of a possible buy, which turned out to be an antiquated and deteriorating sloop. Slocum thoroughly rebuilt the vessel, keeping her old name, *Spray.* She was 36-feet nine-inches long by 14-feet two-inches wide, measuring 12.71 tons gross. The conversion cost him $553 plus 13 months of his own labor.

On April 24, 1895, he set out from Fairhaven, Massachusetts, on his world cruise. It was not a nonstop affair; if a port struck his fancy, he would stop for a week or even longer. Somehow, the cruise had ample and widespread publicity, and he received cordial hospitality from governors, admirals, and other notables, with generous gifts and assistance.

His first major port of call was Gibraltar; on leaving, he was chased by a Moorish piratical felucca which he managed to outsail and arrived at the Cape Verde Islands. He ran into the doldrums taking two days to travel 300 miles, but eventually arrived at Pernambuco and went on down the coast to Rio de Janeiro and Buenos Aires. He encountered very heavy seas en route to the Straits of Magellan, where he had further weather difficulties in addition to trouble with the natives of Tierra del Fuego. For part of the passage, he had to double back, but finally emerged in the Pacific, which he reached on April 13, 1896, two months after he had entered the strait.

He stopped at Juan Fernández, Robinson Crusoe's island, and then spent 72 days sailing nonstop to Samoa, where the hospitality included several talks with the widow of Robert Louis Stevenson. Then came Australia with a stopover of several weeks at Sydney, followed by Melbourne and Tasmania. He proceeded northward to Queensland and the Great Barrier Reef, passing through Torres Strait and on out into the Indian Ocean with stops at a few islands, especially Keeling with its tall legends. The southeast coast of Africa was stormy; on reaching Durban, he had two talks with Henry M. Stanley. His longest stopover was at Cape Town, where the *Spray* spent three months in drydock while Slocum visited the Boer country. Finally, he was homeward bound with stops at St. Helena and Ascension. Just north of the equator on May 14, 1898, he encountered the battleship *Oregon* on her famous run to participate in the Spanish-American War. She signaled, "Are there any men-of-war about?" Slocum whimsically replied, "No; let us keep together for mutual protection." On June 27, he reached Newport and later proceeded to his starting point at Fairhaven. For the next 10 years, he spent much of his time lecturing and writing. In 1909 he put to sea once more and was never heard from again.

(See J. Slocum, *The Voyages of Joshua Slocum,* rev. ed., 1958.)

Maine

The *Maine,* entering the harbor of Havana. *(Naval Historical Center)*

The *Maine* became the best-known ship of the "New Navy" after a mysterious explosion sank her at Havana in 1898. Even today it is not known for certain who was to blame, but the cry "Remember the Maine" helped to draw the United States into the Spanish-American War.

The *Maine* had a borderline status. Rated as an armored cruiser when she was commissioned, she was later promoted to "battleship, second class," like the similar *Texas.* She measured only 6650 tons, carried four 10-inch guns in two turrets, and had a speed of some 17 knots.

Her construction was a very slow process. She was authorized in 1886; her keel was laid in New York (Brooklyn) Navy Yard in October 1888; she was launched in November 1890, but she was not completed and commissioned until September 1895. The navy yards had not had experience in building steel ships, and after this the navy for many years built all its new ships in private yards.

The *Maine* first put to sea in November 1895 and went up to Portland to get Maine's gift of a silver service; because Maine was a "dry" state, it did not give the traditional punch bowl. For the next two years she was up and down the coast as part of the North Atlantic Squadron. She lost three men in a fierce gale off Hatteras, and she was at New Orleans for the Mardi Gras celebrations. The scholarly-appearing Captain Charles D. Sigsbee assumed her command.

The *Maine*'s career became more tense late in 1897. Cuba had been having a bitter revolt for three years and there were still serious rumblings. The *Maine* was standing by at Key West when orders came to proceed to Havana. Neither the American consul general nor the Spanish government wanted her at the moment; the initiative seems to have come from the State Department. Captain Sigsbee and the others were received with cold politeness, but there was no overt hostility.

The *Maine* was in Havana harbor when, on February 15, there was a sudden sharp blast followed by a tremendous roar. The forward part of the ship was shattered and there was a heavy loss of life among the crew who were quartered there; most of the officers, whose cabins were aft, escaped. Crews from other ships in the harbor rescued some of the sailors from the water, but altogether fewer than 100 of the ship's 350-man complement were saved.

The exact cause of the explosion was, and still remains, a mystery. A court of inquiry, composed of three prominent American officers, studied the divers' reports and declared that the explosion was external. A Spanish court declared that the explosion was internal, perhaps caused by internal combustion. The American public, stimulated by yellow journalism, was convinced that the Spaniards were to blame (not considering just why the Spaniards would want to blow her up). The cry "Remember the Maine" went up and partly because of that, the United States on April 24 declared war on Spain. The war gave the Americans two easy naval victories and a generous overseas empire.

The rusting wreckage of the *Maine* rested in Havana harbor until 1910, when Congress voted to have it removed. A cofferdam was built, a seasoned American court of inquiry examined the exposed remains and again came to the conclusion that it was an external explosion, with a bomb touching off a magazine explosion. On March 15, 1912, the hull, with proper ceremony, was towed out beyond the three-mile limit, the seacocks were opened, and she sank to a deep grave.

For more than sixty years after that examination of the hulk, the question of an explosion was raised again and again without a definitive answer. Finally, in 1975, a very definite opinion was brought forward by Admiral Hyman Rickover, the brilliant and irascible "father of the atomic submarine." With the assistance of two of the Navy's experts, he declared in positive terms that it must have been an internal explosion, possibly caused by spontaneous combustion in the coal bunkers. In conclusion, the admiral wrote, "There is evidence that a mine destroyed the *Maine*." The belief in an external explosion had led to the stripping of Spain's colonial empire and the emergence of the United States as a world power.

(See J. E. Weems, *The Fate of the Maine*, 1958.)

Olympia

The cruiser *Olympia*, in the Battle of Manila Bay, May 1, 1898. *(Naval Historical Center)*

The protected cruiser *Olympia* won the high regard of the American people because she served as Dewey's flagship in the Battle of Manila Bay on May 1, 1898. The 5870-ton ship came from the Union Iron Works, which was at the same time building the battleship *Oregon*. Launched in 1892, the *Olympia* had four 8-inch and 5-inch guns and a speed of 24 knots.

Early in 1898 the *Olympia* was about to return from a tour with the Asiatic Squadron when, with the possibility of war, she was retained to serve as flagship of Commodore George Dewey, who had been hand-picked by Assistant Secretary of the Navy Theodore Roosevelt. (Incidentally, Dewey did not become rear admiral until after the battle.) Roosevelt had sent out word to be ready to move against the Philippines in case war developed with Spain in the Caribbean.

Dewey was with the *Olympia* and the other vessels of his squadron at Hong Kong when news came of the declaration of war with Spain. For reasons of neutrality, he had to move over to Mirs Bay in China before setting out for Manila. At a farewell dinner for the Americans, one of the British officers remarked, "They are grand fellows but we will never see them again."

Dewey's little squadron consisted of the *Olympia, Baltimore, Raleigh,* and *Boston,* the gunboats *Concord* and *Petrel,* and the revenue cutter *McCulloch.* Small as the American vessels were, they thoroughly outclassed the little decrepit veterans of Admiral Montojo at Manila—the flagship was almost too leaky to stay afloat and one of the larger ships had a wooden hull. In preparation for the fight, Dewey had arranged for coal and other supplies.

While there was little to worry about from the Spanish ships, there was an element of risk from mines and fortress guns. The Spaniards had originally planned to lie in wait at Subic Bay but, knowing the likelihood of defeat, moved into Cavite close to shore in Manila. More vigorous opponents would have mined the narrow channel and would have used the shore guns to better effect.

Consequently, Dewey's ships, approaching in line-ahead formation with the *Olympia* leading, were well in before they were discovered. The Spaniards fired first but their shots fell short. At 5:41 Dewey told his flag captain, "You may fire when you are ready, Gridley"—that, like "Don't give up the ship," and "Damn the torpedoes! Full speed ahead"!—became part of the navy's legends. The *Olympia* opened with an 8-inch gun and the other ships followed. The Spaniards bravely tried to fire back, but the flagship and the wooden ships were soon ablaze with heavy loss of life. Most of the smaller vessels were also in difficulty. Suddenly at 7:35 Dewey ordred his squadron to withdraw. It had been reported to him that his 5-inch ammunition was almost exhausted, which quickly proved a false alarm. After having breakfast, the Americans speedily sank the only Spanish cruiser still in condition to fight. They then turned their fire against the shore installations. The firing ceased at 12:30. The Spaniards had suffered some 167 killed and 214 wounded; the Americans had no one killed or wounded, but one man had died.

Altogether, the action had been a very one-sided affair. Dewey was the luckiest of the American commanders—the nation went madly enthusiastic. In contrast, when the major action of the war, in Cuban waters, came two months later, the squabbling between the devotees of Admiral Sampson and Admiral Schley robbed both of adequate recognition.

Dewey's position was by no means secure even after the battle. The Spaniards still held Manila proper and Dewey did not have men enough to dislodge them. A German naval force under an arrogant admiral came in and acted in a threatening manner; Germany saw a chance to pick up some additional empire. But then a British captain arrived, making clear his support of Dewey, and on June 30 the first reinforcements came from home—2500 troops convoyed by the cruiser *Charleston*. On the way the *Charleston* had taken Guam, whose governor did not know there was a war. More troops came in mid-July and in August, two monitors, the *Monterey* and the *Monadnock*, whose big guns gave ample support, arrived.

The *Olympia* had varied service around the world until 1906, after which she took the Annapolis midshipmen on cruises for three years and for a while was barracks ship at Charleston. During World War I

she was flagship of the Atlantic Patrol Force, and at the close of the war
went to Murmansk and Archangel in connection with the Allied anti-Bolshevik operations. In 1921 she brought the body of the Unknown Soldier back from France for burial in Arlington Cemetery. She was decommissioned in 1922 and laid up at Philadelphia Navy Yard as a shrine.

(See N. Sargent, *Admiral Dewey and the Manila Campaign,* 1947.)

Oregon

The *Oregon* in the Battle of Santiago, July 3, 1898. *(Naval Historical Center)*

In 1898 the new battleship *Oregon* thrilled the nation by racing from California around South America—some 14,000 miles—in 65 days, to get to the Spanish-American War on time. Although she arrived in the Caribbean in time to play an active role in the Battle of Santiago, her voyage was instrumental in calling attention to the need for a canal between the Atlantic and Pacific Oceans.

Until 1890 the United States Navy had been almost entirely a cruiser navy, devoted to commerce protection and commerce raiding. But in 1890 an American naval officer, Captain (later Admiral) Alfred Thayer Mahan, caused a sensation with his *The Influence of Sea Power Upon History, 1660–1783,* stressing the importance of command of the seas. This meant being able to come and go at sea unhindered, but in time of war to hinder the enemy. Sea command, he argued, could not be achieved with cruisers but called for fleets of maximum-power battleships. Mahan's book was probably influential in the authorization by Congress of three first-class battleships, produced in 1893 as the *Indi-*

ana, Massachusetts, and *Oregon.* The first two were built at the Cramp yard at Philadelphia. The *Oregon* was built by the Union Iron Works at San Francisco, which was also building the cruiser *Olympia* which would be flagship at the Battle of Manila Bay. The three battleships were identical with a displacement of 10,288 tons, 348 feet long, and 69 feet in beam. Each cost some $3,000,000. Their main battery consisted of four 12-inch guns in turrets, in addition to eight 8-inch and four 6-inch guns.

As the Cuban situation threatened to develop into war with Spain, the United States was worried at the remoteness of the *Oregon* out on the West Coast and decided to bring her to the Atlantic. On March 19, 1898, she left San Francisco on her famous run, under the command of Captain Charles E. Clark. She was accompanied by the little 1300-ton gunboat *Nashville,* which had two of the tallest funnels in the navy. The gunboat served two purposes: first to go on ahead to make arrangements for coaling at Callao and elsewhere, and second to take precautions against a Spanish torpedo boat rumored to be lurking in the Straits of Magellan. After coaling at Callao, the *Oregon* went on southward without touching at Valparaiso, where there had been incidents. The use of the Straits of Magellan cut off several hundred miles as compared with rounding Cape Horn, but the passage required constant vigilance because of rocks and gales. Once in the Atlantic, there was additional concern because of Admiral Cervera's squadron en route from Europe; much thought was given to the proper handling of a possible encounter with his several cruisers. The *Oregon* coaled at Rio de Janeiro and at Barbados, then moved on to join the American forces in the Caribbean; on May 24 she arrived in Florida where she joined Admiral Sampson's fleet. She figured in the Battle of Santiago on July 3, 1898, reporting the beginning of the escape from Santiago, with the *Brooklyn* pursuing the speedy *Colon* far up the coast until she ran ashore.

After the war the *Oregon* was refitted at New York, then returned to the Pacific, arriving at Manila in March 1899 and cooperating with the army against the Philippine Insurrection. In 1900, after visiting Japan and Hong Kong, she was moving north to take part against the Boxer Rebellion when she struck an uncharted rock and was laid up for repairs. She had another tour in Asiatic waters until 1906, then with diminishing activity spent much of her time on the West Coast. In 1921 a move was made to preserve her as a historic relic at some Oregon port, and in 1925 she was loaned to the State of Oregon and laid up at Portland. In World War II, because of the need for scrap steel, a start was made in dismantling her, but that was halted and she was taken out to Guam to serve as a hulk, or breakwater. In 1948 she broke loose

during a typhoon and drifted to sea. She was located by planes and
spotted 500 miles south of Guam and towed back. In 1956 she was sold
for scrapping in Japan.

(See F. B. Freidel, *The Splendid Little War*, 1958.)

La Bourgogne

The French liner *La Bourgogne*, built about 1885. *(Peabody Museum, Salem)*

The most shocking disaster in the long story of transatlantic passenger travel was the sinking of the French liner *La Bourgogne* in collision with a big sailing vessel in a heavy fog just south of Cape Sable on July 4, 1898. The crew, plus some of the passengers, wantonly rushed the boats, slashing passengers with knives and throwing them overboard. Of the 725 aboard, only 164 survived, of whom 105 were crew and 59 were passengers. Only one of the more than 200 women aboard survived, and all 50 infants perished. The crew broke about even, with 105 saved and 118 lost. However bad the conditions had been on the sinking Collins liner *Arctic* in 1854, they were mild in comparison with those of the *Bourgogne*.

The *Bourgogne* (named for Burgundy, France) measured 7385 tons, one of four medium-sized ships built for the French Line in the mid-1880s. Under the command of Captain De Loncie, she had left New

York on July 2, 1898, on the regular run to Le Havre. Before the fatal collision occurred, she was already taking two inexcusably irregular steps which threatened trouble. She was way off her course, running some 160 miles north of the normal eastbound lane, and she was speeding through intense fog at 17 knots, almost her maximum speed.

The 1462-ton British iron-bark *Cromartyshire,* bound from Dunkirk to Philadelphia, was proceeding cautiously at about four knots, sounding her fog signal. Captain Oscar Henderson, who would emerge from the affair with flying colors, was warned by his wife about 5 A.M. of the fog whistle of another vessel. Suddenly, at close range, the black bulk of the *Bourgogne* appeared off the bow of the *Cromartyshire,* and before she could change her direction, the bark crashed into the liner. Her bowsprit transfixed the *Bourgogne's* bridge and her sharp bow cut in deep between the funnels, causing a flooding of the engine room. The two ships separated in the fog, neither aware of the other's identity or how badly she was damaged. On the bark, the bulkhead behind the crushed bow held fast and she could hear the liner's siren sound briefly and then cease.

Aboard the *Bourgogne* there was utter chaos. With the deck officers killed or incapacitated in the crash, the burden of command fell upon Second Officer Delinge, who did what he could before he went down with the ship. Three Catholic priests did valiant work in trying to restore order. But all officers were not worthy; Fourth Engineer Laisne went to the opposite extreme. He was quoted as saying, "Damn the passengers! Let them save themselves. We save ourselves first. If I had a pistol I would shoot the passengers."

The crew, along with some Austrian sailors and some passengers, quickly ran riot. The most comprehensive testimony came from a second-class passenger, Christopher Brunen. He told of a passenger killed by the blow of an iron bar, after which his body was dumped into the water. Brunen went on to say:

> Men fought for positions in the boats like raving maniacs, women were forced back from the boats and trampled on by the human beasts who invoked the first law of nature and made self-preservation their first object. On board were a large number of Italians who cared little for human life. The fiends stopped at nothing. In one boat was a party of forty women, but so great was the panic that not a hand was raised to assist her launching.

> So desperate was the situation that an Italian passenger drew his knife and made a thrust at one who, like himself, was endeavoring to reach the boats. Immediately the action was imitated in every direction. Knives were flourished in every direction and used with deadly effect.

Women and children were driven back to an inevitable death at the point of weapons, the owners of which were expert in their use. Even sickness was not respected and according to the stories of some of the survivors, women were stabbed like so many sheep. The situation in the water was even worse. Many of the unfortunates who were struggling in the water attempted to drag themselves into the boats and on rafts. They were rudely pushed back to their watery grave.

Page after page of individual episodes bear out those grim remarks. A few of the boats reached the *Cromartyshire*, which had come back to the scene of the trouble. Captain Henderson recorded with disgust that the first two boats were filled with crew whose clothes were dry—they had not been overboard. Fifteen minutes after the crash, the *Bourgogne* went down. Although wireless still lay a few years in the future, the Allen liner *Grecian* bound from Glasgow to New York came on the scene, taking on survivors and towing the crippled *Cromartyshire*, which had 14 feet of water in her hold, into Halifax.

There was an almost worldwide roar of shock and indignation when the stories of the survivors were told to reporters. Although French officials tried to whitewash the matter, blaming the steerage ruffians, the French Line remained under a cloud for some time to come. The remark was made that with the British, you are sure of arriving safely but the food is not inspiring; the French will wine and dine you well but you may not arrive; the Germans are first rate both in safety and in cuisine.

(See R. L. Hadfield, *Sea-toll of Our Time: A Chronical of Maritime Disasters during the Last Thirty Years*, 1930.)

Portland

The night boat
Portland, a
passenger and cargo
cruiser.
(Mystic Seaport)

For a whole century, from the 1820s to the 1920s, "night boats" plied the waters north of Boston with services, extending to Portland, Maine, the Kennebec River, Penobscot Bay, and the Maritimes. Most of them were white wooden sidewheelers, carrying both freight and passengers. Northbound they carried varied cargo for the wholesale distributors of Maine; southbound they carried fish, canned corn, and other Maine products less bulky than the lumber, granite, and ice, which went by schooner. These coastal steamers also provided a comfortable night at sea for passengers who preferred the salt air to travel by rail and who appreciated the traditional dinner of roast beef cut from a huge steamship roast. Despite frequent fog along the rockbound coast, the steamers made their nightly rounds with relatively few mishaps.

But late in November 1898, the *Portland* provided New England with its worst maritime disaster. In a violent, record-breaking northeaster, which became known in down-east tradition as the "Portland Gale," the *Portland* went down with all 190 aboard; 140 other vessels with many additional lives were also lost in the wild hurricane.

The *Portland* was built in 1889 and measured 2400 tons; she was a fine specimen of the traditional night boat sidewheeler. She and her sister ship, the *Bay State,* were built at Bath. The two maintained a shuttle on the better than 100-mile run between Boston and Portland, sailing from each port at 7 o'clock in the evening and passing each other en route, and arriving very early the next morning.

In 1898 the Thanksgiving weekend found a large number of Maine residents prepared to return home after the holiday by the pleasant and convenient night boat. On Saturday, November 28, they gathered on the *Portland* at India Wharf in Boston. Though the weather had been moderate during the day, there were indications of an approaching storm. Indeed, at Portland, Maine, the decision had been made to keep the *Bay State* at her pier for the night. But Captain Hollis H. Blanchard of the *Portland* had decided to sail and his judgment prevailed. Afterward a question arose as to whether the officials ashore had played a sufficiently strong role in determining the course of action. At any rate, the *Portland* pulled out of India Wharf at 7 o'clock and started down the harbor, passing several vessels, including a night boat returning to port rather than risk the perils of the oncoming storm.

In the meantime, two separate hurricanes were about to converge in midevening north of Boston to form the violent gale which swept the coast. At 9:30, just before the hurricanes struck, the *Portland* still seemed to be all right off Thatchers Island near Gloucester. Apparently she continued a little farther up the north shore, but about 11 o'clock, when two vessels sighted her, she was headed south, possibly in trouble. As nearly as can be determined, Captain Blanchard, unable to reach shelter in Gloucester, had decided to stand out to sea. One of the weak points of sidewheelers was that if one wheel became damaged, the ship, like a bird with a broken wing, might be unable to hold her course. Whether this had happened to the *Portland* is not known.

During the night the *Portland* caught the full force of the gale. Apparently she was driven from Cape Ann southward past Massachusetts Bay to the tip of Cape Cod. Shortly after 5 o'clock on Sunday morning, the keeper of Race Point Light near Provincetown heard four blasts of a steamer whistle—the signal of distress. Later, when the weather lifted briefly, two steamers were sighted offshore; apparently one was the *Portland* and the other a small screw freighter.

The weather shut in again and the gale raged all day Sunday and all night. Shortly before midnight wreckage began to drift ashore; the bodies of 36 of the 190 aboard the *Portland* followed. Their watches had stopped between 9:15 and 9:30 apparently the time the ship went down. There is evidence also that the granite-laden two-masted *Addie E. Snow* had crashed into the *Portland,* as divers later found the two hulls close together.

Monday morning the storm began to ease up, revealing the destructive effect ashore as well as at sea. Wires were down and roads were blocked deep with snow. One energetic newspaper correspondent managed to struggle into Boston Tuesday morning with the first news of the disaster.

Because so many of the victims came from the vicinity of Portland, their relatives formed an association which met yearly on the anniversary of the disaster and threw a wreath into Portland Harbor. The *Bay State* continued in the Boston-Portland service until 1916, when in heavy fog she crashed ashore on the rocks of Cape Elizabeth near Two Lights Lighthouse outside Portland.

(See G. W. Hilton, *The Night Boat,* 1968; A. A. Hoehling, *Great Ship Disasters,* 1971.)

V

THE TWENTIETH CENTURY

(1897–1977)

Turbinia	Scharnhorst
Holland	Lusitania
Pruessen	Seeadler
Gjöa	Mont Blanc
General Slocum	Cyclops
Suvoroff	Quistconck
Potemkin	Resolute and Reliance
Mauretania	Langley
Dreadnought	Bremen
Kronprinzessin Cecilie	Vestris
(Mount Vernon)	Morro Castle
Republic	Normandie
Waratah	(Lafayette)
Wyoming	Queen Mary
Titanic	Queen Elizabeth
Empress of Ireland	U-47
Emden	Admiral Graf Spee

Jervis Bay

Bismarck

Arizona

Prince of Wales

Lexington

Enterprise
(CV-6)

Fort Stikene

Yamato

Missouri

United States

Kon Tiki

Andrea Doria

Nautilus

George Washington

Triton

Torrey Canyon

Manhattan

Glomar Explorer

V

THE TWENTIETH CENTURY
(1897–1977)

A further major development in steam power came with the high-speed turbine engine, first successfully operated in 1897 in the British torpedo-boat *Turbinia*. The turbine would ultimately replace the reciprocating engine as the principal means of marine propulsion until challenged itself first by the diesel and then by nuclear power. Warships underwent other major changes in the twentieth century. In the *Dreadnought* class of battleships (1906) the British first combined the massive throw-weight of an "all-big-gun-ship" with heavy armor protection, immediately rendering all pre-*Dreadnoughts* obsolete. The battleship reached its ultimate development during World War II in the German *Bismarck*, the American *Missouri*, and the Japanese *Yamato* classes. By that time, however, two other developments had further revolutionized naval warfare. One was the submarine, greatly advanced by Germany's U-boats of World War I and perfected in mid-century by America's nuclear submarines such as the *Nautilus* (1958). The other change came with the aircraft carrier, introduced by the United States in 1922 with the *Langley* and further developed during World War II with the fast carrier task force centered on such vessels as the *Lexington* and *Enterprise*. By 1946 the battleship itself had virtually passed into oblivion.

Meanwhile, the world's merchant fleets also underwent major change. The first half of the twentieth century was the heyday of the luxury liner. From the majestic *Mauretania* (1906) to the elegant *Queen Mary* (1937) these vessels indeed made "getting there half the fun." But the fastest liner of all, the *United States* (1952), was shortly rendered obsolete by the introduction of jet air transportation over the North Atlantic. The supertanker *Torrey Canyon* (1967) represents the ultimate development of the merchant ship in our era, with its enormous size, complex ownership and leasing arrangements, and most significantly, its ultimate threat to the very seas upon which the world depends for so much.

Turbinia

The substitution of the turbine for the reciprocating engine at the turn of the century was a revolutionary change for fast ships. Instead of the traditional piston pushed up and down in the steam cylinders, in the new compact turbine high-velocity jets of steam spun multibladed fans, which were geared to turn the propeller shaft at optimum speed.

This was the invention whereby Charles A. Parsons, fourth son of the Earl of Rosse, achieved both fame and fortune. In 1894 he was instrumental in forming the Marine Steam Turbine Company. For experimental work Parsons built the little 42-ton *Turbinia* in which he ultimately developed 2400 horsepower.

To advertise her unique capacity, Parsons staged a brazen demonstration among the warships of many navies gathered to observe Queen Victoria's Diamond Jubilee in 1897. The *Turbinia* raced at the incredible speed of 34.5 knots among the ships drawn up for review "in an astonishing display of maneuverability and speed defying the efforts of the patrol boats which attempted to cut her off."

With the turn of the century, tangible results began to appear. The Royal Navy built two fast destroyers, the *Cobra* and the *Viper*. The Cunard Line, before going ahead with the *Lusitania* and *Mauretania*, built two fairly identical liners, one with reciprocating engines and the other with turbines. The latter behaved so well that turbines were installed in the two big liners, with excellent results. At the same time, the Admiralty's "Dreadnought Board" decided on turbines for Admiral Fisher's revolutionary new battleship, in which, as in the Cunarders, the turbines established new speed records, and quickly supplanted the old reciprocating engine. The Parsons concern developed a thriving business furnishing motive power for the British and other navies.

(See R. H. Parsons, *The Steam Turbine and Other Inventions of Sir Charles Parsons*, 1942.)

Holland

The inventor John P. Holland in his submarine, the *Holland*. (Naval Historical Center)

News of one of the most important events of maritime history received only scant notice on the day it happened. On May 17, 1897, the *New York Times* reported that "the *Holland,* the little cigar-shaped vessel owned by her inventor, which may or may not play an important part in the navies of the world in the years to come, was launched from Lewis Nixon's shipyard this morning." It would be three years before that first successful submarine was finally purchased by the United States for $150,000 on April 11, 1900, and six months more before she was commissioned on October 12, 1900, as the U.S.S. *Holland,* the nation's first official submarine. After 1900 the development of the submarine moved swiftly; when World War I broke out in 1914, almost 200 submarines were enrolled in the world's leading navies.

The idea of an "undersea boat," as the Germans call it, was by no means new. In the United States the *American Turtle,* invented by David Bushnell, fresh from Yale in 1775, tried to fasten a bomb to Lord Howe's flagship but could not penetrate the copper bottom. Then came the *Nautilus* of the versatile Robert Fulton, and later the Confederate *H. L. Hunley,* which carried six crews to their deaths but sank a Union cruiser. Despite their mechanical ingenuity, they all had one essential drawback—they were dependent upon human muscle for propulsion.

Not until the internal combustion engine and the storage battery were developed would the submarine reach its full stature. And John Philip Holland would combine these motive sources to launch the first real submarine.

The motive for Holland's submarine development was the burning Irish desire to sink Britain's Royal Navy—a bitterness sharpened by his boyhood memories of the potato famine. Born on the bleak western coast in a little port of County Clare, he was the son of a coast guardsman. An ardent Catholic, he attended the local school and then that of the Christian Brethren, where he stayed on to teach from 1858 to 1872. He became interested in submarines even before he emigrated to America in 1873. He settled in Paterson, New Jersey, where he taught as a lay Christian Brother in a parochial school.

With some financial aid from the violently anti-British Fenians, in 1878 he built the first of his six submarines, a little one-man affair which managed to stay submerged for an hour in the Passaic River. Then with heavier Fenian backing, Holland produced a really impressive boat, the *Fenian Ram*. It had many of the final important submarine features and performed well. However, some of the Fenians were impatient for action and ran off with her across the Sound. Although Holland's progress was now slowed down, he made contact with a naval lieutenant (ultimately a rear admiral) who paved the way for naval backing. In the meantime, other inventors began to experiment with submarines, but none of them could approach Holland in all-around competence.

In 1888 the navy announced a competition for submarine design with several rigid specifications; the winner would receive an appropriation to build his submarine. Holland won the first award, but the appropriation was postponed largely through the machinations of another inventor with political influence. There were numerous official and unofficial trials, based at first in lower New York Bay and later out near Montauk Point. The John P. Holland Torpedo Boat Company was founded in 1893 and business was transacted in its name, even the quest for foreign contracts. On March 7, 1895, the naval contract was finally awarded. Holland constructed three experimental vessels before the final Holland VI was produced.

This first real submarine (sometimes called "Holland VI") was built in the yard of Lewis Nixon, a former naval officer, at Elizabeth, New Jersey. She was 58 feet 10 inches long, 10 feet 3 inches in beam, and had a displacement of 64 tons. Like Holland's earlier versions, she was powered by a motor for surface work and by storage batteries for underwater cruising—it was this combination that made the modern submarine possible. She was called "the first submarine having power to run submerged for any considerable distance." Her crew of seven included an operator, engineer, and gunner. She had three torpedo tubes either for dynamite missiles or Whitehead torpedos. She was launched on May 17, 1897, and was soon taking part in various successful trials. She was purchased by the navy on April 11, 1900, after making a surface trip via Annapolis to the Potomac, where she underwent further trials. She had received enthusiastic backing from Assistant Secretary Theodore Roosevelt and constant support from Admiral George Dewey, who remarked that with two such boats the Spaniards could have kept him out of Manila Bay. In maneuvers off Newport, the submarine claimed to have "sunk" the new battleship *Kearsarge*. With this accomplishment, she was formally commissioned as the U.S.S. *Holland* (later SS-1), the navy's first submarine. Lieutenant Harry H. Caldwell, Dewey's aide, became the first submarine commander.

Business began to boom for Holland. The navy ordered five more submarines and the British Admiralty in 1901 ordered five. The John P. Holland Torpedo Boat Company was absorbed as the principal subsidiary of the new Electric Boat Company, headed by Isaac L. Rice, law school professor and founder of the *Forum,* but more pertinent, virtual monopolist of the storage battery industry. With this power shift, Holland was gradually crowded out of control of his submarine and of all but a meager share of the profits. The Electric Boat Company flourished, becoming the leading builder of submarines. Orders came from most of the principal navies, either buying the boats outright or getting royalty permission on its patents. One competitor did manage to cut in on an otherwise strong monopoly—Simon Lake of Baltimore developed a submarine somewhat similar to Holland's. Lake established his company at Bridgeport and produced eight submarines. One of these submarines, along with one of Electric Boat's, was ordered by Russia for its war with Japan. They were shipped overland on the Transsiberian Railway from Kronstadt to Vladivostok but did not arrive until the fighting was over. Neither did the two submarines made by Electric Boat for Japan. Holland later received a Japanese decoration.

The original *Holland* spent four years as a training submarine at Annapolis, then the rest of her career at Norfolk. She was dropped from the Navy Register in 1910 and was sold for scrap in 1913, with her purchaser having to post a bond that she would not be used as a submarine.

Holland died on August 12, 1914, two weeks after the outbreak of World War I. By that time, France had 77 submarines, Great Britain 55, the United States 38, and Germany 28, with still more in the smaller navies. Had Holland lived six weeks longer, he would have learned of an illustration of his original anti-British purpose in undertaking sub-

marine invention. The German *U-9* sank, in rapid succession, three
British armored cruisers—the *Cressy, Hogue,* and *Aboukir*—with the
loss of 1400 lives. In February 1915 submarines began to punish commercial shipping, threatening Britain's survival.

(See R. K. Morris, *John P. Holland, 1840–1914: Inventor of the Modern
Submarine,* 1966.)

Preussen

Wreck of the bark
Preussen, after
colliding with the
Brighton off English
coast in 1910.
(Mystic Seaport)

Sailing vessels reached their maximum size just before World War I.
Both major types were represented. Heading the square-riggers was the
5081-ton bark *Preussen,* carrying nitrate from Chile around Cape Horn
to Hamburg. Largest of the fore-and-aft ships was the 3730-ton *Wyoming,* bringing coal up the coast from Hampton Roads to New England.
Each was appropriate for its route: the square-rigger was best for the
wide-open spaces of the high seas, whereas the fore-and-aft vessel was
most suitable for longshore work, where it was possible to claw off a lee
shore. Neither ship lasted long; each met a violent end. Sail was at least
ending in a blaze of glory; it had its last chance for usefulness in World
War I, after which it virtually disappeared.

The *Preussen,* largest of all sailing ships, was the main member of the
large and successful "Flying P" ship line of F. Laeisz & Son of Hamburg. Ferdinand Laeisz had started with a small brig in 1839 on the
Cape Horn run, with some tramping to other areas. By 1867 he had
decided to concentrate on the neglected Chilean trade of copper ore,

guano, and especially nitrate, and that year he purchased six moderate-sized wooden barks. The line soon expanded, gradually concentrating on steel four-masted barks, in addition to the five-masted *Potosi* and *Preussen*. Eventually there were some 20 ships, all with names beginning with "P." This custom, it is said, went back to the *Pudel*, named for Carl Laeisz's attractive wife with her poodle hairdo.

The line was run with taut efficiency, reflecting the Germans' "infinite capacity for taking pains," afloat and ashore. In his comprehensive instructions to his captains, Laeisz always started with the words, "My ships can and shall make *fast* voyages." And they did—strongly built and driven hard. Whatever the relative advantages of steam and sail on other runs, Laeisz was convinced that his big barks were the best for the Chilean run. The *Preussen* could carry 8000 tons of nitrate and maintain a better average speed than the ordinary steam freighter. Such speed made a very important saving in fuel, as not much coal was bunkered in that remote area. The passion for speed extended to the time in port—not an hour was wasted in needless delay—everything was ready for immediate action. This efficiency was reflected in the round-trip figures—the best round trip between Hamburg and Iquique and back was 146 days. The exports to Chile covered a wide variety of goods and contributed importantly to the profits. Altogether, the line's profits were high—and the family gave generously at Hamburg. Laeisz laid great stress on the qualities of his captains. He had a most remarkable one in Robert Hilgendorf, long master of the *Potosi*. Hilgendorf was offered command of the *Preussen* when she was built in 1902, but being determined to retire at age 50, he nominated Boye Petersen, who was later succeeded by Heinrich Nissen.

The *Preussen* lasted only eight years. Outward bound near Dover in 1910, she was rammed by the freighter *Brighton*, which had violated the rules of the road. The *Preussen* was not sunk, but her internal structure was so disturbed that, when she ran into a storm shortly afterward, she was driven ashore with her back broken. The line was disrupted by World War I and some of its vessels shifted to other flags, but it continued after a fashion until World War II.

(See R. L. Hadfield, *Sea-toll of Our Time, A Chronicle of Maritime Disasters during the Last Thirty Years*, 1930; A. J. Villiers, *The Way of a Ship*, 1953.)

Gjöa

The *Gjöa*, under the command of Roald Amundsen. *(Peabody Museum, Salem)*

In August 1906 the Norwegian explorer Roald Amundsen, in a 47-ton former herring smack, first completed the elusive Northwest Passage across the top of America from the Atlantic to the Pacific. For more than three centuries since the days of Frobisher and Davis this quest had led to scores of efforts by explorers, chiefly English, some of whom had perished in the icy wastes. Amundsen had been particularly impressed by the valiant but fatal efforts of Sir John Franklin in 1845–1847, who found the connecting link but did not survive. Dozens of follow-up missions, chiefly by the Royal Navy, did not find the passage.

Amundsen consulted that other great Scandinavian explorer, Vilhjalmur Stefansson, who gave him helpful advice. In 1901 Amundsen purchased the 47-ton *Gjöa* which was built in 1872 for the Norwegian herring fishery, strengthened her hull with three-inch oak plank and iron strapping, and installed a 13-horsepower kerosene-burning motor. With a Danish lieutenant as second in command, a cook, four young men, and six dogs, he set out from Norway on June 16, 1903, and made an initial run to Greenland for more supplies.

He proceeded on to Beechey Island and then to King William Island, where he found a sheltered harbor which he named Gjöa haven. There, frozen in, he spent three winters (September 1903–May 1906).

Advancing through Simpson Strait and along the ice pack of Queen Maud Gulf, he crossed Victoria Strait to Cambridge Bay, where Captain Sir Richard Collinson had wintered. He had now "passed through the hitherto unsolved link in the Northwest Passage."

On August 30, 1906, after passing through several straits, he sighted Nelson Head on Banks Island. The next morning Lieutenant Hansen **311** rushed into the cabin, calling out "vessel in sight, sir." It was a San Francisco schooner, and with her arrival from the Pacific, Amundsen knew that he had found the Northwest Passage. He went overland to Eagle City, Alaska, an army base, before returning to the *Gjöa*. At last, with the weather moderating, he reached Point Barrow after a gale and encountered some more ships, including a revenue cutter with mail for them. On August 13, 1906, they received a tumultuous welcome at Nome, a preview of what would later happen at San Francisco, where the *Gjöa* was enshrined in a little park before finally returning to Norway, where it is now on exhibit at Oslo's maritime museum.

(See E. S. Dodge, *Northwest of Sea,* 1961.)

General Slocum

The excursion boat
General Slocum in
the East River.
(Mystic Seaport)

New York's worst and most tragic local maritime disaster was the burning of the excursion steamer *General Slocum* in the East River on June 15, 1904, with the loss of more than 1000 lives. It was particularly tragic because the victims were largely German women and children on a picnic. The worst of it was that the deaths were unnecessary; the steamer was not provided with proper lifesaving equipment, and her pigheaded aging captain refused to take the measures that could have prevented most of the casualties.

The *General Slocum,* named for a Civil War commander with local political connections, was a wooden sidewheeler of 1284 tons, built in

Brooklyn in 1891. Her captain, with the good old New York name of Van Schaick, was rather more superannuated, some 61 years old with long experience in New York excursion steamers. With her shoddy sister ship, the *Great Republic,* she belonged to the equally shoddy Knickerbocker Steamship Company, and had been chartered by the St. Mark's Lutheran Church for $350 for a 40-mile cruise to Lucust Grove on Huntington Bay, Long Island.

The excursion marked a great day in Lutheran circles and drew large numbers; since many of the husbands and fathers were at work, women and children were heavily represented. With banners flying and the band playing "Ein feste Burg ist unser Gott," the *Slocum* pulled out of her pier at Third Street on the East River. A 14-year old boy later told the clearest story of the first hint of trouble: "I was near the pilot house and saw smoke coming up from below. The captain was in the pilot house and I shouted to him that there was a fire on board. He shouted back: 'Shut up and mind your own business!' The boat was then opposite East 83rd Street." Instead of running the steamer ashore at once, Captain Van Schaick kept her speeding up through Hell Gate to North Brother Island off 138th Street, more than two miles away.

The fire apparently started in a little cubbyhole cabin used for oil, paint, and similar material, where the crew often used matches to locate what they wanted in the dark. Because the fire started forward, the steamer's speed drove the flames back through the ship. This became quickly obvious to outside observers; tugboats and factory whistles sounded distress signals, and there were shouts of "Why don't they stop her?" But the stubborn old captain kept steadily on at 12 knots. As the flames enveloped much of the ship, the passengers faced the cruel decision of whether to burn or to drown—few of them could swim.

The inquiries after the accident revealed some shocking conditions aboard the *Slocum.* The first mate was unlicensed and incompetent. Most of the life preservers dated back to 1891 and were filled with pulverized cork which gave no support, while the outer covers were so rotten that a thumbnail could rip them open. Plugs prevented a flow of water into the hose which, it seemed, had been bought very cheaply and was badly kinked. The lifeboats were not put over.

It was small wonder that the death toll was heavy. Of the 1358 people aboard, the dead numbered 938 and the missing 93, a total of 1031. In addition, 109 were injured, and only 218, including all but three of the crew, were uninjured. The blow fell particularly hard on St. John's Lutheran Church, which had 114 funerals with nearly 200 bodies; its pastor lost his wife and his daughter. So great was the total of young deaths it was feared the Lutheran Churches might suffer from a "lost generation."

Hearings on the accident were held by both the coroner's jury and by the Federal grand jury with fairly similar findings. The inquiries were quite searching, ranging all the way from corporate responsibility to faulty life preservers. The coroner's jury for the Bronx issued warrants charging manslaughter in the second degree against Captain Van Shaick, Mate Edward Flanagan, and "Commodore" Pease, as well as the president and the board of directors of the Knickerbocker Line, and United States Steamboat Inspector Henry Lundberg. A month later, the Federal grand jury indicted Captain Van Schaick. He was subsequently convicted and received a 10-year sentence. The *Slocum* disaster led directly to a tightening of the steamboat inspection service.

(See H. D. Northrop, *New York's Awful Steamboat Horror*, 1904.)

Suvoroff

The Russian predreadnought *Suvoroff,* flagship of the Baltic Fleet. *(Mystic Seaport)*

One of the most spectacular and tragic major naval operations of history was the 18,000-mile odyssey of the Russian Baltic Fleet to the Far East, where it was virtually annihilated by the Japanese at Tsushima in 1905. The Russians had no ice-free ports on the open sea in Europe and only two out in the east coast of Asia. Two major fleet units, the Baltic and Black Seas, had to pass through bottlenecks, so the Russians were making the best of their bases at Vladivostok and the newly acquired base at Port Arthur. When war started with Japan in 1904, these bases might threaten Japanese movement of troops to the mainland in Manchuria. Japan was particularly eager to eliminate the Port Arthur threat.

The Russo-Japanese War found the two contestants fairly even in armament—it was a period of rapid growth in military development; the great powers sent out senior observers to report on how their untried equipment worked. On land, there were machine guns, siege howitzers, and barbed wire. At sea, in addition to torpedoes and mines, there was the predreadnought battleship with armor, speed, and heavy 12-inch guns. On paper, Russia and Japan were fairly even in ships—the Japanese flagship *Mikasa,* built in Britain, was similar in size and speed to the Russian *Suvoroff*—the big difference was in upkeep. The Russians had crowded large amounts of extra equipment and luxury items aboard, permitting routine ship affairs to become messy; the Japanese were shipshape and efficient on all counts, including gunnery.

The situation was complicated by international relations which were leading up to the alliance systems that would fight in World War I. The longest standing of these, and the one that would affect the cruise of the Baltic Fleet most strongly, was the Franco-Russian alliance formed about 1890—the Russians would rely heavily upon the far-flung French colonies for coal. Offsetting that relationship was the 1902 Anglo-Japanese alliance, important because it ranged England strongly against the Russians. A complication that weakened the Russo-French alliance was that in 1904 England was forming its Entente Cordiale with France. Germany did not appear strongly in the picture except that Russia was able to secure the services of numerous Hamburg-American colliers.

Coal was the crux of the problem—it would take 500,000 tons or so to get the Russian ships out to the Orient. And the British controlled much of the bunkerage along the route—in every worthwhile port was a stock of good Cardiff prime steam coal available to the friends of Britain—which the Russians definitely were not. Russians depended primarily upon what France's widely scattered colonial empire could provide. Some coal could be gotten in port, but much of it had to be transferred at sea from colliers—a very dirty, backbreaking job.

The Baltic Fleet (sometimes called the Second Pacific Squadron), set sail from Libau in the Baltic on October 15, 1904, under the command of Rear Admiral Zinovi Petrovich Rozhdestvenski, a controversial, ambitious officer with capability in ordnance, but no experience in sea command. The strength of the fleet centered on four new, identical, strong predreadnoughts, built in Russian yards—the flagship *Suvoroff* (named for an eighteenth-century general), *Alexander III, Borodino,* and *Oriel.* The mission of the fleet was to unite with the strong Port Arthur fleet—together they might threaten Japan's contact with the mainland.

The cruise started with a fiasco which threatened serious results. Debouching into the North Sea, the Russians were convinced that they were being attacked by Japanese torpedo boats. Actually, they were in the midst of a swarm of herring trawlers out of Hull, but in panic they started firing. Several trawlers were hit and their crews injured or killed; some Russian warships were also hit. With the cessation of the shooting, the Russians moved on, ignoring the damaged trawlers. If the Russians looked ridiculous in the fray, the British were highly indignant and were considering a strong protest. The Russian squadron put into Vigo in Spain, with strong British naval units standing guard over them. They later moved down to Tangier, where part of the Russian force broke off to go through Suez by itself.

The main force continued on the course around Africa, stopping at various minor colonial ports and giving the British at Cape Town a wide berth. In January 1905 they reached Madagascar, a French colony where they remained nearly three months, during which the Suez squadron joined them. At this time there was a progressive deterioration of morale in the fleet. A petty officer named Novikov-Priboi left a violent antiadministration account aimed at the stupidity of the czarist officers and the steadily declining morale of the sailors. He told of a stoker insulting the executive officer who replied, "What does it matter; we'll all be feeding fish shortly." He also told of the admiral's insulting attitude toward his captains. While they were at Madagascar, word came that Port Arthur had fallen, and there was the general question of whether it was worth while to continue on under the circumstances. The admiral offered to go on home.

The fleet continued on eastward, passing Singapore and going on to Indo-China. They made long stops at Haiphong and adjacent ports, taking on coal. Once again, as at Madagascar, the fleet's morale disintegrated. To complicate matters, the Russians found that they were wearing out their welcome with the French. Under international law, a belligerent vessel was allowed only 24 hours in a neutral port and the French decided to enforce the ruling.

In the meantime, a third force had been sent down by the Russian Admiralty. It included a swarm of old vessels—delinquent in speed and gunfire—in the mistaken notion of reinforcing the attackers by a few dozen extra vessels; they were simply using up precious coal.

With the purpose of getting through to reinforce the Russian force at Vladivostok, Admiral Rozhdestvenski decided to go through the narrow strait between Japan and Tsushima Island instead of going outside where there was more freedom of action but possibly more chance of difficulty in reloading coal in the rougher water.

On the critical day, May 27, 1905, Admiral Togo was lying in wait for the Russians, with his *Mikasa* and the rest of his fleet. The Russians came up in two lines, the flagship *Suvoroff* leading the main line. As they came within range of the Japanese, Rozhdestvenski did what he should have done hours before—shifted into a single line. This was a difficult enough operation under ordinary circumstances, but under fire it was fatal. The Russian ships became doubled up and the big battleship *Oriel* was crowded out of line.

At the same time (it was remarked that the battle was really decided in the first hour), Togo pulled his mass strike. It was already recognized in naval tactics, that a "T" was the proper way to offset an enemy line-ahead formation. Togo led his battleships, headed by the *Mikasa*, across the head of the Russians coming up behind the *Mikasa*. As a result, each Russian battleship, as she came up, was subjected to the concentrated force of eight Japanese battleships. This famous tactic—crossing of the T—was the basic pattern of the fighting. Both the Japanese and Russians concentrated on the flagships which were leading their respective lines. The *Suvoroff*, as a result, was taking particularly heavy punishment. The armored conning tower, containing Admiral Rozhdestvenski and his staff, was badly hit and the admiral was severely wounded; the *Suvoroff* finally drew off to one side, but the Russians had been told to follow her. Before long, in this heavy pounding of 12-inch shells, two more of the Russian "big four" battleships, the *Alexander III* and the *Borodino*, were sunk—the fourth one, the *Oriel*, which had been crowded out of line, stayed at one side in isolation.

From that point onward, the play-by-play story of the battered Russians is too intricate to follow here. As night came on, the torpedo boats took over with such effect that by morning the Russian fleet was much further depleted. As the pounding of the Russian flagship *Suvoroff* became more intense, the injured Rozhdestvenski was transferred to a Russian destroyer. A junior Russian admiral surrendered the remaining ships. Three of the smaller Russian vessels sped safely to Vladivostok; but all told Tsushima was a very famous victory. It was estimated that the Russians lost 4850 killed and about 5917 prisoners—an all-time record for naval battles—while the Japanese lost only 117 killed.

(See R. A. Hough, *The Fleet That Had to Die*, 1963; A. Novikov-Priboi, trans. by E. Paul and C. Paul, *Tsushima*, 1937.)

Potemkin

A well-publicized naval mutiny took place on the Russian predread-nought *Potemkin* in the Black Sea in 1905 as one of the first acts of the Russian Revolution. The crew shot some of the officers, hoisted the red flag, and mixed in with the fighting ashore. The revolutionaries, then and later, made much of the *Potemkin* as a sort of birthplace of the 1905 revolution, and a film has kept the episode alive.

The *Potemkin,* named for a powerful favorite of Catherine the Great, was a new ship, one of the strongest in the navy. Measuring 12,680 tons, she had the usual predreadnought armament of four 12-inch plus lesser guns, and a crew of 675. She was similar to the *Suvoroff* which had just been sunk by the Japanese at Tsushima. More to the point here, she was the strongest of all the ships in Russia's Black Sea Squadron.

The mutiny story, beginning on June 27, 1905, consisted of a series of related episodes stretching over more than a week. The initial impact came from several sides of allegedly maggoty beef. The *Potemkin* had come from the Sevastopol base for repairs at an island near Odessa. The attendant torpedo boat was sent to Odessa for supplies, including several sides of beef which were hung up on deck. The crew's attention was called to the maggots swarming over the beef and to the unpleasant odor. Complaints quickly arose; the surgeon was sent for and pro-nounced the beef all right to be converted into stew. The captain was easygoing but the second in command, Commander Hipollit Gilairov-sky, a highly unpopular disciplinarian, decided to take a strong hand. He ordered everyone in the assembled crew who was ready to eat the stew to step forward. Only a few did. He repeated the order, with the same result. So he sent for a firing squad. Cries came from the crew, "Get yourselves rifles and ammunition; we're taking over the ship." Some sailors ran for the armory and helped themselves to rifles, and Gregor Vakulinchuck fired the first shot; the commander returned the fire and the seaman fell, mortally wounded. Another shot rang out and the commander fell dead. The mutiny was on—in the next half hour, seven officers were killed and several were wounded; some officers jumped over the side.

The real leader of the mutiny was now appearing. The Social Demo-cratic Party had been planning mutiny in the navy and had planted leaders aboard each ship. The leader on the *Potemkin* was Afanasy Matushenko, the torpedo quartermaster. He had seen what the mag-goty meat could do to whip up feeling and had already been stirring up discontent. Since the officers were shot, wounded, or missing, he quickly assumed authority. Most of the crew were newly-conscripted peasants, not seasoned seamen. They were puzzled by the whole situation and followed the leadership of the few strong personalities. Matushenko found a potent coadjutor in a young university student, Constantine Feldmann, already prominent in the Social Democratic Party. Feldmann proved to be a tireless and effective haranguer.

The second day, June 28, the land situation was in the ascendancy, with things relatively quiet aboard the *Potemkin*. A general strike was already under way in Odessa and now the workers staged a big parade. The Cossacks fell on them with swords and rifles—altogether some 6000 are estimated to have died. By nighttime, fire had broken out in some of the waterfront warehouses and spread over about a quarter of the city. The body of the sailor killed by the commander was set up ashore as a sort of shrine; the next day an impressive funeral was held.

In the meantime, the ship and city revolutionaries discussed the value of bombarding Odessa. Obviously the battleship's big guns would raise havoc, but the question was where to shoot—this problem had been raised with the shore liaison. Since the military chiefs were having a conference on plans, a few shots dropped into the theater might be effective—or perhaps the threat itself might break up the meeting. But the military was not intimidated. The bombardment was a fiasco—there was no map of Odessa on the ship and no one knew just where to aim. Two six-inch shells were fired and overshot the theater, taking the roofs off two residences. That was the end of the bombardment project.

The third day, June 29, the rest of the Black Sea Squadron came briefly into the picture and then withdrew. There were six battleships in the squadron, though none was as strong as the *Potemkin* and there was no knowing how their crews might behave. The *Catherine II* was in such questionable condition that she was left behind. In the first attempt to restore control three battleships—the *Holy Trinity, Twelve Apostles,* and *George the Conqueror*—were sent to handle the *Potemkin*. They appeared off Odessa but hurried back to sea when they saw the *Potemkin*'s signal flags: "Surrender or we will fire." The three ships returned, reinforced by two more battleships, the *Botislav* and *Sinope*. They approached Odessa in two parallel lines, barely a mile apart. And then came a fantastic development: the *Potemkin* sailed between the two lines, at almost point-blank range. As the *Potemkin* passed *George the Conqueror*, her hatches were thrown open and her crew poured out on deck, waving their caps and shouting "Hurrah for the *Potemkin;* greetings to our comrades." The *George* soon indicated a desire to come alongside the *Potemkin*. The *George* entered Odessa alongside the

Potemkin where enthusiasm ran high—it looked as if the naval revolution was succeeding. The commander in chief, who had been absent at St. Petersburg, returned to Sevastopol. Realizing that some of the other ships might follow the *George*'s example, he sent the entire personnel at Sevastopol home on indefinite leave, with only a few technicians retained for caretaker purposes. "The Black Sea Fleet has virtually ceased to exist," declared the London *Times*.

That happy picture changed rapidly. There had been uncertainty on the *George*; she announced that she was sailing to Sevastopol and invited the *Potemkin* to follow. Then she ran into a mudbank. One of the *Potemkin*'s officers had played a treacherous role. The *Potemkin* was short of coal, and there were indications that the army might be bringing up heavy artillery. Disheartened, disillusioned, and dreading an awful punishment, the crew decided to surrender—not to the Russians, which would have been suicidal, but to the Romanians. Dissatisfied with their reception at Constanta, the *Potemkin* made for Feodosiya in the Crimea where she was fired on. So it was back to Constanta on July 8. Romania assured the crew that they could settle there and would not be returned to Russia. They piled ashore, greatly relieved. At the order of Matushenko, who was giving effective leadership to the end, the battleship's seacocks were opened and she sank to the bottom of the shallow bay. However, she was soon pumped out by the Russians, and remained at Sevastopol, under a new name, until 1919, when she was sunk again just before the Bolsheviks arrived.

(See R. A. Hough, *The Potemkin Mutiny*, 1963.)

Mauretania

The *Mauretania*, as camouflaged World War I troopship. *(Naval Historical Center)*

During 1906 the British launched three remarkable and important vessels. The all-big-gun *Dreadnought* was a landmark in battleship construction. Existing ships became obsolescent almost overnight, and a new word was introduced into naval language. The Cunarder *Lusitania* was a superlative ship. She was sunk by a German submarine, with a loss of more than 1000 lives; this wanton warfare was one of the reasons for America's entering World War I. Her identical sister ship the *Mauretania* for 20 years held the transatlantic speed record and was a well-loved favorite with travelers.

The American financier, J. P. Morgan, was primarily responsible for those two great Cunard liners. He had already formed the United States Steel Corporation and other great trusts and now contemplated gathering into his International Mercantile Marine (IMM) all the world's great liners in order to impose monopoly instead of the existing competitive rates. While he did not place the United States flag on all his ships, he gained control of the American Atlantic Transport Line and the Belgian Red Star Line, and had an understanding with the great German lines. Most important for the British, he secured their White Star Line, Cunard's close rival.

This economic raiding stirred the British into action. Morgan control of Cunard would not only tighten his monopoly, but would also be a great blow to British maritime pride. In addition, it would involve a serious naval threat, since Britain had subsidized the big liners with the view that in time of emergency they would become either armed merchant cruisers or troop transports.

Consequently, the British government decided to bribe Cunard to stay out of Morgan's IMM. Beginning in 1902, protracted negotiations were held between the Admiralty and Cunard. It was finally agreed that the government would lend Cunard £ 2,500,000 at the generously low rate of 2¾%, and provide an annual operating subsidy. The government wrote into the contract provisions for the potential wartime status of the ships.

The *Mauretania* and the *Lusitania* were almost identical twins, but because of their extreme size it was decided to build them in separate yards—the *Lusitania* in the Scottish Clydeside yard of John Brown & Company and the *Mauretania* on the east coast at the Tyneside yard of Swan Hunter. The ships each had a gross tonnage of 30,386, well ahead of the next largest ship, the 19,503-ton *Kronprinzessin Cecilie* of North German Lloyd, launched that same year.

A prime question was motive power. All the other liners were using the traditional quadruple-expansion reciprocating engine. But a new rival method had recently come up in Parson's turbine, demonstrated when his little *Turbinia* had impudently sped around the British fleet in 1897. Cunard decided to try out the two types of engines in two good-sized liners that it was building. The *Caronia* got reciprocating engines and the *Carmania*, turbines. Based on results in these two ships, Cunard decided on turbines for the *Mauretania* and the *Lusitania;* this was a major reason for their subsequent remarkable speed record. The Admiralty that same year decided on turbines for its new battleship *Dreadnought* with similar good results.

A major aim in liner rivalry at the time was the attraction of the wealthy first-class passenger traffic. Following the lead of the Germans who had done well in that respect, Cunard gave the new liners luxurious fittings to attract the rich trade.

The so-called blue riband of the Atlantic, bestowed on the fastest ship, had been held by the Germans ever since the North German Lloyd's *Kaiser Wilhelm der Grosse* had taken it from the Cunarder *Lucania* in 1897. The Germans held it until 1905, when the Cunarder *Etruria* took it over, holding the record until superseded by the *Mauretania* in 1909. Except for two *Lusitania* passages, the *Mauretania* held the record for 20 years. From the turn of the century to the early 1920s, the record crossing was five days and 10 hours, with an average speed of about 23 knots. Toward the end of 1928, after she had changed from coal to oil, the *Mauretania's* record average speed was 26.20 knots. In July 1929 the North German Lloyd *Bremen* captured the blue riband at 27.02 knots. The *Mauretania* then went into cruising.

In contrast to the dramatic role of the *Lusitania*, the *Mauretania's* career was relatively uneventful. At the time her sister ship was sunk,

she was 100 miles away at Bristol, loading troops for the Dardanelles,
and she engaged in various wartime services without incurring damage. After the war, she alternated on the Atlantic shuttle with the new Cunard *Aquitania*, which, although not a record-breaker, also had a long and popular service. A second *Mauretania* was launched in 1939, "the largest merchant ship ever built in England," but was soon outdone by the two "Queens," the *Queen Mary* and the *Queen Elizabeth*.

(See N. R. P. Bonsor, *The North Atlantic Seaway*, 1955.)

Dreadnought

The British *Dreadnought,* a first-line battleship. *(Naval Historical Center)*

The launching of the British battleship *Dreadnought* in 1906 was one of the most significant events in modern naval history. From that time on, capital ships found their way into the language as predreadnoughts, dreadnoughts, and superdreadnoughts. The main difference lay in their big guns, of 12 inches or more. The previous battleships had four 12-inch guns, supported by a considerable number of 8-inch or 9-inch guns. The *Dreadnought* was an "all-big-gun" ship with ten 12-inch guns instead of the previous mixture. This meant that in a showdown against a predreadnought, the *Dreadnought* could stay out of range of the 8- or 9-inch guns and smother the smaller ship with a 10 to 4 advantage in the great guns. For that reason, the predreadnoughts were almost immediately regarded as obsolete.

The British had more of the older ships than any other nation, and were deliberately wiping out that huge backlog of obsolescent naval strength. When armor had first come in and rendered wooden ships obsolete, the British had let the French bring out the first ironclad, the *Gloire*, in 1859, but then the British rushed into action with their ironclad *Warrior* in 1860.

But now the British felt it was unsafe to hold back. Germany had started a naval race with England in 1900 and was fast building a fleet, concentrating on battleships that might threaten Britain's command of the seas. It normally took about three years to build a battleship, so the British felt that if they could secretly rush through some of these radical, new all-big-gun ships, they would have a valuable head start over the Germans.

The mastermind and driving spirit in this radical project was Admiral Sir John Fisher (later Lord Fisher), the new First Sea Lord, who did more than anyone else to prepare the Royal Navy for its coming showdown with Germany. Although egocentric and overbearing, he was also brilliant and passionately patriotic, and was largely responsible for most of the innovations incorporated in the battle fleet in 1914.

Fisher moved swiftly. He became First Sea Lord on October 21; on December 22 he became chairman of a new Committee on Design, better known as the Dreadnought Committee. The committee studied writings of the brilliant Italian naval architect Vittorio Cuniberti, who had first suggested some of the new ideas. They knew that in battleship design there had to be compromise between hitting power, speed, and armor, and that any increase in one of those factors had to be compensated by diminishing one of the others or else by an increase in overall tonnage. As compared with the five ships of the *King Edward VII* class which were just approaching completion and immediate obsolescence, the committee made increases in all three fields—ten instead of four 12-inch guns, an 11-inch armor belt, and a turbine-produced speed of 21.6 knots. As a result of those changes, the *Dreadnought*'s tonnage was increased from 16,350 to 17,940 tons.

The *Dreadnought* was built with record-breaking speed and with secrecy. Materials were assembled in advance and some partly completed ships were "cannibalized" to save time. She was laid down on October 2, 1905, was launched four months later, and was completed and ready for trials on October 3, 1906, just one year and one day after the keel-laying. This was about one-third the normal time of construction. She burst as a complete surprise upon the nation and upon other nations. At the cost of rendering her former battle fleet obsolete, Britain now had a three-year head start before the Germans completed their first dreadnought, the *Nassau*.

In addition to his all-important, all-big-gun battleship, Fisher also produced a companion brainchild, the misnamed "battle cruiser" in which armor protection was sacrificed to speed. These new ships looked like dreadnoughts; were almost as heavily armed, with eight instead of ten 12-inch guns; and had virtually the same tonnage. Their speed was increased to a nominal 25 knots, actually up to 28, but the extra knots of speed were paid for by reducing the armor belt by five inches. The first three, the *Inflexible, Invincible,* and *Indomitable,* were laid down early in 1906 and completed in 1908. Two of them proved their value as cruiser chasers at Falkland Islands, sinking the *Scharnhorst* and *Gneisenau.* But the big mistake, implicit in the name "battle cruiser," was in putting them in the line of battle with the battleships. In the great showdown at Jutland in 1916, three of them were sunk, though not one of the more numerous battleships suffered that fate. In 1941 two more battle cruisers, the giant *Hood* and the *Repulse,* were sunk; altogether, of 30 battle cruisers built by the various navies, nine were sunk.

The completion of the *Dreadnought* accelerated the "naval race" with Germany, which had internal political repercussions in Britain. The Germans went ahead with their construction, but in England there was opposition to trying to keep ahead of them. The Liberals had just come into power, and were primarily concerned with the novel and expensive "social security" aspects of the Lloyd George budget, which taxed all employers and employees to give new benefits—old-age insurance, unemployment insurance, and the like—just at the time when the naval pressure for more dreadnoughts was becoming acute. Social benefits or not, the British listened to threats to their naval supremacy—reflected in the Tory slogan, "We want eight and we won't wait." As it was, they got both the dreadnoughts and the social benefits. The British managed to maintain at least a 3 to 2 lead, to keep their Grand Fleet strong enough to contain the German High Seas Fleet. At the outset of the race, things were too close for comfort—Britain's lead was in only a few precious hulls—if the Germans could trap a few of them, they might break loose; by 1916, at the Jutland showdown, the lead was more secure:

	1906	1908	1910	1912	1914	1916
			Dreadnoughts and Superdreadnoughts Completed			
Britain	1	1	8	12	18	29
Germany			2	7	13	17
			Battle Cruisers Completed			
Britain		3	3	4	9	10
Germany			1	2	4	8

By 1909 the *Dreadnought* with her 12-inch guns was being overshadowed by the new superdreadnoughts with 13.5-inch guns, and by 1915 there would be 15-inch guns. The latter would be in a remarkable class of five superdreadnoughts which would make an unusual record both in World War I and World War II. There tonnage had expanded to 27,500, in order to accommodate the new features—eight 15-inch guns, armor belts of 13 inches, and a speed of 25 knots. They were the navy's first ships to use oil instead of coal.

The following table indicates the rapid expansion in 10 years from the last predreadnoughts of the *King Edward* class to the superdreadnoughts of the *Warspite* class:

	King Edward VII	Dreadnought	Inflexible (battle cruiser)	Warspite
Date	1905	1906	1908	1913
Tons	16,300	17,940	17,250	27,500
Armor belt, inches	9	11	6	13
Speed, knots	18.5	21.6	26	25
Guns	four 12-inch, four 9.5-inch, ten 6-inch	ten 12-inch	eight 12-inch	eight 15-inch

The powerful new ships distinguished themselves at Jutland in a rearguard action against the main German fleet which had sunk two of the battle cruisers. The *Warspite*, in particular, absorbed very heavy punishment and kept going. Thereafter, the five ships of this class figured prominently in widely scattered actions. Between the wars they received extensive remodeling; in World War II they again served in many actions, but one of them, the *Barham*, was sunk in 1941 in the eastern Mediterranean. Incidentally, naval developments had been moving so rapidly that the original *Dreadnought*, launched in 1906, had dropped rather quickly out of first-line service and was not even included among the large group of dreadnoughts and superdreadnoughts at Jutland.

(See O. Parkes, *British Battleships, 'Warrior' 1860 to 'Vanguard' 1950*, 1957.)

Kronprinzessin Cecilie
(Mount Vernon)

The *Kronprinzessin Cecilie* at Bar Harbor, Maine. *(Peabody Museum, Salem)*

Transatlantic liners reached a temporary peak in size, speed, and luxurious fittings around the turn of the century. They were beautiful big ships, generally with four tall funnels—it was said that the European emigrants judged the merits of a ship by the number of its funnels. But the emigrants were only one source of consideration. The real competition was for the wealthy in first class. It was for the rich trade that interior decorations were carried to sumptuous extremes and that engines were produced in hope of winning the blue riband for speed—a very expensive consideration. Actually, these ships were a matter of costly international prestige; subsidies helped and profits were not too closely scrutinized. Moneymaking could be left to the lesser ships.

During the years up to World War I, four lines competed with varying fortunes for that rich trade. At the outset, the leader was the North German Lloyd Line based at Bremen. At that time they had a lead over the other German line, Hamburg-American, abbreviated as Hapag. In the same league were two British lines: Cunard, which was started in 1840 and White Star, in 1871.

The North German Lloyd Line moved first into the big-ship race in 1897 with the *Kaiser Wilhelm der Grosse* (KWDG), a 14,349-ton ship—the largest up to that time. (Liner tonnage was usually given in gross tons of enclosed space.) Three later members of the line's "express service," named for the royal family, followed: the *Kronprinz Wilhelm* in 1901, the *Kaiser Wilhelm II* in 1903, and the 19,503-ton *Kronprinzessin Cecilie* (named for the Kaiser's daughter-in-law) in 1907. All were built in the Vulcan Yard at Stettin on the Baltic and all attracted a generous share of the rich first-class trade.

At the outbreak of World War I, the *Cecilie* made a dramatic escape at a time when the British were starting to round up all German merchant shipping on the high seas. In the last week of July 1914, the *Cecilie* had left New York with a summer Social Register passenger list and with several million dollars in gold for the Reichsbank. She was scheduled to stop at Southampton before proceeding to Bremen.

On the evening of August 1, when the European alliances were falling into line, the first-class passengers were dancing topside with the moonlight coming through the starboard windows. Suddenly the ship seemed to stop and shiver, then start off in the opposite direction. The dancers saw that the moonlight was now coming in from the port side. Some of them remembered what had happened to the *Titanic* in those waters and nervously urged the captain to go more slowly, but he politely shrugged them off. Later they learned that enemy cruisers were crackling on wireless, hunting for the *Cecilie*.

With a stunning ingenuity, the captain thought of a way out. He realized that British cruisers would probably be lying in wait off Boston, New York, and other major ports, so he must seek refuge elsewhere. He recalled that one of the passengers was a prominent yachtsman who summered at Bar Harbor in Maine. The captain and the yachtsman talked over the problem and decided it would be feasible to take the ship into Bar Harbor. One of the passengers, who had left Bar Harbor a few days before to take the *Cecilie* from New York, awoke one morning to find the ship anchored in front of her cottage at Bar Harbor.

During the several years' internment of the *Cecilie* at Bar Harbor, her crew did what they could to sabotage her machinery, so that the Americans would have a tough repair job when the United States Navy took her over after entering the war in 1917. Renamed the *Mount Vernon,* she was fitted out as a troop transport and made nine voyages to Brest. She had a close call on September 5, 1918, when a U-boat torpedoed her, but she was able to reach Brest under her own power, undergoing repairs there and later at Boston before returning to transport work. With her special amenities, she carried many important passengers during the war, including the Secretary of War, President Wilson's Colonel House, the Chief of Naval Operations, and the Army Chief of Staff. On September 29, 1919, she was decommissioned by the navy and transferred to the army as a transport. She was scrapped in 1935.

(See G. R. Newell, *Ocean Liners of the Twentieth Century,* 1963.)

Republic

Radio, or wireless as it was then called, was first used to summon help when the White Star liner *Republic* was sunk in collision with the Lloyd Italian immigrant liner *Florida* south of Nantucket on January 23, 1909. Marconi's wireless had gone into operation at the close of the century and numerous liners already had the equipment and operators on hand. The collision occurred in the fog in the same general area as the later sinking of the *Andrea Doria*. Jack Binns, the English radio operator, became an international hero.

The *Republic* had been launched as the *Columbus* in 1903, but after two trips her name was changed when the White Star took her over from the Dominion Line. Built by Harland & Wolff at Belfast, she measured 15,570 tons and was, incidentally, the largest ship wrecked up to that time. Her speed was 16 knots. She had sailed on January 22, 1909, on a cruise to the Mediterranean with 211 first-class and 211 steerage passengers and a crew of 300.

At 5:30 in the morning of January 23, proceeding slowly in a dense fog, she was rammed, almost without warning, by the 5018-ton *Florida* bound from Naples to New York, with 800 immigrants. She cut the *Republic* down to the waterline. Three of the *Republic*'s passengers were killed and several injured in the crash. Within 10 minutes the engine room was filling with water; to avoid a boiler explosion, the engine room crew bravely managed to let off the steam. Captain Sealby gave orders for the abandoning of the ship and also ordered the wireless operator to send out a call for aid.

This was the famous "first time" which would bring lasting fame to Jack Binns, the operator who immediately sent out "CDQ" which was then the distress call—it would be later supplanted by the more recognizable "SOS" with its three dots, three dashes, three dots. The wireless cabin had been smashed in the collision and the ship's lights were out, but Binns was able to send out for a while with emergency power. His message was received by the big wireless station at Siasconset on Nantucket, which relayed it to all available craft for rescue.

In the meantime, Binns was also in contact with the wireless operator of the *Florida* and, since her condition was not serious, it was decided to send almost everyone from the *Republic* over to her. An attempt was made to run the *Republic* ashore but she filled rapidly and sank. Captain Sealby went down with her, but managed to stay afloat until rescue came.

The responses to the wireless distress calls brought numerous would-be rescuers, including some revenue cutters. The main rescuing was done by another White Star liner, the *Baltic,* which had great difficulty in locating the darkened *Republic.* Binns, who stuck to his post, sending out some 200 messages, could see the *Baltic's* lights and could give her directional messages. It was decided to take everyone from both the *Republic* and *Florida* into the *Baltic.* When the *Florida's* immigrants learned that the *Republic's* passengers would go first, panic and rioting almost broke out on the part of the Italians, many of whom had just come through the Messina earthquake and were in a nervous condition. Some of the men started to push women and children aside in a rush for the boats, but a small, tough little *Republic* steward waded into the crowd, knocking down some overwrought men, and announcing that the next troublemaker would be thrown overboard. That saved the situation.

The rescue had received worldwide attention. In New York and then at home in England, Binns and Captain Sealby were heroes of the hour, while Captain Ransom of the *Baltic* received a medal from Lloyd's and a silver gift from the White Star Line. The whole episode did much to enhance the importance of wireless, whose value would be increased still further in the *Titanic* disaster five years later.

(See R. L. Hadfield, *Sea-toll of Our Time, a Chronicle of Maritime Disasters during the Last Thirty Years,* 1930.)

Waratah

The passenger and freight liner *Waratah*. *(Mariners Museum)*

There are few places in the world where the winds howl as fiercely and continually as around the southern tip of Africa. Bartholomeu Dias, the first European to visit the area, told the king of Portugal that he had named it the "Cape of Storms." The king changed the name to "Cape of Good Hope," but it has remained a stormy threat to ships, with the South Atlantic coming in from the west and the Indian Ocean from the east.

Naturally, down through the centuries many ships have had trouble there. Seriously overloaded Portuguese galleons, homeward bound from India, came to grief on the inhospitable southeast coast of Africa, while other ships piled up on the desolate "Skeleton Coast" on the southwest side. In more recent times, the stormy waters have produced a major mystery of the seas. In 1909 the substantial passenger and freighter liner *Waratah* disappeared without a trace between Durban and Cape Town.

The new, 9350-ton ship, named for a popular red Australian flower, belonged to Lund's Blue Anchor Line, whose ships plied between London and Australia with stops in South Africa. On this particular passage, the *Waratah* stopped at Durban to discharge cargo from Australia, then sailed on July 26 (midwinter in South Africa) for Cape Town, not far down the coast. The fine clear weather deteriorated rapidly. The captain of the freighter *Clan McIntyre*, which sailed at the same time, wrote, "We experienced a great storm—I never met with anything like it in thirty years in the trade. The wind seemed to tear the water up and was of quite exceptional fierceness and power, rising at   331 times to hurricane force. There was a tremendous sea." But the *Clan McIntyre* passed the *Waratah* enroute and reached Cape Town safely.

Nothing was heard from the *Waratah,* however. A search, with naval vessels from the Simonstown base, a salvage vessel, and a chartered ship, found no trace of her. Inquiries at ports all the way from Peru to Australia yielded no news. Hope was not abandoned completely. Since wireless had not yet become general, no direct word could be expected. It was possible, therefore, that the ship was still afloat, perhaps with a broken propeller shaft, always a dangerous possibility with single-screw ships. There were recollections of the liner *Waikate,* bound from London to Australia, which broke her propeller shaft 180 miles from the Cape of Good Hope. She had drifted without power for 14 weeks before she was picked up and towed into Western Australia. News of the *Waratah,* if still afloat, would have to wait until she was actually sighted.

But much more than 14 weeks passed with no word of the *Waratah.* Among the speculations as to her fate, the question of her stability kept recurring because she had developed a bad name for crankiness. She would roll over and stay off balance until she recovered with a jerk. Ultimately, after a formal investigation, the theory was fairly well accepted that the *Waratah,* a vessel of doubtful stability and perhaps improperly loaded, had developed an excessive list and capsized in her first real storm. All hands were lost, including her veteran captain, 92 passengers, and crew. The loss of the *Waratah* also marked the end of the Blue Anchor Line, which was sold to the Peninsular and Oriental Line.

(See A. J. Villiers, *Posted Missing,* rev. ed., 1974.)

Wyoming

The six-master
Wyoming, largest
schooner ever built.
*(Peabody Museum,
Salem)*

As mentioned in connection with the German *Preussen*, sailing vessels reached their maximum size just before World War I when they were about to become obsolete. This held true for both major types: the square-riggers on the long ocean runs, and the "great coal schooners of New England" for duty on the Atlantic coast.

Down to the Civil War period, the numerous schooners had been largely two-masters, but thereafter the expanding cargoes and increasing size of the sails led successively to three-, four-, five-, and six-masters, and for a short time there was one seven-master. Ice from Maine and timber from the South accounted for most of the cargoes carried by the early multiple masts, but the major incentive of expansion came from the hauling of bituminous coal from Hampton Roads after the Chesapeake & Ohio Railroad reached Newport News in 1881 and the Norfolk & Western reached Norfolk two years later. Large cargoes for Boston and Portland were now available and the schooners expanded in size and numbers to meet them. The first five-master appeared in 1888—there was a 10-year gap and then 44 more five-masters. The first two six-masters came in 1900 and by the launching of the *Wyoming* in 1909, eight more.

Like virtually all the others, the *Wyoming* was a product of the Maine coast. She was built on the Kennebec in the important yard established by Captain Samuel R. Percy and Frank D. Small in 1894. They soon ran up an impressive total of schooners, including five of the 10 six- **333** masters. (Incidentally, their yard is being restored by the Bath Marine Museum.) Like the much older Sewall yard, they managed the ships which they built.

At 3730 tons, the *Wyoming* was the largest wooden ship ever built in America, except for Donald McKay's unfortunate *Great Republic*. There was a limit, on account of the size of the trees, to the effective size of a vessel, and even with iron strapping there was a danger that their keels would "hog." With iron or steel, of course, there was no such limit— the steel-riven–master *Thomas W. Lawson* ran to 5212 tons but was a failure in the coal trade. In the early years of American shipbuilding, Maine could underbid the British because oak, pine, and other timber grew almost to the water's edge. That advantage had passed by 1830, and the Maine builders had to go considerable distances for their timber. The oak frames of the *Wyoming* came from Chesapeake Bay, her planking was of southern pine, and her masts and spars had to be brought by rail from Oregon. Timber transport was one reason why she cost $190,000.

The Hampton Roads bituminous coal came up the coast 527 miles to Boston or 568 miles to Portland, the two chief receiving ports. Under normal circumstances, the voyage took three weeks—one week southbound, one week loading, and one week returning northward. A sixmaster could carry about 5000 tons, at about 80 cents a ton. The crews were about 10% American, and the rest were German and Scandinavian. When desertions occurred in Hampton Roads, one could usually bail out replacements from the local jail; one skipper recounted that when the jailer said he had a likely Scandinavian, the sailor asked, "What's your ship, Captain?" "*Wyoming.*" "Hell, I'd rather stay in jail."

Up to 1907 the coal schooners paid good dividends, and the business was flourishing. Percy and Small sought far and wide for capital—often reflected in the names of the vessels. One heavy western investor, in fact, got two ship names—the five-master *Governor Brooks* and one for his state *Wyoming*. Prosperity in the coal trade reached its peak in 1907 and then fell off sharply—the *Wyoming* did not come on the scene until the tide had turned. One hint of the new concern came from steam colliers. In 1907 the Sprague concern put three steamers on the run—the *Everett, Malden,* and *Melrose*—named for north-side suburbs of Boston. Against this competition, the schooners had several advantages— cost of construction, fuel, and crew—about half the cost for steamers. But the steamers had still greater advantages. With their quicker loading and transit, they could make better than 40 voyages a year to 11 or 12 for the schooners. What was more, the port authorities in Hampton Roads often kept the schooners waiting while the steamers got in first to the berth. Profits under sail began to fall off, and it was only World War

I with its heavy demand for anything which would float that gave the schooners a final chance.

The *Wyoming* was still operating after a fashion when she came to her end on March 24, 1924. She was northbound with a light cargo of 3500 tons from Hampton Roads to St. John, New Brunswick, when a north-easter caught her in the dangerous waters and shoals south of Cape Cod. She was last seen anchored and laboring heavily as night came on. The next morning she was gone—so too were Captain Charles Gleaser and all the crew. It was thought that either she grounded or the gale simply pulled her bows out.

(See W. J. L. Parker, *The Great Coal Schooners*, 1948.)

Titanic

The *Titanic*, on the eve of her maiden voyage.
(U.S. Naval Institute)

On the night of April 14, 1912, the White Star liner *Titanic*, on her maiden voyage, crashed into an iceberg which ripped part of her bottom out. Within two hours, the supposedly "unsinkable" ship foundered with the loss of some 1500 lives out of about 2200 aboard. There were several tragic aspects to the sinking. First, there were lifeboats enough for only about half of those aboard. Second, six wireless warnings about icebergs had been received but not acted upon. Third, if the wireless operator on the Leyland liner *Californian*, a few miles away, had stayed at his key another half hour before turning in, everyone might have been saved.

The *Titanic*, at 46,329 gross tons (66,000 tons displacement), was the largest ship afloat, 1005 gross tons larger than her sister ship *Olympic*. They were built at the Harland & Wolff yard at Belfast in Northern Ireland. The *Titanic* was 852 feet long, 92 feet wide, and measured 175 feet from the keel to the top of the four tall funnels—"she was, in short, 11 stories high and four city blocks long. Her engines were a mixture of quadruple expansion operating two wing propellers, and a turbine driving the central one, altogether totalling 50,000 horsepower, with a little extra to spare. She was capable of 24 to 25 knots. She had capacity for 2,584 passengers—1,054 in first class, 510 in second, and 1,020 in third. Her interior fittings were sumptuous."

She had sailed on this maiden voyage from Southampton on April 10 and had stopped at Cherbourg and on April 11, at Queenstown. Her master, Captain Edward J. Smith, with 38 years' service in White Star, "was more than just senior captain of the line; he was a bearded patriarch, worshipped by crew and passengers alike." At age 59 he was about ready to retire, "but he traditionally took White Star ships on their maiden voyage." Another important figure who would also go down with the ship was Thomas Andrews, managing director of Harland & Wolff, who came along to observe the performance of the great ship his yard had just built. The third important person, and perhaps the most controversial figure aboard the ship, was J. Bruce Ismay, managing director of the White Star Line—White Star was sometimes called the "Ismay Line"; it had been started in 1871 by Thomas H. Ismay. Bruce Ismay, a self-important figure, presented a problem similar to what the navy would call civilian interference. Though not in the formal chain of command, he did not hesitate to "throw his weight around"; he even directed a change in the proposed time of arrival without consulting Captain Smith. His role in the coming sinking would add anything but luster to his name.

One vital question that has remained unanswered was the matter of responsibility for ignoring the half-dozen wireless ice warnings from other liners. Just before lunch on the fatal day, Captain Smith was walking with Ismay and handed him the strong ice-warning message from the *Baltic*. Ismay put it in his pocket without comment and later showed it to two of the prominent women on board; just before dinner Captain Smith sent for the message to post on the officers' bulletin board. The last of the messages, just before the crash, came from the wireless operator on the nearby *Californian*. Without even waiting for the full message, the *Titanic* operator told him to shut up—he was busy communicating with Cape Race. And so the *Titanic* kept speeding into the darkness at about 18 knots.

At 11:20 P.M. on April 14, the lookout suddenly spotted an iceberg close at hand. He banged the warning bell and called the bridge, whose officers tried too late to alter course. Some ice fell on deck but only gradually was the significance of the slight grinding noise appreciated. The underpart of the iceberg had ripped a long gash into the first five bulkheads. Andrews, who knew the ship well, realized the potential danger. It had been felt that the ship could stay afloat with four bulkheads gone, but five was one too many. The bulkheads farther aft were low, and the water could come in over them.

As the situation steadily deteriorated, Captain Smith at 12:05 ordered the chief petty officer to uncover the boats. Then he proceeded to the wireless shack and told the operator to send the call for assistance, giving him a slip showing the ship's position. The operator immediately sent out CQD, the conventional distress call, later adding the new, more easily recognizable SOS. The most hopeful chance was the nearby *Californian* but her wireless operator, Cyril Evans, who had been told to shut up when he tried to warn the *Titanic,* was tired after a busy day and closed his set down at 11:30. And so the *Californian,* which could have been on the scene quickly, "didn't get the word," and did not even respond to the rockets fired from the stricken ship. On the other hand, the Cunarder *Carpathia* responded quickly. Though she was 58 miles away, Captain Arthur H. Rostron immediately jumped into action, putting on all possible speed and preparing thoroughly for his rescue role. But it would take four hours to reach the scene and the *Titanic* could not stay afloat that long.

The dramatic tragedy centered on who got into the lifeboats and who did not—it was literally a matter of life and death. Statistically, the *Titanic's* lifeboats had a capacity of 1178 persons, just about half of the 2200 aboard. It was the line's fault for not having enough room for all. But within that frame there was the further question of how many made those lifeboat seats. Actually, the boats were only about half full. Some of the officers had been extremely strict about "women only," but others had been quite permissive.

Fortunately, we have a remarkably detailed picture of what was going on among the passengers in that trying time. In his story *A Night to Remember,* Walter Lord developed a "mosaic" technique, bringing together scores, if not hundreds, of recollections by passengers and crew members. These give the "feel" of the situation, from the reactions to the first grinding jolt down to the last hour of those who expected death. Unfortunately, no such account was possible when the *Lusitania* was torpedoed three years later—she sank only 18 minutes after the first shock.

On the whole, there was an admirable observance of the "women and children first" principle. The Edwardian caste system (Edward was dead only two years) was still influential. Of the 143 first-class women, only four died, and three of those by choice. In the second class, 15 of the 93 women died, while all 23 of the first- and second-class children were saved. In the third class, or steerage, however, 81 of the 179 women and 23 of the 76 children died. As Walter Lord remarked, "Neither the chance to be chivalrous nor the fruits of chivalry seemed to go with third class passage."

Of all the many Lord case histories, that of Isidor Straus and his wife seems to strike the most responsive chord. Straus and his brother had gained control of Macy's and made it the biggest department store in the world; Straus had declined Grover Cleveland's offer of a cabinet post; and he and his wife, a woman of "sweetness and strength," had a remarkable record of philanthropy. She refused to get into a boat—"I have always stayed with my husband; so why should I leave him now? . . . We have been together for many years; where you go, I go." One of their friends said to Straus, "I'm sure there would be no objection to an old gentleman like you getting in. . . ." "I will not go before other men," replied Straus. He and his wife sat together on deck chairs and awaited the end.

In the loading of the boats, there was a big difference in the attitude of the officers in immediate charge. John Jacob Astor led his young, pregnant wife to a lifeboat and asked if he could join her, as she was in "a delicate condition." "No, sir," replied the officer. "No men are allowed in these boats until the women are loaded first." But the opposite in extreme permissiveness was the case of Lifeboat No. 1, with a capacity of 40, but which put off with only 12—Sir Cosmo Duff Gordon, his wife and her maid, three other men, and six stokers who were put aboard to row. When one of the stokers cried out, "It's time to go back and pick up anyone that's in the water," Duff Gordon overruled him.

Even more flagrant, in the eyes of the public, was Ismay's escape. When one of the last lifeboats was ready to pull off, Ismay slid into a vacant seat. He had been rather officiously trying to assist on deck when one exasperated officer told him to "get the hell out." In the British inquiry, he came in for some tough questioning. He was asked why, if there were no women on deck for the boat, he had not gone elsewhere to find others. Lord Mersey, conducting the case, said, "Having regard to his position it was his duty to remain upon the ship until he went to the bottom." By the time he had been rescued by the *Carpathia*, he was a nervous wreck and had insisted on being alone. He later resigned from the company and acquired a home in western Ireland.

For hours, the orchestra had been playing ragtime but as the end approached, it shifted to the Church of England hymn "Autumn."

Some of the passengers were on their knees, and the Lord's Prayer was frequently heard.

When the *Titanic* finally sank at 2:20 A.M., three hours after the crash, the 1500 who had been waiting on her decks were cast into the sea. Only about 60 were rescued by the lifeboats. Mrs. Charles Hays, wife of the president of the Grand Trunk Railway, kept calling, as each boat approached, "Charles Hays, are you there?" But there was no response.

The memorial to one of the victims has given the name Widener lasting significance in the world of scholarship. George D. Widener, Philadelphia traction magnate, with his son Harry, saw Mrs. Widener and her maid off in their lifeboat, but both men went down with the ship. Harry, an enthusiastic bibliophile, had willed his 3000 rare books to Harvard, when it would have accommodation for them. To meet that need, Mrs. Widener gave Harvard a magnificent library building, built around Harry's personal library. Some of us have been using the richly stocked Widener Library for more than half a century.

By the time the *Carpathia* arrived on the scene, she was able to pick up the lifeboats, but there were no more cries from those in the water. She arrived at New York with some 700 rescued from the lifeboats. Captain Rostron of the *Carpathia* was the hero of the occasion, whereas Captain Stanley Lord of the *Californian* was the only individual actually penalized for his part in the affair. Because of his passive role, in view of the rockets and other evidence of the *Titanic's* distress, he was dismissed from the Leyland Line but soon found another command. A half century after the disaster, a book on the *Titanic* and the *Californian* aimed at clearing his reputation.

There were three investigations, one in the United States and two in Britain. It was made clear that White Star was at fault in the lifeboat situation and in not slowing down after all the ice warnings. One of the results of the disaster was the requirement for enough lifeboats to accommodate everyone and for a 24-hour wireless vigilance and, in addition, for an international ice patrol of the North Atlantic danger zone during the bad months. The *Titanic's* sister ship *Olympic* served as a troop transport and then returned to the North Atlantic shuttle. In 1934 she sank the Nantucket lightship in a heavy fog; she was scrapped the following year.

(See R. L. Hadfield, *Sea-toll of Our Time, a Chronicle of Maritime Disasters during the Last Thirty Years*, 1930; W. Lord, *A Night to Remember*, 1963.)

Empress of Ireland

The worst maritime disaster in Canadian waters occurred on May 30, 1914, when a coal-laden Norwegian tramp, on the foggy St. Lawrence River, crashed into the crack Canadian Pacific liner *Empress of Ireland*, which sank almost immediately with the loss of more than 1000 lives.

The 14,191-ton liner was built in Glasgow in 1906. She was one of the newest additions to the Canadian Pacific Railway's "Empress" fleets which, on the Atlantic and Pacific, connected with the railway's 3000-mile transcontinental run, forming, under one head, a so-called "all red route" from Britain to the Orient. The *Empress of Ireland* had left Quebec at 4:30 P.M. for Liverpool with 1477 aboard—a considerable number of her passengers were delegates to an international Salvation Army conference. Nine hours later, at 1:30 A.M., she had dropped her pilot and picked up last-minute mails from two steamers near Rimouski.

Captain Kendall, who was taking every precaution, noticed a steamer some six miles away, coming up the river. She was, as it turned out, the Norwegian freighter *Storstad,* carrying 11,000 tons of Cape Breton coal up the river from Sydney, Nova Scotia, to Montreal. Her first mate, the man most responsible for the tragedy, was navigating her. After the first view from the *Empress,* the fog suddenly came in very heavily and the *Storstad* disappeared from view. Captain Kendall reversed his engines to full speed astern and so indicated with whistle signals. Suddenly the *Storstad* appeared out of the fog close at hand, and, instead of a parallel course, she had changed to come in on the *Empress* from the side—it was too late to do anything. The *Storstad* hit the liner a crushing blow; water was rushing in at an estimated rate of 263 tons a second—the liner keeled over sharply to starboard with less than a quarter hour to stay afloat. Since her steam went off almost immediately, there was no chance to run her ashore. She did, however, get off the distress signal SOS which brought in the little mail steamers.

Aboard ship there was chaos but no panic. A few boats were gotten off, but with the lights gone some passengers stumbled through darkened passageways and many others were trapped in their cabins. Later, divers recovered some 800 bodies from the wreck. Some passengers slid into the water and were eventually picked up.

The Dominion government set up hearings to determine responsibility; Lord Mersey, the British admiralty law peer who had presided over the 1912 *Titanic* hearings and would also preside at the *Lusitania* hearings, offered his services and conducted rigidly searching examinations. The court found that the *Storstad* was entirely to blame. Her mate was judged at fault in changing his course in the fog and in not calling the captain. Of the 1477 aboard the *Empress*, 1014 died and 463 were saved.

(See R. L. Hadfield, *Sea-toll of Our Time, a Chronicle of Maritime Disasters during the Last Thirty Years*, 1930.)

Emden

The wreck of the *Emden*, off the Cocos Islands in the Indian Ocean. *(Naval Historical Center)*

History may not repeat itself exactly, but there was a remarkably close parallel between the raiding of the German light cruiser *Emden* and that of the Confederate cruiser *Alabama*, just a half century earlier. In each case, a bold and highly competent commander took a heavy toll of enemy merchant shipping, created a state of alarm which ran up war-risk insurance rates, diverted numerous enemy cruisers in search of him, incurred no death or injury among the merchant crews he captured, and finally had his ship sunk by one of the enemy cruisers that had been searching for him.

The *Emden* had been out on the China station in the years before World War I, one of the lesser members of Germany's Imperial Asiatic Squadron, commanded by Admiral Graf von Spee. She was a very light cruiser, measuring some 3200 tons, and armed with 4.1-inch guns. Her one distinctive asset was her speed of 25 knots. Her commander, who would receive much of the credit for her success, was Captain Karl von Mueller, slender, serious, and rather shy, with a somewhat hawklike expression which mellowed under special circumstances. He had a very competent executive officer, Lieutenant Commander Helmuth von Muecke. The *Emden* had a complement of some 320 officers and men.

With the rest of the Asiatic Squadron she was based at Tsingtao when World War I started. On August 2 she was sent north to intercept the Russian Vladivostok-Shanghai mail steamer, which she accomplished and returned to base. On August 8 the *Emden* joined Spee's squadron in the Marianas; to von Mueller's delight, the admiral detached him on special duty to raid enemy commerce.

The *Emden* moved southward, looked in on the German base at Yap where British cruisers had destroyed communications equipment, and then moved down to what would be her great raiding area in the Indian Ocean, with its particularly busy shipping lanes from Calcutta southward. In preparation for this raiding in enemy waters, the executive officer had a clever inspiration: at that time most German cruisers had three funnels whereas the British had four; so he had a dummy fourth funnel rigged up, which could be hoisted into place when needed. On September 10 the *Emden* took her first prize, a typical British tramp en route to Bombay to pick up troops and horses for France. Her crew was taken off and she was sunk with dynamite bombs. Thereafter the prizes came fast as the *Emden* followed up the coast toward the Bay of Bengal. Some of the ships, especially those loaded with coal, were ordered to trail along behind the cruiser. One prize was a British liner with a cargo for America; when the boarding officer entered the captain's paneled cabin, he was surprised to encounter the captain's wife and young son. Captain von Mueller himself soon came over in full dress, was charming in conversation, and announced that he was sparing the ship to carry 300 captured crewmen back to Calcutta; as he left the ship, the liner's crew gave three cheers. But other contacts were not that amiable. One ship had two thoroughbred racehorses aboard; they were shot

before the vessel was scuttled. Those captures were only a beginning—
there would be plenty more in the next few weeks.

But, as in the case of the *Alabama,* the psychological effects of the raiding were more important than the physical ones. The *Emden*'s bold and surprising incursion into the Bay of Bengal was disrupting British shipping; vessels were remaining in port; and war-risk insurance rates were rising fast. Also, British warships were being diverted from important duties to hunt for the *Emden;* more than a dozen were in the quest, most of them stronger than the little German cruiser. Two of them, the *Hampshire* and the *Minotaur,* continued uncomfortably close to her; sometimes their lights could be seen in the distance.

To intensify the enemy alarm, von Mueller made two spectacular and well-publicized port raids. The first was Madras, a major port in southeast India. On the rainy night of September 22, the blacked-out *Emden* swept past and set afire two big, white, storage oil tanks of Burma Oil Company; the flames were visible nearly 100 miles away. The next target was Penang, an island in the busy Straits of Malacca between Sumatra and Malaya. Again, the *Emden* swept in undetected in the darkness. The port was full of merchant shipping, but this time von Mueller was after warships. Regretting that no British were present, he sank the Russian cruiser *Jemtchug* and the French destroyer *Mousquet,* then escaped before dawn.

Von Mueller finally headed for the Cocos Islands, after visiting the Sunda Strait, where he found no further prey. He had captured 24 vessels, totaling some 100,000 tons; there had been casualties on the two warships at Penang, but not a single civilian, noncombatant victim.

The Cocos, or Keeling, Islands were a mere dot on the map about midway between Perth, Australia, and Ceylon, and far from anywhere else. They were, however, an important communications center with a wireless and cable station on Direction Island. Von Mueller hoped to put the station out of commission. Arriving at Cocos, he sent his executive, von Muecke, with a demolition crew to destroy the equipment and bring off whatever he could find in the way of codes and records. The manager, a Briton, accepted things philosophically, even after they cut down the wireless tower, smashed all the equipment, and started to cut the cables to distant ports. But before that destruction had started, the warning had gone out: "SOS Cocos! SOS Cocos . . . Very urgent. Do not reply. Warship here, three funnels. Landing men at 7 A.M." That was picked up at Perth and relayed out to the convoy.

Von Mueller's luck was beginning to run out. A major convoy, carrying the first Australian troops to France, was being escorted by several strong cruisers. The Australian cruiser *Sydney* went off to handle the situation at Cocos; the Japanese cruiser started to go also but was called back. The *Sydney* definitely outclassed the *Emden*—nearly twice her size and a knot more in speed. Her 5.9-inch guns could easily outrange the *Emden*'s 4.1-inch guns. The result was a foregone conclusion. The Germans got in a few good shots at the very outset, but then the Australian shells began to rip into the fragile hull and upper works of the *Emden*, causing heavy casualties. Controls and steering gear shot away and burning fiercely, she was grounded on a nearby island. Her crew suffered critically before relief could reach them. In the meantime, von Muecke with his demolition crew had not been able to reach the cruiser; they escaped in a decrepit schooner and later transferred to another vessel.

The toll of casualties was heavy—117 killed and 65 wounded; only 117 were unhurt. One of the amazing aspects of the *Emden*'s capture was the favorable British reaction to von Mueller. The London *Daily Telegraph* wrote: "He has been enterprising, cool, and daring in making war on our shipping, and has revealed a nice sense of humour. He has moreover shown every consideration to the crews of his prizes. . . . There is not a survivor who does not speak well of this young German, the officers under him and the crew obedient to his orders. The war on the sea will lose some of its piquancy, its humour and its interest now that the *Emden* has gone." The only other German to receive such an enemy appreciation was Count von Luckner who, later in the war in an auxiliary sailing ship, captured a similar number of merchantmen without inflicting any loss of life. Such men were all the more appreciated when submarine warfare got under way a few months after the loss of the *Emden*; throughout the Anglo-Saxon world the U-boat was regarded with horror.

(See A. A. Hoehling, *Lonely Command: A Documentary*, 1957.)

Scharnhorst

Admiral von Spee's flagship, the armored cruiser *Scharnhorst.* *(Naval Historical Center)*

The most dramatic naval episode of World War I was the experience of the German East Asiatic Squadron under Admiral Maximilian von Spee in his flagship *Scharnhorst*. At the outbreak of the war, he and his powerful cruiser force disappeared from their base in China, crossed the Pacific, destroyed a British squadron off Coronel in Chile, and then, five weeks later, were themselves destroyed by a British squadron off the Falkland Islands in the South Atlantic.

Britain and Germany were concentrating their major forces in the North Sea, with the dreadnought battleships of the British Grand Sea Fleet trying to keep Germany's High Seas Fleet from breaking out. They sat there at Scapa Flow and Wilhelmshaven in a four-year siege, broken only by one major indecisive action, the Battle of Jutland. The British navy's other major concern was in guarding the 80,000 miles of vital sea lanes, on which England depended for her essential foodstuffs, minerals, and other supplies. To protect these lanes, she had scores of cruisers to guard the shipping on those supply routes. Before the submarines came into the picture in 1915, Germany had only a handful of cruisers for commerce raiding.

Most impressive of those German ships was the cruiser force on the China station, based at its attractive new colony, Kiaochow. It was an elite force, to which Germany sent some of its best ships, officers, and men. It consisted of two of the newest and best of the armored cruisers, the *Scharnhorst* and the *Gneisenau,* named for two leaders of Prussia's **345** national revival in Napoleon's time. Germany would have two other ships with those same names in World War II. Built in 1906, the *Scharnhorst* and *Gneisenau* measured some 11,600 tons and carried eight 8.1-inch and six 5.9-inch guns. The 8.1-inch guns could throw a 240-pound projectile more than seven miles. The ships were capable of 25-knot speed. They were beautiful, sturdy vessels with four tall funnels. Supporting them were several fast light cruisers. Altogether, this squadron had been called "the most formidable group of fighting ships of their class in the world." They were consequently a menace to Britain's command of the seas. Britain's many cruisers were scattered out on convoy patrol duty around the world and could be at the mercy of a concentrated force like the East Asiatic Squadron.

The commander in chief of the *Scharnhorst* was then Admiral Maximilian von Spee, a 53-year-old, highly skilled professional officer, "a stern, religious and dedicated warrior-aristocrat, with interests in natural history and the intricacies of auction bridge." He came of a Prussian family that traced its ancestry back to 1166. The family had a castle in the Rhine province and a house at Lucerne in Switzerland. His mother was a Dane. At age 16, in 1877, he had entered the Imperial German Navy as a cadet. He had developed a lively interest in Germany's colonial expansion and had extensive service in that field; in fact, he had been an officer on the little gunboat *Moewe* in 1884 when she planted the German colonies in West Africa.

A realistic officer, he had spent much of his time thinking of the problems which would face him when war came. Among other things, he had read the memoirs of Raphael Semmes describing his problems in trying to keep the raider *Alabama* supplied with coal. On his long, remote cruising, coal would be one of his gravest problems, and Spee began to consider arrangements for colliers to meet him at particular distant points.

When war came, Spee slipped out of Kiaochow on August 6 to avoid capture by the British, or possibly the Japanese. His first important jumping-off place was the island of Pagan in the Marianas. The harbor was filled with liners, supply ships, and potential colliers, so that for the moment the squadron's needs were well met. At Pagan he lost one of his light cruisers. Captain von Mueller of the *Emden* requested permission to operate alone in the Indian Ocean. Spee's first reaction was negative, but later in the day he sent over his permission, and wrote in his diary "a single light cruiser . . . will be able to maintain herself longer than the whole squadron in the Indian Ocean."

At last the squadron set out on its long voyage, with its destination a mystery to all but a few of Spee's intimates. The Royal Navy, the Japanese, and the rest of the world would be speculating as to his whereabouts and the British would be actively hunting him. The one ship he most wanted to avoid was the powerful battle cruiser *Australia;* with the rest he felt relatively confident. He was most happy that Berlin had decided that "he must have complete liberty of action." Lesser men might have dreaded the full responsibility but he reveled in it.

On September 22, in mid-Pacific, he revealed his whereabouts to the outside world, indicating that he was headed for Chile. He did this by swooping down on Papeete in Tahiti, sinking the French gunboat *Zelee,* and blasting the batteries, but found that the French were burning their coal to keep it out of his hands. Then came the first real shore leave for the crews—six days at Nuku Hiva in the tropical delights described by Melville in his *Typee.* Then on to the more barren atmosphere of Easter Island and Mas Afuera.

And now the British were on their way, with a squadron under Admiral Sir Christopher Cradock, a longtime friend of Spee. Cradock was famous as a man of action, full of the aggressive Nelson spirit. He was to "search and destroy," but the Admiralty had been niggardly in providing the ships for that job. He had two armored cruisers—the *Good Hope* and the *Monmouth*—older, slower, and less heavily armored than the *Scharnhorst* and the *Gneisenau.* He did have the *Glasgow,* one of the best of the light cruisers with one of the best cruiser captains; he also had a merchant cruiser, the *Otranto,* a "white elephant." There was one other ship which could have enabled this scratch force to stand up against Spee. This was the old, slow, obsolete predreadnought *Canopus,* built in 1897. She had been sent along because of her four 12-inch guns, which could have stood off the German cruisers. She was 250 miles to the southward, but Cradock would have none of her. It was counter to his Nelsonian emotions to fall back on her big guns. With that decision went the chance to check Spee.

The confrontation took place on November 1 off the little coaling port of Coronel south of Valparaiso. Contact was established late in the afternoon, but the shooting did not start until 7:02, just after the sun had set. Spee knew that until then the sun would be in the eyes of the German gunners, but the moment it set, the reverse would be true and the British ships would be silhouetted against the sunset. The rival squadrons were in line-ahead formation in parallel columns a few miles apart, the flagships paired off against each other. One of Cradock's two big 9.2-inch guns was put out of action at once, then the *Scharnhorst's* shells began to rip the *Good Hope* apart. The weather was bad; a heavy sea was running and the British could not use all their lower guns. As darkness set in, the *Good Hope* showed a mass of flames below. No one knows about those last hours on the flagship, and no one saw her go down. There were no survivors. Admiral Cradock, his faithful little dog, and 900 officers and men went to the bottom, thanks to the gunnery of the *Scharnhorst.*

Some men were still alive on the *Monmouth* when the little *Glasgow* regretfully pulled away to escape. Later, the cruiser *Nürnberg*, joining battle, threw her searchlight on the blazing hull of the *Monmouth* with the flags still flying, giving the survivors a chance to surrender, which they did not take. The *Nürnberg* fired once more and the *Monmouth* rolled over with her entire crew of 700 joining the *Good Hope*'s 900 as victims of the German raiders.

The Spee squadron put into Valparaiso where the numerous Germans hailed them as heroes. An episode throws an interesting light on Spee who felt keenly about Cradock's death. At a club gathering, a drunken German civilian proposed a toast "for the damnation of the British navy." Spee stood and raised his glass to Cradock, "I drink to the memory of a gallant and honorable foe," and without waiting for compliance, drained the glass, threw it on one side, picked up his cocked hat and made for the door. His squadron moved on down the coast, experienced a terrific gale, ran low on coal, and rounded Cape Horn. Then Spee decided to attack the Falkland Islands.

The battle cruisers were now coming into the picture. As soon as Admiral Lord Fisher, the man who had done more than anyone else to put the Royal Navy in condition, returned to power as First Sea Lord, his reaction to Coronel was to order two battle cruisers, the *Inflexible* and the *Invincible,* to get Spee. These were his special brainchildren, part of the dreadnought program. They were virtually the size of dreadnoughts and, with eight 12-inch guns, almost as strongly armed. The difference was in speed and armor. They were several knots faster but had several inches less of armor. It was a general principle that a battleship should be able to absorb the same sort of punishment she dealt out, but the battle cruisers were not able to do that. In fact, it was a mistake to call them battle cruisers and include them in the line; three were sunk at Jutland, including the *Inflexible* which had gone after Spee. But for this work against armored cruisers, with their superior speed and guns, the role of the battle cruisers was perfect. Overriding the objections of the Grand Fleet, Fisher detached the *Inflexible* and the *Invincible* for immediate service against Spee.

The Falkland Islands action on December 8, 1914 (38 days after Coronel) was a matter of complete surprise to both sides—neither knew that the other was in the vicinity. Vice Admiral Sir Doveton Sturdee, rejected by Fisher as chief of staff, received the command as a sort of face-saving gesture. Twice he would have to be prodded into action and finally arrived at Falkland Islands on December 7, giving orders to start coaling the next morning. When a lookout on a hilltop sighted the

Germans, it took two hours to complete coaling and get up steam. In the meantime Spee, suspecting nothing, sent the *Gneisenau* and *Nürnberg* ahead to reconnoiter. The atmosphere was heavy with smoke; in fact, all day smoke would be a prime nuisance. The *Gneisenau*'s gunnery officer thought he saw the tripod masts of battle cruisers, but his captain said that was ridiculous—there were none on this side of the Atlantic.

The moment of truth came in midforenoon. Spee's ships began moving off at top speed and the British followed in pursuit. "Two vessels soon detached themselves from the number of our pursuers," wrote a German officer later. "They seemed much bigger and faster than the others, as their smoke was thicker, wider and more massive. . . . No British battle cruiser carried fewer than eight 12-inch guns and every British battle cruiser could steam five knots faster. . . . We choked a little at the neck, the throat contracted and stiffened, for this meant a life and death struggle, or rather a fight ending in an honorable death." The battle cruisers started off at 26 knots, a thrilling sight, but Sturdee cut them down for 80 minutes to give the slower ships a chance to catch up. At 12:45 he signaled, "Open fire and engage the enemy," but the British gunnery was slow and ragged. At 1:20 Spee detached his light cruisers to give them a chance to escape, and a gunnery duel of the four big ships began at 1:30 at a range of about eight miles. For a while the German gunnery was more effective than the British, and Spee tried maneuvering.

By 3:00 P.M. the fight was approaching a climax with both sides firing steadily. The German ships were now taking real punishment, particularly the *Scharnhorst*. "Her upper works seemed to be but a shambles of torn and twisted steel and iron, and through the holes in her side could be seen dull red glows as the flames gradually gained the mastery between decks." By 4:19 she was barely moving and her fire was wonderfully steady. She turned over on her beam, all flags still flying, and Spee sent a last message to the *Gneisenau*: "Keep away and try to save yourself." Not a soul survived. The *Gneisenau* kept up the fight for nearly two hours. But three-quarters of the ship's company were dead or wounded, the engines had stopped, and not a shell was left. There was to be no surrender; such an act was unthinkable. Captain Maerker ordered the survivors on deck and gave orders for the ship to be flooded. She sank a few minutes past 6 o'clock, with some 400 struggling in the water, many of them wounded. The British cruisers put out boats and rescued about a third of them.

In the meantime, British cruisers had gone in pursuit of the detached German cruisers which put up their own valiant fights. The *Kent* sank the *Nürnberg,* and the *Glasgow* and *Cornwall* sank the *Leipzig*. Those were tragic hours for Countess Spee; her husband was lost on the *Scharnhorst,* her son Heinrich on the *Gneisenau,* and her son Otto on the *Nürnberg.* The only ship to escape was the *Dresden,* finally sunk by the *Glasgow* in mid-March off Robinson Crusoe's barren island west of Chile. With this action, Germany's surface cruiser force disappeared, just as her new raiders, the U-boats, were going into action. Spee's reputation in Germany was so high that when, in the late 1930s, three new "pocket battleships" were built, one of them was named the *Admiral Graf Spee.*

(See G. M. Bennett, *Coronel and the Falklands,* 1962; R. A. Hough, *The Pursuit of Admiral von Spee,* 1969.)

Lusitania

The *Lusitania,* passing Old Head of Kinsale on south coast of Ireland. *(Mariners Museum)*

By a grim coincidence, two of the largest, fastest, and supposedly safest liners in the world went to the bottom three years apart—the White Star *Titanic* in April 1912 and the Cunarder *Lusitania* in May 1915. In each case, more than 1000 lives were lost. But there the resemblance ceases. The *Titanic* was a purely marine disaster, with her bottom ripped out by an iceberg. The *Lusitania,* on the other hand, was a wartime victim—her torpedoing by a German submarine started the United States on its way to participation in World War I.

The *Lusitania's* disaster has been called "the world's most controversial sea tragedy." More than a half century later, there is still a crop of unanswered questions. No small part of the trouble lay in the fact that submarine commerce destruction, with its whole new set of practices, had come into being only three months before the disaster. Because of the vulnerably thin hull of the submarine, it dared not stand by, as surface cruisers did, to stop and search a suspected craft. So out of that came the terribly deadly practice of torpedoing without warning. Eventually, the world would grow used to that grim practice, but in May 1915 it ran counter to the traditions of sea warfare.

From the very outset, the *Lusitania* sinking produced a series of charges, some of which still remained current into the 1970s:

1. She carried a heavy cargo of explosive munitions, which not only damaged her status as an innocent liner but also accounted for her sinking in 18 minutes.

2. The Germans deliberately set a trap for her, with a submarine lying in wait to sink her.

3. The British, especially Winston Churchill, believed that her sinking would help to bring the United States into the war on their side, and left her approach unguarded.

Even after the British opened their secret archives 50 years later, some of those beliefs still persisted. They gained new credence when a British newspaperman, Colin Simpson, brought out his book *The Lusitania* in 1973, repeating some of the strongest charges, based in part on a vivid imagination. The effect of the book was increased when the British Broadcasting Corporation produced a documentary film repeating the same charges. That brought on a valid counterattack in 1975 from two Americans—Thomas A. Bailey, distinguished Stanford historian, and naval Captain Paul B. Ryan—in their book *The Lusitania Disaster*. With thorough, professional research, Bailey and Ryan demolish the old rumors and place the blame on two men—the 30-year-old Lieutenant Schweiger of the *U-20* who, on his own responsibility, loosed the fatal torpedo, and Captain William Turner, the pigheaded veteran skipper of the *Lusitania* who placed her in a vulnerable position.

The *Lusitania* and her sister ship *Mauretania*, named for the old Roman provinces of Spain and Morocco, were built in 1907 and at once began to alternate as the fastest liners afloat, thanks in part to their novel turbine engines. The *Lusitania* had completed 200 Atlantic crossings when she undertook her final trip. Up to then, the Cunard Line had not lost a passenger or a piece of mail entrusted to it. Samuel Cunard had insisted on safety and speedy delivery in his orders to the captain of the original *Britannia* in 1840.

When the British government promoted the *Lusitania*'s original construction, they had made provision, as with other major liners, for her use as an auxiliary armed merchant cruiser. There were places on the ship for 12 large guns, but they were not put aboard—the *Lusitania* had such a voracious appetite for coal, 1000 tons a day, that the government decided not to use her as an armed cruiser. Although she was not taken into the Royal Navy, she was subject to direction both from the Admiralty and the Cunard Line.

The day the *Lusitania* sailed from New York (May 1), a sensational advertisement appeared in numerous newspapers:

NOTICE!!

TRAVELERS intending to embark on the Atlantic voyage are reminded that a state of war exists between Germany and her allies and Great Britain and her allies; that the zone of war includes the waters adjacent to the British Isles; that in accordance with formal notice given by the Imperial German Government, vessels flying the flag of Great Britain, or of any of her allies, are liable to destruction in those waters and that travellers sailing in the war zone on ships of Great Britain or her allies do so at their own risk.

IMPERIAL GERMAN EMBASSY
Washington, D.C. April 22, 1915

It had originally been planned to publish this advertisement on April 22, more than a week before the sailing, but some technical difficulties caused a postponement. The advertisement was received with indignation as an unwarranted threat, infringing on Americans' rights to sail on whatever ship they pleased. Very few passages had been canceled when the time came for sailing.

The main Atlantic crossing was uneventful; it was only as the *Lusitania* approached the Irish coast that complications arose. Even in those opening days of submarine warfare, certain important precautions were being adopted under Admiralty direction. It was felt that the big fast liners should simply plow ahead at top speed, not slowing down for anything—with submarines capable of only 15 knots or so, the liners should be safe. As a matter of fact, that rule held in both world wars with remarkable safety results. The speed of the *Lusitania* had already been cut down from about 25 to about 21 knots by shutting off some of her boilers, but this speed should have been enough to outstrip a submarine. In addition, the ships were to zigzag, changing direction at frequent intervals to throw off a submarine's target sighting. Finally, the ships were to stay well off shore—the channel between Ireland and southwest England was wide enough to give security. In particular, there was strong advice to stay away from headlands and to pass all ports with particular speed.

Unfortunately, the *Lusitania*'s crusty captain, William Turner, stubbornly chose to disregard repeated advice or orders and to do as he pleased with "his" ship. He cut down the speed to 18 knots, and for three hours even to 15. To make matters still worse, he went in close to shore and slowed down to take a navigational fix on Old Head of Kinsale, close to where the fatal torpedoing would come.

In the meantime one lone submarine, the *U-20*, was operating in the area and its confrontation with the *Lusitania* would be a chance encounter rather than a plotted ambush. The *U-20*, under the able and ambitious 30-year-old Lieutenant Karl Schweiger, had left Emden and sailed around the north of Scotland and Ireland to the Irish Sea. In the two days before the fatal May 7, she had sunk one small vessel off Old Head of Kinsale and two large ones some 80 miles to the northeast. That news had been sent by the Admiralty concerning submarine activity in the area; there is nothing in the records to show any German message regarding the *Lusitania*. On May 6 Schweiger decided not to proceed toward Liverpool as originally instructed but to return homeward on the same route by which he had come. He had only three torpedoes left and he felt the need to conserve fuel oil.

And then, at 1:40 P.M. on May 7, the two ships came together. Captain Turner, thanks to his insistence on slow speed, his failure to operate in midchannel, and his refusal to zigzag, had brought the great Cunarder into a vulnerable position. And Lieutenant Schweiger was ready to transform that contact into a tragedy. He recorded that, at a distance of about 13 miles, "Starboard ahead four funnels and two masts of a steamer with course at right angles to us. . . . The ship is made out to be a large passenger steamer. . . ." He submerged and ran toward her; she suddenly turned to make a perfect target. There were several other big four-funneled ships and he apparently was not sure which this was. At any rate, the sinking of so much tonnage would be helpful to his career. The actual sinking was his own personal decision, without assistance from higher up. He launched his missile from the forward torpedo tube at a distance of 700 meters.

The results were amazing. The torpedo struck fairly well forward on the starboard side. It was followed almost immediately by a dull roar, accompanied by smoke and debris. Some claimed that a second torpedo was fired; the German war diary gives no indication of that. Another popular explanation was that the cargo of munitions had exploded. Actually, the small quantity of munitions on board was not explosive— 4200 cases of rifle ammunition which would simply fizzle out, plus empty shrapnel shells and nonexplosive fuses. These, moreover, were far ahead of where the torpedo struck. The exploding boilers were clearly the cause of the damage. The ship quickly developed a very sharp list to starboard. The *Titanic*, with her bottom ripped open by an iceberg, stayed afloat more than three hours—the *Lusitania* went to the bottom in 18 minutes.

This time there were enough lifeboats for everyone—the *Titanic* experience had produced that result—but with the sharp list to starboard most of them could be launched only with difficulty, if at all. The crew, moreover, proved most inadequate—there had been no drill in launching the boats or in instructing the passengers about life jackets. There were only a few grim minutes of chaos and then the ship slid bow foremost into the sea, about 12 miles from Old Head of Kinsale and 20 miles from Queenstown. An SOS call brought small rescue vessels out, but that took time and many of those struggling in the frigid water succumbed before help came. Altogether, of the 1959 persons aboard (including 700 crew), 1198, or 61%, were reported dead; of the 187 Americans aboard, 128 died. Particularly tragic was the loss of 35 of the 39 infants. The bodies of 761, including the multimillionaire Alfred Gwynne Vanderbilt, were never recovered. Captain Turner was picked up by a boat after three hours in the water.

Some criticism was leveled at the Royal Navy and particularly Winston Churchill for failure to provide naval protection for the *Lusitania*—the few trawlers had been absent at the time of the sinking and the obsolete cruiser *Juno* was too weak to be of any assistance. On the other hand, there was no real call for naval protection—the big fast liners were too speedy for a U-boat and did not need an escort as long as they plowed ahead at full speed; actually they did just that in both World Wars.

There were two investigations of the disaster. Lord Mersey, the British legal power in charge of Admiralty cases, presided at one; the other, in New York, was a civil suit in the Federal Court. Reflecting the general wartime feeling against Germany and its submarines, both inquiries concentrated the blame on Germany, rather than probing British shortcomings afloat or ashore. The principal beneficiary of this attitude was Captain Turner, who escaped virtually scot-free. In the American inquiry, Cunard escaped what could have been very heavy damages. Captain Turner was given command of a smaller transport but after she was also torpedoed, he went ashore to stay.

It was almost two years before the United States went to war against Germany, but the sinking of the *Lusitania* was a start in that direction. During that intervening period the Germans toned down their submarine warfare until they were ready to strike in full force in February 1917.

In assessing blame for the loss of the two great liners, it has been remarked that Captain Smith of the *Titanic*, despite constant warnings, went too fast, while Captain Turner of the *Lusitania*, despite constant

(See T. A. Bailey and P. B. Ryan, *The Lusitania Disaster,* 1975.)

Seeadler

$\mathbf{A}$t the close of World War I, Lowell Thomas made household words of two of the war's most romantic raiders. His *Lawrence of Arabia* told of blowing up Turkish rails in the desert, whereas *Count Luckner, the Sea Devil* told of a German square-rigger which sent tons of Allied shipping to the bottom. The chief characters in these two accounts became far more widely known than the commanders in chief at the Somme and Jutland. Lawrence need not concern us here, but Luckner strove valiantly with tongue and pen to keep alive his reputation not only for courage but also for humanity toward the crews of the vessels he captured. His second biographer labeled him "Knight of the Sea." But just as Lawrence's luster diminished with time, the concept of Luckner's chivalry has been dimmed by recently revealed records of his final actions when he sailed away and left his prisoners marooned on a mid-Pacific atoll with inadequate food and water.

Luckner's raiding took place between December 21, 1916, and August 2, 1917, in the 1571-ton *Seeadler* (Sea Eagle), Germany's only sailing raider, built in 1888 as the *Pass of Balmaha.* She had been sold to an American firm in 1915 and was on her way to Archangel with a cargo of cotton when she was stopped by a British cruiser and then captured by the Germans who took her into their navy. The Germans had had a few surface raiders, the *Emden* and the steamships *Wolf* and *Moewe,* but they could see the advantage of a sailing vessel because of freedom from the problem of coal.

This unique assignment was given to Lieutenant Commander Count Felix von Luckner, whose ancestors for centuries had held high cavalry commands. Luckner himself was a blond Nordic giant with a booming voice and a hearty manner. As a youth, he was bored with school and ran away to become a common seaman. He later decided to learn navigation and became a petty officer and then officer in a steamship line. Luckner joined the naval reserve and came to the attention of his uncle, an admiral, and of the Kaiser, who predated his commission so that he would have a chance with others of his grade. He served aboard a cruiser in West Africa and then aboard a dreadnought at Jutland.

Luckner was meticulous and thorough in fitting out the *Seeadler* for her unique mission. While he preserved the external appearance of a Norwegian freighter, he stripped her internally to provide quarters for several hundred prisoners, and equipped her with folding bulwarks which could be let down for the two 4.2-inch guns and with an auxiliary engine for use on special occasions.

The prime concern was to get the *Seeadler* from Hamburg through the tight three layers of the British blockade. To preserve the Norwegian nautical appearance, Luckner gathered a nucleus of Norwegian-speaking sailors who were to remain on deck while the German crew hid below. Norwegian clothing was provided for all crewmen and to give verisimilitude to the deception, there were prepared letters from "home" with proper postage stamps. Then, as a master stroke, Luckner himself went up in disguise to Copenhagen to steal, from under the captain's mattress, the actual log in a square-rigger similar to the *Seeadler*.

Since the British patrols might be scattered, it was decided to wait for a real gale before sailing. The *Seeadler* finally sailed on December 21, 1916 (just six weeks before the start of unrestricted submarine warfare). The gale effects were well simulated in the cabin with water thrown over the ship's papers to make them less legible to the boarding officer. For the final coup, a delicately featured sailor was rigged up with wig and dress to represent the captain's wife.

Luckner congratulated himself on apparently getting through all three layers of the British blockade. But on Christmas morning the 15,000-ton armed merchant cruiser *Avenger* signaled, "Stand by, or we fire." A small boat with two officers and 16 sailors rowed over. The boarding officer was pleasant but thorough, and the ordeal went through without misadventure. Then the *Seeadler*, discarding the Norwegian disguises, moved southward into the Atlantic.

The first victim, on January 9, was the 3600-ton British freighter *Gladys Royal*, typical submarine fodder, with Cardiff coal for Buenos Aires. The British crew was housed below in the *Seeadler;* time bombs were set in the *Gladys Royal*, and the ship soon went down by the stern. Next came another British freighter, the *Lundy Island*, with sugar from Madagascar for the French army. Later, on March 11, a third steamer, the *Horngaeth*, with corn from the Plata to Britain, plus a generous amount of champagne and cognac, was sunk.

Aside from those three freighters, the rest were all sailing ships, eight in the Atlantic and three in the Pacific: four French, two Canadian, one British, and one Italian in the Atlantic; and three United States ships in the Pacific. The cargoes were varied, ranging from saltpeter to salt fish. Luckner explained his emotional regret at having to sink sailing vessels,

sailed as a seaman from San Francisco to Liverpool. Sentimentally, he
went aboard her and found his name carved on the rail.

Luckner took special pride in his humane and hospitable treatment of
his prisoners. Only one life had been lost in this raiding. In an effort to
smash the radio shack on the *Horngaeth* before an alarm could be sent
out, one shell had fatally injured a junior officer. For the others, however, he declared that the *Seeadler* had "degenerated into a breed of
passenger ship."

> Our passengers were our prisoners. That made the situation somewhat
> unusual and added a bit of spice. I've served on a dozen or more liners,
> and have seen all kinds and strata of society aboard. . . . But no group
> of passengers on a liner ever enjoyed such happy comradeship as we
> did aboard our buccaneering craft. The fact that we were captors and
> captives only seemed to make it all the jollier. We took the greatest
> pleasure in making the time agreeable for our prisoners, with games,
> concerts, cards, and story-telling. We tried to feed them well, and I
> think we did, which helps a lot as you will agree. In fact, we served
> special meals for all the nations whose ships we captured. One day,
> our own German chef cooked, and that boy was *some* cook as you say.
> The next day, an English cookie, then the French chef, and then the
> Italian to make us some *polenta*. The English food was the worst. It
> usually is. . . .
>
> The prisoners seemed to appreciate our intentions thoroughly. They
> wanted to do everything they could for us in return. . . .

During the period of those seizures, the *Seeadler* had been down
between the bulges of Brazil and West Africa, where a half century
earlier the Confederate *Alabama* had found such good hunting. But by
late spring, the time was coming to head for the Pacific. Consequently,
Luckner put his 262 captives, plus two wives, into the ship *Cambronne*
for Rio de Janeiro, cutting down her upper masts so that she would not
arrive too soon and spread the alarm.

The British were not unaware of the German raider and its Norwegian disguise. On April 26, 1917, the *Illustrated London News* contained
a center-fold sketch of the raider with a caption headlined, "An Armed
Sailing Ship Used as a German Raider: Ready to Sink the Victims she
has attracted by False 'SOS' Wireless Signals of Distress." The report
stated that ships coming to the rescue find "a sailing ship hove to,
flying Norwegian colors and distress signals. . . . The unsuspecting
rescue ships are caught by the raider's hidden guns and are sunk one by
one. . . . This despicable trick violates the most cherished principles of
chivalry at sea. . . . Even a Barbary pirate might have shrunk from the

act here illustrated." As the *Seeadler*'s records show, her primary mission had been to disrupt British shipping and boost war-insurance rates. In fact, she did send false distress signals, purportedly from British ships in trouble, in order to harry and disrupt duties of the cruisers and to keep insurance rates prohibitively high.

Out in the Pacific the pace slowed down; between June 8 and July 8 she captured three American four-masted schooners, the *A. B. Johnson, R. C. Slade,* and *Manila,* all bound for Australia. Since America had not entered the war until April, its ships had not been fair game earlier. The United States had let its foreign trade fall to foreign-flag shipping; less than 10% of its imports and exports were carried in American-flag vessels. With the coming of the war, however, German shipping was out of the picture and British was tied up in war duties. A rich and broad array of foreign markets was thus thrown open to the Americans. But they had almost no seagoing freighters to take advantage of the commerce. To meet this need, every sailing vessel that would float was pressed into service on the long runs to South America, Asia, Africa, and Australia. World War I was the final period of importance for sail, and in 1917 the emergency fleet program of steel Hog Islanders was started.

On the whole, the *Seeadler* cruise was an essentially machismo affair; but there were female prisoners, including a bride and a wife from each of two of the Atlantic ships; the women were pleasant and amiable and presented no problems. As Luckner told it:

> We had noticed a woman aboard the captured ship. The skipper in question presently introduced me to his helpmate, and a knockout she was, pretty, petite and—well just a bit roguish. By Joe, I thought, the skippers of these days are marvellous fellows. Where do they get these swell-looking wives? When I was in the forecastle it was different. . . .
> The captain had not been long aboard before he took me aside and made an awkward and somewhat embarrassed confession. He had been thinking things over. "Count," he said, "in your reports you may say something about my having my wife along." "Yes," I replied. "Well, by Joe," he continued, "I wish you wouldn't say anything about my having a wife along. My real wife might find it out, and then there would be hell to pay."

> Everything went all right until the second captain took a shine to the girl, too. It was funny business. She kind of liked him. I took the two captains aside and said to them, "I don't care what arrangements you two fellows make with your fair playmate, but it has got to be kept quiet. The sailors must think that she is the wife of the captain of the ———."

Luckner decided that it was necessary to find a place where the ship could be hauled out to have the bottom scraped of marine growth. So he headed for Moorea, a coral atoll in the Society Islands, where they arrived on July 31, 1917. It seemed a fair site. Since the channel through the coral was too narrow for the ship, she was swung parallel to the reef, leaving only an anchor to keep her off it. Luckner asked if it was safe to anchor close to the reef and was told that vessels frequently did so. (At this point our narrative shifts from Luckner to the Americans.) They knew how changeable the winds and currents could be but did not feel it their duty to advise their German enemies.

On the third day, disaster struck. Luckner and the captains were ashore on a picnic, leaving one officer aboard the *Seeadler*. An American mate noticed that she was drifting. "They made the mistake of hauling up sail, which increased the forward motion. . . . When we finally hit, the keel was cut through in five places. That was the end of the *Seeadler*."

Luckner was dismayed at losing his ship but equally concerned with saving face. With his proud reputation as a shiphandler, he could not let it be known that his carelessness had lost the ship. He called in his officers and swore them to secrecy and invented a story of a tidal wave 30- or 40-feet high which caused the damage. An American cabin boy, who knew German, overheard the conference. Luckner told this lurid tale to Lowell Thomas; but there was no record of a tidal wave in the area.

On August 23, after three weeks ashore, Luckner with three officers and two men set off in a 38-foot launch and sailed west with the trade winds. They were finally arrested in Fiji. On September 5 a schooner from Tahiti put in for her semiannual visit to pick up copra from the natives. The Germans still on Moorea seized her by surprise, imprisoned her French crew, and sailed away, leaving the 29 American prisoners and the Frenchmen marooned on the island with "15 bags of flour, two cans of coal oil, rice, biscuits, beans and matches, much of it in a deteriorating condition." Some of the Americans went off for relief in an 18-foot dinghy, but after nine days they had to put back. On September 19 another American group put out again in the dinghy and sailed 1100 miles in the leaky boat, reaching American Samoa nine days later. The naval commander notified the American consul in Tahiti, where a British vessel set out for the remaining Americans and Frenchmen at Moorea and brought them safely back. Though Luckner had talked with the British and Japanese, he had not mentioned the needs of those on Moorea.

His callousness did not cramp his exuberant style on his extensive lecture tours with his charming countess. He was hail fellow well met with anyone and everyone and would tear a Manhattan telephone book in two with his bare hands to demonstrate his Viking vitality.

(See E. P. Hoyt, *Count von Luckner, Knight of the Sea,* 1969.)

Mont Blanc

Careless shiphandling on the part of the French munitions ship *Mont Blanc* touched off an explosion in the cargo which caused terrible devastation at Halifax, Nova Scotia, on December 6, 1917. The damage and loss of life was even heavier than in the similar explosions of the *Fort Stikene* at Bombay in 1944 and the *Grandcamp* at Texas City in 1947.

The 3124-ton *Mont Blanc,* built at Middlesbrough, England, in 1899, was a freighter belonging to the Compagnie Général Transatlantique and hailing from Saint-Nazaire. She had come to Halifax to join a transatlantic convoy assembling there. She had an extremely deadly cargo: 2300 tons of picric acid, 10 tons of guncotton, 200 tons of highly sensitive trinitrotoluene (TNT), and 35 tons of easily flammable benzol in thin steel drums around the hatches on deck. As she entered the convoy assembling area in the Bedford Basin, she collided with another freighter, the old Norwegian ship *Imo,* which had the right of way; later investigations proved quickly that the French ship was in the wrong.

The collision punctured some of the benzol drums on the deck of the *Mont Blanc,* whose crew took to their boats and hurried for the woods ashore. The ship began to burn furiously. The Halifax fire department sent over its new pumper, and from the dockyard the cruiser *Niobe* sent over a boat with firefighters. None of them survived; at 9:05 A.M. the *Mont Blanc* disappeared in a terrible explosion, vanishing in a pillar of smoke reaching a mile into the sky. The blast shattered windows 60 miles away but had far more deadly effect closer at hand. Whereas the Bombay and Texas City explosions were felt particularly in industrial areas, this one almost wiped out the mile square Richmond residential district with its preponderance of wooden houses. It was estimated that more than 1400 men, women, and children were killed outright or were buried in the ruins of their houses and burned to death. Some 600 others died of injuries. Tragically, large numbers were blinded by splinters of flying glass from shattered windows.

The property damage was tremendous. The freighter *Imo* was driven ashore in damaged condition. An anchor shank from the *Mont Blanc* landed two miles away. The only railroad station was a total loss, as was the railroad yard. The dockyard and barracks were badly damaged, as were many industrial plants; in one printing establishment nearly everyone, including 30 girls, were killed, and only three men escaped from a foundry.

Relief operations for the 2000 injured or blinded were extremely difficult, since the hospitals were already full of war cases. To make matters worse, a howling blizzard with freezing temperatures settled down on the stricken city. Besides what could be provided locally, however, relief from outside areas was prompt. Generous financial assistance came from all over Canada, while Massachusetts and other parts of New England rushed relief materials of every kind to the scene of the disaster.

Cyclops

The collier *Cyclops* of the Naval Auxiliary Service, Atlantic Fleet. *(Naval Historical Center)*

In what has been called one of the greatest of American naval mysteries, the 19,000-ton collier *Cyclops*, bound north from Rio de Janeiro with manganese, disappeared without a trace early in 1918, during the later months of World War I. For a while it was supposed that she had been torpedoed, but when the opportunity came to examine the submarine logs, it was clear that no U-boat had been in the vicinity at the time. No trace of her, or the 308 men aboard, ever appeared.

The *Cyclops* was one of a group of seven large naval colliers launched between 1909 and 1912. The need for large, relatively fast colliers capable of accompanying naval operations had been demonstrated by the world cruise of American battleships in 1907–1909, and behind that was the dramatic and traumatic experience of the Russian Baltic Fleet in 1905, on its way to destruction at Tsushima. During the preceding decades Britain had gained substantial control of overseas bunkerage, essential during the period of coal. In almost every worthwhile port around the world, there was an ample supply of good Welsh steaming coal—for the right people approved by Britain. It seemed desirable, however, for the Americans to be able to carry fleet supplies with them. And so these seven large colliers, all with classical names—*Cyclops, Jason, Jupiter, Neptune, Nereus, Orion,* and *Proteus*—came into being between 1909 and 1912. With their high ranks of loading frames, they were rather ugly ships, but they served their purpose. The *Jupiter* would later achieve fame as the first aircraft carrier, *Langley*.

The ships were given semimilitary status in the Naval Auxiliary Service, Atlantic Fleet. The *Cyclops,* launched at the Crump yard in Philadelphia on May 7, 1910, made one voyage to the Baltic and then served along the coast. Later she coaled ships on patrol in Mexican waters. When the United States entered World War I, she was formally commissioned into the navy, made one voyage to France, and then served along the eastern coast until January 9, 1918, when she was assigned to the Naval Overseas Transport Service to service British ships in Brazilian waters.

The United States being short of commercial tonnage, the *Cyclops* was ordered to bring a cargo of manganese, essential for steel production, from Rio de Janeiro. She sailed on February 16, 1918, with 308 men aboard, touched in briefly at Barbados, and was never heard from again.

A new and controversial theory was advanced in the 1970s by Charles Berlitz in his book *The Bermuda Triangle*. He claims that more than 100 ships and planes have disappeared without a trace in the area bounded by Bermuda, South Florida, and Puerto Rico, and implies that some very strong influence has been at work to produce such strange results. The *Cyclops* was mentioned as one of the most prominent of the victims. Informed persons, however, with good marine reputations, have laughed that off. The *Cyclops* remains a challenging mystery.

(See *Dictionary of American Naval Fighting Ships*, 1959.)

Quistconck

The steel freighter *Quistconck*, a product of Hog Island. *(Peabody Museum, Salem)*

Toward the end of World War I the United States returned to the distant sea lanes in great strength after a half century of neglect. There had been active coastal shipping during the so-called "Dark Ages" after the Civil War, but American-flag vessels were carrying less than 10% of the trade with other countries. The British, Germans, and other nations were giving good service, and no strong need was felt for American-flag shipping. Then came World War I in August 1914 and the United States realized what it meant to be caught without one's own ships— the German merchant marine was virtually eliminated and the British had too much on their hands to take over the neglected markets in Latin America and elsewhere. These rich markets were now available for American exports and imports, but there was almost no adequate shipping to take advantage of the opportunity. Then in 1917 the Germans speeded up their submarine warfare to take a terrific toll of British and other merchant ships; this was very serious since England was largely dependent upon food from other countries.

It was this combination of circumstances that led the United States Government to undertake an Emergency Fleet program which would produce large quantities of seagoing cargo ships. The task was assigned to the new Emergency Fleet Corporation under the new United States Shipping Board. Since the established shipyards were busy with complex naval construction, new shipyards were set up at government expense. The most elaborate of these was Hog Island, on a dreary patch of marshland on the Delaware River just below Philadelphia. Fifty separate shipways were set up, thousands of workers assembled, and prefabricated ship material brought in from many distant points. Hog Island was so important, both for its size and the relative excellence of its products, that "Hog Island" tended to become the generic name for the whole program.

Its first product was the steel freighter *Quistconck,* typical of the yard's construction. She measured some 8500 deadweight tons, 5100 gross tons, and 3100 net tons. (For the Liberty Ships of the World War II emergency program, the corresponding figures were 10,400; 7200; and 4400.) She was 390 feet long and 54 feet in beam. Her engines developed 2500 horsepower, and at their best 10½ knots speed—usually it was much less. Hog Islanders were far from beautiful but, unlike some of the jerry-built contemporaries from the other yards which "spat rivets all over the seven seas," they proved tough. Designed to eliminate curves for greater speed in building by green workers, they were wall-sided, flat-bottomed, bluff-bowed, and square-sterned. Durable and satisfactory products of honest workmanship, they became the backbone of the new merchant marine, carrying over the world the strange names that Mrs. Woodrow Wilson had chosen for them.

The name "Quistconck," which she selected for the first ship, was the local Indian name for Hog Island, or for "the place of the hogs." She christened the ship on August 5, 1918, just six months after the keel was laid—building would be much faster as time went on. Only three months later, on November 11, 1918, the war ended with Germany's surrender. The emergency fleet was barely started—of the 1741 steel emergency ships contracted for, only 107, including the *Quistconck,* had been completed. Some of the contracts were canceled, but the government decided to go ahead with the bulk of the program, and the last ship was not launched until 1921. The United States found itself with the largest merchant marine in the world. Since very few of the new ships had had time for any useful service before the war ended, those not actively engaged were anchored in sheltered waters in "laid up fleets." A real problem then arose of what to do with the huge fleet, all still the property of the United States Shipping Board.

The solution, which affected the *Quistconck* and many of the others, was to put them on essential trade routes to develop American commerce. It was desired to place them in private ownership as soon as practicable. The ships were sold at auction, at a fraction of their original $200-a-ton cost, to operators who would agree to maintain regular service on a particular run for a period of years. In 1934, after many of the other lines were established, the Gulf firm of Lykes Brothers made a huge package deal with the Shipping Board to acquire, at the extremely low rate of $5.00 a ton, ships enough to serve seven different routes from Gulf ports. The *Quistconck* remained in this service until World War II, later shifting to the Lykes coastwise runs and hailing from Houston, Texas; then she disappeared from the record.

It was a tribute to the Hog Island yard that all but 12 of its 112 "Class A" freighters were still in service by the beginning of World War II. Twenty years was considered the normal life of a ship, and many of the emergency freighters built by other yards had disappeared.

(See W. C. Mattox, *Building the Emergency Fleet*, 1920.)

Resolute and Reliance

The liner *Resolute*, transferred to Panamanian registry. *(Peabody Museum, Salem)*

Two 19,000-ton liners, originally laid down by Hamburg-American and then put in other fleets, won an accidental distinction as the initial ships to fly the "flags of convenience," which later would expand into two of the major merchant marines of the world. These "flags of easy virtue," notably the Panamanian and Liberian, would offer very flexible freedom from the normal restrictions of regular national registry. Most important, they would enable United States shipowners to man their vessels at a fraction of the cost of American union wages. They also allowed bargain terms in taxation, an escape from wartime commandeering of shipping, and various other loopholes. The vessels might have "Panama" or "Monrovia" painted on their sterns as hailing ports, which they might never visit. The whole thing was a brazen fiction which somehow won official recognition.

The *Resolute* and *Reliance* had been laid down before World War I as the *William Oswald* and *Johann Heinrich Burchard* for Hamburg-American's South American service. After the war and the seizure of Germany's merchant shipping, they were completed as the *Brabantia* and *Limburger* of the Royal Holland Lloyd. In 1922 they passed to United American Lines, headed by Averell Harriman, son of the railroad magnate. Renamed *Resolute* and *Reliance,* they were placed on the New York–Hamburg run, but their chance for distinction came when they were advertised for Caribbean cruises. Then Attorney General Harry Daugherty ruled that the Volstead Act, forbidding the sale of liquor, would apply to American-flag ships. Most of the cruise reservations were quickly canceled. Thereupon one of the Harriman staff had a brilliant inspiration—to transfer the ships to Panamanian registry. Panama had almost no merchant marine, but it did have a flag. The permission of the Shipping Board was secured and, with the bars now open, the cruise passengers returned. The *Resolute* and *Reliance* in 1926 returned to Hamburg-American. In 1935 the *Resolute* went under the Italian flag as the *Lombardia;* in 1943 she was destroyed in an air attack on Naples. The *Reliance* also came to a violent end; in 1926 she was gutted by fire and in 1941 she was scrapped.

During the late 1940s the Panamanian merchant marine encountered an even more potent rival. A syndicate headed by Edward Stettinius, former Secretary of State, was granted a charter to develop the economic interests of Liberia. Again, a New York lawyer had an inspiration; the syndicate would operate a new flag of convenience for a fee and give Liberia a share of the profits. Swelled by tankers owned in Greece and the United States, it was soon one of the largest merchant marines in the world. Honduras and Costa Rica also developed flags of convenience on a smaller scale.

(See N. R. P. Bonsor, *The North Atlantic Seaway*, 1955.)

Langley

After nine years as the naval collier *Jupiter,* the *Langley* in 1922 became the navy's first, though rather limited, aircraft carrier. It would be another five years before the first full-sized fast carriers, the *Lexington* and the *Saratoga,* would come on the scene.

Originally, the *Jupiter* was one of the seven big 11,900-ton colliers,
like the ill-fated *Cyclops* which "went missing." She was built at the Mare Island Navy Yard in Vallejo, California; she was launched on August 24, 1912, and commissioned on April 7, 1913. The first electrically propelled ship in the navy, she served briefly on the Mexican Pacific coast during the revolutionary troubles and then, on October 12, 1914, was the first vessel to transit the Panama Canal west to east.

During World War I, assigned to the Naval Overseas Transport Service, she spent most of the time on coaling duty in the Atlantic. But by that time, with oil gradually replacing coal as fuel in the navy, the need for colliers was diminishing and she was decommissioned as a collier on March 23, 1920.

Before World War I the navy had flown a plane from a cruiser and had landed a plane on a cruiser, but the initiative in developing the carrier had rested with the British. Now the *Jupiter* was converted to a carrier at Norfolk Navy Yard, where she was recommissioned as the *Langley* on March 20, 1922, and given the designation "CV-1" as the first carrier. She was named for Samuel Pierpont Langley, the distinguished astronomer, physicist, and inventor. He developed an apparently successful airplane and, with the backing of Theodore Roosevelt as Assistant Secretary of the Navy, a trial flight from a barge on the Potomac was arranged in 1898. An accident robbed Langley of his fame as inventor of the plane—on launching, a wire became entangled in the craft and the plane dropped into the Potomac. The trial was not repeated, so the way was left clear for the Wright brothers at Kitty Hawk. The navy remained loyal to Langley, naming not only the carrier but also a major airfield for him.

The *Langley* participated in numerous experiments which played an important part in the development of American naval aviation. After taking part in maneuvers and training of various sorts, she went in 1924 to the Pacific for 12 years of similar duty. In 1936 she was converted at Mare Island into a seaplane tender attached to the Aircraft Scouting Command, operating from Sitka, Seattle, Pearl Harbor, and San Diego.

On the day after the Pearl Harbor attack, the *Langley* left Cavite for Borneo and Australia; she was assigned to the hopelessly outnumbered ABDA (American, British, Dutch, Australian) command which was seeking to check the spread of Japanese power. On February 27, 1942, after departing from Fremantle, Australia, she left the convoy to deliver 32 planes to Tjilatjap, Java, with two destroyers as an escort. Japanese planes attacked her, the aircraft cargo caught fire, and she went dead in the water. There was nothing to do but abandon ship; the two destroyers fired 4-inch shells and two torpedoes into her, and she went down some 75 miles south of Tjilatjap. Sixteen lives were lost.

Another carrier *Langley* (CVL-27) was added to the fleet in 1943.

(See A. D. Turnbull and C. L. Lord, *History of United States Naval Aviation,* repr., 1972.)

Bremen

The *Bremen* a blue-riband winner on the North Atlantic run.
(Peabody Museum, Salem)

During the decade after World War I, the German merchant marine made an amazing comeback. In 1914 it had been the largest in the world—Hamburg-American had 203 seagoing ships and North German Lloyd, 131. All of them were taken away and scattered among other fleets at the end of the war. By 1922, the German revival had set in. On the North Atlantic run, the *Mauretania* was maintaining Cunard primacy, but the German ships were soon giving vigorous competition. In 1926 North German Lloyd carried nearly as many passengers as Cunard or White Star and considerably more than Hamburg-American or the French Line. Late in 1926 the Germans determined to recover the blue riband they had lost 20 years before.

The Germans ordered two remarkable vessels which would restore the old primacy. They laid down the *Bremen* at Bremen and the *Europa* at Hamburg. The ships were almost identical, averaging 50,000 tons and engined with turbines driving four screws, with bulbous bows to improve speed. They had accommodation for 2000 passengers—600 first class, 500 second class, and in place of steerage because of the new American immigration restrictions, 300 tourist, and 600 third class. In

appearance, they broke sharply with tradition in the matter of funnels—in place of the majestic look of four tall funnels, they had two
squat ones.

German enthusiasm was unbounded over the two new vessels which
were launched a day apart—the *Europa* on August 15, 1928, at Hamburg and the *Bremen* the following day at Bremen. A fire damaged the
Europa while she was fitting out, and so the *Bremen* got to sea first. On
her maiden run in July 1929, she took the blue riband from the *Mauretania* at 27.83 knots average, and slightly improved that speed on the
return passage. The two ships had things pretty much their way for
much of the decade, except that the new Italian liner *Rex* in 1933 took
the westbound record. The *Bremen* and *Europa* continued on the North
Atlantic run until 1938 and were strong favorites with the traveling
public.

On the eve of hostilities in 1939 the *Bremen*, to avoid internment at
New York, made a spectacular dash to Murmansk in the Soviet Union,
which at that time was allied with Germany. She later returned to
Germany but was destroyed by fire during an air raid at Bremen. The
Europa was in Bremen when the war started, but avoided serious
damage from air attacks. At the close of the war she made two voyages
to America as a transport and then became the *Liberté* of the French
Line. During a gale at Le Havre she broke loose, crashed into the hulk of
the burned-out *Paris,* and was scuttled. Later, however, she was
repaired and served on the North Atlantic run.

(See N. R. P. Bonsor, *The North Atlantic Seaway,* 1955.)

Vestris

The *Vestris,* listing badly, sank off the Virginia coast on November 12, 1928. *(Peabody Museum, Salem)*

The loss of the Lamport & Holt liner *Vestris* on November 12, 1928, was chiefly caused by the pigheadedness of her captain who refused to summon aid to his slowly sinking ship until it was too late. As a result, 69 passengers and 56 crew lost their lives. It was also charged that overloading and improper stowing of cargo at the dock in Hoboken was a cause.

The *Vestris* was a passenger and cargo ship of 10,494 tons, built at Belfast in 1912, along with the *Vandyck* and *Vauban,* for the Lamport & Holt Line, whose ship names all began with "V." They traded primarily with the east coast of South America either from Liverpool or New York.

The timetable on that fatal weekend (Saturday, November 10–Monday, November 12) is an important part of the story—ships have seldom been so slow in going down. She sailed from Hoboken on Saturday at 3:45 P.M. with Captain William J. Carey in command. She carried 129 passengers and a crew of 197. Of the 326 aboard, 125 did not survive.

By Sunday morning the weather was not good, and it was noticed that the *Vestris* already had a list to starboard. The wind increased during the day, and by late afternoon waves were sweeping her decks.

In addition, she was leaking badly. Water was coming in through the starboard half-door, and also through the starboard ash-ejector. There was so much water that the stokers had to hold onto chains for support. The engineers helped to feed the furnaces for a while. About 7:15 a huge wave came piling onto the portside, causing much damage. The ship heeled further over to starboard and never righted herself again.

It was obvious to virtually everyone aboard that the situation warranted calling for help. But Captain Carey, hour after hour, refused to send an SOS. He was apparently afraid of getting in wrong with the company which might not approve of an unnecessary call for help. At the inquiry, it was declared that by 4 A.M. Monday the situation positively called for an SOS, but it was not until six hours later, at 9:56, that the call went out; an hour later Carey ordered the lifeboats to be prepared. With the ship listing so badly, this was a difficult operation and the lowering was rather bungled.

As for the distress call, relief was extremely slow in coming and the *Vestris* was sinking lower and lower into the water. In the case of the distress calls from the *Republic, Titanic,* and *Andrea Dorea,* the vessels were all on well-traveled sea lanes and help came relatively quickly. The *Vestris,* cutting across for South America, was in a more lonesome sea. Ironically, the *Montrose* was only six miles away, but having no wireless knew nothing of the situation until she reached Boston later. Some of the ships that did rally to the scene were badly delayed—the radioed latitude and longitude were erroneous; the sun goes down early in November and some of the ships wasted hours hunting in the dark. They ranged in size from the battleship *Wyoming* and the 15,000-ton former German liner *Berlin* down to the little 1237-ton *Miriam.* Altogether they picked up eight boats with 200 survivors aboard, but the rest went down. Eight of the 27 women aboard were saved, whereas all 12 children perished. As the *Vestris* foundered at 2:30 P.M. on Monday, Captain Carey and Second Officer Watson were thrown into the sea. Watson, who was finally picked up, said that the captain had refused to put on a lifebelt and his last words were, "My God, my God, I am not to blame for this."

Carey's innocence, however, was not the verdict of the Board of Trade inquiry in London which called the delayed SOS the chief cause of the unnecessary disaster. There was a generally messy atmosphere about the whole affair. The Board of Trade report declared, "Speaking generally the evidence is unsatisfactory, contradictory, inconsistent and piecemeal. Much of it is unreliable, some of it is untruthful."

(See R. L. Hadfield, *Sea-toll of Our Time, a Chronicle of Maritime Disasters during the Last Thirty Years,* 1930.)

Morro Castle

In the early hours of September 8, 1934, the Ward Line's luxury passenger liner, the *Morro Castle,* returning from a Labor Day weekend cruise to Havana, burned off the New Jersey coast with a loss of 126 lives. About 1:45 A.M., smoke was noticed in a writing room. With amazing speed the fire spread through much of the ship, while she plowed ahead at full speed into a gale. She finally went aground on the beach at Asbury Park, a total loss.

There were numerous strange factors, material and human, which contributed to the disaster. The 11,500-ton ship was built in 1930 for the Ward Line at a cost of $4,800,000 as part of the program made possible by the Jones-White Act of 1929. She was rated as "the finest and most luxurious vessel yet placed in the coastwise service." She had most of the proper safety devices, but certain shortcomings played their part on that September night. She had fire-detection equipment in the state-rooms and other key places, but none in the public rooms, such as the one where the fire started. (Twenty years later, the only particle of wood aboard the new liner *United States* was the butcher's block; tighter control of flammable materials was partly the result of what had happened on the *Morro Castle.*) The plywood paneling between the state-rooms, impregnated with glue and varnish, was highly flammable and did much to spread the fire. She was provided with fireproof doors to block off the passageways, but they were not closed in this emergency. She had more than enough lifeboats, but they were allowed to go off only partly filled or else were left on the davits.

The lack of adequate overall control was the greatest human failing. The *Morro Castle*'s master, Captain Robert Willmot, had died that evening, possibly from indigestion or a heart attack. The command fell to Chief Officer William F. Warms, who was suddenly faced with crisis after crisis which he was not competent to handle. He was not an impressive figure—certainly not the rugged sea-dog type. He tried hard but made a series of grave mistakes, compounded by a gale of almost hurricane force. The chief engineer, Eban S. Abbott, was far more blameworthy, skulking into one of the first lifeboats in his dress whites without going near the engine room where his third engineer, Arthur Stamper, was struggling to stave off further disaster. The boatswain was too drunk to get the hoses into action.

But as the picture eventually developed, there was a strong suspicion that the real villain was the chief radio operator, George Rogers. One radio operator had already been fired and another was under suspicion. Thomas Gallagher dug deeply into the Rogers story in his book *Fire at Sea* and presented a quite convincing story that Rogers, for revenge, had planted explosives in the writing room locker where the fire started. The crew as a whole were below par and many were untrained. It had been company policy to omit lifeboat and fire drills because they might scare away passengers. Unlike the *Bourgogne* and the *Arctic*, no unseemly rush for the lifeboats appears to have occurred, but it was recorded that in the first boats only three of the 96 occupants were passengers.

Many passengers died in their staterooms, others were killed in jumping from the decks, while a few did manage to swim the eight miles or so to shore. Those who emerged from the dark and crowded corridors tended to congregrate at the stern where, with the ship heading into a gale, the flames were driven back in their direction. One of the major charges against Captain Warms was that he had not earlier headed for shore. Another serious charge was his long delay in sending out an SOS call for help. An SOS could not go out without the captain's permission, and five times the second radio operator fought his way through the smoke before the necessary permission was given. The *Morro Castle* was in a major sea lane, and when the SOS call finally went out, three vessels were quickly at hand to assist in the rescue. The shore communities also participated. For the moment, Rogers, the chief radio operator, was a popular hero for having stayed at his post while the flames closed in.

The Coast Guard cutter *Tampa* tried to tow the *Morro Castle* northward from Sea Girt, but the gale was increasing in strength and the 12-inch towline parted. The *Morro Castle* drifted onto the beach close to Convention Hall at Asbury Park, where she would remain for some time as a major attraction. The hulk was finally sold for $33,605 to the Union Shipbuilding Company. She was towed first to Gravesend Bay and then down to Baltimore for scrapping.

In December, Captain Warms and Chief Engineer Abbott were indicted. The charges against Warms, who had been captain for only eight hours, included failure to divide the sailors into equal watches; to keep himself advised of the extent of the fire; to maneuver, slow down, or stop the vessel; to have the passengers aroused; to provide the passengers with life preservers; to take steps for the protection of lives; to organize the crew to fight the fire properly; to send distress signals promptly; to see that the passengers were put in lifeboats and that the lifeboats were lowered; and to control and direct the crew in the lifeboats after they were lowered. In January 1936 Warms was sentenced to two years' imprisonment, and the still more reprehensible chief engineer Abbott was sentenced to four years. In April 1937 both sentences were reversed by the Court of Appeals.

The Ward Line also came in for retribution. Henry E. Cabaud, executive vice president of the line, was fined $5000 and given a one-year suspended sentence for "willful negligence." The company was fined $10,000 on the same charge, and the judge remarked that he regretted that the statute would not permit a stiffer sentence. By that time the Ward Line had lost another ship under circumstances that were not creditable: its *Mohawk* was sunk on January 25, 1935, with the loss of 45 lives, in a collision in the same waters off Sea Girt; and still a third Ward Liner was wrecked, far off her course. Because of the cumulative bad publicity, the company dropped the name Ward Line and used its corporate title, "New York & Cuba Mail Steamship Company."

(See T. M. Gallagher, *Fire at Sea: The Story of the Morro Castle,* 1959.)

Normandie
(Lafayette)

The French liner
Normandie, before
World War II.
*(Peabody Museum,
Salem)*

The 1930s saw a spectacular race between England with her *Queen Mary* and France with her *Normandie* to have the largest and fastest steamship afloat. For years the French had been overshadowed in this field by the British and the Germans, but now there seemed to be a chance to gratify France's thirst for glory. The two ships were laid down a month apart in December 1930 and January 1931; even then there was keen public interest. The *Normandie* was launched in 1932; because of the depression, work was suspended on the *Queen Mary* for two and a half years, and she was not launched until 1934.

An enthusiastic author of a book on Atlantic liners calls the *Normandie* "one of the most notable ships ever built." Less conventional in design than her rival, she had a round stern and a bulbous lower bow to give added buoyancy. She had four screws, turbo-electric power, and three rather squat funnels—the Germans had already discarded the old very tall funnels. The *Normandie's* accommodations were sumptuous. The first-class dining saloon was 305 feet long, and seated 700 passengers. Because of the new American immigration restrictions, steerage was less prominent than in earlier days. Her passenger accommodations included 848 first class, 870 tourist, and 454 third class.

When launched, the *Normandie* measured 79,280 gross tons, which was topped by the *Queen Mary's* 81,237. Thereupon French pride resorted to a technical trick. Gross tonnage is the cubic content of all enclosed space. So enough deck space was glassed in to raise the *Normandie* to 82,790 tons, the largest ship afloat until the *Queen Elizabeth* came along with 83,673 tons.

375

The competition quickly extended to speed. The old *Mauretania's* long-held blue-riband record had passed to the North German Lloyd's *Bremen* in 1929 at 27.83 knots average and a passage of 4 days, 14 hours; the *Europa* of the same line about equaled that in 1939. But then the *Normandie* and *Queen Mary* began to put these figures in the shade. On her very first voyage in 1935, the *Normandie* hit 29.92 knots westbound and 30.36 knots homeward—ever since the days of the square-rigged packets, the eastbound passage was faster because of the following winds. The *Queen Mary* beat that in mid-1936 and then for a while they alternated. "It has been shown," declared the historian of Atlantic passages, "time and again the publicity value of speed record is incalculable, but from most other points of view it has little value. For example, an increase of speed from 30 to 31 knots reduced the time for the North Atlantic crossing by a mere three hours."

The two ships kept up their neck-and-neck performance until the outbreak of World War II in 1939 when, because of war conditions, the *Normandie* was laid up at a North River pier in New York. On December 12, 1941, she was seized by the United States, which had entered the war that week, renamed the U.S.S. *Lafayette,* and work was started to convert her into a troopship. On February 9, 1942, a spark from a blowtorch set fire to some waste and she was soon ablaze. However smooth her exterior might look on the surface, large amounts of flammable wood were found underneath—the French in fact had recently lost several ships by fire. The local naval commandant gave the order to flood her; she soon became topheavy and turned over in her pier. A year was spent in salvage operations to clear the pier, but the *Normandie (Lafayette)* was too far gone to warrant further expense, and the "most notable" ship was towed away to be dismantled.

(See N. R. P. Bonsor, *The North Atlantic Seaway,* 1955.)

Queen Mary

The *Queen Mary,*
with her distinctive
three-funnel feature.
(U.S. Naval Institute)

For 30 years (1937–1967) the Cunarder *Queen Mary* was one of the largest, fastest, and finest ships afloat. For part of that time she shared those honors with her companion (not exactly a sister ship) the *Queen Elizabeth.* On top of the proud 1907–1934 record of the *Mauretania,* Cunard enjoyed a half century of transatlantic leadership.

By 1930 Cunard was considering plans for recovering the long primacy held by the aging *Mauretania.* The ambitious goal was a two-ship weekly service between Southampton and New York. When the designers first got to work, they started with a length of almost 1000 feet. In the meantime the French Line was setting 981 feet for its projected *Normandie,* which would be a close rival of the *Queen Mary.* On December 1, 1930, the contract was awarded to the yard of John Brown on the Clyde near Glasgow; he had built the ill-fated *Lusitania.* The keel was laid that month, but just a year later, when the ship was only in frame, financial difficulties stemming from the world depression forced a two-year cessation of construction until April 1934; during that interval, to improve the financial situation, Cunard was merged with its ailing rival to form the Cunard-White Star Line. The ship was launched on September 20, 1934, by Queen Mary, for whom she was named.

A delightful legend, long believed but now discredited, grew up about the naming of the ship. According to the legend, the name originally planned was "Victoria." This would fit the century-old practice of ending all Cunard names in "ia." The story goes that while grouse hunting with King George, one of the company directors asked him for permission to name the ship for "the most illustrious and remarkable woman who has ever been Queen of England." The King's

377

alleged response was, "I shall ask Her Majesty's permission when I return to the Palace. She will be most appreciative of this great honor you have bestowed upon her." And so the name became "Queen Mary." The story is flatly denied.

When the *Queen Mary* started her career, she was the largest ship afloat, at 81,237 gross tons, but the French, glassing in one of the *Normandie*'s decks, raised her tonnage from 79,280 to 82,790 tons. Then the *Queen Elizabeth* topped them both at 83,673 tons. While the *Mary* was being built, there was no drydock long enough to accommodate her; Cunard had to use all its persuasion to get an adequate drydock at Southampton. The *Mary* had four sets of single-reduction-geared turbines, each developing 160,000 shaft horsepower and each driving one of the huge, 18-foot propellers. At normal speed she consumed 1020 tons of fuel oil every 24 hours; at maximum speed the consumption was higher; her total bunker capacity was 8630 tons. Her officers and crew totaled 1285 men and women.

The *Queen Mary* had accommodations for 2038 passengers, 704 in first class, 751 in second class, and 583 in tourist. First-class passengers loomed very large in the arrangements. Every effort was made to lure as many as possible aboard—one of the considerations in undertaking such a superlative ship was to win back some of the rich Americans who had been attracted by the *Bremen* and *Europa*. Both prestige and profit were involved. At the outbreak of World War II the airlines were on the verge of transatlantic service. As soon as the war was over, Pan American started regular service, but it was a relatively slow and tiring trip in the old propeller planes. Cunard met the situation with the slogan, "Getting there is half the fun!" Leisurely transportation lost somewhat of its lure when jet planes took over the run in 1958, cutting the crossing time from five days eventually to five hours.

The *Queen Mary* sailed from Southampton and Cherbourg on her maiden voyage on May 27, 1936. Cheering spectators turned out in tens of thousands—the British were inordinately proud of their new ship. There was similar enthusiasm on her arrival at New York—one can still feel the thrill of seeing the majestic liner coming up through the Narrows into New York harbor. She did not really let out her speed until August, when she beat the *Normandie*'s record at 30.14 knots westbound and 30.63 eastbound. The two rivals alternated for a while and then in 1938 the *Mary* made a blue-riband record of 30.99–31.60, which lasted until the new *United States* bested it in 1952. It was cited as quite an achievement in those depression years that the unsubsidized *Mary* had met expenses and actually made a profit.

Then came World War II in 1939. To avoid bombing and submarining, the *Queen Mary* remained laid up at her pier on the North River in New York until March 1940. There she was joined briefly by her "consort," the *Queen Elizabeth*, for the first time. Without waiting for completion, the *Elizabeth* had made a secret five-day dash across the Atlantic to be out of the way of bombing. For the same reason, both ships made their way to Sydney, Australia, to prepare for long and valuable work as army transports. The *Mary's* elaborate fittings were taken out and stored and bunks were set up in their place—starting at 8000 capacity, they soon were crowding 15,000 aboard. After service to the Middle East they were shifted to the North Atlantic shuttle; by the end of the war they had transported 320,000 American troops to Europe. The *Mary* made one exception in her cramped quarters. Winston Churchill, for his visits to Washington and the staff conferences, chose to travel by ship rather than by plane; very comfortable quarters were secretly set up for him and some of his important associates.

A tragic accident occurred in the transport service in October 1942, when the cruiser *Coracoa* was sunk in a collision off the coast of Ireland. The *Mary* was en route from New York to the Clyde with troops. As in both wars, these "Monsters," as they were called, crossed the Atlantic at full speed without convoy. For the submarine-infested coast of Ireland, however, it seemed wise to provide convoy, remembering that the *Lusitania* had had no escort in Irish waters. On this occasion there were several destroyers well out ahead, while close at hand (too close) was the 4200-ton antiaircraft cruiser *Coracoa*. There was a mistake about zigzagging and the *Queen Mary* cut the cruiser in two and rode over her—she went down in five minutes, carrying 338 officers and men to their deaths; 101 survived. Under the rigid antisubmarine regulation, it was forbidden for the liner to stop to pick up victims. When the question of responsibility came up, it was ruled that the liner was one-third to blame and the cruiser two-thirds.

At the close of hostilities, the liners engaged in the repatriation of soldiers to America; the *Mary* also made several voyages with the babies of overseas troops. Both ships went through a lengthy restoration of their lush furnishings. The *Elizabeth* completed the restoration in October 1946 but it was July 1947 before the *Mary* joined her in the originally planned weekly sailings. There was little to break the orderly routine. In 1949 stabilizers were installed to check her bad rolling. At that time the "White Star" disappeared from the line's name. In 1952 the *Mary's* blue-riband record was shattered by the new *United States*, which cut it heavily. Actually, speed was no longer a prime concern— with the planes slashing days off the Atlantic crossing, a few hours did not matter much. And so the big liners came and went from their row of West Side docks in New York.

By 1967 the *Queens* came to the end of their careers. The *Mary* had been losing some £2,000,000 a year. With full respect for their past, the line had to look at the financial aspect. Scrapping could bring about

£2,000,000, but they sought other possibilities. The city of Long Beach, California, offered £3,400,000, provided she made a special cruise by Cape Horn to Long Beach. The excursion was a success and the *Mary* was finally eased into her resting place at a Long Beach pier. She was stripped, for the third time, and the new activities were set up. Two decks were given over to a Museum of the Sea. Another attraction was the hotel accommodations; staterooms became hotel rooms, and ample restaurant facilities were established. It looked as though all was set to interest crowds and turn in a good profit, in contrast to the burned-out hull of the *Elizabeth* at Hong Kong.

(See N. Potter, *The Queen Mary: Her Inception and History*, 1971.)

Queen Elizabeth

The *Queen Elizabeth*, with only two funnels due to improved boiler efficiency. *(U.S. Naval Institute)*

The Cunarder *Queen Elizabeth*, a "consort" of the *Queen Mary*, was the largest liner ever built—83,673 gross tons. They were planned, as early as 1930, to be fast enough for a two-ship weekly transatlantic service. Because of the depression and then World War II, it was not until 1947 that they settled down to regular weekly passenger service. They were not exactly "sisters"; the distinguishing feature was the number of funnels: the *Mary* had three and the *Elizabeth* two. In the years between their inception, boilers had become so much more efficient that the *Elizabeth* needed only 12, and so the third funnel was discarded.

The keel of the *Elizabeth* was laid in October 1936, as soon as the John Brown Clydeside yard had finished with the *Mary*. She was launched in September 1938, and was named for the Queen Mother. Her interior was not yet entirely finished when World War II broke out. To avoid the danger of bombing, she was rushed across the Atlantic, docking close to the *Mary* in the North River in New York. In early 1940 both ships left for refitting at Sydney, Australia. For a while they carried troops from Australia and then troops from America to Britain. When the war was over, they engaged in repatriation crossings. The *Elizabeth* was fitted out for peacetime work in October 1946, nine months ahead of the *Mary;* both ships maintained weekly service as originally planned. The *Elizabeth* never really "let herself out" in the matter of speed—with the coming of transatlantic aviation there was no purpose in that costly endeavor.

The two ships were taken out of active service in 1967, but the *Elizabeth* did not share *Mary*'s arrangements for a long and comfortable retirement. She was purchased by a Hong Kong group which spent $11,000,000 in refitting her as the *Seawise University*. While lying in Hong Kong harbor, however, a fire started and burned her out completely. Her ragged skeleton lies stretched out along the harbor.

In 1969, Cunard in a move of doubtful wisdom, built a liner of moderate size as the *Queen Elizabeth 2*, often abbreviated as the "*QE 2*," for shuttle or cruising service. She has not been particularly successful, breaking down on her trial run and again on a West Indian cruise, when another ship had to rescue her passengers. Cunard also built two smaller cruise ships, the *Cunard Adventurer* and *Cunard Ambassador;* the latter was badly damaged by fire. Cunard's good fortune seemed to have dissipated.

(See L. A. Stevens, *The Elizabeth: Passage of a Queen,* 1968.)

U-47

The German submarines in both World Wars spent much of their effort in sinking merchant shipping, an effort that more than once promised victory. But the most spectacular submarine feat was the sinking of a British battleship in the supposedly ultrasecurity of the great British base at Scapa Flow in the Orkneys, north of Scotland. Britain had built Scapa Flow just before World War I as its main fleet base to keep the Germans from getting out of the North Sea into the Atlantic. Throughout World War I, the Grand Fleet had rested there in perfect security.

Early in World War II, Scapa Flow's very security tempted the Germans to try to violate it. The base was built among a ring of islands, with the channels between the islands blocked by sunken hulls except for the entrance, which was blocked by movable antisubmarine nets. The entrance was naturally guarded with extreme vigilance. But German reconnaissance found another channel that was inadequately protected.

Germany picked one of its boldest submarine officers, Lieutenant Commander Günther Prien of the *U-47*, to attempt penetrating the fleet base. On Friday, October 13, 1939, he made his approach. Strong tidal currents pushed him toward the narrowest entrance between the block ships and the rocks, but with masterly maneuvering he traversed the gap at top speed; he grounded briefly but managed to work himself free. When he surveyed the base, he found that much of the normal Scapa fleet had gone to sea. Then he sighted a likely target. His first torpedo from the *U-47* hit its bow, causing no alarm; and the second did not explode either. The Germans, like the Americans later, were having trouble with duds. Prien moved away, reloaded, and then loosed three more torpedoes, all of which took effect. A great spray accompanied the explosion of the target's ammunition. As the ship sank, Prien managed to speed out through the gap.

The torpedoed ship was the dreadnought *Royal Oak,* completed at Plymouth in 1916 just in time to take part in the battle of Jutland. The explosions ripped out her bottom and she rolled over in 11 minutes. Very few had time to save their lives; 24 officers and 809 men were lost.

Prien was given a hero's welcome in Berlin. Hitler, proud at this spectacular blow to British naval pride, rewarded Prien with the Iron Cross. He was now known as the "Snorting Bull of Scapa Flow." A few months later he was up at Narvik in the Norwegian operations. There he fired torpedoes at several targets, including a battleship, but the torpedoes proved to be duds. The British depth-charged the U-boat heavily but she managed to escape. Prien died in March 1941, south of Iceland, when the *U-47* was depth-charged and destroyed with all on board.

(See G. Cousins, *The Story of Scapa Flow,* 1965.)

Admiral Graf Spee

The *Admiral Graf Spee,* damaged by British cruisers off Montevideo, December 13, 1939. *(Naval Historical Center)*

In the early 1930s the Germans produced three so-called "pocket battleships" which caused the British serious concern in the early months of World War II. The Treaty of Versailles at the end of World War I had limited Germany to cruisers no larger than 10,000 tons, the size of heavy cruisers of other nations. With cleverness and a little cheating, the Germans crowded into a nominally 10,000-ton hull (actually 12,000) six 11-inch guns plus 14 smaller ones (no normal cruiser had more than 8-inch guns), and installed diesel engines to get a speed of 28 knots. Consequently, the German cruiser could run away from any enemy ship that she couldn't beat up. The Germans had also economized on tonnage by welding instead of riveting and had provided the high speed by the use of three sets of novel diesel engines, capable of generating 56,800 horsepower. The first of these pocket battleships in 1930 was the *Deutschland* (later renamed *Lützow*); the other two were named for World War I admirals—the *Admiral Scheer* for the commander in chief of the High Seas Fleet, and the *Admiral Graf Spee* for the commander in chief of the East Asian Squadron, who went down in his flagship *Scharnhorst* at the Falkland Islands, after first sinking a British squadron at Coronel in 1914.

383

The British realized that even without capturing too many ships, these misnamed pocket battleships could disrupt commerce and draw British warships in pursuit. They knew their naval history well enough to realize that Britain had faced a similar threat in the War of 1812. For example, in the War of 1812 the three American 44-gun frigates— *Constitution, United States,* and *President*—were also supercruisers, considerably stronger than any conventional frigate. After losing the *Guerrière, Java,* and *Macedonian* in single-ship duels, the British sent out groups of two or three ships to handle the big ones. In 1815 the big frigate *President* had been captured by the Sandy Hook blockading squadron in an action similar to the one which would check the *Admiral Graf Spee;* the largest British frigate took punishment in slowing down the *President* and then the smaller British frigates completed the capture. In 1939 the British formed eight forces, of two ships or more, to try to run down the pocket battleships—Force M, off South America, under Commodore Henry Harwood, would be the one to handle the *Spee.*

By a coincidence the *Spee* and Force M came together on December 13, 1939, just 25 years and five days after Admiral von Spee had lost his life in action in those same waters. Captain Langsdorff thought that he was up against one British heavy cruiser, the *Exeter,* and a couple of destroyers. Actually, the destroyers were the light cruisers *Ajax* and *Achilles.* In theory, the *Spee's* 11-inch guns should have been able to smash the *Exeter* before her 8-inch guns could get into range. In practice, the *Exeter* quickly closed in and began exchanging shots with the Germans. The gunnery was good on both sides and continued strenuously for an hour and a half. After the action the *Exeter* was barely able to limp away to the Falkland Islands, the two light cruisers had sustained some damage, but the upper works of the *Spee* were a shambles. Langsdorff headed for the River Plate, hoping to get repairs at Montevideo. Under international law he could remain there only briefly unless his damages were too severe to get to another port. He was allowed three days, after which it was get out or be interned. It is rumored that the British naval attaché gave the Uruguayan authorities information on the seriousness of the damages. Meanwhile rumors were spreading that the British were gathering in force off the port to catch Captain Langsdorff if he came out. In fact, there was only one heavy cruiser in the *Exeter's* place, plus the two little light ones.

Captain Langsdorff called Berlin for advice—rumor has it that Hitler talked with him. The *Spee,* followed by a merchant ship, sailed out into the shallow Plata delta on December 17 and was set afire by explosions. The merchantman took the Germans across the delta to Buenos Aires, where in his hotel room Langsdorff committed suicide. For his victory Commodore Harwood was promoted to rear admiral and knighted.

(See H. W. Baldwin, *Sea Fights and Ship Wrecks*, 1955.)

Jervis Bay

Early in November 1940 a British armed merchant cruiser won a lasting place in Royal Navy tradition by her gallant sacrifice play in protecting the 37-ship convoy with whose safety she had been entrusted. So weak a ship should never have been entrusted with such a responsibility, but when she encountered the German pocket battleship *Admiral Scheer* in the North Atlantic, she boldly went into action and quickly disintegrated under a storm of 11-inch shells, but not until most of her convoy had scattered to safety in the growing dusk.

The *Jervis Bay* was an aging 13,850-ton veteran of the Australian Commonwealth Line and, like her four sister ships, was named for an Australian bay. Like scores of other liners of medium size, she was equipped with guns and a naval crew. Such vessels did their most useful work as cruisers to overhaul suspicious merchantmen. It was not normally expected that they would be lone escorts for a big convoy.

At Cape Town a cruiser's officers were sitting in the wardroom when two radio messages came in saying that the Halifax convoy was being attacked by a pocket battleship. "Which poor b— Armed Merchant Cruiser is doomed?" asked one officer. The answer came quickly in another dispatch: "Halifax Convoy HX 84 attacked in position 52°26'N, 32°34'W by *Admiral Scheer*. I am attacking. *Jervis Bay*."

Captain E. S. F. Fegen, who sent the message, had determined, at whatever cost, to give his three-dozen merchantmen a chance to scatter under a smokescreen and the fast approaching dusk. The *Jervis Bay* herself might have made an escape but instead went into suicidal action with her meager battery. She kept between the *Scheer* and the convoy as long as her engines held out. The 11-inch German shells simply knocked the unprotected hull to pieces. The very first hit had torn off one of Captain Fegen's legs and smashed the other. But he kept the command, while the surgeon bandaged the stump. In 22 minutes it was all over, with the battered liner's last gun firing as she went down.

Those 22 minutes, bought at such a cost, enabled all but five of the 37 ships of the convoy to escape. One big Canadian Pacific freighter kept firing for several hours at the *Scheer*. A big tanker caught fire and was abandoned, but her crew later returned and saved her. A Swedish freighter saved 65 of the *Jervis Bay*'s crew from boats and rafts. Captain Fegen was awarded a posthumous Victoria Cross. From that time on the British sent a battleship or other strong warship with their important convoys.

Another armed merchant cruiser, whose name has often been associated with the *Jervis Bay*, was the Peninsular & Oriental liner *Rawalpindi*, named for a city in western India which would be temporarily the capital of Pakistan. A 16,600-ton liner, built in 1925, she met her fate in the same northern waters. On November 23, 1939, she encountered the two small battleships, or battlecruisers, *Scharnhorst* and *Gneisenau* (named for Admiral Spee's two armored cruisers). Unable to escape, the *Rawalpindi* engaged in a hopeless battle, succumbing to the 11-inch shells as the *Jervis Bay* had done.

(See C. R. V. Gibbs, *British Passenger Liners of the Five Oceans*, 1963.)

Bismarck

For four days in May 1941 the British were in a state of near-panic. The German superdreadnought *Bismarck*, one of the most powerful ships afloat, was at large in the North Atlantic where she might be able to completely disrupt all communications on that most vital sea lane. The Royal Navy threw everything it could—48 surface vessels plus scores of planes—into the pursuit and managed by a lucky hit from a plane to slow her down and then crowd in on her. The tough ship withstood terrific battering before she finally sank with almost all hands.

German prewar strategy included massive raiding. In World War I the concentrated dreadnoughts of the High Seas Fleet had spent four years in port, facing the British Grand Fleet across the North Sea; there had been one indecisive fleet action and that was all. However, in 1937 Admiral Raeder, the German commander in chief, drew up his "Plan Z," which called for a quite different use of the naval forces. Instead of passive fleet action, they would devote themselves to commerce destruction, stretching out the British naval defenses to the limit. Raeder had planned a strong force of various sizes of warships, which were only partly completed when war broke out in 1939.

Most powerful of the German warships were the *Bismarck* and the

Tirpitz, measuring 41,700 tons, with eight 15-inch, twelve 5.9-inch, and sixteen 4-inch guns, an extremely heavy armor belt of 12.6 inches, and engines capable of 128,000 horsepower and 30-knot speed. They were a little stronger than the new 35,000-ton superdreadnoughts which Britain and the United States began to build after the "naval holiday" in 1936.

The British maintained constant aerial reconnaissance over the various ports where these German ships were stationed, in order to give speedy alarm should they try to break out. An alarm was sounded when the *Bismarck* and the heavy cruiser *Prinz Eugen* sailed from Gdynia near Danzig on the Baltic Sea on May 18, 1941, and headed for Denmark Strait, almost on the Arctic Circle between Iceland and Greenland, a passage narrowed by the extensive ice field on the Greenland side. Two British heavy cruisers were on watch in these foggy waters. Late on May 23 the cruiser *Suffolk* sighted the German ships seven miles away. By a lucky chance, at her captain's insistence, the *Suffolk* had just been equipped with search radar which was not yet general in the navy. Dodging into the mists before the Germans could fire, she followed their movements on radar and sent off word to the high command at Scapa Flow.

The British rushed out two great ships which, on paper, looked even stronger than the two German ships. One was the *Hood,* the huge battle cruiser which for more than 20 years between the wars had been the largest warship afloat. She was equal to the *Bismarck* in guns and size and almost equal in speed. But she was a battle cruiser with the inadequate armor belt of that unfortunate class. Her consort, the *Prince of Wales,* went to the opposite extreme of being too new—she was not yet really shaken down and some of the dockyard technicians were still aboard, making last minute adjustments. In contrast, the two German ships were in good shape with their crews in a state of readiness.

The four ships came together at 6 A.M. on May 24. The fight was over in 20 minutes—the *Hood* lasted barely five minutes. The German shells touched off some antiaircraft ammunition which had been stored unwisely on deck and another German salvo set off scattered fires; then an explosion of her magazines caused her bow and stern to rise high in the air as she broke in two amidships and disappeared, carrying down all but three of the 1419 men aboard.

The *Bismarck* then concentrated on the *Prince of Wales,* inflicting considerable damage. The British ship, however, did get in three hits which slowed down the German ship a bit and caused a serious loss of fuel oil. The *Prince of Wales* withdrew from the brief fight, leaving the two radar-equipped cruisers to try to keep track of the *Bismarck* in the fog.

The *Bismarck* started off as though she were heading southwest into the western Atlantic. Very soon, however, she confounded her pursuers by changing course and heading southeast for Europe; her fuel loss was serious enough to cause her to abandon the originally planned raiding. The British in the meantime were assembling every possible ship for pursuit of the *Bismarck* under the general command of Admiral Tovey in the new *King George V*. In addition to the warships in home waters, ships strained themselves rushing in from the Mediterranean and America. The British were fully aware of what the *Bismarck* might do if not checked.

During the first day a few contacts were made by radar and plane, but for 30 desperate hours (from 4 A.M. on May 25 to 10:30 A.M. on May 26) there was no track at all of her whereabouts. Then during a short break in the clouds, an aircraft sighted her and reported her position some 690 miles northwest of Brest in western France.

A critical stroke of luck for the British came about 9 P.M. on May 26, when a force of torpedo planes from the carrier *Ark Royal* attacked the *Bismarck*. Despite "low rain clouds, strong wind, stormy seas, fading daylight, and intense and accurate enemy gunfire," two torpedoes hit the *Bismarck*. One hit the armor belt with no particular damage; the other hit the stern and damaged the propellers, wrecked the steering gear, and jammed the rudders. "It was this hit that sealed her fate," for she might otherwise have escaped to safety.

Some destroyers closed in on the *Bismarck*, firing torpedoes; then about 9 A.M. the battleship *Rodney* and the cruiser *Dorsetshire* began pouring armor-piercing shells into her at close range. "By 10:15 the giant battleship had been reduced to a floating shambles, and all her guns were silent." The *Dorsetshire* fired two torpedoes into her port side and one into the starboard. "At 10:35 the *Bismarck* had disappeared in 48°16′N and 16°12′W, with her flag still flying. She had fought gallantly to the finish, even after overwhelming strength had been concentrated against her." About 110 survivors were rescued, but the threat of submarines curtailed further rescue work. More than 2200 were lost.

The *Bismarck*'s potent sister ship *Tirpitz* spent much of her time in Norwegian fiords, where she was carefully observed by British planes and succumbed to their bombing in 1944.

(See R. Grenfell, *The Bismarck Episode*, 1949.)

Arizona

The *Arizona*, after the Japanese attack on Pearl Harbor, December 7, 1941. *(National Archives)*

The most tragic victim of the Pearl Harbor attack on December 7, 1941, was the superdreadnought *Arizona*, blown up by a Japanese aerial bomb. She still lies on the bottom at Pearl Harbor, with more than 1000 of her officers and men buried in her torn and burned-out hull.

She was one of the best of the new American superdreadnoughts that were built during and just after World War I. She had been launched in 1915 and was a sister ship of the fleet flagship *Pennsylvania. Jane's Fighting Ships* declared that they represented "one of the most successful, if not the most successful, of all Dreadnought designs to the present time." She measured 31,900 tons, had ten 16-inch and twenty-two 5-inch guns, a 14-inch armor belt, and the conventional 21-knot battleship speed.

A surprising thing about the *Arizona* and her companions in the battle fleet at Pearl Harbor was their age—averaging a quarter century. In contrast to the 16 battleships of the Great White Fleet which made the world cruise in 1907–1908 and were obsolete while still new, these ships were caught in the long "naval holiday" imposed by the Washington Naval Conference in 1922. New construction was forbidden, but the *Arizona* and the others received some extensive modification. They had spent their time in cruising in majestic line-ahead fleet formation.

As trouble with Japan was threatening, they were held at Pearl Harbor over the very strong protest of their commander in chief, who finally went to Washington to urge President Roosevelt to move them; instead, he moved the admiral. The Americans had cracked the Japanese radio code but failed to make use of the information received.

In the Japanese attack about 8 A.M. an aerial bomb hit the *Arizona* and blew up her forward magazines. The original belief was that the bomb had gone down her funnel, but later investigation showed that the wire screen at the top of the funnel was still intact. It seems "likely the bomb landed alongside the second turret, crashed through the forecastle, and set off the forward magazines. In any case, a huge ball of fire and smoke mushroomed 500 feet into the air." Hundreds of men had no chance—they perished in a single searing crash. Rear Admiral Isaac C. Kidd and Captain Franklin van Valkenbergh were killed on the bridge. Some of the crew on deck were able to slide down to the tender *Vestal,* which lay alongside.

Nearly every ship in Battleship Row was damaged—the only others sunk were the *Oklahoma* and the *Utah,* but not with the terrific loss of life as on the *Arizona.* There are still 1002 victims entombed in her hull, which has become a memorial. Many of the other ships were repaired and found their way out to the Pacific during the war. But partly because of this blow at the battle force, the traditional line-ahead formation of superdreadnoughts no longer represented maximum striking power afloat—that passed rapidly to the "fast carrier task force." Fortunately, the carriers were absent on that disastrous Sunday morning of December 7.

(See W. Lord, *Day of Infamy,* 1963; S. E. Morison, *The Two-ocean War,* 1963.)

Prince of Wales

Many warships went through their entire active service without hearing a shot fired in anger. The American "Great White Fleet" of 18 battleships which made its world cruise in 1907–1909 was, with one possible exception, in that category. But the opposite extreme was reached by the British superdreadnought *Prince of Wales* in 1941. Before she had been commissioned for a year, she had fought the German *Bismarck* in the Arctic waters of Denmark Strait, had brought Winston Churchill to the summit meeting off Newfoundland which produced the Atlantic Charter, and then had been sunk by Japanese aerial attack in the tropical waters off Malaya.

She was part of Britain's revival of battleship construction in 1936, after Japan withdrew from the international "naval holiday" restrictions. After the long period of "time out," Britain, the United States, Germany, and Japan all began to build ships of 35,000 tons or more. The *Prince of Wales* was one of five new superdreadnoughts, equipped with only 14-inch guns, which were the largest available.

The *Prince of Wales* was barely commissioned and still had civilian dockyard technicians aboard when she was ordered out to join the giant but weak *Hood* to pursue the mighty *Bismarck,* which had broken loose from British surveillance. In the action in Denmark Strait between Iceland and Greenland, the *Hood* suddenly blew up. The *Prince of Wales* was somewhat mauled, but not before her three shots had caused the *Bismarck* so much loss of fuel oil that she could not carry out her original plan of raiding in the western Atlantic.

In her second 1941 episode, the *Prince of Wales* took Winston Churchill to Newfoundland for his summit conference with President Roosevelt, which produced the Atlantic Charter, a statement of Allied aims.

Then for the third major episode of her brief but hectic career, she was ordered out to Southeast Asia where war with Japan was threatening. The British had long advertised Singapore as their supposedly impregnable eastern bastion. Their strategy assumed that a land attack would have to come down the long narrow Malay Peninsula which could easily be blocked, while warships prevented any flank attacks by the enemy. The *Prince of Wales,* with the battle cruiser *Repulse,* came out for that purpose under the command of Admiral Tom Phillips, one of Britain's ablest commanders, fresh from his post as Deputy Chief of Staff. Then comes one of the war's mysteries—why the Singapore command was so passively open to Japanese attack, and why no adequate air support was given Phillips' ships. They steamed up the coast on rumor of a Japanese landing and then turned back to meet another landing—but still no air support from Singapore. On December 10, three days after Pearl Harbor, Japanese planes swarmed in on the two British ships, and between aerial bombs and torpedoes both quickly went to the bottom. The British destroyers rescued 1285 of the *Prince of Wales* complement of 1612, but Admiral Phillips was lost. A similar proportion of the *Repulse's* crew was saved. This sinking of a battleship underway at sea by airpower alone had a shock effect even greater than the sinking of the American battleships at Pearl Harbor.

(See R. A. Hough, *Dreadnought: A History of the Modern Battleship,* 1964; O. Parkes, *British Battleships, 'Warrior' 1860 to 'Vanguard' 1950,* 1957.)

Lexington

For a decade the carrier *Lexington* and her sister ship, the *Saratoga,* played a most important role in the development of American naval aviation. Except for the little *Langley,* they were the navy's only real carriers until just before World War II. They played a part in the development of both air strategy and the tactics of fighting, dive bombing, torpedo bombing, and scouting. As a result, when the war came, naval aviation was well prepared for action.

The carriers had been started as battle cruisers, a type the British had introduced just before World War I along with the battleship *Dreadnought.* The battle cruisers were almost the same as the battleship in size and hitting power, but their armor protection was weakened in the interest of speed. At the Battle of Jutland in May 1916, just at the time the *Lexington* and *Saratoga* were authorized by Congress, three British battle cruisers were sunk, demonstrating, in the slang phrase of the day, that they could "dish it out but could not take it." Construction on the two ships was postponed during the war in order to build destroyers, but was resumed in 1921 when the *Lexington* was laid down at Bethlehem Quincy (Fore River). In 1922 the Washington Naval Conference saw the United States make a self-sacrificing disarmament play to produce a capital ship ratio of 5:5:3 with Britain and Japan. Construction on a big new battleship fleet was halted and one ship actually sunk at sea; similar treatment was planned for the two battle cruisers: the *Lexington* was one-third completed and the *Saratoga,* a little further along.

At this time, the prime promoter of naval aviation was Admiral William A. Moffet, head of the new Bureau of Aeronautics, who stepped into the picture. He won support for his proposal that instead of destroying the two battle cruisers, converting their hulls into aircraft carriers, a type in which the United States quota still allowed room. Their conversion was authorized by Congress on July 1, 1922, at the close of the conference. The *Lexington* was launched on October 3, 1923, at Fore River, but the full conversion was time-consuming; she was commissioned on October 14, 1927, as CV-2 (the *Langley* was CV-1).

In the very thorough conversion, two major aspects of the battle cruiser stage remained. Like the *Saratoga,* the *Lexington* measured 33,000 tons and had a speed of 33.9 knots. Both were larger than any of the subsequent wartime American carriers. The *Essex* class of 17 carriers, which began to come on the scene in 1940, measured 27,100 tons. Their 34-knot speed became the norm for the carriers themselves and for the escorts designed to keep up with them. That was far faster than the 24 knots of the battleships at the beginning of the war. Later in the war the *Missouri* and three other battleships had a speed of 33 knots to keep up with the carrier task forces.

In addition to the size and speed, many entirely new features were built into the hulls. Most conspicuous was the 900-foot flight deck, flat and smooth except for the "island" at the side with the funnel and the seat of authority. Planes took off over the bow, with the ship headed into the wind, and came in over the stern. They were housed just below on the hangar deck, with room for 80 planes or so—the "Wildcat" fighters, the "Dauntless" dive bombers and scouting planes, and the "Devastator" torpedo bombers. These were brought up to the flight deck on the two elevators. Opposite the island were the huge tanks of fuel oil and dangerously flammable aviation gas. There was much else in the rabbit warren below; the *Lexington* had some 600 separate compartments. All these features were designed for usefulness, not gracefulness. No one ever called a huge, bulky carrier a thing of beauty.

The question of command, so vital a consideration to all ambitious officers, raised a difficult problem. Because of the special techniques involved, an early ruling stipulated that every carrier should be commanded by an aviator. But the aviation service was so new that the fliers had not had time to reach four-stripe command rank. To meet this need, some of the older captains were encouraged to earn their wings as fliers or observers. This happy solution brought several active, progressive officers into the carriers, and gave the service some strong champions against the conservative battleship admirals, who had long been in the saddle. Outstanding among these new "aviators" were Joseph M. Reeves, Harry E. Yarnell, William F. Halsey, and Ernest J. King, who later became the wartime commander in chief. Aboard the ship the fliers formed a "group" under an aviation commander. The carrier, or carriers, were part of a task force (TF), including the cruisers and destroyers of the escort. This very flexible phrase could include everything from a single carrier to two or several. With their escorts, the commander, usually the flag officer, was not necessarily an aviator.

During their first decade the "Lex" and the "Sara," as they were nicknamed, undertook all the earlier carrier experimenting. They participated in maneuvers in the Pacific and the Caribbean. An important maneuver had one carrier attacking and another carrier defending Panama. Another maneuver was the Sunday morning attack on Pearl Harbor under Admiral Harry Yarnell in 1932; such a successful demonstration might have served as a warning of the vulnerability of Pearl Harbor; the Japanese attack on Pearl Harbor on December 7, 1941, showed that the earlier raid had been forgotten.

The Pearl Harbor attack precipitated a major revision in American naval strategy and tactics, with the "fast carrier task force" supplanting the line-ahead formation of battleships. The conservative senior admirals who, as the proaviation enthusiasts said, "could not see beyond the splash of a 16-inch gun," resisted new carrier dvelopments and stuck to the Jutland pattern. Most of the battleships were at Pearl Harbor when the Japanese struck and five were sunk—that was the end of the line-ahead formation. It was a godsend for the Americans that no carriers were in port exposed to attack. The *Enterprise* was just approaching port, the *Lexington* was far out in the Pacific, and the three others were also at a safe distance. Under the circumstances, the carrier task force took over from the old battleship formation, and maintained its supremacy.

There was a need for carriers out in the western Pacific, where the Japanese, having seized Indonesia and other territories, were gathering for an attack on New Guinea and Australia. The *Lexington* made its first contact off Rabaul on New Britain Island; Japanese bombers swarmed out but were driven back; a lieutenant won the Congressional Medal of Honor by knocking off five Japanese planes, causing the enemy to withdraw. Continuing on across the Coral Sea, the *Lexington* and *Yorktown* joined in an attack on the Japanese in the little New Guinea ports of Lae and Salamaua, their planes swarming over the tall mountains to sweep down with a smashing raid on March 10.

The *Lexington* came to her end in the Battle of the Coral Sea, a landmark in naval history, on May 8, 1942. In this first carrier-versus-carrier action, the accompanying surface ships did not come within sight of each other or exchange a shot, while the planes shuttled across the 200-mile gap. A powerful Japanese force was planning to sweep down to the tip of New Guinea, where it could definitely cut off all contact between America and Australia.

To prevent this Japanese maneuver, a two-carrier task force with the *Lexington* and the *Yorktown* moved into the area. On May 7 they demolished a small Japanese carrier. On May 8 two new big Japanese carriers, the *Shokaku* and the *Zuikaku,* with several heavy cruisers and numerous destroyers, were 200 miles north of the two American carriers and their surface ships. The American planes went north in force, badly damaged the *Shokaku,* and inflicted heavy losses on the Japanese planes. But in the meantime the Japanese planes came south to attack the lightly guarded American carriers. In some 20 minutes of late forenoon, torpedo bombers and dive bombers pounded the *Lexington* mercilessly. When the attack let up, the damage control parties went to work to make repairs. About an hour later, there was a very heavy internal explosion. At first it was thought to be explosions of gasoline fumes from ruptured tanks. The explosions continued faster than they could be checked and by late afternoon, flames were rapidly spreading throughout the ship. At 5 o'clock the order was given to abandon ship; Captain Frederick Sherman and his executive, the last to leave the ship, slid down ropes and were taken aboard a cruiser. A destroyer fired two torpedoes to sink the gutted hull. The *Yorktown* had suffered less severe damage.

So far as damage was concerned, the Coral Sea Battle was pretty much a draw but, strategically, it was an important American victory. It had saved Australia and New Zealand from the spread of Japanese influence, and the Japanese forces concentrated on other warfare. The Navy launched a new *Lexington* (CV-16) early in 1943. The *Saratoga* fought on through the war and was one of the warships sunk at Bikini Atoll in 1946 to test the effectiveness of the atomic bomb.

(See C. G. Reynolds, *The Fast Carriers: The Forging of an Air Navy,* 1968.)

Enterprise
(CV-6)

The carrier *Enterprise* had an amazing record of important activity for three and a half years of the United States Navy's Pacific war during World War II. She lived a charmed life and happened to be on hand for almost every event of interest. She participated in many different actions, sinking numerous ships. We are not concerned here with all the little island-hopping, but rather with the major events.

She was launched on October 3, 1936, at the big private yard of the Newport News Shipbuilding and Drydock Company, and was commissioned on May 12, 1938. She measured 19,200 tons, had an 800-foot flight deck, and was capable of the usual carrier 33-knot speed. Though smaller than other fleet carriers, she was nicknamed "Big E."

One of the fortunate aspects of the Pearl Harbor attack was that the few precious carriers of the United States (only five in the Pacific) escaped damage. The *Enterprise* was just returning from delivering planes in mid-Pacific when she almost became a victim of the attack.

On April 8, 1942, the *Enterprise* with her escorts left Pearl Harbor on a mysterious mission. Several days later, in chilly air toward Asia, she rendezvoused with the new carrier *Hornet* on whose forward deck were 16 strange large planes. A signal ended the mystery: "This force is bound for Tokyo." Lieutenant Colonel James H. Doolittle of Army Air Force and his B-25 bombers left the carriers 500 miles east of Japan, dropped their bombs, and flew on to China, where some of the air crews were captured and executed by the Japanese.

Next came participation in one of the most decisive battles of the war. The United States Navy had broken the Japanese radio code; this was a tremendous advantage in learning the enemy's plans. The Navy discovered that the Japanese were planning a big raid on Midway Island and the Aleutians, and immediately devised a counterattack. Late in May the *Enterprise* left Pearl Harbor, leading a task force commanded by Admiral Raymond A. Spruance, a taciturn, brilliant nonaviator. They were joined by the *Yorktown* and her escorts, with orders to defend Midway and inflict maximum damage on the enemy, who had hoped to catch the Americans unaware.

The climax of the encounter off Midway came on June 4, 1942, when Japan's four carriers were sunk—Japanese air power and Japanese naval effectiveness would not be the same again. The Americans performed this feat with three carriers—the flagship *Enterprise*, the *Hornet*, and the *Yorktown*, which, repaired after Coral Sea, was now sunk. The planes of the *Enterprise*, with their slashing attack, sank the *Kaga* and the *Akaga*; the *Yorktown* planes sank the *Soryu*; the *Hiryu*, which had stayed away from the rest, fell victim to the *Yorktown* and *Enterprise* planes. A grim aspect of those carrier sinkings was that their fliers had no decks on which to land and eventually fell into the sea. Japan's original "first team" of pilots had been excellent, but she had not built any "second team" to take their place. Altogether, Midway was one of the decisive naval battles of history, and it gave the United States leadership in the Pacific war.

Just two months after Midway, the Japanese landed on Guadalcanal in the Solomon Islands just east of the Coral Sea, and for several months there was bitter fighting in that area. It was a trying situation in those confined waters, and more than once the *Enterprise* and the other carriers were damaged. This hard fighting terminated with the fierce Battle of the Solomon Islands in mid-November 1942. From May through October the *Enterprise* had a period of "time out," refitting first at the Pearl Harbor Navy Yard and then in the Puget Sound yard at Bremerton. She was the first carrier to receive a Presidential Unit Citation.

By late 1943, the United States Navy was in a position to assume the offensive in the Pacific. This meant an island-hopping drive right through the mid-Pacific. The *Enterprise*'s battle citations included attacks on the Caroline and Marshall Islands, Kwajalein, and the powerful island base of Truk. In the course of this fighting, she made the first night-raider bombing attack.

There was bitter fighting for the Marianas, including the old colony of Guam and Saipan, because with these in hand, the great army bombers could reach Japan itself. Starting on June 6, 1944, the *Enterprise* joined in assisting the hard-fought landings in the islands. On June 19 the situation expanded into one of the greatest sea fights, known formally as the Battle of the Philippine Sea. Knowing how serious it would be if

American bombers were to fly from Marianas bases against Japan, a huge Japanese fleet was sent out to prevent American takeover of the Marianas.

Admiral Ozawa had nine carriers, with full quotas of planes and strong warship escorts. Ozawa stayed outside of range for a while, but on June 19 came the fiercest carrier plane battle yet, with the American fliers taking a tremendous toll—one enthusiastic flier called out, "It's just like an old fashioned turkey shoot"; the action became known as the "Marianas Turkey Shoot." The *Enterprise* was in the thick of battle; the climax came on June 20, when some of the Japanese carriers were cut down, ending the threat. The great difficulty was that the Japanese did not come within range until just before sunset. The American fliers were faced with the problem of flying out into the darkness, exhausting their fuel, and losing their way back. But as they returned toward the darkened carriers, Admiral Mitscher ordered the carriers to turn on their lights. Admiral Spruance, of Midway fame, and Admiral Mitscher were in command of the overall American force, consisting of 15 carriers, seven battleships, 12 cruisers, and 58 destroyers; the *Enterprise* was in one of the task groups with three other carriers. Like Midway, it was a striking American victory. Ozawa limped back to Okinawa after losing six carriers and more than 426 planes and airmen. Midway had cost Japan its "first team" of aviators; now Philippine Sea had left the Japanese severely shorn of naval air power.

After several intermediate operations, the *Enterprise* participated with distinction in a still greater action—the Battle of Leyte Gulf in mid-October 1944, the most extensive sea fight in all history, even exceeding Jutland. As the Americans closed in on the Philippines as a springboard against Japan, the Japanese threw all their depleted naval forces into an effort to prevent the success of the operation. It was a complicated story, the culmination of two major American drives: one under the navy proper across the Pacific, and the other under General MacArthur "up the ladder" past New Guinea. They arrived under two separate commands, the Navy's Third Fleet under Admiral Halsey, and MacArthur's Southwest Pacific command with its naval forces under Admiral Kinkaid. The main trouble was that each was independent of the other, with no superior authority short of Washington.

The separate actions which are collectively known as the Battle of Leyte Gulf involved covering three distinct phases: (1) the southern approach by Surigao Strait, a relatively simple job for the old battleships; (2) the main central approach with major force by San Bernardino Strait; and (3) the most controversial aspect, the carrier force at Cape Engano to the northward, which was simply the Japanese design to distract the Americans from the main scene of action—and Admiral

Halsey fell for it. The *Enterprise* participated in both the second and third phases. In San Bernardino, she inflicted the principal punishment upon the Japanese flagship, the *Musashi*, which, with her sister ship *Yamato*, was one of the two largest battleships ever built—she even carried 18-inch guns. The *Enterprise*'s dive bombers exploded 11 of 18 bombs on the great ship, while eight torpedo bombs added to the punishment, from which she later sank. Although the Japanese still had several strong ships left, they unaccountably gave up the San Bernardino attack. Originally, the Americans had San Bernardino guarded, especially with the new fast battleships. But Halsey stripped those forces to dash north against the distant carriers at Cape Engano. The *Enterprise* went north with that group, in what one correspondent gave the lasting nickname of "Bull's Run." In this greatest of sea fights, the Americans had left San Bernardino unguarded but their error was more than offset by the Japanese unnecessarily turning back from the undefended strait.

The two remaining major naval actions were undertaken so that fighter planes could protect the bombers—Iwo Jima in February–March 1945, and Okinawa in April, along with devastating fast carrier air raids on the mainland of Japan. One major concern of the American warships was the Japanese use of "kamikaze," or suicide, attacks. No longer able to furnish fuel for regular air activities, Japan found patriotic fliers ready to take out planes, with fuel enough only for an outward bound attack on an American ship. On May 14, 1945, 250 miles southeast of Japan, a kamikaze hero accomplished what the rest of the Japanese navy had been unable to do for three and a half years—put the *Enterprise* definitely out of action. The carrier crew saw the Japanese plane coming and let loose a heavy volume of antiaircraft fire but the plane kept coming and went down the forward elevator shaft, where the pilot loosed his heavy bombs. Calling cards found on his body showed that he was Chief Pilot Tomi Zai. The explosion started fires but the efficient damage-control group quickly checked them. Admiral Mitscher shifted his flag to another carrier and the *Enterprise* made her way across the Pacific to Ulithi, Pearl Harbor, and Puget Sound. She later received welcoming honors in New York and also from the British at Southampton. She made two voyages returning troops from Europe, then was laid up in "mothballs" for 10 years at Bayonne, New Jersey. Vigorous efforts to raise enough funds to preserve her as an historic relic failed; she was broken up by shipbreakers in 1959. Her name, however, lasted on with great distinction on the navy's first huge nuclear carrier.

(See C. G. Reynolds, *The Fast Carriers: The Forging of an Air Navy*, 1968.)

Fort Stikene

The *Fort Stikene*, a munitions and cargo freighter. (*U.S. Coast Guard*)

Munition-laden ships presented a serious port problem in both world wars and resulted in two particularly disastrous explosions. In November 1917 the cargo of the French freighter *Mont Blanc* devastated a considerable section of the port of Halifax, and in April 1944 the British freighter *Fort Stikene* caused similar destruction when her cargo exploded at Bombay.

The 7142-ton *Fort Stikene* had been built at Prince Rupert, British Columbia, as part of Canada's ambitious program of "Fort" freighters. Launched in April 1942 and hailing from London, she was chartered to the British Ministry of War Transport. On April 13, 1944, she arrived at Bombay from Karachi and was berthed in the Victoria dock. Her cargo included dried fish on top of baled cotton, and ammunition, with 300 tons of trinitrotoluene (TNT) in her 'tween decks. Normally the ammunition would have been removed first, but with the tendency in wartime to take chances whether necessary or not, this precaution was not observed. As baled cotton makes one of the most dangerous of shipboard fires, this situation was highly risky. The vessel was not even flying the usual red explosives flag at her masthead.

Fire was discovered in the No. 2 hold just after luncheon on April 14. The crew used hose lines, but for 40 minutes the Bombay Fire Brigade was not notified that a cargo of explosives was on fire. The colonel in charge of port fire-fighting operations faced a grave dilemma. He might order the *Fort Stikene* towed to sea and sunk, but that involved risk in the tortuous passage out of port. He decided to leave it to the fire brigade. An ordnance officer suggested that the vessel be scuttled where she lay but the master refused to accept responsibility; two of the top naval officers had such authority but were not consulted.

About 4 o'clock the TNT cases started to burn and the *Fort Stikene* blew up with a terrific explosion which created havoc over a large area.

Every one of the 40 Indian firemen was killed and the only trace of them ever found was their steel helmets. Great quantities of debris and burning cotton set fire to warehouses, dock buildings, and other ships in the harbor. The *Fort Stikene*'s boiler was found a half mile away. A huge tidal wave crossed the dock, tore vessels from their moorings, and smashed them against the quays. A 5000-ton coaster actually landed on top of a low warehouse building. A second great explosion, a half hour later, caused further serious damage. The entire poop deck of the 3935-ton freighter *Jalapadama*, lying alongside the *Fort Stikene*, was blown over buildings 40 feet high to land 200 yards away in the main road outside the docks. The whole dock area and some 25 ships were all afire. Though the army was called out, it was four days before the last major fire was out, and two weeks more before smaller fires smoldering in the warehouse ruins were extinguished.

The casualties amounted to 231 killed and 476 injured among the services, the fire brigade, and the dock employees. In addition, some 500 civilians were killed and 2408 injured. Twelve ships, totaling about 50,000 tons, were sunk and another 12 ships were damaged. Naturally, that was a serious blow to the Allied logistics in the area.

(See F. Rushbrook, *Fire Aboard: The Problems of Prevention and Control in Ships and Port Installations*, 1961.)

Yamato

In World War II the Japanese had the two largest battleships with the largest guns in history, but they failed to effectively use the *Yamato* and *Musashi*. There was almost no firing of their huge 18.1-inch guns, and both were sunk by aerial bombs. When the naval powers began rebuilding their fleets in the late 1930s, after the long treaty truce, the Americans and British started at about 34,000 tons whereas the Germans went up to 41,000. The Japanese, however, almost doubled the tonnage at 72,000. As against the maximum 15-inch or 16-inch gun of the Western powers, the Japanese had 18.1-inch guns.

In 1937 the Japanese started planning for three giant battleships—the *Yamato* and *Musashi* were virtual twins in construction; the *Shimano*, however, was converted to a carrier after the Japanese carrier losses at Midway and she was quickly sunk by torpedo. The ships were built with great secrecy—high walls were put up about the *Yamato* at Kure and the *Musashi* at Sasebo. The *Yamato* was completed in December 1941, the month of Pearl Harbor. Her big guns fired 3200-pound projectiles with a range of 22½ miles. (The 16-inch shells of the other navies weighed 2700 pounds.) The *Yamato's* four turbines generated 150,000 horsepower with a speed of 27 knots. She had a complement of 2767 officers and men. The statistics for the *Musashi* were virtually identical.

Considering the partly successful raiding of the *Bismarck,* the record of the giant Japanese sisters seemed strangely futile. Together, they composed a division and were on hand in the big actions such as Midway and Philippine Sea but did not participate in the shooting—they were simply an impressive "fleet in being."

This seeming invulnerability was punctured in the great Battle of Leyte Gulf in October 1944 when the *Musashi* met her end; the *Yamato,* however, played a strange role on her own. They were in Admiral Kurita's central force headed for Leyte Gulf, when American aviators caught them out in the Sibuyan Sea, with virtually no adequate air cover. The *Musashi* absorbed more than a dozen aerial hits plus 10 torpedo hits and suddenly rolled over with heavy loss of life.

Then came what Samuel Morison has called the most remarkable action of the Pacific war. Both sides made a serious mistake, but the Americans had enough force so that they could afford it. The American mistake, which one writer named "Bull's Run," was Admiral Halsey's being lured off by the northern decoy force, taking carriers and the big battleships and leaving Leyte Gulf itself stripped to the very light defense of escort carriers and destroyers. This ploy seemed to leave Leyte wide open for Kurita's main force, including the mighty *Yamato,* to close in on the apparently undefended area. It was guarded only by a few escort carriers and destroyers, some of which were feeling the effects of the very few blows that the *Yamato's* monster guns fired. Inexplicably, when the American position seemed desperate, Kurita moved the *Yamato* and the rest of his force back through the San Bernardino Strait.

The *Yamato* had one further strange role to play, and it would be her final one. In the last months of the war with their resources, especially oil, dwindling, the Japanese evolved a practice that was probably uniquely their own: this was the "kamikaze," or suicidal, attack in which a flier went out, with no return gasoline, to crash down on an American warship off Ikinawa. In April 1945 the *Yamato* became involved in a seaborne kamikaze-type attack to lure the Americans off on the day of the major kamikaze attack on Okinawa. Just what the Japanese expected to gain from this sacrificing of their great warship was hard to tell—going out without air cover, there was no chance of success. She emerged from the Inland Sea and was soon spotted by American aviators who trailed her. For two hours during the afternoon the *Yamato* succumbed to the incessant air attacks. A surviving ensign told of the deck slanting at a 35° angle, with the staff officers tumbled into a pile. They extricated themselves and saluted the admiral; everyone stood in somber silence and then the admiral went into his cabin to try to save the picture of the emperor. Of the 2767 aboard, only 23 officers and 246 men survived.

Missouri

Fleet Admiral Chester W. Nimitz signing peace terms after the surrender of Japan aboard the *Missouri*. (Naval Historical Center)

The *Missouri* was the most distinctive of the four last American battleships built during World War II. After a long "naval holiday" following the Washington Disarmament Conference in 1922, the United States and Britain began building new battleships in the late 1930s. The *North Carolina, Washington,* and others joined the fleet, but they had one serious shortcoming. With the sudden revolution in tactical roles, the battleships, fighting in line-ahead formation, were no longer the major embodiment of naval fighting strength. They were replaced by the "fast carrier task force," composed of one or more carriers whose planes could project their hitting force far beyond the 20 miles of a naval gun. But against that extra offensive force, the carrier itself was vulnerable to attack. In contrast with the battleship, whose heavy armor enabled her to withstand the same sort of blow she dealt out, the carrier lacked the armor and guns and, moreover, was loaded with highly flammable aviation gas. Consequently, it was necessary to protect the carrier with a screen of destroyers and cruisers, all of which could keep up with the 33-knot speed of the carriers.

But even the newer World War II battleships were capable of only some 28 knots, which was too slow for the screen. Not until 1943–1944 did the fleet have battleships fast enough to protect the carriers. At that time four new ships appeared: the *Iowa, New Jersey, Wisconsin,* and *Missouri.* They had virtually the same armor and 16-inch guns of the earlier World War II battleships; the one basic difference was their 33-knot, instead of 28-knot, speed, which required enlarging their tonnage from 35,000 to 45,000. Their new role meant a diminution in status— rather than being units of maximum power, they were now auxiliaries to the new carriers. Instead of a Jutland line-ahead role, their major functions were to ward off attacks on the carriers and to engage in shore bombardment.

The *Missouri,* laid down on January 6, 1941, at New York Navy Yard (renamed Naval Shipyard), was not launched until January 29, 1944, and was commissioned in June—the last battleship completed by the navy. Despite the slow start, she had two roles of high distinction: the treaty ending the war with Japan on V-J Day was signed on her deck in Tokyo Bay, and she engaged in a spectacular play of "showing the flag" to support Turkey against Soviet threats. She also avoided the ignominy of her 45,000-ton sister ships in the so-called "Bull's Run," where Admiral Halsey used their costly 33-knot speed to carry them away from Leyte Gulf where they were sorely needed.

The *Missouri's* active Pacific career lasted only seven months. She had trials off New York and later transited the Panama Canal, arriving at San Francisco, whence she sailed for active duty in mid-December, arriving at Ulithi in the Carolines in January. A month later she was part of the screen of the carrier *Lexington* in Admiral Mitscher's Task Force 38, which launched the first air strikes against Tokyo since the initial Doolittle raid in 1942. From that time on, her service consisted of supporting several more such raids, plus effective heavy short bombardment off Iwo Jima and Okinawa.

The *Missouri's* really distinctive claim to fame came with the cessation of hostilities. There has been speculation whether these distinguished engagements were due to her being named for President Truman's home state—incidentally, his daughter Margaret had christened her. The handling of Japan's surrender, which the Americans felt they had earned the right to conduct alone, contrasted sharply with the termination of hostilities with Germany, cluttered up with rival claims of the United States, Britain, the Soviet Union, and even France. The *Missouri* ceremonies were the special province of two American leaders: Fleet Admiral Chester W. Nimitz, Commander in Chief, Pacific Fleet and Pacific Ocean Areas, and General of the Armies Douglas MacArthur, Supreme Commander of the Allies. The third principal participator was Japanese Foreign Minister Mamoru Shigemitsu. The ceremonies lasted only 23 minutes. The next day the *Missouri* started for home by way of Guam and Pearl Harbor.

The *Missouri*'s next important assignment came eight months later, on March 21, 1946. As the postwar international setup became manifest, it was clear that two major powers—the United States and the Soviet Union—were far ahead of all others, and a few Americans were beginning to be concerned about the threat of Soviet expansion. In particular, the Soviets seemed to be threatening Turkey and Greece, after already overrunning central Europe. Someone in the State Department suggested that now was an admirable opportunity to "show the flag." The Turkish ambassador at Washington had just died, so it was decided to send his body home in the *Missouri,* fresh from her honors in Tokyo Bay. When she sailed up through the Dardanelles and Bosporus, the Turks went wild with joy at this tangible demonstration of American friendship, and the Soviets also got the point. In April 1946 the same enthusiastic reception occurred at Piraeus, the port of Athens. This goodwill was followed shortly by the creation of the American Sixth Fleet in the Mediterranean: a force of carriers, cruisers, and destroyers, which ever since has shown the flag from port to port, ready, as the old phrase went, "for a fight or a frolic." This show of force and friendship was quite effective. The Truman Doctrine, which backed up threatened governments, was part of this support project.

The *Missouri* took President Truman to Rio de Janeiro for the Inter-American Conference on Hemisphere Peace and Security, with the signing of a treaty broadening the Monroe Doctrine assurances. In 1950 the *Missouri* encountered her one major embarrassment by grounding firmly on a mudbank in Hampton Roads—the captain was criticized for publicly blaming his navigating officer. After two weeks she was floated with the help of pontoons, just as the army at Fort Monroe was ready with a placard stating, "The battleship is here to stay."

In 1950 and 1951, the *Missouri* participated in Korean actions—partly with gunfire bombardments and partly in carrier protection. Late in 1950 she provided gunfire support to cover the retreat of the 3rd Infantry to the sea. For her remaining active years, she had varied duties until she was decommissioned at Puget Sound Naval Shipyard in Washington, where the "Mighty Mo" continued to receive thousands of admiring visitors.

(See R. A. Hough, *Dreadnought: A History of the Modern Battleship*, 1964.)

Kon Tiki

Certainly the most unconventional vessel in this collection of famous ships was the raft *Kon Tiki*, in which six young men drifted across the Pacific 4000 miles from Peru to Tahiti in 1947. The purpose was to demonstrate that the Polynesians of Tahiti could have made such a voyage 1500 years earlier. The exploit caught worldwide attention—the memoirs went through many editions and the vogue went so far that South Sea restaurants still bear the raft's name.

The idea originated with Thor Heyerdahl, a Norwegian anthropologist and geographer, born in 1914. During his graduate work at the University of Oslo, he spent some time studying in the Marquesas Islands. He became intrigued with the three outstanding Polynesian peoples—far advanced over the other Pacific islanders—who had reached Tahiti, Hawaii, and New Zealand. He absorbed the Polynesian legends and became particularly interested in the story of Kon Tiki, a leader defeated in his Peruvian homeland who had sailed away by raft into the far Pacific.

Heyerdahl decided to test whether or not a primitive raft could perform such a voyage. He managed to secure both official and unofficial support, albeit with much skepticism. He enlisted five men as colleagues and then built a raft on the old model, that is, without nails, spikes, wire cable, or other modern elements. The basis of the raft consisted of five big logs of balsam (the lightest of woods) brought down from Ecuador and laid side by side, fastened with rope. She had one large square sail and was steered with a heavy oar, at which the crew stood two-hour shifts. A cabin was built for shelter. Altogether, the raft was 30 feet square, with the central log extending at bow and stern. The whole project was based on being carried along by wind and current, which were expected to give steady support. Steering could bring only a minimal change of course—the *Kon Tiki* was a clumsy but stable craft, even when waves swept over her. On the two-hour night shifts, the helmsman tied a rope around his waist to prevent being swept overboard, since there was no railing.

The 100-day voyage started from Callao on April 27, 1947, with a proper, if skeptical, official send-off. The *Kon Tiki* was christened with coconut milk and put to sea, flying the Norwegian flag, towed by a navy tug—the last artificial power on the long voyage. At the outset the raft was under the influence of the cold, northbound Humboldt Current, which carried her parallel to the coast. The voyagers feared that they might not clear the Galapagos Islands, but before long the South Equatorial Current took over; coupled with the southeast trade winds, the raft had a steady push to the westward. "The *Kon Tiki*," according to the highly readable account of the passage, "did not plow through the sea like a sharp-prowed racing craft. Blunt and broad, heavy and solid, she splashed sedately forward over the waves. She did not hurry, but when she had once got going she pushed ahead with unshakeable energy."

The principal item of interest during the long passage was the almost constant contact with fish. Every morning there were numerous flying fish, useful as bait to attract larger fish. There were dolphins, bonito, and squid, and frequent adventures with sharks, including an ugly-visaged whale shark.

In the course of the voyage the men became concerned about a landfall, as most of the Pacific Islands were ringed with high coral reefs, and the clumsy craft could not easily navigate the narrow openings. The first landfall came on the ninety-seventh day, off Anagatau in the Tuamotu Archipelago. Friendly natives came out by canoe and one of the crew went ashore, but it clearly was not feasible to try to bring the raft inside the reef, so they moved on to a more trying experience. Ahead of them, for mile after mile, stretched the perilous Raroia reef, surrounding a huge lagoon. They realized, on the one-hundredth day out, that they were drifting toward certain shipwreck. When they were finally driven against the reef, they managed time and again to hang on, and eventually to get over into the quiet lagoon. They established themselves on an island and with the radio—one of the few concessions to modernity aboard—they got word to the outside. Help came first from natives on the other side of the lagoon and then from the colonial headquarters. A schooner towed the battered but still fairly intact craft to safety. There was extensive joyous wining and dining first by the lagoon natives and then by the Tahitians. The voyagers took their time going home; they stopped in Washington and were received by President Truman.

Summing up his feelings on the whole affair, Heyerdahl wrote: "My migration theory, as such, was not necessarily proved by the successful outcome of the *Kon Tiki* expedition. What we did prove was that the South American balsa raft possesses qualities not previously known to scientists of our time. . . ."

United States

The liner *United States*, a blue-riband winner in the 1950s. *(Mystic Seaport)*

The American liner *United States* became the fastest merchant vessel in the world, but she came on the scene when fast ships were giving way to fast aircraft. Six years before she was launched in 1951, transatlantic air service had started and by 1958 several-hour jet service was a deadly blow to the liners. On top of that, the American-flag liners were under the handicap of very high wages imposed by the maritime unions. The extra speed had been called for by the navy which hoped to use her as a troop transport; as a result, the government paid more than half of her $80,000,000 cost, but she was never used by the navy, not even for Vietnam.

Designed by William Francis Gibbs, she was regarded as his masterpiece and he superintended every detail with loving care. She was built in a drydock by the prestigious Newport News Drydock and Shipbuilding Company. Laid down in 1950, she was floated out of dock in 1952 and immediately showed her superlative speed, restoring to the United States the blue riband which had not been held by an American ship since the Collins Line's *Baltic* a century earlier. At 53,000 tons, she was much smaller than the Cunard "Queens."

She served on the New York, Le Havre, Southampton run, alternating with the 26,000-ton *America*. On her maiden voyage in 1952 she cut the crossing time to three days, 10 hours, and 40 minutes at an average speed of 35.59 knots, with a highest daily average of 36.31 knots. She cut the previous blue-riband eastbound record of the *Queen Mary* by 3.9 knots and the westbound by 3.5 knots, the largest margin in the blue-riband records. As time went on and plane speeds increased, there was no point in trying to equal or beat the blue-riband records.

408

In view of her prospective naval transport service, carrying 14,000 troops at a time as compared with 15,000 for the "Queens," she was built with numerous special defense features. For protection against fire, the only wood in her whole construction was the butcher's block. To reduce weight, aluminum was used instead of steel wherever stresses were not too great.

She had passenger accommodations for 871 first class, 508 cabin, and 549 tourist. During her first two years she carried 139,000 passengers, and during her whole career, more than 1,000,000.

In 1969 she was laid up in "mothballs," tied up at a dock in Newport News, near her birthplace. Numerous suggestions were made as to useful disposal, but on the two occasions of a call for bids, nothing suitable resulted.

(See F. O. Braynard, *By Their Works Ye Shall Know Them: The Life and Ships of William Francis Gibbs, 1886–1967,* 1968.)

Andrea Doria

The *Andrea Doria,* sinking after colliding with the *Stockholm,* July 26, 1956, south of Nantucket Lightship. *(U.S. Naval Institute)*

In July 1956 the maritime world was amazed and shocked by a collision near the Nantucket shoals on the main approach to New York. The Swedish-American liner *Stockholm* rammed and sank the Italian liner *Andrea Doria*—the first time that two major passenger liners had ever collided. There were several surprising aspects to the accident. Both ships were relatively new, embodying the 1948 international safety features. Both ships had sighted each other by radar but did not give way in time. The blame was even enough so that each side agreed not to sue the other.

The Italian ship was the larger and more distinguished of the two, the pride of Italy's new fleet of crack liners named for famous Italians from Caesar to Cavour with special emphasis on the Renaissance period, including not only the great artists but also Andrea Doria, Genoa's outstanding naval commander. Backed with generous government subsidies, they were built by the Ansalso yard near Genoa, the headquarters of the Italian Line. In addition to luxurious equipment, the *Andrea Doria* carried a magnificent collection of art.

The *Stockholm* was somewhat older and less impressive, overshadowed by the succession of Swedish-American's well-run *Gripsholm* and *Kungsholm*. She was built in 1948 and, like the *Doria,* was engaged at that time in transatlantic passenger service. A few years later, with the advent of jet planes, ocean liners would spend part if not all their time cruising.

	Andrea Doria	*Stockholm*
Owners	Italian Line	Swedish-American Line
Built	1952	1948
Tons	29,100	12,165
Horsepower	35,000	14,600
Speed, knots	23	19
Passengers	1134	548
Run	Genoa, Naples, New York	New York, Copenhagen, Gothenburg

At 8 P.M. on July 25, the four officers who would be on the respective bridges at the time of crucial decision came on duty for the 8 to 12 watch. There were three on the *Doria:* the veteran Captain Piero Calami, who always stayed on the bridge at critical times, and two other officers. The *Stockholm* was in full charge of the 26-year-old Third Officer, Ernst Carstens-Johannsen. Captain Gunnar Nordensen had turned in, with orders to call him if anything special occurred. The ships were in the vicinity of Nantucket Lightship, marking the edge of the shoals running back 50 miles to Nantucket Island—it was a point which all transatlantic shipping had to pass. The little red lightship was something of a nerve-wracking post for its crew, knowing that liners were speeding down on its beam, often in the fog, to turn aside just in time—if a liner failed to do so, the lightship would go down with all hands. Coming in from the sea, the *Doria* passed the lightship at 10:20 without seeing it in the heavy fog.

Aside from the events leading to collision, there were two circumstances of culpable responsibility. The regulations stipulated that in fog

a ship should slow down so that it could stop within half the range of
visibility. Instead, both ships were going at virtual full speed—the fog
was not nearly as thick on the *Stockholm*'s approach but it did obstruct
seeing the other ship. In addition, the Swedish-American line made a
practice of using the westbound lane instead of the eastbound. Use of
the wrong lane was admitted reluctantly in the hearings. To avoid the
danger of head-on collisions, many of the leading shipping lines had
agreed for years to follow the separate eastbound and westbound lanes,
about 20 miles apart. This was not mandatory, however, and Swedish-
American followed the inside, westbound lane because it saved time en
route to Scandinavia.

Observance of separate eastbound and westbound lanes was
optional, but observance of the basic Rules of the Road was not.
Normally, passing ships, like automobiles, kept to the right, or "left to
left" as the phrase went. If circumstances made it desirable to turn left
for a "right to right" passing, ample notice was to be given. It was the
violation of that rule, more than anything else, that brought the two
ships together. Each ship finally saw the distant pip denoting a passing
vessel, but there was no telling just where it was headed or how fast it
was going. To answer those questions, the *Stockholm* had a plastic
maneuvering board on which the pip was noted at intervals to indicate
speed and direction. On the *Doria* the officers did not bother with the
board—it was shut away in a drawer. The ships were quite close before
the fog lifted enough for them to come into view.

With the two ships almost on a collision course, Carstens-Johannsen
made arrangements for a conventional left-to-left passing. Captain
Calami made the unfortunate decision for a right-to-right passing
toward the open sea. "Four degrees to the left and nothing to the right,"
he told the helmsman. The *Stockholm*'s lights appeared and she tried to
swing further to the left, which was right into the *Doria*'s path.

At 11:20 the *Stockholm* crashed into the *Doria* on her starboard side
just below the signal bridge. The bow of the white Swedish ship
punched a great hole in the *Doria*, 40 feet wide and tapering toward the
bottom. The bow had been reinforced with heavy steel for passage
through ice. The builders of the *Doria* had counted on not more than 15°
list, but with water rushing in it was quickly 20° and then almost 30°.
This meant that the decks were at a very sharp angle and that, as on the
Lusitania, the lifeboats on the port side could not be used.

Most of the 50 casualties were in the forward starboard staterooms all
the way from the deluxe topside suites down to the tourist rooms,
chiefly filled with Italian immigrants. Many of them were crushed in
their rooms and there were numerous harrowing stories, recounted in
Alvin Moscow's excellent account, along the line of Walter Lord's

mosaic in his *Titanic* story. There were relatively few injuries aboard the *Stockholm*, but a strange, almost unbelievable event occurred on her bow. Responding to a girl's cry, a sailor found 14-year-old Linda Morgan, who had been carried to the smashed bow of the *Stockholm* from her wrecked stateroom on the *Doria*, where her father and sister were killed. There was general bewilderment but no real panic. The behavior of the officers and crew was on the whole excellent, but when the *Doria*'s first few boats reached the *Stockholm*, the Swedish sailors were disgusted to see mess attendants and other nonsailor types from the steward's department.

The *Stockholm* had pulled out of the *Doria*'s side, with her bow crumpled back to the first bulkhead, but apparently in no danger. There were two main problems on the *Doria*: first, how long she would stay afloat and second, with the port lifeboats unavailable, how the passengers and crew could be gotten off. The lifeboats of the two ships were nowhere near enough. An SOS was sent out; the Coast Guard's well-organized Sea and Air Rescue Coordination Center in New York did excellent work in arranging aid—first a United Fruit freighter, then two army transports, a tanker, and a swarm of Coast Guard cutters. Most welcome and helpful of all was the giant aging *Ile de France* of the French Line, commanded by a gracious French count. She had left New York that noon, along with the *Stockholm,* and had quickly drawn ahead of her; she now turned back. Her 11 lifeboats, along with those from the other ships, got nearly everyone off. Captain Calami wanted to go down with his ship, but his staff captain virtually carried him into the lifeboat. They drew away from the *Doria* just as the sun was rising on the stricken ship. She stayed afloat until 10 A.M., 11 hours after the collision.

Both companies wanted to have the question of responsibility, with its financial implications, settled as soon as possible. A searching inquiry quickly got under way in the Federal District Court in New York. Millions of dollars were at stake and the admiralty lawyers undoubtedly made a handsome profit. The Italian Line suggested splitting the cost of the multimillion dollar *Doria,* but one of the counsel for the Swedish Line, after studying the reports on stability, brought out a point which let his line off easy. It was claimed that if the tanks, which had held some 4000 tons of oil and fresh water, had been refilled with salt water, as they should have been, the *Doria* would probably have retained her stability. Draining and cleaning the oil tanks was an expensive and time-consuming chore, however, so the *Doria* evaded the regulation.

Before the *Doria*'s engineers could testify, the case was settled out of court. The Italian Line and its insurers agreed to pay for the $30,000,000

Doria, and the Swedish Line for the *Stockholm*'s $1,000,000 new bow and a similar amount for her lost voyage. Both lines dodged the private claims for loss of life and property, which might have totaled $100 million or more, taking advantage of the minimum amount, in absence of proven negligence, of some $6,000,000 to be paid jointly by the two lines. Captain Calami, aged and upset by the experience, did not go to sea again, but Captain Nordensen and Carstens-Johannsen, now promoted, went to sea on the line's new *Gripsholm*.

Twenty years after the collision, the matter came prominently to life through the initiative of Peter Gimbel, one of the heirs of the department-store fortune. He had always been interested in diving—in fact he had dived down to the *Doria* wreck the day after the collision. He had maintained a continued interest in the whole affair, particularly in why she sank so quickly. He had picked up a rumor that in addition to the two forward compartments, a third one, the main generator room, had also been flooded by the absence of a connecting door.

Early in 1976 the *Doria* was again prominent news due to a television documentary that Gimbel directed in cooperation with the actress Elga Andersen. Dozens of descents, some of them by Gimbel himself, produced pictures in color with vivid clarity, showing fish swimming around the encrusted hull. The condition of the bulkhead prevented locating the missing door, but Gimbel announced his intention to go ahead with the quest, including a trip to Italy to interview some of the old engine room force of the unfortunate liner.

(See A. Moscow, *Collision Course*, 1960.)

Nautilus

The *Nautilus*, being launched at Groton, Connecticut, January 21, 1954. *(National Archives)*

The Nautilus had a double distinction. She was the first of all nuclear-powered submarines as well as the first to brave her way under the polar ice cap from the Pacific to the Atlantic by way of the North Pole. She was laid down in 1952 at the Electric Boat Company yard at Groton, opposite New London, Connecticut, and President Truman spoke at the ceremony. She was launched January 21, 1954, and commissioned September 30, 1954. Under Captain Eugene P. Wilkinson, she first put to sea on January 13, 1955, reporting, as she pulled out, "under way on nuclear power."

That was a momentous first in the Navy's history; once started, the nuclear power program developed quickly. Using a reactor the size of a melon in place of tens of thousands of tons of diesel fuel, the atomic submarine could travel thousands of miles, submerged if necessary, without a refill. Tactically, also, such a submarine was at a great advantage over its conventionally powered predecessors, which had to surface, sometimes in vulnerable positions, to recharge their storage batteries. With surface vessels, nuclear power was not as essential—it gave certain advantages but there was little that the nuclear-powered surface vessel could do that other vessels could not. As a result, in the two decades after the *Nautilus* debut, while the submarines had gone almost completely atomic, the Navy had built only three atomic carriers, one atomic cruiser, and one atomic frigate, along with numerous conventional types.

414   In its conception and overall direction, the atomic power program

was essentially a one-man affair, and that one man, Captain (later Admiral) Hyman Rickover, maintained a jealous proprietary interest in it. He was an "engineering duty only" officer in the Bureau of Ships—a category of scientific specialists not in line for command—specializing in shipboard electrical equipment. At the close of World War II, he conceived the idea of harnessing nuclear power, already demonstrated in the atomic bomb, into propulsive power for submarines, a problem calling for extreme compression. That innovation demonstrated only some of his unusual attributes: He was a superb technician and, essential in the Washington setup, a masterly aggressive "operator," making himself generally unpopular among naval officers. He had a cantankerous disposition and more than once the very proper selection boards turned him down for retention or promotion, but outside civilian backers were able to offset that. Although there was lack of both sympathy and support for a while, both came at last from Admiral Chester W. Nimitz, Chief of Naval Operations, who ordered the establishing of a Naval Reactor Branch with Rickover at its head. Then, since the Atomic Energy Commission also had a voice in the matter, Rickover secured the creation of their Atomic Reactor Branch, which he also headed; from then on power was well concentrated in his hands. For the experimental development of the first submarine, he established a prototype setup in the desert at Arco, Idaho, with a full-dress model on which crews could be trained. (There would later be a second one at West Minot, N.Y.) Out of that the original *Nautilus* came. Rickover, in civilian dress, energetically moved from place to place, keeping a close eye on everything and even insisting on selecting the officers.

During her first two years, under Captain Wilkinson, the *Nautilus* underwent numerous tests and visited many places. Among other things, she traveled 1381 miles and was submerged for 89.9 hours on her shakedown cruise. By the time her new challenging task came, she had traveled 110,000 miles, with only one reactor refill.

In 1956, Commander William R. Anderson, after the usual scrutiny by Admiral Rickover, was transferred to the Naval Reactor Branch to prepare for the challenging command of a cruise under the polar ice cap. Like some of her other cruises, this was a top secret matter, and the Navy went to all lengths to keep it so. In addition to the ultimate publicity value of a successful experiment, the Navy would not want to admit failure in the event of an unsuccessful one. In the case of the Arctic, moreover, it was essential to keep the plans from the Russians, who might have closed in on the lone ship near their Siberian waters. An additional Arctic hazard was the danger of being trapped in the ice unless there was ample clearance over the bulky "sail" on top and the keel far below.

As it was, the *Nautilus* experiment lasted more than two years, with a midway trial run north of Greenland in 1957, and the full Pacific–Atlantic–North Pole run in 1958. Several scientists with especially pertinent experience went along on each cruise. The 1957 cruise started from New London (Groton) on August 19, 1957. A smaller conventional submarine went along to be a helpful "buddy ship" for the first part of the way. The *Nautilus* made her way up through the Atlantic north of Iceland and on September 1 pushed her way under the ice cap. She damaged both periscopes under the ice and had trouble with the gyrocompass, but competent technicians aboard made the necessary repairs. She came within 180 miles of the North Pole, then turned eastward to head for her arranged destination in England. She had gone 60,000 miles submerged; it was pointed out that this equalled the *Twenty Thousand Leagues under the Sea* which Jules Verne had written about his fictional submarine *Nautilus*.

Back home, Commander Anderson was called down to Washington, where he had conferences at the Pentagon and a talk with the President's naval aide, who was greatly interested in the matter of polar exploration. Before long, Admiral Arleigh Burke, the Chief of Naval Operations, and President Eisenhower himself were supporting a top secret proposal for a run from the Bering Sea over the top of the world to England. Again keeping spouses, crew, and almost everyone else in darkness as to plans, the *Nautilus* left London for Panama and the West Coast on April 25, 1958. Panama was used as a blind more than once—social invitations were accepted there and the crew made purchases on the outward transit to be picked up when they got back.

The trip fell into two parts—a June start that had to fall back because of shallow water, then the main run from Hawaii to Portland, England, from July 23 to August 12. It was realized that there might be difficulty on the Bering side until the full summer thaw. Given a choice of which side of the St. Lawrence Island to use on the approach to the strait, they used the western Siberian side first, despite the danger of observation by the Russians. Finding it to be blocked by ice, they turned back and tried the eastern Alaska side. The ship made its way fairly easily through the Bering Strait, then faced near-disaster in the large, shallow Chukchi Sea, which lay across the approach to the Arctic Ocean. On June 17, eight days out from Seattle, the captain was called to the control room and shown that the ship had sailed under 63 feet of ice. There was only eight feet clearance above the ocean floor. Then came a huge chunk of ice that was cleared by only five feet! The inevitable consequences would be severe damage to the ship—perhaps even slow death for those on board.

The *Nautilus* managed to escape from that trap, but prospects of more such danger lay ahead in that shallow sea. With great reluctance, possible to proceed. Word came back to head for Pearl Harbor and perhaps try again when warmer weather might have melted some ice. Elaborate deceptive devices preserved secrecy by creating the impression that the real object was Panama. The submarine received a warm reception, with "Anchors Aweigh" and dancing girls. Anderson and a few other ship members went to Washington. Four weeks later the ice cap cruise was resumed, but during the elapsed time the crew did not leak the facts. The navigator, disguised as a Pentagon staff officer, made a series of observational flights over the Chukchi Sea to determine when it would be feasible to try again.

The *Nautilus* left Pearl Harbor on July 23, and all went well. With the turbines purring along at 20 knots or so, it was hard to believe that they were in the same water which had been so troublesome two months earlier. The whole ship was quite comfortable. With the small reactor replacing the thousands of tons of diesel oil, a roominess now existed which was impossible in earlier submarines. Life was very pleasant aboard ship with good, hot meals, movies, music, and even a ship's newspaper. The only equipment that did not work properly was the garbage disposal, which was soon fixed.

After traversing the Chukchi Sea and rounding Point Barrow, they entered the Barrow Deep Sea Valley with a good approach to the northward. The climax came on August 3, 1958, at 11:15 P.M. On reaching 90°N latitude, the *Nautilus* would be at the North Pole. There was a general air of excitement aboard ship. Commander Anderson, with his eye on the distance indicator, gave the countdown for the crew: 10 . . . 8 . . . 6 . . . 4 . . . 3 . . . 2 . . . 1 . . . MARK! It was a moment that no one aboard would ever forget. There was a brief silence followed by cheers from the crew, and then a special celebration. The fathometer showed the water depth to be 13,410 feet; there was, of course, solid ice overhead.

The rest of the cruise on the shorter distance to the Atlantic went quickly. Dodging occasional ice, they came down the east coast of Greenland, near where they had cruised the previous year. On August 7 they passed the nuclear submarine *Skate*, which was headed north. Then they went eastward to England, reaching Portland on August 12, nine days from the North Pole. They were welcomed enthusiastically in Portland; then they sped across the Atlantic to land at New York, where they were greeted with boat whistles and hose spray, and later a ticker tape parade up Broadway.

George Washington

During the so-called "Cold War" with the Soviet Union in the 1950s, grave concern was felt in the United States that, without warning, the enemy might start a war by a surprise bombing of the American land-based missile sites. But thanks to the ingenuity of two naval officers, the navy developed a potent deterrent. It might be possible to prevent such a Soviet attack by leaking information that if a surprise bombing should happen, hidden submarines could launch long-range missiles on Moscow, Leningrad, and other vital centers with disastrous effects.

To accomplish such a reprisal, the Polaris program called for 41 special submarines. They combined two vital features. One was the nuclear-powered submarine, developed by Captain (later Admiral) Hyman George Rickover, which had already demonstrated its capabilities with the *Nautilus* in 1958. The other feature was the Polaris inter-continental ballistic missile developed by Rear Admiral William F. Rayburn. The plan was that the submarine, with 16 Polaris missiles aboard, would lie hidden on the sea bottom, with her missiles aimed at Moscow and the other vital centers, ready to let fly if word came of a Soviet attack.

The first of the 41 Polaris submarines was the *George Washington,* built by the Electric Boat Company at Groton, Connecticut, just across the river from New London and just below the navy's big submarine base. Using the hull of a submarine already under construction, a

midship section of 130 feet was added for the missiles. The *George*
Washington was launched on June 9, 1959, and was commissioned on
December 30, 1959. The abbreviation SSBN stood for Submarine Ballis-
tic/Missile Nuclear.

Special arrangements were made for the crews, partly because of the
unpleasantness of lying on the bottom for two months without sending
out any communications. Unique in the navy was the system of two
whole crews—the Blue and the Gold—complete from commanding
officer down to the ordinary enlisted man. They would alternate every
six months, taking over the whole ship. While one crew was on cruise,
the other was whisked back to Groton by air for rest and recreation and
further training. They were a handpicked lot—each man had a technical
specialty and equally important, a stable nervous system—there was no
room for neurotics during those weeks on the bottom. The subs were
normally based at Holy Loch, just below Glasgow in Scotland or at Rota
on the beautiful bay of Cadiz in southern Spain. Occasionally, there
were operations from Charleston, South Carolina.

The first Polaris missile made a practice flight on July 20, 1960, after
leaving Cape Canaveral for the 1100-mile target range. The commanding officer sent the joyously triumphant report: "Polaris, from out of the
deep to target. Perfect." The program moved on steadily, with a constant record of success. The Polaris subs were strictly a "silent service,"
and Soviet curiosity was not gratified as to their resting places.

The 41 subs were named mostly for American presidents and prominent statesmen, but there were a few gracious additions such as *Simon
Bolivar*, named for the Latin American liberator, and *George Washington
Carver*, named for the black scientist. Eventually, the program was
expanded for the more effective Poseidon weapons.

Triton

The *Triton*'s claim to fame was that in 1960 she made the first submerged circumnavigation of the world. Like the voyage under the North Pole in 1958 by the *Nautilus* and the firing of the first Polaris missile by the *George Washington,* this was one of the spectacular achievements of the new nuclear-powered submarines, accomplishing what would not have been possible for the older conventional submarines.

Like the *Nautilus* and the *George Washington,* the *Triton* was a product of the Electric Boat Company at Groton, opposite New London, Connecticut, a short distance down the Thames River (locally pronounced to rhyme with dames) from the great submarine base. Launched on August 19, 1958, she was by far the largest submarine to date, displacing some 6000 tons on the surface and some 8000 tons submerged. She was so large that part of her had to be cut away and assembled later to clear the launching obstructions. She was unique in having two separate reactors and engines, each operating a propeller. She was formally commissioned, after trials, in November 1959.

The *Triton* was starting off with an unusually competent handpicked crew, which had had ample opportunity to become acquainted with each other and with the submarine aboard the prototype at West Minot, New York. The prospective commanding officer, Commander Edward Beach, possessed an unusual combination of qualities. He had a thorough knowledge of the sophisticated aspects of the mechanism of a supersubmarine—a know-how that would show when, on cruise, he had to make final decisions on many intricate matters. In addition, as a "navy junior," he was well grounded in the traditions of the service and was qualified to express himself competently on the subject. Whereas **420** many British naval officers can write excellent accounts of their experiences, American officers usually have to resort to a ghost-writer. Beach had already written a factual account of American submarines in World War II, as well as a fictional version entitled *Run Silent, Run Deep*. He had also written a report of the Caribbean tidal wave that had swamped his father's armored cruiser. In addition to formal duties, he had served as White House naval aide to President Eisenhower. He had a good sense of humor and got on famously with his officers and enlisted men. All the officers were first rate and had been individually approved by Admiral Rickover. There was a very high proportion of ratings in specialized fields among the enlisted men—the account of how so many of them handled special emergency problems was most impressive. The submariners were an elite lot, and the *Triton*'s men were the cream of the crop. She was a happy ship and a most effective one.

Shortly after commissioning, Beach was summoned to Washington and asked if his ship was in proper condition. He allowed that it was and then came the question that took his breath away, "Could you take her around the world submerged?" Beach said that he could and plans got under way for the great circumnavigation. It became linked up with Magellan—later a bronze plaque in that explorer's honor was put ashore at Cadiz. As in the case of the *Nautilus* in the Arctic, a top secret classification was imposed on the project—even the wives were not told.

The *Triton* sailed from Groton on the Thames and some distance out of Montauk Point at the tip of Long Island, she submerged, not to surface again for three months. She headed for a small target just off the coast of Brazil, St. Peter's and St. Paul's Rocks, once a guano center with a lighthouse but now abandoned. The Rocks were important to the cruise because the circumnavigation proper started there and would return there 60 days later, coming up from the South Atlantic.

Despite the Magellan example, it was decided not to use the Straits of Magellan because that would give away the voyage to the Chileans. They therefore continued south for Cape Horn and ran into some of their most vexing problems. On one particular day, down near the Falkland Islands, the fathometer, which indicates the depth of water below the ship, went bad and despite tinkering was out of commission for the rest of the cruise. Then there was a scare that one of the reactors was in trouble; the engine was slowed down but an error in calculation was revealed as the trouble. The third crisis threatened the whole cruise. One of the enlisted men came down with a kidney stone which caused intense pain; treatment was beyond the scope of the ship's medical equipment and the illness might possibly be fatal. Beach was faced with a grave dilemma; if nothing was done, the patient might die; but if the *Triton* put into port the secrecy of the circumnavigation was blown. Beach hit upon a way out. He knew that the cruiser *Macon* was down in those waters as flagship of a task force, and he personally knew the admiral and the captain. A rendezvous off Montevideo was arranged. The *Triton*'s main hull remained below the surface (in order not to hurt the submerged story), and a boat came over from the cruiser and took off the patient, who recovered completely.

After doubling Cape Horn, the ship moved out into the Pacific for the long crossing to Guam. On approaching Hawaii, they had a lush luau with the traditional food and costumes. When off the longitude where the first *Triton* had gone down in World War II, a memorial service was held, including "taps." Almost the only other events were "baby-grams"—several wives had been pregnant when the *Triton* left home and birth announcements came through naval channels. In the Philippines where Magellan had met his death, ceremonies were held.

It had been planned that the *Triton* would make other special studies along the line. Despite the loss of the fathometer, observations were made of special irregularities along the bottom. The psychiatrist aboard made tests of the effect of air conditions and for 10 days required everyone to refrain from smoking.

The way around the Cape of Good Hope was without incident, as was the route up through the South Atlantic to St. Peter's and St. Paul's Islands, which technically rounded out the circumnavigation. After a shift to helicopter at the mouth of Delaware Bay, the *Triton* continued on to her home port, New London–Groton, where she arrived on May 11, 1958. On the circumnavigation from St. Peter's and St. Paul's Rocks and back, she had covered 26,723 nautical miles (30,763 statute miles) in 60 days, 21 hours. She had been submerged until the final approach to New London.

(See E. L. Beach, *Around the World Submerged*, 1962.)

Torrey Canyon

By the 1960s, coastal communities were beginning to regard the increasing number and size of tankers with keen concern over the danger of oil spills. There had already been some, but the classic spill occurred on March 18, 1967, when the tanker *Torrey Canyon* ran on a dangerous reef off Land's End in England. She broke in two and a large part of her 118,000-ton cargo of crude oil spread out to pollute the beaches of Cornwall, Devon, and distant Brittany.

It was an inexcusable accident, occurring on a bright, clear day at high tide. A lightship had been stationed to warn ships away from the Seven Stones rocks. Its crew were amazed to see the big tanker disregarding the warning and heading directly for the danger. Signals of every sort were made, even to whistles and firing a gun, but she kept on. Drunk or otherwise incapacitated, the captain kept on until she crashed; she split in two and the oil began to pour out.

There were international complications on her status. She belonged to the Union Oil Company, an American company, but she was under charter to British Petroleum to bring oil from Kuwait in the Persian Gulf to refineries in Wales. She was under Liberian registry and had an Italian crew, including the highly culpable captain. The British had done much of the marine underwriting.

The chief cause for alarm was the steadily increasing oil slick, headed for the beaches of Cornwall and Devon, and gradually reaching over to France. The $300,000,000 tourist business was threatened, while some 15,000 sea birds were killed when their wings became clogged with oil, and there was fear of damage to fish and shellfish. Bombers were brought in to set the hulk afire, with eventual success. Meanwhile along the extensive beaches bulldozers plowed the sludge under.

The *Torrey Canyon* spill was notorious. The methods used to control and counteract the adverse effects of oil spills are now widely used. Concern about oil spills is no longer limited to coastal areas; it has become an international issue.

Manhattan

The *Manhattan*, plowing through broken ice in the Northwest Passage. *(Naval Historical Center)*

Between August and November 1969, the big American tanker *Manhattan* traversed the Northwest Passage from the Atlantic to Alaska and back. It was the first time that any major ship had performed that feat; only a few small ships had done so since Amundsen's initial passage in the *Gjöa*. The *Manhattan*'s voyage was occasioned by the recent discovery of huge oil deposits on Alaska's Northern Slope behind Prudhoe Bay, just east of Point Barrow. If the sea route by the Northwest Passage should prove feasible, it would be cheaper than the alternative of a pipeline overland to Valdez in southern Alaska. The tanker voyage was an experiment to determine how practicable the route might be.

The voyage came at the time of a tremendous boom in tanker size. The "T-2," the standard government-built tanker of World War II, had been 18,000 tons deadweight, then considered the maximum size. By 1958 tankers were reaching 45,000 tons, and in the boom of the early 1960s they grew from 100,000 to 200,000 tons before the end of the decade. These tankers were given a new name—VLCC (Very Large Crude Carriers)—there were 388 VLCCs by 1974, and 498 were under construction or on order. By that time, the new initials ULCC (Ultra-Large Crude Carriers) were used for ships over 400,000 tons, the maximum being the 476,000-ton *Global Tokyo*.

The *Manhattan*, at 103,000 tons, had been one of the maximum new
424 tankers when she was launched at the Bethlehem Quincy Yard in 1962

for the Greek shipowner Niarchos. Because of her deep draft, she could
serve very few harbors, and Niarchos, making a good tax loss, sold her
as a "white elephant" for a fraction of her cost. She was engaged in
trade when the oil interests hit upon her as the perfect ship for their
Arctic venture. Time was pressing in 1969 and a rush job was necessary.
She was cut into four parts; some sections went down to the Gulf of
Mexico and one section to Newport News; major coordination was
done at the Sun Shipbuilding Company yard at Chester on the Delaware. A special reinforced bow, designed at Massachusetts Institute of
Technology, was built at Bath Iron Works. After these parts were
rapidly assembled at Chester, the *Manhattan* was a ship of some 150,000
tons, with much reinforcement and engines of 43,000 horsepower.

The whole operation was under the direction of the Humble Oil
Company, subsidiary of Esso, which put up most of the $70,000,000
cost, with small amounts from Atlantic Richfield and British Petroleum,
which also had some interest in the Prudhoe oil fields. Humble's
authority centered on Stanley B. Haas, a tall, blond Missourian, "the
chief visionary, advocate and strategist" for the expedition. After painstaking preparation, he went along on the voyage in general authority.
The chief maritime authority was vested in the master, Captain Roger
A. Steward, from the Boston area, a mariner with long and broad
experience. He had two staff captains in order to always have a captain
on the bridge. The Canadians contributed importantly to the experiment. They had a distinguished Arctic navigator aboard, and their
tough icebreaker, the *Sir John A. Macdonald,* named for the first Canadian prime minister, accompanied the *Manhattan* throughout the voyage, rendering essential assistance. There were underlying delicate
questions, because much of the voyage would be through the Canadian
archipelago.

The *Manhattan* sailed from Chester on August 24, 1969, with some
130 persons of various interests aboard. Some of these VIPs went only
part way, being exchanged with others at different spots along the line.
The expedition made a stop at Halifax, partly to show the flag, then took
the time-honored Arctic approaches past the coast of Greenland to
Thule and into Baffin Bay. That led into the Northwest Passage proper
in the long reach of Lancaster Sound. Some of the earlier Elizabethan
and post-Elizabethan voyages had gone that far. But a long hiatus had
followed until the idea was revived by the Admiralty after 1815. The
map of the area is littered with the names of British officials and
worthies. Parry Channel led further westward. The tragic climax of the
ambitious, well-prepared expedition of Sir John Franklin which had
"gone missing" in the late 1840s had led to many search expeditions.

By the time the *Manhattan* reached Viscount Melville Sound, the ice was beginning to cause trouble. The tanker could butt through it fairly well, but now and then when the ice was too deep she was blocked and the *Sir John Macdonald* came to her assistance, breaking out the ice on either side. At the western end of the Viscount Melville Sound, a problem arose as to the final breakthrough to the Pacific. They first tried the more difficult route through McClure Sound, only to find the ice impassable. They then doubled back and went through the easier Prince of Wales Sound, finally reaching the end of the Northwest Passage at Sachs Harbor on the Beaufort Sea, a spot which incidentally was 4000 miles equidistant from New York, London, and Tokyo.

From here on the rest of the voyage was easy. They went up the Alaska coast, leaving Canadian for American waters and resting far offshore at Prudhoe Bay, the nominal goal of the oil efforts. There was no question of taking on a real oil cargo but as a symbol, a 55-gallon gold-painted barrel was filled with North Slope crude and brought aboard, placed conspicuously at the bow—the *Manhattan* had brought back some Alaskan oil.

She continued on to Point Barrow, the northernmost tip of Alaska and the local seat of American authority, where they made only a brief stay to give the crew their first short shore liberty.

The return voyage was something of an anticlimax. As autumn approached, the weather turned more somber. Ice became troublesome in places, and ever-present was the realization of having to get out before the ice closed in. Considering the experimental aspect of the voyage, there was the constant problem of whether tankers, and probably bigger ones than the *Manhattan*, would be able to maintain monthly service throughout the year with conditions definitely worse in the winter months. At any rate, general relief was felt on getting back to Halifax, where a cordial final celebration was held with the Canadians. The *Manhattan* arrived at New York on November 12, with whistles blowing and fireboats spraying and an elaborate dinner at the Plaza Hotel.

As a result of the voyage of the *Manhattan*, the final decision was that the Northwest Passage tanker route was not feasible, and efforts at once shifted to the 48-inch Alaska pipeline, held up for a while by the efforts of the conservationists.

(See W. D. Smith, *Northwest Passage*, 1970.)

Glomar Explorer

The *Glomar Explorer,* the most recent and most fantastic of all our famous ships, raised part of a sunken Soviet submarine three miles from the bottom of the Pacific Ocean in 1974. The secret conception and completion of the vessel involved cloak-and-dagger shenanigans by the Central Intelligence Agency (CIA) with the cooperation of Howard Hughes.

The 4000-ton, 18-year-old submarine was a valuable source of information. She had been refitted to carry three atomic missiles in addition to torpedoes. Based in Vladivostok, she was some 750 miles northwest of Hawaii when one or more explosions sent her to the bottom with all hands. Sophisticated Soviet and American sound-ranging devices located her hull and the Americans even got photographs of the wreck. But the three-mile depth put her beyond the range of existing recovery equipment.

The CIA was determined to raise her, hoping to recover her coding devices and to examine the Soviet atomic missiles. It went to extreme measures to ensure secrecy, particularly in view of possible Soviet reactions. There were even secret staircases at headquarters so that the comings and goings of staff would not be observed. A high wall was erected outside the building area. Because of the publicity that would attend seeking funds in the normal way from Congress, Howard Hughes agreed to advance temporarily the necessary funds—eventually $500,000—through his Summa Corporation, which contracted with the Global Marine Company (whence the name *Glomar*) for construction by the Sun Shipbuilding Yard at Chester, Pennsylvania. To further ensure secrecy, the yard was told that the new ship was designed to raise nodules of manganese and other minerals from the sea bottom. Construction extended from May 1971 to May 1974.

The resultant *Glomar Explorer* was a good-sized ship of 36,000 tons, 618 feet long and with a beam of more than 115 feet. Her diesel electric machinery could develop 42,000 horsepower. Her topsides were cluttered with all sorts of gear. The most conspicuous item was a giant claw to grapple the sunken target—to it was attached a series of prongs to fasten along the sunken hull. The hoisting line from the ship operated inside a pipe, ultimately three miles long.

In addition to the *Glomar Explorer* there was a huge submersible barge the size of a football field, built by the Lockheed plant at San Diego on the West Coast. The barge was to be carried below the *Glomar Explorer* until it was needed, when it would be raised and pumped out to carry any rescued material to the surface.

On July 4, 1974, the new apparatus was put to the test at the site of the wreck northwest of Hawaii. The results fell short of expectation. The submarine was grappled and the forward third of it was brought to the surface. Apparently, the rear prongs had been damaged and could not support the main part of the submarine. As a result, the things that were sought most eagerly—the coding machinery and the atomic missiles—did not come up. That was the formal and generally accepted report. One of the articles that reported the story claims that everything came up but it did not seem wise to let the Soviets know that the Americans were examining their secrets.

The next step was the sudden stripping away of the ship's strict secrecy for reasons not entirely clear; the story was given to the newspapers, where it produced various reactions. Publicity was attributed to such factors as loan reimbursement and incomplete secrecy. Burglars reputedly raided one of the Hughes offices and found an outline of the whole operation. Also, with the ship tied up at a West Coast port the local authorities presented a tax bill for the whole value; it was necessary to explain that she really belonged to the United States Government. The navy therefore was told that it would have to make good the $500,000 that Hughes had advanced. The navy was not happy; many of its officers had felt that the whole project was not worth what it cost, but the amount had to be paid out of Navy research funds.

The *Glomar Explorer* has remained inactive on the West Coast since its 1974 experience. Its future is uncertain; there have been projects to use it for recovering manganese nodules, and she has even been offered for sale, apparently without takers. But there is the possibility, probably not overlooked either in Washington or Moscow, that if an important ship or plane goes down in those very deep waters, the *Glomar Explorer* might be called upon to go after the secret material.

Index

429